Read This First

The information in this book is as up to date and accurate as we can make it. But it's important to realize that the law changes frequently, as do fees, forms, and other important legal details. If you handle your own legal matters, it's up to you to be sure that all information you use—including the information in this book—is accurate. Here are some suggestions to help you do this:

First, check the edition number on the book's spine to make sure you've got the most recent edition of this book. To learn whether a later edition is available, go to Nolo's online Law Store at www.nolo.com or call Nolo's Customer Service Department at 800-728-3555.

Next, because the law can change overnight, users of even a current edition need to be sure it's fully up to date. At www.nolo.com, we post notices of major legal and practical changes that affect a book's current edition only. To check for updates, go to the Law Store portion of Nolo's website and find the page devoted to the book (use the "A to Z Product List" and click on the book's title). If you see an "Updates" link on the left side of the page, click on it. If you don't see a link, there are no posted changes—but check back regularly.

Finally, while Nolo believes that accurate and current legal information in its books can help you solve many of your legal problems on a cost-effective basis, this book is not intended to be a substitute for personalized advice from a knowledgeable lawyer. If you want the help of a trained professional, consult an attorney licensed to practice in your state.

10th edition

Everybody's Guide to

Small Claims Court

by Attorney Ralph Warner

Illustrated by Linda Allison

Tenth Edition	JUNE 2004
Editor	LISA GUERIN
Illustrations	LINDA ALLISON
Production	SUSAN PUTNEY
Cover	KEN ARMISTEAD
Proofreading	MU'AFRIDA BELL
Index	MICHAEL FERREIRA
Printing	CONSOLIDATED PRINTERS, INC.

Warner, Ralph E.
    Everybody's guide to small claims court / by Ralph Warner ; illustrated by Linda
Allison.-- 10th ed.
        p. cm.
    ISBN 1-4133-0034-0 (alk. paper)
    1. Small claims courts--United States--Popular works. I. Title: Small claims court. II.
Title.

KF8769.Z9W37 2004
347.73'04--dc22

                                                                2003070160

For information on bulk purchases or corporate premium sales, please contact the Special Sales Department. For academic sales or textbook adoptions, ask for Academic Sales. Call 800-955-4775 or write to
Nolo at 950 Parker Street, Berkeley, CA 94710.

Thank You

A number of talented friends have read the manuscript of this book and made helpful suggestions for improvement. With enough help, even a tarnished penny can be made to shine. Thanks to Steve Elias, Susan Cornell, and especially Ilona Bray, who have labored hard to round up many of my errant thoughts while making numerous suggestions for improvement. Thanks, too, to Judge Roderic Duncan, Mary Alice Coleman of the California State Department of Consumer Affairs, and Jeanne Stott— San Francisco's recently retired small claims court legal advisor; they don't always agree with what I write, but are nonetheless unfailingly helpful.

Ella Hirst, Stanley Jacobsen, and Beth Laurence compiled the research for all material appearing in the Appendix. Their thorough, patient, and dedicated work has made this a better book.

Linda Allison's wonderful drawings speak for themselves. Working with her is like catching the first ray of sunshine on a clear morning.

For Toni,

the light, the heart, and the love of my life

Contents

Introduction

Filing a case in small claims court is a highly cost-effective strategy for resolving all kinds of disputes. In most states, the maximum amount you can sue for has increased substantially in recent years, and court judgments have become far easier to collect. In addition, many states have implemented innovative mediation programs for small claims, which can spare you the time and tension of presenting your case to a judge. So, while more can and should be done to make small claims court a true people's court, it is an efficient forum that gives participants an opportunity to resolve most personal consumer and small business disputes.

The goal of this book is to help people bringing or defending a small claims case do the best possible job. I provide you with the tactical, strategic, and, above all, practical information necessary to succeed. From deciding whether you have a good case or defense, to adopting a savvy pretrial settlement strategy, gathering evidence, and planning your courtroom presentation, you'll find answers to all your key questions here, including:

- "How does small claims court work, step by step?"
- "Do I have a case worth pursuing or defending?"
- "How can I settle a case when my opponent won't even talk to me?"
- "What is mediation? Should I give it a try?"
- "What witnesses and other evidence will I need in court?"
- "What's the best way to organize my courtroom presentation?"
- "What are the tips and traps of using eye and expert witnesses?"
- "How do I deal with a lying opponent?"
- "Can I appeal if I lose?"
- "How do I collect my judgment?"

Small claims court offers participants an opportunity to see justice served, but that doesn't mean you can just waltz into the courtroom and expect an easy victory. Even a good case can be lost if it isn't properly researched or presented. That's why it's so important to take the time to learn the effective case preparation techniques I discuss in this book.

Just as important as knowing when and how to bring or defend your small claims action is knowing when not to. You don't want to waste time and energy dragging a hopeless case to court—or even a winning one, if collecting your judgment will be difficult or impossible. So I also explain the key differences between cases in which you have a good chance of both winning and collecting your judgment and those in which it will be hard to do either. Once you understand this information, it will be up to you to keep the losers at home.

This new tenth edition contains expanded material on how to settle and mediate small claims cases. As many pleased readers of this book have reported over the years, you can sometimes achieve all of your objectives without ever setting foot in a court-room. Instead, armed with good negotiation and mediation techniques, you and the other party can craft your own mutually satisfactory settlement. By so doing, you can keep control over your own dispute, reducing the possibility that a poor or inattentive judge might make a wrong decision that one or both of you might hate. And best of all, when cases are compromised out of court, the person who owes money is far more likely to pay promptly, thus avoiding exhausting and expensive collection problems.

In addition to studying the information you'll find here, I strongly urge you to carefully review the materials made available by your state's small claims court. Important technical details such as when and where court is held, what types of evidence are allowed and prohibited, and how much it will cost to collect a judgment are covered in more detail in these materials than I can possibly do in this 50-state guide. Fortunately, accessing this material is easy—it's usually available online as well as in free pamphlets available at your small claims court clerk's office. You'll find the URL for your state's small claims website in the state-by-state appendix.

Finally, let me say a few words about the frequent mention of other Nolo self-help law books and Nolo's website throughout the text. Lest you think my only goal is to try to sell you another book, let me make three points. First, Nolo is by far the longest established and most comprehensive publisher of self-help law materials in the United States, which means there are many legal subjects on which Nolo really does publish the only decent materials aimed at nonlawyers. Second, Nolo's website, including its comprehensive legal encyclopedia, is free. Third, Nolo books are available at virtually every American public library, which means that you can look up the information you need at no cost.

Icons Used in This Book

Look for these icons to alert you to certain kinds of information.

 Warning: A caution to slow down and consider potential problems.

 Fast Track: Lets you know when you may skip reading some material that is not relevant to your situation.

 Tip: Gives practical suggestions for handling a legal or procedural issue that may come up.

 Recommended Reading: Suggests references for additional information.

 Cross-Reference: Refers you to other chapters or sections of the book that deal with a particular subject.

CHAPTER

In the Beginning

A. First Things

Small claims procedures are established by state law. This means there are differences in the operating rules of small claims courts from state to state, including the maximum amount for which you can sue; who can sue; and what papers must be filed, where, and when. There are even differences among names used for small claims court (or its equivalent) in the different states, with "justice," "district," "municipal," "city," "county," and "magistrates" court among the names commonly used.

While the details of using small claims courts vary from state to state, the basic approach necessary to prepare and present a case properly is remarkably similar everywhere. But details are important, and you should do three things to make sure you understand how small claims court works in your state:

- Look up the summary of your state's rules in the 50-state Appendix to this book.

- Obtain your local small claims rules from your small claims court clerk's office.

- Check out your state's small claims rules online at Nolo's free Small Claims Center. You'll find this in the Legal Research area of Nolo's home page, at www.nolo.com. Or access your state's small claims information by entering the URL you'll find near the top of your state's listing in the Appendix.

The purpose of small claims court is to hear disputes involving modest amounts of money, without long delays and formal rules of evidence. Disputes are normally presented directly by the people involved. Lawyers are prohibited in some states, including Michigan and California (except to argue their own disputes), but are allowed in most. However, the limited dollar amounts involved usually make it economically unwise to hire a lawyer. The maximum amount of money for which you can sue (in legal jargon, the "jurisdictional amount") is set by state law, too. For example, the limit is $5,000 in the District of Columbia, $5,000 in New York, and $7,500 in Minnesota. These amounts are typical, although there is considerable variation. Some states allow small claims court cases up to $15,000, while others limit cases to no more than $2,000. (See the Appendix.)

In recent years, the maximum amount for which suits can be brought has been on the rise almost everywhere. Don't rely on your memory, or what a friend tells you, or even what you read here. Look up the small claims court on the Web (see the Appendix for a list of state websites), or call the small claims court clerk and find out exactly how much you can sue for. You may be pleasantly surprised.

There are three great advantages to using small claims court:

- You get to prepare and present your own case without having to pay a lawyer more than your claim is worth.

- Filing, preparing, and presenting a small claims court case is relatively easy in most states. The gobbledygook of complicated legal forms and language found in other courts is kept to a minimum. To start your case, you normally need only fill out a few lines on a simple form—for example, "Honest Al's Used Chariots owes me $5,000 because the 2000 Neon they sold me in supposedly 'excellent condition' died less than a mile from the car lot." When you get to court, you can talk to the judge in plain English without a whole lot of "res ipsa loquiturs" and "pendente lites." Even better, if you have helpful documents or witnesses, you can show them to the judge without complying with the thousand years' accumulation of rusty, musty procedures, habits, and so-called rules of evidence of which the legal profession is so proud.

- Small claims court doesn't take long. Most disputes are heard in court within a month or two after the complaint is filed. The hearing itself seldom takes more than 15 minutes. The judge either announces a decision right there in the courtroom or mails it out within a few days.

But before you decide that small claims court sounds like just the place to bring your case, you will want to answer a basic question: Are the results you are likely to achieve worth the effort you will have to expend? Unless your case involves the simple failure to pay an undisputed debt, it will probably take ten or more hours to prepare and present and, depending on your personality, may cause you a few sleepless nights.

In order to clearly assess whether your case is worth the effort of bringing it to court, you will want to understand the details of how small claims court works. Understanding who can sue, where, and for how much, is a good start. You will also want to learn a little law: Are you entitled to relief? How much? And how do you compute the exact amount? Finally, and most important, comes the big question so many people overlook, to their later dismay: Assuming you prepare and present your case brilliantly and get a judgment for everything you request, can you collect? Unfortunately, many plaintiffs who go through the entire small claims procedure and come out winners have no chance of collecting a dime, because they sued people who have neither money nor any reasonable prospect of getting any.

The purpose of the first dozen chapters of this book is to help you decide whether or not you have a case worth pursuing. These are not the chapters where grand strategies are brilliantly unrolled to baffle and confound the opposition—that comes later. Here we are more concerned with such mundane tasks as locating the person you want to sue, suing in the right court, filling out the necessary forms, and getting them properly served. Perhaps it will disappoint those of you with a dramatic turn of mind, but most cases are won or lost at the preparation stage, long before anyone enters the courtroom.

Occasionally throughout this book we reproduce forms used in California and New York. Forms used elsewhere may look somewhat different, but you will find that the differences are usually more a matter of graphics than of substance. The basic information requested—who is suing whom about what—is very similar everywhere. Blank copies of all forms are available at your local small claims clerk's office, and often online (see the Appendix for your state's small claims website).

B. Checklist of Things to Think About Before Initiating or Defending Your Case

Here is a preliminary checklist of things you will want to think about. Each of these areas will be covered in more detail in later chapters. But let me remind you again, if you haven't already gotten a copy of your local Small Claims Court rules, do it now. It's silly to come to bat with two out in the ninth and the bases loaded and not know whether you are supposed to run to first or third.

QUESTIONS A PLAINTIFF NEEDS TO ANSWER

☐ 1. Do you have a good case? That is, can you establish or prove every element of a valid legal claim? (See Chapter 2 for a discussion of what you'll need to prove to win contract, debt, property damage, and other common types of cases.)

☐ 2. How much money are you asking for? If it is for more than the small claims maximum, do you want to sue for the maximum and give up your right to the rest? (See Chapter 4.)

☐ 3. Have you made a reasonable effort to contact the other party to demand payment and, if appropriate, offer a compromise? (See Chapter 6.)

☐ 4. Is your lawsuit brought within the proper time limit? (See Chapter 5.)

☐ 5. Which small claims court should you bring your suit in? (See Chapter 10.)

☐ 6. Whom do you sue, and how do you identify this person or business on your court papers? In some types of cases, especially those involving businesses, automobiles, and landlords, this can be a little more technical and tricky than you might have guessed. (See Chapter 9.)

☐ 7. If mediation is offered or required by your small claims court, do you understand how it works and how best to use it? (See Chapter 7.)

☐ 8. Can you prove your case? That is, do you understand what evidence you'll need to bring to court to convince a judge you are in the right? (See Chapters 15 through 23.)

☐ 9. Can you make a convincing courtroom presentation? The key here is practice, practice, practice. (See Chapter 16.)

☐ 10. And again, the most important question—assuming that you can win, is there a reasonable chance you can collect? (See Chapters 3 and 25.)

QUESTIONS A DEFENDANT NEEDS TO ANSWER

☐	1.	Do you have legal grounds for a countersuit against the plaintiff? Or put another way, are you the one who's been wronged, such that the plaintiff really owes you money? (See Chapters 11 and 13.)
☐	2.	Do you have a partial or complete legal defense against the claim of the plaintiff? Or put another way, has the plaintiff filed a bogus lawsuit? (See Chapters 2 and 13.)
☐	3.	Has the plaintiff sued for a reasonable or an excessive amount? (See Chapter 4.)
☐	4.	Has the plaintiff brought suit within the proper time limit? (See Chapter 5.)
☐	5.	Has the plaintiff followed reasonably correct procedures in bringing suit and serving you with the court papers? (See Chapters 12 and 13.)
☐	6.	Have you made a reasonable effort to contact the plaintiff in order to arrive at a compromise settlement? (See Chapters 6 and 13.)
☐	7.	If mediation is offered or required by your small claims court, do you understand how it works and how to use it? (See Chapter 7.)
☐	8.	Assuming you'll contest the case in court, have you gathered the evidence (letters, estimates, photos, and witnesses) that you'll need to prove that your version of events is correct? (See Chapters 14 through 17.)
☐	9.	Are you prepared to present your side of the case convincingly in court? (See Chapter 16.)

Defendants may want to file their own lawsuit. In addition to their right to vigorously defend themselves, defendants can also file their own cases against the plaintiff. (See Chapters 11 and 13.) You will want to do this if you believe that the plaintiff is legally responsible for monetary losses you suffered. Defendant's claims commonly develop out of a situation in which both parties were negligent (say in a car accident) and the question to be decided is who was more at fault. If your claim is for less than the small claims maximum, you can file your claim there. (See Chapter 11, Section C.) But if it is for more, you will want to carefully check your state's rules. Typically, you'll learn that you should file your case in a different court (and have your opponent's case transferred there), but your state may use a different system.

C. Legal Jargon Defined

Mercifully, there is not a great deal of technical language used in small claims courts. But there is some legal jargon that may be new to you. Don't try to learn all of these terms now. Instead, refer back to these definitions if and when you need them. Here we give you the most widely used version of most terms. In some states, jargon may vary slightly, but the substance will be remarkably similar everywhere.

Abstract of Judgment: An official document you get from the small claims court clerk's office that indicates that you have a money judgment against another person. Filing it with the county recorder places a lien on real property owned by the judgment debtor.

Action: Synonymous slang for "lawsuit." Lawyers often call a lawsuit an "action" or a "cause of action."

Adjournment: See Continuance, below.

Agent for Service of Process: The person a corporation designates to be served with court papers (see Service of Process, below). If the corporation is based in another state, the agent in your state may be called a "resident agent."

Appeal: Some states allow only a defendant to appeal; others allow the parties to appeal based only on law—not facts. Many require you to post a bond when you file an appeal. (See Chapter 24 and the Appendix.)

Appearance: Lawyer slang for showing up or "appearing" in court.

Arbitration: A voluntary system under which a case is heard by arbitrators rather than in a court setting. Arbitration is not available in most states, but is used widely in New York City night courts. Ask your court clerk for local rules, if any.

Calendar: A list of cases to be heard by a small claims court on a particular day. A case taken "off calendar" is removed from the list. This usually occurs because the defendant has not been served or because the parties jointly request that it be heard on another day.

Civil Code (CC) and Code of Civil Procedure (CCP): The Civil Code is the name many states give to the book containing much of their basic law. The Code of Civil Procedure typically contains the state's legal procedures. However, a number of states call these legal codes by other names, such as "Revised Statutes," "Rules of Civil Procedure," (RCP) and "Rules of Court." No matter what their name, state laws are available at most large public libraries, at law libraries, and online (see the Legal Research Center on the Nolo website at www.nolo.com).

Claim of Defendant: A claim by a defendant that the plaintiff owes him or her money. A claim of defendant, also called a "Defendant's Claim," is filed as part of the same small claims action that the plaintiff has started.

Claim of Exemption: A procedure by which a "judgment debtor" can claim that, under federal and/or state law, certain of his or her money or other property is exempt from being grabbed to satisfy a debt.

Claim of Plaintiff: In many states, this is the name for the document that is filed with the small claims court clerk to initiate a lawsuit. Some states refer to this form as a "Complaint." You may also encounter other names, such as "Statement of Claim" or "Affidavit and Claim."

Commissioner: A court employee designated to hear small claims cases in certain states, such as California. Usually a commissioner has the same powers to hear and decide cases as does a judge.

Complaint: See Claim of Plaintiff.

Conciliation Court: Minnesota's term for small claims court.

Conditional Judgment: When a court issues "equitable relief" (nonmoney relief such as the return of a piece of property), it has the power to grant a conditional judgment. A conditional judgment consists of actions or requirements that depend on other actions (for instance, "return the property in 15 days or pay $2,000").

Continuance: Called an adjournment in some states, this is a court order postponing a hearing to a later date.

Counterclaim: Basically the same as a Claim of Defendant or a Cross Complaint. Different states use different names.

Default Judgment: A court decision given to the plaintiff (the person filing suit) when the defendant fails to show up for a hearing or to file an answer after having been served with a claim.

Defendant: The person or "party" being sued.

Dismissed Case: A dismissal usually occurs when the plaintiff drops a case. If the defendant has not filed a claim, the plaintiff simply files a written request for dismissal. If the defendant has filed a claim, both plaintiff and defendant must agree in writing before a dismissal will be allowed. If a plaintiff does not show up in court on the appointed day, the judge may dismiss the case. Most cases are dismissed "without prejudice." This means that the case can be refiled at any time as long as the statute of limitations has not expired (see Chapter 5). But if a case is dismissed "with prejudice," it means that it can't be refiled unless the dismissal is first successfully appealed.

Equitable Relief: In many small claims courts, this comprises several very specialized legal remedies—called "rescission," "restitution," "reformation," and "specific performance"—in which a small claims court judge has the power to issue judgment for something other than money. For example, the judge may order a party to return "one-of-a-kind" property (a family heirloom vase, for example), end a fraudulent contract, fix a mistaken contract, or do one or more of the acts discussed in more detail in Chapter 4, Section E. Equitable relief is allowed in some, but by no means all, states. Check your state's website (listed in the Appendix) to see whether your state allows some or all of these legal remedies in small claims court.

Equity: The value of the portion of a particular piece of property that you actually own. For example, if a car has a fair market value of $2,000 and you owe a bank $750 on it, your equity is $1,250.

Execution: Executing is legal jargon for either fulfilling your obligations under a contract or completing a document by signing or acknowledging it to make it legally valid. It can also refer to seizing property under a court order.

Exhibit: Some states use this term to describe physical evidence such as letters, photos, and documents you present to the judge as evidence in a small claims case.

Formal Court: As used here, this term refers to the regular "lawyer-dominated" state courts. The states call their trial courts by all sorts of names (municipal, superior, district, circuit, supreme, civil, etc.). For example, in California, claims too large for Small Claims Court are heard in Superior Court. All of these courts require a knowledge of confusing language and procedure, and you will want to do some homework if you decide to bring a case in one of them. If your claim is really too big for Small Claims Court, see *Represent Yourself in Court: How to Prepare & Try a Winning Case*, by Attorneys Paul Bergman & Sara J. Berman-Barrett (Nolo). Or, if you choose to hire a lawyer, see *The Lawsuit Survival Guide: A Client's Companion to Litigation*, by Joseph Matthews (Nolo). With or without a lawyer, you'll find guidance on certain important pretrial procedures in *Nolo's Deposition Handbook*, by Paul Bergman & Albert Moore (Nolo).

Garnish: To legally take money directly from its source—usually wages, commissions, or a bank account—for payment of a debt. Called an attachment in some states, a creditor must get a court order to garnish or attach wages or a bank account.

Hearing: The court trial.

Homestead: Homestead laws allow homeowners to protect a certain amount of the equity in their homes from attachment and sale to satisfy most debts. Homestead laws can work in one of two ways. In some states, the homeowner must file a paper called a "Declaration of Homestead." In other states, simply owning a home (and having the deed recorded) is enough to entitle the homeowner to homestead protection. (See Chapter 25, Section C.)

Injunction: Injunctive relief, which typically consists of getting an injunction to order a defendant not to do something (don't cut down that tree or fill that swamp) can't usually be granted in small claims court. This type of lawsuit must be filed in formal court.

Judge: In many states, small claims cases are heard by full-time judges who also hear cases in other courts.

Judge Pro Tem: A lawyer who pinch hits for a regular judge on a temporary basis. A pro tem judge can hear your case only if you consent, in writing.

Judgment: The decision rendered by the court.

Judgment Creditor: A person to whom money is owed under a court decision.

Judgment Debtor: A person who owes money under a court decision.

Jurisdiction: Jurisdiction refers to the court's authority to hear various types of cases. A small claims court has jurisdiction to hear cases involving money damages up to a certain amount—for example, $7,500 in Alaska, $1,800 in Kansas. (This is often called the "jurisdictional amount.") Some small claims courts also have jurisdiction over certain types of nonmoney cases, such as unlawful detainer (eviction) actions, and some may award nonmoney remedies, as discussed in Chapter 4.

Levy: A legal method to seize property or money for unpaid debts under court order. For example, a sheriff can levy on (sell) your automobile if you refuse to pay a judgment.

Lien: A legal right to an interest in the real estate (real property) of another for payment of a debt. To get a lien, you first must get a court judgment and then take proper steps to have the court enter an "Abstract of Judgment." You must then take the Abstract to the county office where property deeds are recorded in a county where the judgment debtor has real estate.

Magistrate: Another word for judge.

Magistrate's Court: Georgia's term for small claims court.

Mediation: Many small claims courts recommend or require that parties meet with a neutral third party (called "the mediator") to try to settle their dispute voluntarily. Mediation sessions typically last an hour or two and take place in a conference room at the courthouse or other public building. If no settlement is mutually agreed to (mediators have no power to impose a decision), the case moves on to small claims court.

Motion to Vacate a Judgment: The motion the defendant must file to reopen a proceeding in which the judge entered a default judgment because the defendant didn't show up. (See Chapter 11.)

Order of Examination: A court procedure allowing a judgment creditor to question a debtor about the extent and location of his or her assets.

Ordinance: A law or statute adopted by a local government, such as a city or county.

Party: A participant in a lawsuit. Thus the plaintiff or defendant may be referred to as a party—and both together as the parties—to a small claims suit.

Plaintiff: The person who starts a lawsuit, by suing the defendant.

Prejudice: A term used when a case is dismissed. A case dismissed "without prejudice" can be refiled at any time as long as the statute of limitations period has not run out (see Chapter 5). A case dismissed "with prejudice" is dead (can't be refiled) unless the dismissal is first successfully appealed.

Process Server: The person who delivers court papers to a party or witness. (See Chapter 12.)

Recorder (Office of the County Recorder): The person employed by the county to make and record documents. The county recorder's office is usually located in the main county courthouse.

Replevin: A type of legal action in which the owner of movable goods is given the right to recover them from someone who shouldn't have them. It is commonly used in relation to buyers and sellers; for example, a seller might bring a replevin action if the seller delivered goods to a buyer who then failed to pay for them. Replevin is allowed in a few states' small claims courts.

Satisfaction of Judgment: A written statement filed by the judgment creditor when the judgment is paid. (See Chapter 24.)

Service of Process: The required delivery of copies of legal documents or court papers such as subpoenas and complaints, usually by personal delivery to the defendant or other person to whom the documents are directed.

Settlement: An agreement between plaintiff and defendant to resolve their dispute prior to trial. In some states, a settlement (sometimes called a Stipulated Judgment) can be presented to the judge and made into a formal court judgment.

Statute: A law adopted by a state or the federal government. In small claims court, state law is applicable in almost all situations. (See Section D of this chapter for information on how to look up the law.)

Statute of Limitations: The time period within which you must file your lawsuit. It is normally figured as a set number of years from the date the act or omission giving rise to the lawsuit occurred. The time limit will vary depending on the subject matter of the suit. (See Chapter 5.)

Stay of Enforcement: When a small claims court judgment is appealed by the losing party, enforcement (collection) of the judgment is stayed (stopped) until the time for appeal has expired.

Stipulation: An agreement to compromise a case (often called a settlement) that is entered into by the parties and then presented to the judge. If the judge approves, it is called a "stipulated judgment" in many states. See Settlement.

Submission: A judge who wants to delay decision on a case until a later time, "takes it under submission." Some judges announce their decision as to who won and who lost right in the courtroom. More often, they take cases under submission and mail out decisions later.

Subpoena: A court order requiring a witness to appear in court. It must be served on (given to) the person being subpoenaed in order to be valid. (See Chapter 15.)

Subpoena Duces Tecum: A court order requiring that certain documents be produced in court.

Substituted Service: A method by which court papers may be served on a defendant who is difficult to serve by other means. (See Chapter 12.)

Transfer: The procedure by which the defendant can have a small claims case transferred to a "formal court." In most states this can be done when the defendant has a claim against the plaintiff for an amount exceeding the small claims maximum. In a few states, the defendant can transfer a case simply to get out of small claims court. In many states, a defendant who wants a jury trial can also transfer to formal court. See the Appendix for details.

Trial De Novo: The rehearing of a small claims case from scratch after the defendant files an appeal. In this situation, the previous decision by the small claims judge has no effect, and the appeal takes the form of a new trial (trial de novo). This is allowed only in some states. Check the Appendix.

Unlawful Detainer Proceeding (known as "summary dispossess" and "forcible entry and detainer" in some states): Legalese for "eviction." Unlawful detainer proceedings may be brought in small claims court in some states but are not allowed in most. Check the Appendix.

Venue: The proper location (court) in which to bring a suit (see Chapter 10). If a suit is brought in the wrong place, it can be transferred to the right court or dismissed, in which case the plaintiff must refile in the right court.

Wage Garnishment: After a judgment has been issued (and the defendant's time to appeal, if any, has elapsed), the small claims court clerk will issue a writ of execution upon request. This may be turned over to a sheriff, marshal, or constable with orders to collect (garnish) a portion of the judgment debtor's wages directly from his employer.

Writ of Execution: An order by a court to the sheriff, marshal, or constable of a specific area (in most states, this is either a city or county) to collect a specific amount of money due.

D. Legal Research

As part of using small claims court, you may need to look up a state law or city or county ordinance. This is particularly likely to be true if your case is based on the other party's violation of a consumer protection, landlord-tenant, or other statute (law). In many states, laws are roughly divided by subject matter, often into sets of books that are called "codes" or "statutes." Thus, there may be a civil code, probate code, penal code, vehicle code, and many more. Other states follow a less organized system under which all laws are lumped together in one seemingly endless numerical sequence. In either case, a subject index (often in the last volume) will be available.

1. Law in the Library

You can find your state laws at any large public library, publicly funded law school library, or county law library (usually located in the main county courthouse or in larger branch courthouses). All of these are open to the public.

Ordinances are laws passed by cities and counties. Among other things, ordinances often include zoning rules, building codes, leash laws, parking restrictions, view and tree-cutting rules, and minor vehicle violations. Usually, you can get copies of local ordinances from city or county offices. Collected sets are commonly available at the public library and, for more populous cities and counties, online.

If you do your research at a law library, you may have an opportunity to look up state laws in the annotated codes. In addition to the basic laws, these codes also list relevant court decisions (called "cases") interpreting each law. If you find a court case that seems similar to your situation, you may want to read it. If it seems relevant to your case, point it out to the judge as part of your small claims presentation. (See Chapter 24, Section D, for an example.)

2. Legal Research Online

You can also find your state's statutes or local court rules online.

a. State Statutes Online

You'll find links to the statutes for every state by going to Nolo's website, at www.nolo.com. Go to the Legal Research Center and click "State Laws." Then click your state.

If you're lucky, your state's website will offer you at least three options for searching or viewing:

- the table of contents
- a keyword search, or
- a statute number search.

Start with the table of contents if it's available. This allows you to access broad subject categories, thus minimizing the risk of overlooking important sections. Most states have conveniently bundled all their small claims court laws under one subheading (usually under a broader heading like "Courts" or "Judiciary"). Reviewing these will allow you to find specific information on some of the issues I've covered in this book. For example, if you are a landlord and wonder whether your resident manager can handle a small claims case for you, you'll probably find the answer here.

The table of contents search can also be helpful for researching substantive legal issues, especially if you don't have a good keyword to work with. Let's say you are in a dispute over a car accident. If you are sure the other driver must have done something wrong, you might just want to find the vehicle code and scan the whole darned thing. Or if you are in a landlord-tenant dispute and want to know more about your overall rights, the state statute may lay them out for you. Similarly, if you feel you have been ripped off by a dishonest business, you'll want to check out your state's consumer protection and false advertising laws.

The keyword search method is more hit or miss. It might take you straight to what you're looking for. For example, if you were a landlord who has been sued over a security deposit issue, entering "security deposit" might well pull up the statute that tells you that you returned the deposit on time. On the other hand, typing in "small claims maximum" might get you nowhere if your state happens to call it "jurisdictional limit" or doesn't give it a name at all.

The last option is a search by statute number. The 50-state Appendix to this book gives you a list of the statute numbers applicable in small claims courts. If your state's website does not offer a table of contents option, use these numbers to access general small claims court information.

b.   Local Courts Online

Don't stop with your state statutes. Most small claims courts put their rules, forms, and other helpful information online. Nolo's Small Claims Center (in the Legal Research area at www.nolo.com) has links to websites for all the state and local courts that handle small claims cases. I also list URLs for each state's small claims forms and information in this book's 50-state Appendix.

For a more thorough exploration of legal research options, see *Legal Research: How to Find & Understand the Law*, by Stephen Elias & Susan Levinkind (Nolo), an easy-to-read book that provides step-by-step instructions on how to find legal information, in the library and on the Internet. ■

CHAPTER

2

Do You Have a Good Case?

A. Stating Your Legal Claim in Court Papers

One of the advantages of using small claims court is that you are not required to state theories of law. Instead, you simply lay out the facts of the dispute and rely on the judge to fit them into one or another legal theory of recovery. All you really need to know to file a small claims case is that you have suffered monetary damage and that the person or business you are suing caused your loss.

To illustrate how this works, let's jump ahead and take a look at the form you will fill out when you file your case. Turn to Chapter 11 and find the form entitled "Plaintiff's Claim" (this form may be called by another name, such as a "Complaint", in your state). Look at Line 1. As you can see, there is no space to state a lengthy legal argument. Indeed, there is barely room to describe your dispute and list the date on which it occurred or began. Depending on the facts of your case, you should use this space to describe your dispute more or less like this:

- "John's Dry Cleaners ruined my jacket on December 13, 20xx."
- "Defendant's dog bit me on the corner of Rose and Peach Streets in Dover, Pennsylvania, on April 27, 20xx."
- "The car repairs that Joe's Garage did on my car on July 11, 20xx were done wrong, resulting in an engine fire."
- "Defendant refused to return the cleaning deposit when I moved out of my apartment on August 11, 20xx even though I left it clean."
- "The used car I purchased from Robert Yee on January 26, 20xx blew a gasket the next day."
- "The $5,000 I lent defendant has not been repaid by July 12, 20xx, as promised."

Don't try to argue your case until you get to court. When you state your case on the court papers, your goal is to notify the other party and the court of the issue in dispute. You don't need or want to try to list your evidence or otherwise try to convince anyone that you are in the right or that the law is on your side. Your chance to do this will come later, in court.

Time to Get Organized

Even before you file your case, you should set up a good system to safeguard key records and evidence. It's no secret that more than one case has been won (or lost) because of good (or bad) recordkeeping. One excellent approach is to get a couple of manila envelopes or file folders and label them with the name of your dispute (for example, Lincoln vs. Williams Ford). One folder or envelope can be used to store evidence, such as receipts, letters, names and addresses of potential witnesses, and photographs. The other is for your court papers. Once you get them organized, make sure you store your folders in a safe place.

B. But Is My Case Really Any Good?

If you read the little pamphlets small claims court clerks hand out, you will learn pretty much what I have just outlined in Section A of this chapter. Almost always you will be advised to:

- briefly state the nature of your dispute on a written form
- organize any evidence and witnesses you think will help back up your version of events
- practice your court presentation in advance
- come to court on time
- be polite, and
- let the judge decide if your case is any good.

While this approach allows you to expend little effort or thought while the judge does the heavy legal lifting, it comes with a huge built-in disadvantage. You are being told to present your case without understanding the legal rules the judge must apply to render a decision. Here are the main problems with this "dumb and trusting" approach.

- If you don't understand the law that applies to your situation, you won't know your chances of winning—which means you run a high risk of wasting time and energy pursuing an obvious loser.
- Even if you have a decent case, you won't know which facts or arguments are most important if you don't understand the legal rules that underlie it. You probably won't prepare as well as you would have if you'd been fully informed.
- If you win—or especially if you lose—you won't know why.

If the "dumb and trusting" approach sounds like a poor way to prepare your case, perhaps you are open to considering a better one: taking just a few minutes to understand the basic legal rules that underlie your position. Or put another way, it means understanding your dispute on the same legal terms that a judge will ultimately use to decide it.

Defendants need the same legal knowledge as plaintiffs. To defend a case well, a defendant needs to understand the essential legal elements of the case the plaintiff is attempting to prove. Once armed with this information, the defendant will be in good shape to try to convince the judge that at least one key legal element is missing—and therefore, that the plaintiff should lose.

Start by reading the rest of this chapter. It discusses the legal theories most commonly used to establish legal liability. In many instances, this will be all the information you need to properly prepare your case. Occasionally, you will want to do additional legal research, as would be true if the exact wording of a statute or key court decision has a direct bearing on your case. (See Chapter 1, Section D, for more on legal research.)

Below I list the most common legal theories (causes of action) and the requirements (lawyers call them elements) you need to prove to establish each. In the rest of this chapter I'll review each in detail, so you can see if the facts of your loss fit the requirements of at least one of them.

Here is an outline of the key legal theories that underlie 99% of Small Claims cases:

- **Breach of Contract:** The person you are suing broke one or more terms of a valid contract (written, oral, or implied). As a result, you have suffered a monetary loss. (See Section C, below.)

- **Bad Debt:** A type of contract case. To prevail, you need to prove the debt exists, its amount, when payment was due, and that the person you are suing hasn't paid it or has paid only part of it.

- **Breach of Warranty:** A merchant has breached a written or implied warranty and, as a result, you have suffered a monetary loss—for example, a new car suffers mechanical problems while still covered by warranty. (See Section D, below.)

- **Negligence:** The careless behavior of the person you are suing has caused you to suffer a personal injury or property damage resulting in a monetary loss. (Negligence that results in damage to property is covered in Section E1, below. Negligence resulting in a personal injury is covered in Section F, below.)

- **Intentional Harm:** The intentional behavior of the person you are suing has caused you to suffer personal injury or property damage resulting in a monetary loss. (See Section E2, below, for cases involving property damage and Section F, below, for those involving personal injury.)

- **Personal Injury:** The negligent or intentional behavior of the person you are suing has caused you to suffer personal injury. (See Section F, below.)

- **Product Liability:** You or your property were injured by a defective product and the manufacturer is responsible for the damages you suffered under the doctrine of "strict liability." (See Section G, below.)

- **Failure to Return a Security Deposit:** Another variety of contract case that commonly arises between tenants and landlords. As discussed in more detail in Chapter 21, for a tenant to prevail, you need to prove that you made a deposit, that the landlord didn't return it or returned only part of it, and that you left the premises sufficiently clean and undamaged that the landlord owes you some or all of the amount withheld. (In most states you may also be eligible for additional damages if the landlord had no good reason for withholding your deposit or followed improper procedure.)

- **Violation of a Statute:** Your rights under a statute have been violated and, as a result, you have suffered a monetary loss. This would be the case if your opponent had broken a consumer protection, landlord-tenant, employment or other law, resulting in your being out some money. (See Section H, below.)
- **Professional Malpractice:** A lawyer, doctor, or other professional's failure to use the ordinary skills of members of that profession has resulted in your suffering harm or a monetary loss. (See Section I, below.)
- **Public and Private Nuisance:** Someone created a health or safety hazard affecting you (and perhaps other neighbors or nearby property owners), or does something that interferes with your ability to use and enjoy your property—for example, a factory makes so much noise that you and other nearby residents are kept awake all night. (See Section J, below.)

Other legal theories exist. As noted above, these legal theories (lawyers call them "causes of action") make up the overwhelming majority of small claims cases. I have no space to list the technical legal requirements for the dozens of more obscure types of lawsuits—for example, libel and slander lawsuits—that are allowed in some states' small claims courts but prohibited in many others. However, if your case isn't covered here, you may sensibly want to do some additional research to determine whether your case qualifies (contains the correct "legal elements," or criteria) under a different legal theory (cause of action).

Now, before we consider each of these legal theories individually, here is an example of why it's so important to establish not only that you have suffered a loss, but that someone is legally liable to make it good.

Example 1: A thief enters the open, unlocked garage in Sue's apartment complex, smashes her car window, and steals her fancy, $1,000 sound system. After the landlord refuses to pay for Sue's loss, she files suit against him in small claims court. In preparing for her day in court, Sue gets several witnesses to testify that her car had been vandalized in the garage and obtains a copy of the police investigation report. She also gets several estimates as to the cost of repairing the damage to the car window and replacing the sound system.

Unfortunately, Sue overlooks one thing: Under the circumstances, the building owner isn't legally liable (responsible). He has never promised to keep the garage locked. In addition, he has never locked the garage or otherwise led Sue to believe that he would do so. Once the judge determined that all the tenants knew the garage was open, and that no previous crimes had been committed that would have put the landlord on notice of a theft problem in the garage, he concluded the building owner was not liable for Sue's loss. As the judge explained to Sue, there was simply no contract giving her the right to park in a locked garage, so under the circumstances the landlord was not legally negligent (careless).

Example 2: Let's assume the same situation, except that this time the lease (contract) signed by Sue and the landlord states that Sue would be assigned a parking place in a "secure garage." Let's also assume that the garage had always been locked until the lock broke a week before the theft occurred. Finally, let's posit that Sue and other tenants had asked the owner to fix the lock the day after it broke, but that he hadn't "gotten around to it." In this situation, Sue should win. The landlord made certain contractual promises to the tenants (to keep the garage locked) and then failed to keep them in a situation where he had ample opportunity to do so. The failure presumably allowed the thief access to the car. So in this case, it's fair to say that the landlord's failure to live up to his promise caused Sue to suffer a monetary loss.

C. How to Approach a Breach of Contract Case

A contract is any agreement between individuals or businesses in which one side agrees to do something for the other in exchange for something in return. For example, A asks B to paint his kitchen for $3,000 and B agrees. The agreement can be written or oral (in most situations), or implied from the circumstances. Contracts made by minors can be disaffirmed (found invalid) if they are made before the minor turns 18. However, in most states, if a minor makes a contract, then honors it after turning 18, the contract is valid and can no longer be annulled.

All contracts come with an obligation that each party carry out its terms in "good faith." This means each contracting individual or business will deal with the other fairly and honestly under the circumstances so that the common purpose set out in the agreement can be achieved. On the other side of the coin, courts have found "bad faith" when one party does something that evades the spirit of the agreement or violates community standards of fairness and reasonableness.

Practically, it's important to understand that all contracts contain an unwritten good faith requirement, because it means that a small claims judge often won't find in favor of a party who sues based on a highly technical—but obviously unfair or unreasonable—interpretation of contract language. For example, if X agrees to landscape Y's yard in two weeks, but on the last afternoon doesn't quite finish because she is called to the bedside of a sick child, a court will not agree with Y's contention that he doesn't have to pay for any of the work because X technically missed the 14-day deadline. Instead, a judge will almost surely rule that Y's duty to carry out the agreement in good faith requires him to allow X to finish the job a few days late.

1. Common Contract Rules

Here is a short summary of basic contract principles designed to help you understand whether you've got a valid contract in the first place:

- **A gift is not a contract.** As every law student learns on the first day of contracts class, a promise to make a gift is not a contract. The reason is simple: The gift's recipient hasn't promised to do anything in return. Or put another way, an enforceable contract absolutely depends on an exchange—or a promise to exchange—something of value, such as money for services.

- **A loan is a contract.** In contrast to the gift scenario just above, a loan, or a promise to make a loan, is normally a valid contract. That's because each party provides the other something of value—the lender agrees to advance the borrower the money, and the borrower agrees to pay it back with interest.

- **An agreement to exchange goods, services, or money is a contract.** The most common type of contract occurs when A agrees to pay money to B in exchange for B agreeing to work for A or provide A with valuable goods. Thus, if A agrees to pay B to fix A's computer, remodel his kitchen, or walk his dog, a contract exists. Here is an example of how a typical contract is formed: Fred calls electrician Ivan and asks him to repair his faulty wiring. Ivan says, "I'll do it for $2,000." Fred says, "Start Monday."

- **Most oral contracts are valid if proven.** The great majority of spoken agreements are valid and enforceable, assuming their existence can be established to the satisfaction of a judge. But there are several major exceptions to this rule. Generally speaking, oral contracts are not valid if they: 1) can't be accomplished within a year, 2) are for the sale of real estate or 3) involve the sale of goods or property worth more than $500. (But this third type of transaction needs very little written proof—a faxed order or a letter confirming a deal will be enough.) Because the great majority of oral consumer contracts—whether to fix a kitchen, repair a car, or deliver a bed—can easily be carried out in less than a year (even if it actually takes longer), most oral contracts that can be proven to the satisfaction of a judge can be enforced in small claims court.

- **Someone's unjust enrichment can prove a contract.** A contract can be implied where one party has obviously benefited from the other and the other expects to be paid for goods or services. This is a tricky area of contract law that occasionally surfaces in small claims cases. The judge will be particularly interested in evidence that the party who received the benefit knew that the service provider expected to be paid.

Example: Next door neighbors Al and Sara agree that it would beneficial to both to construct a wall on the property line between their yards. Al builds the wall over several weekends while Sara watches. When he finishes he asks Sara to pay for half of the cost of the materials. When Sara refuses, Al sues her in small claims court. In explaining why he is ruling for Al the judge says, "Under these circumstances, Sara would be unjustly enriched if she didn't pay her share."

More help to understand contract law. The law student outline *Contracts,* by Melvin A. Eisenberg (BarBri Group; *Gilbert Law Summaries* series), does an excellent job of explaining contract law. It is particularly good at presenting all the many rules (called "offer and acceptance") that cover whether a contract was formed in the first place.

2. Proving and Defending Contracts Involving Unpaid Debts

Every business day, thousands of Americans are sued in small claims court for failing to pay the phone company, the local hospital, a friend (now a former friend, undoubtedly), a fine to the public library, or some other debt. (See Chapter 19 for more on small claims suits for money owed.) Technically, this is just another contract case, but because it's so common I'll address it separately here. In many situations, getting a judgment for an unpaid debt involves no more than stating that the defendant committed to buy certain goods and/or services, that they were in fact provided, and that a legitimate bill for X dollars has not been paid. In a few states it's even possible to get a judgment in an uncontested case by submitting written documentation of the unpaid bill or loan to the court clerk—you won't even have to enter the courtroom.

To win an unpaid debt case, a plaintiff must normally prove:

- the identity of the debtor
- that the plaintiff kept his or her side of the bargain (for example, lent the money, provided the goods, or did the work)
- the existence of a contract with the debtor, and
- that the debt hasn't been paid.

To establish a winning defense, a defendant usually must prove that either:

- the goods or services were delivered late or not at all, or were seriously defective
- the plaintiff never lent the money in the first place
- the defendant already paid back some or all the money the plaintiff claims is owed
- the plaintiff agreed to a subsequent contract to forgive the debt or give more time to pay, or
- the transaction violated a consumer protection law.

How to convince the judge that a loan contract existed. If you lent a defendant money under the terms of a written agreement, simply bring the agreement to court. But if, as is common, you lent the money with no more than an oral promise to repay it, you'll need to be more creative to establish the loan contract's existence. For example, if you wrote the debtor a check, bring a copy. The check, plus your own testimony that the debtor promised to pay you back, should be all you need to get a judgment. But if you suspect the defendant will claim you never advanced him any money—or that if you did, it was a gift—it would be helpful to have a witness who heard the defendant promise to pay you soon or ask you for more time to pay.

3. Proving and Defending Contracts for Services

A case that commonly crops up in small claims is one in which one party claims the other didn't perform services due under a contract. Claims of sloppy, dangerous, or late work are particularly common. Here are several examples:

- A caterer shows up four hours late with the food and drink for an important business party.
- A "professional" wedding photographer uses the wrong film, and all the photos are badly overexposed.
- A freelance writer agrees to produce a history of a business organization for an annual report but gets so many key facts wrong that the work can't be used.
- A contractor does half the kitchen repair work called for in a contract, then stops working for a month.
- An electrician does several thousand dollars worth of work using materials not approved by the local building code, and the job is not approved by the building inspector.

Damages resulting from a breach of contract are normally not difficult to prove. After you show that the contract existed and that the other party failed to live up to its terms, you should testify about the circumstances of the other person's breach of the contract and the amount of damages you suffered as a result. Remember, judges will not look kindly at plaintiffs who rush into court complaining about minor contract issues, so don't march off to the courthouse unless the defendant really blew it.

Example 1: Justine and Bob planned a June wedding. Because the families of both prospective spouses were widely dispersed, this was to be a combination family reunion and wedding. The couple planned a large reception and arranged to have it catered by Top Drawer Deli. The Deli prepared an order listing food and drink, and Justine signed it. When the big day arrived, everything went swimmingly, until the 200 guests arrived at the reception to find that, while the band was playing cheerfully, Top Drawer had not shown up with the food and bubbly. Fortunately, the best man hopped into his SUV, drove to the nearest liquor store, and in less than an hour was back with 10 cases of champagne. (Clearly there was a reason he was picked as best man.) Someone else had the presence of mind to order 30 pizzas. Three hours later, Top Drawer showed up full of apologies. (A key employee called in sick and their van broke down.) Justine and Bob accepted the cake and nothing else. When the bill came, they paid for the cake and told Top Drawer to eat the rest. Top Drawer sued for $4,000 for breach of contract. Bob and Justine countersued for $5,000 for emotional distress. The judge ruled that by being three hours late to a time-sensitive event, the caterer had breached its contract, so Bob and Justine owed nothing. The judge then dismissed the emotional distress claim after remarking that the reception obviously turned into an unforgettable party.

Example 2: Assume the same facts above, except that Top Drawer showed up only 20 minutes late, because its van had a flat tire. Top Drawer also called from the roadside to say they would be there soon. Although the delay caused the bride and groom (and their parents) additional stress, the guests barely noticed and the party was a success. Nevertheless, when Top Drawer submitted its bill, Bob and Justine only paid half, claiming their contract had been breached due to the late delivery. This time the judge ruled for Top Drawer, stating that under admittedly difficult circumstances the spirit if not the letter of the contract had been met.

⚠ Get an expert if the issue is whether professional or technical work was done properly.
If you claim a dentist botched a crown, a car mechanic ruined your engine, or an electrician improperly wired your vacation cabin, you'll normally need to back up your position with the testimony of an expert. Thus, if another dentist, mechanic, or electrician is willing to testify that the first one did substandard work, and that the work resulted in you suffering a monetary loss, you should have a good chance of winning. See Chapter 15 for a full discussion of the crucial role an expert opinion can play in resolving your dispute.

4. Proving and Defending Contracts Involving Defective Products

Most small claims lawsuits over defective products claim that a written or implied warranty has been broken. See Section D, below, for a full discussion of warranty issues.

5. Common Plaintiff's Mistakes in Breach of Contract Cases

Although many contract cases are easy to win, not all of them result in victory. In fact, I've seen a fair number of plaintiffs lose what looked like open and shut cases, either because of their own mistakes or because of creative work by the defendants. Here I highlight several common situations in which a defendant may be able to take advantage of a plaintiff's slip-up:

- **Failure to show a contract existed:** It's always the plaintiff's job to prove that a contract existed. If the contract is in writing, this can be as easy as bringing it to court and showing it to the judge. But if a written contract has been lost, or the contract was oral or implied from the circumstances, the plaintiff will need to find other ways to prove its existence to the judge's satisfaction. I discuss how to develop and present this type of evidence from the plaintiff's point of view in Chapters 14 and 15. Defendants will want to look for a substantial defect in the contract. For example, a defendant could argue that the contract term was over and the contract no longer in force; that the plaintiff broke the contract first; or that the plaintiff seeks to unfairly rely on a technicality and is therefore acting in bad faith. The example below illustrates one situation where the plaintiff believed a contract existed, but the defendant proved otherwise.

Example: Ben, a landlord, sued John, the parent of one of his tenants, for damages John's daughter and her roommates had caused to their rental unit. John was sued because he had co-signed his daughter's lease. Ben easily convinced the judge that the damage had, in fact, occurred, and the judge seemed disposed toward giving him a judgment for the $980 requested, until John presented his defense. He showed that the lease between his daughter and the landlord had been rewritten three times after he originally co-signed it and that he had not added his signature to any of the revised versions, one of which involved replacing several of his daughter's original roommates with others. The judge agreed that because John had not co-signed any of the subsequent leases (contracts), he wasn't liable. The reason was simple: There was no longer a contract between Ben and John. (Leases and rental agreements, including a detailed discussion of the rights and responsibilities of co-signers, are discussed in more detail in *Every Landlord's Legal Guide,* by Marcia Stewart and Attorneys Ralph Warner & Janet Portman (Nolo).)

- **Failure to sue the right defendant:** Surprisingly, many plaintiffs who have suffered a real loss nevertheless sue the wrong person or business. As discussed in Chapter 9, sometimes a plaintiff sues an individual business person when in fact he or she should have sued a corporation or limited liability company (LLC). But a plaintiff's failure to sue the right defendant can also occur where the plaintiff doesn't fully investigate and understand who is legally responsible for the loss. For example, if water from a broken pipe on your neighbor's property floods your land, it would be a mistake to sue the neighbor without investigating who owns the pipe (maybe it belongs to the water company) and how the break occurred (maybe a city worker did it).

Example: Sid sued Acme Dry Cleaners for $650, the cost of replacing a pigskin suede jacket that shrunk dramatically when Acme cleaned it. In court, Sid established that he had taken the jacket to Acme for cleaning and had agreed to pay Acme $80. Acme, by accepting the jacket, clearly implied it would properly clean the jacket, so there was no question that a contract existed. And certainly Sid was very convincing as to his loss when he stood in court and tried to wriggle into his pygmy jacket whose sleeves now barely passed his elbows. Unfortunately for Sid, he had overlooked one big thing: He had sued the wrong defendant.

    This became clear when Vijay, Acme Dry Cleaner's owner, testified that when he saw the jacket after cleaning, he was amazed. His specialized cleaning process should have resulted in no such shrinkage. What's more, Vijay testified that he examined a number of other items in the same cleaning batch and found no similar problem. To determine what happened, he sent the jacket to an independent testing laboratory. Their report, which he presented to the court, stated that because the leather had been severely over-stretched prior to assembly, it was the jacket itself, not the cleaning, that was the problem.

As a result, the judge ruled that Acme had not breached the cleaning contract and suggested that Sid sue the person who sold him the coat for breach of warranty (see Section D, below).

- **Failure to prove a contract was broken:** In addition to proving that a contract existed in the first place, a plaintiff must also show that the contract was broken and that he or she suffered a monetary loss as a result. This is usually a two-step process, especially if the case is vigorously defended.

  For example, if Alan agrees to sell your collection of baseball cards on consignment in exchange for 20% of the receipts, but Alan instead pockets 50% of the money, your first task is to convince the judge that the two of you truly had a contract that included a 20% fee. Once you do this, it's time to make the point that Alan failed to live up to the contract. This second task should be easy if Alan simply sold the cards and pocketed half the money. However, your task will be harder if Alan gets up and testifies that after difficulty selling the cards, he both faxed and emailed you asking for a higher commission, and that after receiving no objection, he redoubled his efforts and finally found a buyer.

  In such a situation, it would greatly help your case if you could prove, for example, that you were out of town and never received the defendant's (Alan's) message or that you talked personally and rejected his request for a higher commission.

  If you end up as a defendant in a breach of contract lawsuit, it may be appropriate for you to claim that although a contract existed, the plaintiff broke it first. If this is the case—and assuming the breach of contract was serious (material)—you are legally excused from continuing to perform your contractual responsibilities. For example, if Helmut and Wolfgang agree to start a small graphics business, with each contributing $5,000 for startup costs by July 1, Wolfgang has no responsibility to continue with the business should Helmut fail to pay his share. If Helmut later sues Wolfgang for breach of contract, claiming Wolfgang knew Helmut was having money troubles and would pay eventually, Wolfgang should win. Although Helmut has an excuse, he still broke the contract in a material way, and can't ask Wolfgang to continue the business as if everything were normal.

Don't stake your case on a minor breach of contract. A minor breach of contract (in the above example, Helmut telling Wolfgang he will pay the $5,000 three days late) usually won't justify a not-very-injured party such as Wolfgang in withdrawing from the contract. An exception is made when the contract itself emphasizes that a tight deadline is an essential part of the contract (look for legal language that says "time is of the essence").

- **Failure to give the other party a reasonable opportunity to fix the problem (cure the breach).** Both parties to a contract must act fairly and in good faith. This requirement helps explain why it is always wise to give the other party a chance to fix a minor breach of a contract before filing a lawsuit. When you present your case, you want to be sure a judge will conclude that you sincerely tried to carry out the spirit, as well as the letter, of your agreement.

  Example: Carlos hired Leah to remodel his kitchen, agreeing to pay her $20,000, with $10,000 paid up front and the remainder due when the job was completed satisfactorily and within 60 days. After getting through about half the work, Leah pulled her crew off the job to finish up another remodel that was overdue. In the meantime, Carlos was left with an unusable kitchen. After listening to half a dozen of Leah's broken promises to return to his kitchen, and then waiting until 60 days had passed, Carlos wrote Leah a letter stating that she was in breach of their contract and asking her to get back to work in five days. When she didn't, Carlos got two bids from other competent contractors. Accepting the lower bid of $13,000, he finally got his kitchen completed. Carlos then sued Leah for $3,000, the difference between her price and the price he had to pay the second contractor to step in on an emergency basis. Finding that Carlos had given Leah a reasonable chance to cure her breach of contract, and that she had failed to take him up on the opportunity, the judge awarded Carlos the entire $3,000.

- **Failure to prove the amount of damages requested.** Once a breach of contract is established, the plaintiff's last big job is to establish the amount of his or her loss. You have to state this figure when you file your small claims case. I discuss this issue in Chapter 4.

 More material affecting contracts:

- How much you should sue for in breach of contract cases (how to value your damages) is discussed in Chapter 4, Section C1.
- Breach of warranty—based on a written or oral contract—is covered in Section D, below.
- How the violation of a state or federal law can make a contract unenforceable is covered in Section H, below.
- Leases and rental agreements—specialized types of contracts—are covered in Chapter 21.
- How to collect on contracts involving unpaid bills is covered in Chapter 19.
- If your contract involves fraud, undue influence, or a simple mistake ($2,000 was mistakenly written as $20,000), you may have a right to have the contract ended or rewritten, or to get your goods back, under the legal doctrine of "equitable relief." See Chapter 4, Section E.

D. How to Approach a Breach of Warranty Case

 In Chapter 18, I discuss warranties as they apply to problems with new and used cars, as well as lemon laws.

Warranty law is extremely confusing, even to lawyers. A principal reason is that, in every state, at least two separate warranty statutes can apply to the retail sale of goods (see "Warranty Law: Where Does It Come From?"). The sad result is that, short of presenting you with a major treatise, it's impossible to thoroughly explain the warranty law of all 50 states. The best I can do in the short space I have here is to give you several basic rules:

- If a new or used product comes with a written warranty, you have the right to rely on it.

- If a seller makes written or oral statements describing a product's features (for example, "these tires will last at least 25,000 miles") or what it will do ("this hair dryer will work for two years"), and you rely on these statements as part of your decision to purchase the product, an express warranty exists. This is true even if the written warranty printed on the package states there are no other warranties.

- In most situations, an implied warranty of general fitness for the intended use or "merchantability" also applies (for example, that a lawn mower will cut grass, a tire will hold air, and a calculator will subtract). This warranty exists in addition to the written and oral or express warranties discussed just above. Again, the warranty applies even if there is a statement (often called a "warranty disclaimer") printed on the product or packaging saying no warranties exist beyond the express written warranty, that no warranty exists at all, or that all implied warranties are specifically disclaimed.

Warranty Law: Where Does It Come From?

The Magnuson-Moss Warranty Federal Trade Commission Improvement Act (15 USC § 2302) is a federal law that applies in every state. In addition, every state has a commercial code, which includes similar laws regulating retail sales and warranty protections for consumers. Some states have enacted separate consumer protection and warranty laws that go beyond the Magnuson-Moss Act and these commercial codes. For example, in California, a warranty or guarantee is still good even if the buyer doesn't fill out and return the manufacturer's form (Cal. Com. Code § 2801), and in Kansas an implied warranty exists even for goods sold "as is," unless the consumer has knowledge of the exact defects in the merchandise (Kan. Stat. Ann. § 50-639). To find out about your state's warranty laws, search your state statutes for "commercial code," "consumer protection," or "warranty" (see Chapter 1, Section D for more on how to do this), or get in touch with your state consumer protection agency.

If you believe a warranty has been breached—for example, a TV set with a six-month warranty on parts and labor breaks the day after purchase—you should notify the seller and manufacturer in writing, keeping copies of both letters. Give them a reasonable chance to make necessary repairs or replace the defective product. Thirty days to accomplish this is usually considered to be reasonable. If they fail to act, it's time to think about filing in small claims court.

In considering whether and how to pursue a breach of warranty case, you should realize that many small claims court judges often evaluate warranty disputes based on their own broad view of what is fair under the circumstances. In other words, if you purchase goods that are clearly defective or don't do what the seller said they would do (either in an advertisement or a personal statement to you), and you have made and documented a good faith effort to have the seller or manufacturer either fix or replace the goods or refund your money, file in small claims court and let the judge worry about the details of warranty law. But do be prepared to document the statement (warranty) of the seller that you relied on.

Example: Alan purchases a computer and some expensive accounting software from ABC Computer. He fully explains his high-end bookkeeping needs to the salesperson and is assured that the computer and software will do the job. The computer contains a written warranty against defects in parts and labor for 90 days. The warranty statement says that all implied warranties are disclaimed. The software contains no written warranty statement. It is apparent to Alan after a couple of days' work that the software simply is not sophisticated enough to meet the bookkeeping needs that he described to the salesperson, and that the salesperson didn't know what he was talking about when he said it was "perfect for the job."

Two days later, the computer breaks. Alan calls ABC and asks for the computer to be fixed or replaced and for his money back on the software. When ABC ignores him, Alan sues in small claims court. As to recovering for the computer, Alan should have no problem—it failed within the written warranty period.

The software raises a different problem. In asking for his money back, Alan claims the seller breached an express warranty (the salesperson's statement that it would meet his needs), as well as the implied warranty of general fitness or merchantability (Alan must show the software really does fall below the reasonable standard for sophisticated small business accounting packages). However, this latter claim might be hard to prove—especially if the software is in wide use and is adequate to accomplish most accounting tasks, just not sophisticated enough for Alan's special needs. In court, Alan will be smart to focus on trying to prove that he relied on the salesperson's express statements that the software would meet his specific bookkeeping needs as part of his decision to purchase it.

How should he do this? If Alan had given the salesperson written specifications of his accounting needs and had a copy, or if he had a witness to the salesperson's overly optimistic promises, he would be in good shape. Otherwise, it might come down to his word against the salesperson's, with the judge left to decide who appears to be telling the truth.

E. How to Approach a Case When Your Property Has Been Damaged by the Negligent or Intentional Acts of Someone Else

After cases involving breach of contract, the most common disputes that land in small claims court involve property damage allegedly caused by the defendant's negligent actions. Less often, the plaintiff claims to have suffered loss because the defendant wasn't merely negligent, but actually intended to damage the plaintiff's belongings.

1. Negligence

A technical definition of negligence could—and does—fill entire law texts. But I don't recommend your reading one, since I remember thinking in law school that the more professors wrote about the subject, the more mixed up they got. Like good taste or bad wine, negligence seems to be easy to recognize, but hard to define.

So I'll breeze right past the "ifs," "ands," and "wherefores" and give you the sort of peasant's definition that always made the most sense to me: If, as a result of another person's conduct, your property is injured, and that person didn't act with reasonable care under the circumstances, you have a valid legal claim based on his or her negligence. In addition, negligence can occur when a person who has a duty or responsibility to act fails to do so. For example, an electrician who fails to check the wiring in a room where you told him you saw some funny sparks and he promised to have a look would be negligent.

Example: Jake knows the brakes on his ancient Saab are in serious need of repair, but does nothing about it. One night, when the car is parked on a hill, the brakes fail and the car rolls across the street and destroys Keija's persimmon tree. Keija sues Jake for $225, the reasonable value of the tree. Jake will lose, because he did not act with reasonable care under the circumstances.

Another obvious situation involving negligence would be one where a car or bus swerves into your driving lane and sideswipes your fender. The driver of the offending vehicle has a duty to operate it in such a way as to not harm you. By swerving into your lane, the driver violated his duty.

Negligence is more difficult to show, however, if the signs of carelessness are less obvious. For example, say your neighbor's tree falls on your car, properly parked in your driveway. Here you have to be ready to prove that, for some reason (such as age, disease, or an obviously bad root system), the tree was in a weakened condition, and the neighbor was negligent in failing to do something about it. If the tree had looked to be in good health, your neighbor probably wasn't negligent, since he had no reason to remove it or prop it up. Here are some additional examples where a person or business failed to act with reasonable care and as a result was negligent:

- While playing with his kids in his small backyard, Kevin hits a ball over the fence, smashing a neighbor's overlooking window.
- While upgrading Eddie's computer, Bill carelessly installs the wrong chip, which crashes Eddie's hard drive and ruins his computer.
- RapidMail Inc., a local courier service, loses several time-sensitive messages and fails to notify the sender of the problem.

Compound negligence exists where more than one person is responsible for the damages you suffer—for example, if you are injured because you fall down a staircase with no hand railing, after someone who is not paying attention to where she is going runs into you. When dealing with any situation in which more than one person may have contributed to your loss, Rule #1 is to sue them all.

Example 1: Sandy comes home from work one day to find her new fence knocked over and Fred's Chevy Blazer in the middle of her front lawn. Fred admits his vehicle knocked over the fence when his brakes failed. To Sandy, this may at first seem like a simple case involving filing suit against Fred, but what if Fred had just picked up his car from Atomic Auto Repair, where he had his brakes worked on? Fred's liability may range from minimal (Atomic is only 50 feet away; he just left the shop with the assurance that the brakes were fixed) to extensive (Atomic is located across town and at the last two stop signs, Fred's brakes acted "funny" but he continued to drive anyway). Sandy would be well advised to sue both Fred and Atomic and let the judge sort out who is most at fault.

Example 2: Now suppose that Fred's brakes are fine, but he claims he was rear-ended at the stop sign by Dana, whose pickup truck pushed his vehicle through Sandy's fence. Again, Fred's liability may be minimal (Dana was drunk and speeding), or it may be extensive (Fred ran a stop sign while turning and was rear-ended by Dana, who had the right of way). Again, Sandy would be wise to sue both parties and let the judge decide who was most at fault.

Negligence concepts are tricky: Don't try to be a judge. There is often no foolproof way to determine in advance whether someone will be judged to be negligent. When it comes to accidents, it's often a close legal and factual question that even lawyers can't predict. If you have suffered a real loss and think someone else caused it, bring your well-prepared case and let the judge decide.

To help you determine whether you have a good case based on someone else's negligence, answer the following questions:

- Did the person whose act (or failure to act) injured you behave in a reasonable way? Or to put it another way, would you have behaved differently?
- Did your conduct significantly contribute to the injury?

If you believe the person who caused you to suffer a monetary loss behaved in an unreasonable way (ran a red light when drunk) and that you were acting sensibly (driving at 30 mph in the proper lane), you probably have a good case. If you were a little at fault (slightly negligent), but the other person was much more at fault (very negligent), you can still recover most of your losses, because courts follow a legal doctrine called "comparative negligence." This involves subtracting the percentage of your negligence from 100 percent to find out how legally responsible the other party is. Thus, if a judge finds that one person (drunk and speeding) was 80 percent at fault, and the other (slightly inattentive) was 20 percent at fault, the slightly inattentive party can recover 80 percent of his or her damages.

More information about negligence. If, despite my advice to keep it simple, you want to get into the gory details of negligence theory, go to your nearest law library and get any recent hardbound legal text on "torts" (wrongful acts or injuries). Or, even easier, if you are near a law bookstore, buy a copy of one of the several competing paperback summaries of torts that law students actually rely on to get through their torts exams (for example, *Torts*, by Marc A. Franklin (Barbri Group; *Gilbert Law Summaries* series)).

2. Intentional Acts

Not all injuries to people or property are accidents. You also have the right to recover money damages from someone who intentionally damages you or your personal property. (I cover personal injuries in Section F, below.)

> **Example:** Basil and Shirley are neighbors who can't stand the sight of each other, despite, or perhaps because of, the fact that both are prize-winning rose growers. When Basil took first place in the local garden club contest for his exotic roses. Shirley, who was angry, frustrated, and jealous, intentionally left her hose running and drowned all of Basil's roses. Basil should be able to recover the value of his roses from Shirley.

In theory, at least, it is also possible to recover punitive damages (additional money awarded to punish the defendant) if you are damaged by the malicious conduct of someone else. However, in part because public sentiment is running strongly against punitive damage awards, they are seldom awarded. Nevertheless, Basil, in the above example, might be tempted to sue Shirley for more than the cost of replacing the roses, based on her bad conduct. Unfortunately, for two reasons, it's rarely possible to be awarded punitive damages in small claims court:

- About half the states simply don't allow claims for punitive damages to be initiated in small claims court.

- Low dollar limits in small claims court mean that even in states where punitive damages can, in theory, be awarded, there is little realistic chance that the judge will do so. In short, if you believe you really might recover punitive damages, you should almost always file your case in a formal court, asking for lots more money than the small claims limit.

But suppose you are convinced you deserve punitive damages and want to sue for an extra few thousand dollars (assuming the small claims limit in your state is high enough). First, check your local court rules. If you find no prohibition, go ahead. The worst the judge will do is to allow you actual damages, while denying your claim for punitives.

 More material on property damage: To determine how much to sue for, see Chapter 4, Section C2.

F. How to Approach a Personal Injury (and Mental Distress) Case

I treat personal injury cases in this separate section because so many people look at them as a different kind of lawsuit. In fact, most personal injury cases are based on a claim that someone has been negligent (and a few are based on claims of intentional injury). The legal theories involved are the same as set out in Section E, above. To prevail, you must show that your injury was caused by someone's negligent or intentional behavior (unless your case qualifies as one of the very few where the law applies the doctrine of strict liability—see Section G, below).

Most personal injury cases involve amounts of money that exceed the small claims maximum and should therefore be pursued in formal courts. However, occasionally a minor personal injury case will be appropriate for small claims.

Example 1: Jenny and Karen are playing softball in a picnic area of a park, where many families are picnicking in the sun. Jenny, never a star fielder, misses a batted ball that hits seven-year-old Willie in the face and chips his tooth. Assuming Willie (with the help of his parents) sues Jenny and Karen for the $500 it will cost to fix his tooth, is he likely to win? Probably. Because Willie was in a picnic area where he had a right to be, we can safely assume that Jenny and Karen were careless (negligent). Why? Because as a society, we have decided that picnic areas are for picnickers—not ballplayers. Because Jenny and Karen's game was inappropriate and dangerous to others, they are going to have to pay for their negligence.

Example 2: Now assume that Jenny and Karen have moved over to a ball field. Their skills still haven't improved and Karen again misses the ball, which again hits Willie, who has escaped his parents and wandered onto the field unobserved. Are Jenny and Karen liable? Probably not. Jenny and Karen took reasonable precautions to avoid hitting picnickers by playing on the ball field. While they may have a responsibility to get little Willie off the field if they spot him, they are probably not legally responsible— that is, negligent—in a situation where he wanders onto the field unnoticed. So this time a small claims judge is likely to award nothing to Willie.

Consider not only your loss, but whether the other party acted reasonably under the circumstances. Before you sue someone for injury, consider whether it was really caused by their negligence. If so, the person is legally liable to make good your loss. If not (you trip and fall down a perfectly safe set of stairs), you have no right to recover, no matter what your injury. (A major exception applies if you were injured by a defective product; see Section G, below.) If in doubt, go ahead and sue, but be prepared to deal with the liability question, and to show the extent of your injury. In Chapters 15 and 16, I give you some practical advice on how to prove your case.

As discussed in more detail in Chapter 4, you do not have to suffer a physical injury to successfully recover in court as a result of someone else's negligent or intentionally obnoxious behavior. Invasion of privacy and the intentional infliction of mental distress are but two of the types of lawsuits that can be based on nonphysical injuries.

> **Example:** Your landlady enters your apartment several times without notice, permission, or good legal reason. You make it clear that this behavior is highly upsetting and ask her to stop invading your privacy. She nevertheless persists in entering your apartment with no good reason, causing you to become genuinely upset and anxious. You file a small claims case based on the intentional infliction of mental distress. Assuming you can convince the judge that you were truly and seriously upset, your chances of winning are good.

Obviously, not every instance of antisocial behavior that makes you mad justifies bringing a lawsuit. Generally, to recover, the other person's actions must:

- be truly obnoxious
- violate a state law or local ordinance (the invasion of a tenant's privacy qualifies, because statutes in most states prohibit a landlord from entering without notice or permission, except in an emergency; for more on this, see *Every Tenant's Legal Guide*, by Attorney Janet Portman and Marcia Stewart (Nolo)), or
- continue after you have asked the person to stop (it's best to do this in writing and to do it more than once).

In addition, you must be able to convince a judge that you have genuinely suffered mental distress as a result of the other person's conduct. (Therapy bills or perhaps evidence of your lost sleep would be good evidence to present to the judge.)

 Damages for pain and suffering are not allowed in many states. As discussed in Chapter 4, small claims courts in some states do not have the power to award damages for "pain and suffering." In these states, actions to recover this type of damage must be filed in formal court.

More material affecting personal injuries. To figure out how much to sue for in personal injury cases, see Chapter 4, Section C4.

G. How to Approach a Case When You Are Injured by a Defective Product (Doctrine of Strict Liability)

Under a legal concept called "strict liability," there is usually no need to prove negligence if you are injured as a result of a defect in a product. (This legal area is often referred to as "product liability.") If your vacuum cleaner, hair dryer, steam iron, lawn mower, car, or other product malfunctions and you are injured as a result, you are entitled to recover from the manufacturer or other defendant (usually the person you bought or rented the product from) without having to prove negligence. Because of the large sums of money often involved, most product liability cases will end up in formal court. Now and then, however, a defect in a product will cause an injury small enough that the damage caused falls within the small claims court maximum. If you find yourself in this situation, it is best to sue both the manufacturer and the seller. Be prepared to prove that the product really did malfunction and that you were injured as a result.

H. How to Approach a Case When Your Rights Under State Law Have Been Breached

There are thousands of laws designed to protect consumers. Everything from the construction of home swimming pools to regulation of retail sales, the moving of household goods, and the types of contracts that you can be offered by health clubs are covered. These laws are too extensive to outline here; however, be aware that if a provider of goods or services has violated one of these laws, you may be able to cancel your deal with no obligation to pay.

One of the most routine consumer complaints (for which specific laws provide remedies) is that advertising was false or deceptive. In general, these laws provide that private parties may recover the money they spent for falsely advertised goods or services. If you believe that the person you have a claim against has violated a state law, and this violation is directly related to the monetary damage you have suffered, call the judge's attention to the law in question as part of your oral presentation in small claims court.

Another common type of consumer protection law involves a cooling-off period, usually a three- to five-day period, during which you can cancel a purchase agreement. For example, the Federal Trade Commission imposes a three-day cancellation period for door-to-door sales (16 C.F.R. § 429.1). You must be given notice of your right to cancel and a cancellation form when you sign the purchase contract. If you don't get the form, your cancellation right extends until the seller sends it to you, even if it takes months.

Most states have adopted laws that also provide consumers' cancellation rights for a number of other types of contracts, often including health club memberships, discount buying clubs, and time-share properties. If you have not been properly notified of your right to cancel, you can raise this as a defense in small claims court.

All 50 states have also adopted some form of "lemon law," protecting buyers of defective cars. Most require that the manufacturer either fix the car or refund the purchase price. For more on motor vehicle purchases and lemon laws, see Chapter 18.

In addition to the specific consumer protection rights embedded in literally thousands of state laws, there are several general legal rules you should know about. One of the most important of these deals with fraud. Generally speaking, if a transaction is fraudulent, the deal can be canceled. Fraud can take the form of intentional misrepresentation, negligent misrepresentation (a statement about a product or service made without adequate information that it is true), fraudulent concealment (hiding a key fact), a false promise (a promise with no intention to fulfill it), or any other act designed to deceive. If you think you have been defrauded, make sure the judge knows about your contention. The judge has the power to "rescind" a sale or other contract that involves fraudulent conduct and order that your money be refunded, along with any damages you have suffered as a result of the fraud.

Not all small claims courts will allow actions for fraud or requests to rescind contracts. Check your state's small claims court rules. In some states, you have to file actions based on fraud in a formal court.

Money Troubles: Legal Strategies to Cope With Your Debts, by Robin Leonard (Nolo), contains additional information about laws that allow consumers to cancel contracts.

I. Professional Malpractice

An increasing number of small claims cases are being filed against doctors, lawyers, accountants, and other professionals. The main reason is that it can be difficult or impossible to get lawyers to represent you in a formal court action. (Lawyers accept only one in 20 medical malpractice cases, according to one study.) As a result, the injured person must decide to either file without a lawyer in formal court or scale down the dollar amount of the claim to fit into small claims court.

As with all lawsuits, to succeed with a malpractice claim, you must establish all its required legal elements as part of your small claims case. These normally consist of:

- **Duty:** The professional owed you a duty of care. This one is automatically taken care of as long as you really were a patient or a client.

- **Carelessness:** The professional failed to use at least ordinary professional skills in carrying out the task (unless he or she claimed to be a specialist, in which case the standard is higher). This one can be tougher to prove. Unless the mistake is breathtakingly obvious, you'll normally need to get the opinion of one or more people (experts) in the same profession stating that the professional screwed up. In theory, you can do this via letter, but because the professional you are suing will almost surely be in court denying all wrongdoing, it's far better to have your expert witness testify in person.

- **Causation:** The professional's carelessness directly caused the harm or injury you suffered. For many types of malpractice, showing that the professional caused your injury isn't a problem (only the dentist could have stuck that drill through your cheek, for example). But in the legal field, the causation issue can be tricky, especially if a failed lawsuit is involved. You typically will need to show not only that the lawyer's mistake caused you to lose, but that you would have won if no mistake had been made. In other words, you need to convince the judge your underlying lawsuit was a winner.

- **Damages:** The harm you suffered at the hands of the professional resulted in actual economic loss to you.

Example: You consult a lawyer about an injury you suffered falling downstairs at a store. The lawyer says he will file a case on your behalf, but forgets to do so before the one-year Statute of Limitations runs out. Several lawyers you consult won't take your malpractice case because your injuries were fairly minor and they aren't sure it will be possible to prove that the store was at fault. (In other words, the lawyer's mistake might not have harmed you, because your case wasn't so hot in the first place.) You sue your lawyer in small claims court. His failure to file your case on time is clearly an act of carelessness (a lawyer using ordinary legal skills would have filed on time), but to win you'll also have to show that your lawyer's careless act resulted in harm to you. This means convincing the judge that, in fact, your case against the store was a winner and that your injuries were serious enough to qualify for the amount of money you are requesting.

Further reading: *Represent Yourself in Court: How to Prepare & Try a Winning Case*, by Paul Bergman and Sara J. Berman-Barrett (Nolo), explores how to bring a malpractice case in formal court.

J. How to Prove a Nuisance Case

Sorry to use arcane terminology like "nuisance," but when you deal with legal theories, gobbledygook often comes with the territory. A private nuisance occurs when someone prevents or disturbs your use or enjoyment of your property. For example, if your neighbor lets his dog bark all night, preventing you from sleeping, that's a private nuisance. If, after you ask that the dog be kept quiet, the barking persists and causes you real discomfort, you can sue.

A public nuisance, by contrast, is an act that causes a group of people (residents of a particular neighborhood, for example) to suffer a health or safety hazard or lose the peaceful enjoyment of their property—for example, if planes suddenly begin flying low over a neighborhood or a chemical plant lets toxic fumes drift over neighboring property, causing people to become ill. Public nuisance suits are often initiated by groups of individuals all filing suits at more or less the same time. One fairly common example of this involves multiple small claims lawsuits against neighbors, or their landlords, who sell drugs. (See Chapter 8, Section C, for more about these so-called class actions.) If you want to know more about the law of nuisance generally, locate one of the several law student course summaries on the field of torts. These are available at specialty law book stores and law libraries.

Try mediation before filing a lawsuit against a neighbor. It is very difficult to put a dollar value on lawsuits against neighbors for antisocial acts, no matter how annoying. In addition, filing suit usually makes long-term relationships worse. For these reasons, I believe disputing neighbors should always try mediation before turning to small claims court. (See Chapter 7 for more on mediation.) ■

Can You Recover If You Win?

This is the shortest chapter and the most important. In it, I ask all of you who are thinking of filing a Small Claims suit to focus on a very simple question: Can you collect if you win? Whenever a dispute develops, it is all too easy to get so caught up in thinking about suing the bastard who did you wrong that you forget to think about how you'll collect. This mistake can compound your loss by wasting valuable time for the dubious and short-lived satisfaction of hearing the judge say, "You win."

Collecting from solvent individuals or businesses isn't usually a problem, because they will routinely pay any judgments entered against them; if they don't, there are numerous legal ways you can force them to do so. Unfortunately, a goodly number of judgment debtors are either broke (lawyers say "judgment proof") or so adept at hiding their assets that collecting your winnings is likely to prove impossible. There are many legal ways for a debtor to protect a long list of assets from creditors armed with court judgments. For example, debtor protection laws prevent you from seizing many types of property, usually including the food from the debtor's table, the TV from his or her living room or even, in most states, the car from his or her driveway. State laws exempt about $1,500–$4,000 of equity in a motor vehicle from being used to pay debts.

What do these facts mean to you? Again, that many people who are not homeless are nevertheless "judgment proof." You can sue and get judgments against them until red cows dance on the yellow moon, but you won't be able to collect a dime.

So a big key to deciding whether to file a small claims case should be figuring out whether you can collect any judgment you win. How can you tell ahead of time? In most situations, it's not hard. The first thing you should investigate is whether the defendant has a job; if a person fails to pay a judgment voluntarily, the easiest way to collect it is to garnish his or her wages. But you can't garnish a welfare, Social Security, unemployment, pension or disability check. So if the person sued gets most of his income from one of these sources, red flags should definitely be flying.

But what about other assets? Can't a judgment be collected from sources other than wages that are not protected by state debtor-protection laws? Sure—bank accounts, stocks and bonds, motor vehicles, and real estate are other common collection sources. And where a business is the judgment debtor, you can often collect by ordering the sheriff or marshal to take the amount of the judgment right out of the debtor's cash register. But remember, many types of personal property are exempt from attachment. In New York, for example, among a long list of exemptions we find "all stoves kept for use in the judgment debtor's dwelling house" and a "pew occupied by the judgment debtor or the family in a place of public worship."

Most states exempt household goods and appliances necessary for everyday living (such as a stove, refrigerator, dishes, or TV set); sentimental items and family keepsakes (such as photos, jewelry, or works of art); and tools or machinery the debtor uses to make a living (such as a computer, professional library, or power saw). A debtor's retirement account, life insurance, pension, and certain types of savings accounts are also protected. Even more significant in terms of assets, a portion or all of the equity in a debtor's home is exempt.

The Law of Wage Garnishments or Attachments

In most states a creditor with a judgment can't take more than 25% of a judgment debtor's net earnings, or the amount by which the debtor's net earnings exceed 30 times the federal minimum wage, whichever is less. (Net earnings are total earnings less all mandatory deductions for such items as withheld income taxes and unemployment tax.)

A few states offer greater protections for judgment debtors; the sheriff or marshal's office in your area can supply you with your state's rules.

Before you file your small claims papers, ask yourself a few questions:
- Does the person you wish to sue voluntarily pay debts, or are you dealing with a person who will make it as difficult as possible to collect if you win?
- If the defendant may not pay voluntarily, does he or she have a job, or is he or she likely to get one in the not too distant future, as might be the case with a student? Or, might the defendant become solvent in some other way: win the lottery, inherit money, or win a personal injury lawsuit, for example? (Most states allow a judgment to be collected for five to 20 years after the date it is entered,

and a persistent creditor can usually renew this right for a longer period (see Chapter 25, Section E).)

- Can you identify some nonexempt assets that you can attach, such as a bank account or real property other than the place where the person lives (in many states, the equity in a home is exempt from attachment up to a fairly hefty amount)?

- If a business is involved, is it solvent, and does it have a good reputation for paying debts? If the answer is no, is there a readily available cash source you can reach, such as a cash register, or does the business own assets, such as valuable office equipment, which you can order attached and sold?

Beware of bankruptcy. If a person or a business declares a straight bankruptcy (under Chapter 7 of the Federal Bankruptcy Act) and lists you as a creditor, your right to recover a small claims court judgment is cut off, just as if you were any other creditor (but if your judgment was based on a secured loan, you do have the right to recover the property pledged as security). One big exception to this general rule exists if the judgment was obtained because you or your property was injured by the malicious behavior of the person declaring bankruptcy. In this situation, your right to collect your judgment should survive the bankruptcy (but you may need to intervene in the bankruptcy proceedings). An example of malicious behavior would be someone getting drunk and then attacking and injuring you.

Chapter 25 explains the mechanics of collecting after you get your judgment. If you think that collection may pose a problem, skip ahead and read this chapter now and, if necessary, do a little research into your opponent's financial affairs. ■

How Much Can You Sue For?

The maximum amount for which you can sue—or be sued—in small claims court varies from state to state. For example, it's $7,500 in Minnesota, $1,500 in Kentucky, and $5,000 in Texas. You'll find the limits for other states in the Appendix, but because these are increased periodically, you'll always want to check by calling your local small claims court clerk or, better yet, obtaining a copy of your local court rules. With some exceptions, small claims courts do not hear cases unless they are for money damages. Thus, you can't use small claims court to get a divorce, stop ("enjoin") the city from cutting down your favorite oak tree, change your name, or do many of the thousands of other things that require a solution other than one side paying money to the other.

One exception to the "money only" rule involves equitable relief, which is available in some states. This is legalspeak for a court's power to order a party to perform a specific act, such as return a uniquely valuable piece of property or change a contract that contains an obvious mistake. Often called by their centuries-old names, such as rescission, restitution, reformation, and specific performance, these remedies are discussed in Section E of this chapter. Another exception to the money-only rule involves evictions. In some states, a landlord can use small claims court to evict tenants in certain situations. (See Chapter 21 and the Appendix for more information.)

A. Cutting Down a Claim That's Over the Limit

It is legal to reduce a claim so that it will fit the small claims court limit. Thus, you could take a $5,300 debt and bring it into small claims court in Oregon (where the dollar limit is $5,000) asking for only $5,000. (Costs for filing and serving papers are recoverable in addition to the dollar limit in most states.) But if you do this, you forever give up your right to the remaining $300. In legal parlance, this is called "waiving the excess." Why might you want to do this? Because the alternative to small claims court involves filing your suit in a formal court with dozens of complicated rules, for which you may need to hire a lawyer, who will surely charge considerably more than $300 to represent you. It is possible to represent yourself in formal court, but doing so requires a good bit of homework and the fortitude to walk into an unfamiliar and sometimes hostile arena. If you do plan to go it alone, see Recommended Reading, just below.

Check out the court just above small claims. In most states, there are several levels of courts, with different monetary limits. A case that doesn't fit into small claims court may be appropriately filed in an intermediate level court (possibly called "circuit," "district" or "county" court, depending on the state). In recent years, these courts, which typically hear cases worth between $10,000 and $25,000, have gradually begun to be "delawyered" as more and more people represent themselves.

By far the best book ever published on handling your own case is *Represent Yourself in Court*, by Paul Bergman and Sara Berman-Barrett (Nolo). It explains in detail what papers to file, how to conduct pretrial discovery and what to do when you finally get your day in court.

B. Splitting Small Claims Court Cases

It is not legal to split one over-the-limit claim into two or more lawsuits to fit each into small claims court. Taking the $5,300 figure used above, this means that you can't sue the same person separately for $3,500 and $1,800 based on the same claim. (Defendants' claims that are over the small claims limit are discussed in Chapters 11 and 13.) As with most rules, however, a little creative thought can sometimes point the way to an exception. It's perfectly okay to bring multiple suits against the same person as long as they are based on different claims, and there is often a large gray area in which it is genuinely difficult to differentiate between one divided claim and several independent ones. This, of course, is where the creativity comes in. If you can reasonably argue that a $5,300 case actually involves two or more separate contracts or injuries to you or your property, you may as well try dividing it. The worst that will happen is that a judge will disagree and tell you to make a choice between taking your entire case to a formal court, or reducing your claim to fit within the small claims dollar limit. But beware of rules limiting the number of lawsuits that you can bring.

> **Example 1:** One morning, a man in the private telephone business came into small claims court with three separate lawsuits against the same defendant, for a combined total of $8,000, in a state where the small claims court maximum is $5,000. One claim, he said, was for failure to pay for phone installation, another was for failure to pay for phone maintenance, and the third was for failure to pay for moving several phones to a different location. The man claimed that each suit was based on the breach of a separate contract. The judge, after asking a few questions, told the man that he was on the borderline between one divided (not acceptable) and several separate (acceptable) claims, but decided to give him the benefit of the doubt and allowed him to present each case. The man won all three and got two judgments for $2,000 and a third for $4,000.

> **Example 2:** Another morning in small claims court in the same state, a woman alleged that she had lent a business acquaintance $3,000 on two separate occasions and was therefore bringing two separate suits, each for $3,000. The defendant objected, claiming that she had borrowed $6,000, to be repaid in two installments. A different judge, after briefly listening to each side of the argument, agreed with the defendant, told the plaintiff that only one claim was involved, and said that if she didn't want to waive all money over $5,000, she should go to Municipal Court, which had a top dollar limit of $25,000.

Think twice before filing separate but related claims on the same day. If you split an over-the-limit claim, you may want to file your separate claims a few weeks apart—that way, they will be heard on different days and, in most metropolitan areas, probably by different judges. Unless the defendant shows up and argues that you have split one claim, you will likely get your judgments without difficulty. There is, however, one possible drawback to this approach. If you bring your claims to court on the same day and the judge rules they are really only one claim, you will normally have a choice to either waive the excess over the small claims maximum in your state or go to a formal court. However, if you go to court on different days and the question of split claims is raised on the second or third day, you may have a problem. If the judge decides that your action in splitting the claims was improper, he or she may throw the second and third claims out of small claims court without giving you the opportunity to refile in a formal court. This is because you have already sued and won, and you are not entitled to sue the same person twice for the same claim.

C. How to Compute the Exact Amount of Your Claim

The exact dollar amount to sue for is often easy to determine—but not always. Before we get to the times when it can be tricky, let's start with Rule #1: When in doubt, always bring your suit a little on the high side. Why? Because the court has the power to award you less than you request, but can't give you more, even if the judge feels you are entitled to it. But don't go overboard—if you sue for $4,500 on a $2,000 claim, you are likely to spur your opponent to furious opposition, ruin any chance for an out-of-court compromise, and lose the respect of the judge.

Ask to amend your claim if you belatedly discover you should have requested more. If you find yourself in court and belatedly realize you have asked for too little, request that the judge allow you to amend your claim on the spot. Some judges will do this and, at the same time, offer the defendant extra time to prepare to defend against the higher claim. Other judges will allow you to dismiss your original case (without prejudice) and start over, which is fine as long as your time to file hasn't run out. (See Chapter 5.)

1. Computing the Exact Amount—Contract Cases

To arrive at the exact figure to sue for in contract cases, compute the difference between the amount you were supposed to receive under the contract and what you actually received. For example, if Jeannie Goodday agrees to pay Homer Brightspot $2,200 to paint her house, but then only pays him $1,800, Homer has a claim for $400 plus the cost of filing suit and serving Jeannie with the papers. (Court costs, which can be added to your judgment, are discussed in more detail in Chapter 16.)

Unfortunately, some claims based on breach of contract are hard to reduce to a dollar amount. This is due to a legal doctrine known as "mitigation of damages." Don't let the fancy term throw you. As with so much of law, the concept behind the mumbo jumbo is simple. "Mitigation of damages" simply means that the person bringing suit for breach of contract must take all reasonable steps to limit the amount of damages he or she suffers. Let's take an example from the landlord-tenant field. Tillie the tenant moves out three months before the end of her lease (remember, a lease is a contract). Her monthly rent is $700. Can Larry the landlord recover the full $2,100 ($700 x 3 months) from Tillie in small claims court? Maybe not. In many states, the law requires Larry to try to limit (or mitigate) his damages by taking reasonable steps to find a new tenant. If Larry immediately rerents the apartment to someone else for $700 or more per month, he has suffered little or no damage (he has fulfilled his responsibility to "mitigate damages"). More typically, it might take Larry several weeks or months (unless he had plenty of advance notice, or Tillie lined up an acceptable tenant for him) to find a suitable new tenant. For example, if it took Larry two months to rerent Tillie's unit, plus $75 worth of newspaper ads, he could recover approximately $1,475 from Tillie, assuming the judge found that Larry had taken reasonable steps to find the new tenant. (For more on landlord-tenant conflicts, see Chapter 21.)

Landlords are not required to mitigate damages in every state. In a few states, landlords have no duty to mitigate a tenant's damages by promptly rerenting. In other states, case law on this issue is unclear. For more information and a state-by-state chart, see Every Tenant's Legal Guide, by Janet Portman and Marcia Stewart (Nolo).

The mitigation of damages concept applies to any contract in which the person damaged can take reasonable steps to limit his or her losses. In the earlier house painting example, if Jeannie Goodday had agreed to pay Homer Brightspot $300 per day for seven days to paint her house and then had canceled after the first day, Homer would be eligible to sue her for the remaining $1,800, based on Jeannie's breach of the contract. However, in court, Homer likely would be asked whether he had earned any other money during the six days. If he had, it would be subtracted from the $1,800.

But what if Homer refused other work and slept in his hammock all week? If Jeannie could show he had turned down other jobs, or had refused to make reasonable efforts to seek available work, the judge would likely consider this a failure to mitigate damages and reduce Homer's recovery.

a. Loan Contracts

How much should you sue for if you lent money to a person who promised to repay it but failed to do so? Bring suit for the total you are currently owed, plus any unpaid interest (assuming it doesn't result in your claim exceeding the small claims maximum). I have seen several disappointed people sue for the exact amount of the debt (say $500) and not include interest (say $50), thinking they could have the judge add the interest when they got to court. This normally can't be done—in most states, the judge doesn't have the power to make an award larger than the amount you request.

Don't invent interest if none was provided as part of the loan. As a general rule, you can only recover interest when it is called for in a written or oral contract. For example, if you loaned a friend $100, but never mentioned interest, you can sue only for the return of the $100.

Special rules apply to installment loans. If you are owed money under the terms of a promissory note (contract) that calls for repayment to be made in installments, you are normally only entitled to recover the amount of the payments that have already been missed (with interest, if it was specified in the contract). You can *not* recover payments that aren't yet due, even if you are sure they will never be paid. But there is an important exception to this rule: You can sue for the entire loan amount plus any interest if your installment contract contains an "acceleration clause"—language stating that the entire amount of the loan is due if one payment is missed.

b. Extra Damages for Bad Checks

In some situations, a statute (law) gives you the right to receive extra damages, over and above the amount of the financial loss. The most common of these involves bad checks (or checks on which the writer stops payment in bad faith).

The majority of states have bad check laws, which allow you to recover the amount of the check plus a penalty of two or three times the amount of the check if the person giving it to you does not make it good within the time period allowed by the statute—usually within 30 days of your written demand to do so. In some states, such as California, this law is mandatory—the judge must award the penalty.

In addition, there are usually some minimum and maximum penalties allowed:

- You can usually sue for some minimum amount in damages, no matter how small the bad check. Thus, in California, which has a minimum penalty of $100, if you get a $25 bad check, you can sue for $125.
- There is usually a top limit on the damages you can sue for, no matter how large the check. Thus, in California, where the maximum penalty is $1,500, for a $600 bad check, the most you can sue for is $2,100 (the amount of the check plus the $1,500 maximum).

Don't forget to demand payment before you sue. If someone gives you a bum check or stops payment on a check and you want to try to collect damages, send him or her a letter by certified mail demanding payment of the amount of your bad check plus any applicable service charge, plus your mailing costs. Wait at least 30 days before filing suit, in order to give the check writer time to pay.

Cover your back if you stop a check payment. If you yourself write a check and then stop payment because you believe that the services or goods you purchased were substandard (or never provided), write a letter to the serviceperson or vendor stating in detail why you were dissatisfied. If you are later sued, your letter will serve as part of your defense.

2. Computing the Exact Amount—Property Damage Cases

When your property has been damaged by the negligent or intentional act of someone else, you usually have the right to recover the amount of money it would take to fix the damaged item.

> **Example:** John Quickstop plows into Melissa Caretaker's new Dodge, crushing the left rear fender. How much can Melissa recover? Melissa is entitled to recover the amount it would cost to fix or, if necessary, replace the damaged part of her car if John won't pay voluntarily. Melissa should get several estimates from responsible body and fender shops and sue for the lowest amount. (See Chapter 20.)

There is, however, a big exception to this rule. This occurs when the cost to fix the item exceeds its market value. Simply put, you are not entitled to a new or better object—only to have your loss made good. Had Melissa Caretaker been driving a 1987 Dodge, the cost to fix the fender might well have exceeded the current market value of her car. If this was the case, she would be entitled to the value of the Dodge, not what it would cost to repair it.

In short, the most you can recover is the fair market value of the damaged item (the amount you could have sold it for) figured one minute before the damage occurred. From this figure, you have to subtract the item's scrap value, if any.

Give yourself the benefit of the doubt when putting a value on property. No one knows exactly how much any used item is worth. Recognizing that reasonable minds can differ, it makes sense to place a fairly aggressive value on property that has been destroyed. But don't be ridiculous, or you'll likely offend the judge and weaken your case.

> **Example:** Let's return to Melissa from our last example. If several used car price guides indicated her 1987 Dodge was worth $1,200, and the fender would cost $1,400 to replace, she would be limited to a $1,200 recovery, less what the car could be sold for in its damaged state. If this was $150 for scrap, she would be entitled to $1,050. However, if Melissa had recently gotten a new engine and transmission, she might legitimately argue that the car was worth $1,700 and, if the judge agreed, she would legally be entitled to recover the entire $1,400 needed to replace the fender.

Knowing what something is worth and proving it are quite different. A car you are sure is worth $4,000 may look like it's only worth $3,000 to someone else. In court, you will want to be prepared to show that your car is worth every bit of the $4,000. The best way to do this is to get some estimates (opinions) from experts in the field (a used car dealer if your car was totaled). One way to present this type of evidence is to have the expert come to court and testify, but, in most small claims courts, you can also have the expert prepare a written estimate, which you then present to the judge (see the sample letter in Chapter 15, Section D). Depending on the type of property involved, you may also want to check newspaper and flea market ads for the prices asked for comparable goods and submit these to the judge. And of course, there may be other creative ways to establish the dollar amount of the damage you have suffered. (You'll find more about proving your case in court in Chapters 17 through 22.)

Replacement costs aren't relevant when figuring how much you are owed when property is destroyed. Many people insist on believing they can recover the cost of getting a replacement object when theirs has been totaled. As you should now understand, this isn't necessarily true. If Melissa's $1,200 car was totaled and she claimed she simply couldn't get another decent car for less than $2,000, she would still be limited to recovering $1,200.

3. Computing the Exact Amount—Cases Involving Damage to Clothing

Clothing is property, so why am I treating it separately? Two reasons: First, disputes involving clothing are common in small claims court, and judges often apply a logic to them that they apply to no other property damage cases. The reason for this is that clothing is personal to its owner and often has little value to anyone else, even though it may be in good condition. It follows that if a judge strictly applied the rules I just described (that you are limited to recovering no more than the current market value of a damaged item), you wouldn't win much more than the few cents your clothes would get at a garage sale. Recognizing this, most judges bend the rules a little and value damaged clothing based on the item's original cost and how long it had been worn.

When suing for damage to new or almost-new clothing, it follows that you should sue for the amount you paid. If the damaged item has already been worn for some time, sue for the percentage of its original cost that reflects how much of its useful life was gone when the damage occurred. For example, if your two-year-old suit that cost $900 new was destroyed, sue for about $450 if you feel the suit would have lasted another two years.

In clothing cases, most judges want answers to these questions:

* How much did the clothing cost originally?
* How much of its useful life was left at the time the damage occurred?
* Does the damaged item still have some value to the owner, or has it been ruined?

Example 1: Wendy took her new $250 coat to Rudolph, a tailor, to have alterations made. Rudolph cut part of the back of the coat in the wrong place and ruined it. How much should Wendy sue for? $250—as the coat was almost new. She could probably expect to recover close to this amount.

Example 2: The same facts as just above, but the coat was two years old and had been well worn, although it was still in good condition. Here Wendy would be wise to sue for about $175 and hope to recover between $100 and $150.

Example 3: This time let's return Wendy's coat to its almost new condition, but have Rudolph only slightly deface the back. I would still advise Wendy to sue for the full $250. Whether she could recover that much would depend on the judge. Most would probably award her a little less on the theory that the coat retained some value. Were I Wendy, however, I would strongly argue that I didn't buy the coat with the expectation I could only wear it in a closet and that, as far as I was concerned, the coat was ruined.

4. Computing the Exact Amount—Personal Injury Cases

Lawyers quickly take over the great majority of cases where someone is injured. These claims are routinely inflated (a painfully sprained neck might be worth $15,000–$25,000 or more), at least in part because it is in many people's selfish interest to place a high value on injuries. Perhaps surprisingly, insurance company adjusters and lawyers are sometimes as much a part of this something-for-nothing syndrome as are the plaintiff's attorneys, who customarily receive a hefty percentage of the total recovery. This makes sense if you consider that if there weren't lots of claims, lots of lawsuits, and lots of depositions and negotiations, insurance companies would have little reason to keep so many adjusters and lawyers on their payrolls.

Another reason why personal injury cases are usually filed in formal court is that, in many states, a small claims judge can only award an injured party the dollar amount of his or her out-of-pocket losses (doctors' bills, lost time from work), but doesn't have the power to award an additional amount to cover the injury victim's pain and suffering, no matter how legitimate. So before filing even a minor personal injury case in small claims court, be sure you check your local rules.

Try to settle or mediate your personal injury claims. If you are seriously injured, you'll almost always want greater compensation than the small claims maximum. But to gain a significant recovery, it's not always necessary to sue in formal court. Many people successfully negotiate or mediate a satisfactory settlement with an insurance company. For information on how to do this without getting skinned, see *How to Win Your Personal Injury Claim*, by Joseph L. Matthews (Nolo).

Despite the potential drawbacks, some small personal injury cases do end up in small claims court. Dog bite cases are one common example. To determine how much to sue for, add up the dollar amount of the following losses:

- Out-of-pocket medical costs, including
  medical care providers $ _____

- Loss of pay or vacation time
  for missing work $ _____

- Pain and suffering (assuming it is
  allowed in your state) $ _____

- Damage to property $ _____

  TOTAL $ _____

Now let's look at each of these categories in a little more detail.

Medical/hospital. The amount of the medical and hospital bills, including transportation to and from the doctor, are routinely recoverable as long as you have established that the person you are suing is at fault. However, if you are covered by health insurance and the insurance company has already paid your medical costs, you will find that your policy says that any money you recover for these costs must be turned over to the company. Often, insurance companies don't make much effort to keep track of, or recover, small claims court judgments, as the amounts of money involved don't make it worthwhile. Knowing this, many judges are reluctant to grant judgments for medical bills unless the individual can show that he or she is personally out of pocket for the money.

Loss of pay. Loss of pay or vacation time as a result of an injury is viewed in a similar way. If the cocker spaniel down the block lies in wait for you behind a hedge and grabs a piece of your derriere for breakfast, and as a result you miss a day of work getting yourself patched up, you are entitled to recover your loss of pay, commissions, or vacation time. However, if your job offers unlimited paid sick time, so you suffer no loss for missing work, you have nothing to recover.

Pain and suffering. The third area of recovery is for what is euphemistically known as "pain and suffering." When you read about big dollar settlements, a good chunk of the recovery routinely falls into the category of compensating the victim for the physical and sometimes mental pain he has suffered. As noted, in many states, small claims judges don't have the power to make awards for pain and suffering. But because most cases involving serious pain and suffering are worth far too much to be brought in small claims court in the first place, this usually isn't a significant limiting factor.

But suppose you are in a state that allows recovery for pain and suffering and you have suffered a minor, but painful, injury that you do want to file in small claims—how much should you ask for? There is no one right answer. When valuing a client's pain and suffering, a lawyer will typically sue for three to five times the amount of the out-of-pocket damages (medical bills and loss of work). Therefore, if you were out of pocket $500, you might wish to ask for $1,500, the overage being for "pain and suffering." Under this approach, if you have no medical bills, it follows that you will find it difficult to recover anything for "pain and suffering." This is why lawyers routinely encourage their clients to get as much medical attention as reasonably possible.

Example 1: Mary Tendertummy is drinking a bottle of soda pop when a mouse foot floats to the surface. She is immediately nauseated, loses her lunch, and goes to the doctor for medication. As a result, she incurs a medical bill of $150 and loses an afternoon's pay of an additional $150. She sues the soda pop company for $900, claiming that the extra amount is to compensate her for pain and suffering. This will probably be considered reasonable and, depending on the judge, she could recover most of this amount.

Example 2: The same thing happens to Roy Toughguy. But instead of losing his lunch, he just tosses the soda pop away in disgust and goes back to work. A few weeks later he hears about Mary's recovery and decides that he, too, could use $900. How much is he likely to recover? Probably not much more than the price of the soda pop—he apparently suffered little or no injury.

Property damage. Often a personal injury is accompanied by injury to property. For example, a dog bite might also ruin your pants. If so, include the value of your damaged clothing when you determine how much to sue for. For information on how to place a dollar value on your property, see Sections C2 and C3, above.

For information on how to negotiate with an insurance company without being skinned—and how to decide how much to sue for if negotiations prove unsuccessful—I recommend *How to Win Your Personal Injury Claim,* by Joseph L. Matthews (Nolo). This book thoroughly discusses how to put a dollar value on injuries in the context of developing a strategy to successfully negotiate with an insurance company.

Don't Count on Recovering Punitive Damages in Small Claims Court

Formal trial courts have the power to award extra damages (over and above out-of-pocket losses and pain and suffering) if an injury is caused by the malicious or willful misconduct (often a fraudulent or criminal act) of the defendant. When the defendant is wealthy, these damages—which are designed to punish the defendant—can run into the millions. About half of the states do not allow punitive damages (sometimes called "exemplary damages") to be awarded in small claims. But even in those states where it is theoretically possible to receive punitive damages, small claims court's low dollar limit largely rules them out—except in a few instances where specific dollar amounts are established for bad checks (see Section C1, above) and failure to return a tenant's security deposit on time (see Chapter 21). If you believe you have been injured by conduct wretched enough to support a claim for hefty punitive damages, see a lawyer.

5. Computing the Exact Amount—Emotional or Mental Distress

As noted in Chapter 2, in our increasingly crowded urban environment, there are all sorts of ways we can cause one another real pain without making physical contact. For example, if I live in the apartment above you and pound on my floor (your ceiling) for an hour at 6:00 a.m. every day, I will probably quickly reduce you to the status of a raving maniac. What can you do about it short of slashing my tires? One remedy is for you to sue me in small claims court based on the fact that my actions constitute the intentional infliction of emotional distress. But how much should you sue for? Unfortunately, it's impossible to provide a formula. It depends on how obnoxious my behavior is, how long it has gone on, and how clearly you have asked me to stop (this should be done several times in writing). And if this isn't vague enough, it will also depend greatly on the personality of the judge, who may be very skeptical of all neighbor disputes, thinking they don't belong in court in the first place. At the very least, you'll need to convince the judge you are an extremely reasonable person and your neighbor is a true boor, before you will be eligible for any recovery.

One way to help try to convince the judge you aren't a hypersensitive complainer is to sue for a reasonable amount. Thus, if you are in a state that permits small claims cases up to $5,000, I would normally advise against suing for any amount over $3,000, unless the other person's behavior clearly makes him out to be first cousin to Attila the Hun.

Try mediation first when neighbors are involved. The process of filing, preparing, and arguing a lawsuit tends to make people madder than they were before. This may be fine if you are suing a large company, or someone you are never likely to interact with again, but given a neighbor's ability to make you miserable in the future, it's usually best to try to amicably settle your case through mediation before going to court. (See Chapter 7 for more on mediation.)

D. Computing an Exact Amount—Malpractice Cases

In theory, most malpractice cases are worth far more than can be awarded in small claims court. But because legal rules are usually tilted to favor professionals and these cases are expensive to bring, it's often hard to find a lawyer to represent you on a contingency fee (an arrangement in which the lawyer doesn't charge you up front but takes a percentage of the settlement), so many are scaled down to fit into small claims court.

For most types of malpractice, you simply need to prove that the dollar value of harm caused you was at least equal to the amount you have sued for (usually the small claims maximum). Thus, if a doctor negligently misdiagnosed an illness and as a result you experienced horrendous problems, you would present the court with:

- all medical, hospital, and drug bills you paid after the misdiagnosis that you claim could have been avoided
- the opinion of a second doctor that the first doctor's handling of your problem did not measure up to accepted medical standards (or, in plain language, that the first doctor screwed up)
- an estimate for your pain and suffering (but first check with your court clerk to be sure pain and suffering damages can be awarded in small claims court), and
- lost pay or vacation time.

Special rules for legal malpractice. As discussed in Chapter 2, Section I, if your suit is based on a lawyer's failure to handle your case properly, you have to be able to prove that you would have won the case if the lawyer had not been a bungler, and that if you had won, your recovery would have been at least as much as you are suing for in small claims court.

E. Equitable Relief (Or, Money Can't Always Solve the Problem)

Nearly half the states allow judges to grant relief (if you ask for it) in ways that do not involve the payment of money, if equity (fairness) demands it. "Equitable relief" is usually limited to one or more of four categories: "rescission," "restitution," "reformation," and "specific performance." Let's translate these into English.

You may need to do more research. If you think you may want to sue "in equity," start by looking in the Appendix for your state. For example, Alabama, Arizona, California, Louisiana, Maine, and Nebraska expressly allow equitable relief in small claims court. If the law says recovery is limited to "payment of money only" or similar words, equitable relief isn't allowed. If you can't tell whether your state offers this relief, your next step will be to look up your state's small claims court law. (You'll find the citation in the Appendix.)

Rescission: This is a remedy that is used to wipe out a grossly unfair or fraudulent contract under any of the following conditions:

- it was based on a mistake about an important fact or

- it was induced by duress or undue influence, or
- one party simply didn't receive what was promised, through the fault of the other.

> **Example:** You purchase aluminum siding from a catalogue. When it arrives, you see that the siding is a different color—and an inferior quality—than the siding pictured in the catalogue. The company refuses to refund your money. In court, you could ask that the contract be rescinded, and your money returned.

Restitution: This important remedy gives a judge the power to order that a particular piece of property be transferred to its original owner when fairness requires the contracting parties be restored to their original positions. It can be used in the common situation in which one person sells another a piece of property (say a motor scooter) and the other fails to pay. Instead of simply giving the seller a money judgment that might be hard to collect, the judge has the power to order the scooter restored to its original owner. Where money has been paid under a contract that is rescinded, the judge can order it to be returned, plus damages. Thus, if a used car purchase was rescinded based on the fraud of the seller, the buyer could get a judgment for the amount paid for the car, plus money spent for repairs and alternate transportation.

Reformation: This remedy is somewhat unusual. It has to do with changing (reforming) a contract to meet the original intent of the parties when some term or condition agreed to by the parties has been left out or misstated and fairness dictates the contract be reformed. Reformation is commonly used when an oral agreement is written down incorrectly.

> **Example:** Arthur the Author and Peter the Publisher orally agree that Peter will publish Arthur's 200-page book. They then write a contract, inadvertently leaving out the number of pages. If Arthur showed up with a 3,000-page manuscript and demanded that it be published in its entirety, a court would very likely "reform" the contract to include the 200-page provision, assuming the judge was convinced that it should have been included in the first place.

Specific Performance: This is an important remedy that comes into play where a contract involving an unusual or "one-of-a-kind" object has not been carried out. Say you agree to buy a unique antique jade ring for your mother's birthday that is exactly like the one she lost years before, and then the seller refuses to go through with the deal. A court could cite the doctrine of "specific performance" to order that the ring be turned over to you. "Specific performance" will only be ordered in situations where the payment of money will not adequately compensate the person bringing suit.

The small claims dollar maximum applies to cases involving equitable relief. In filling out your court papers, you will still be required to indicate that the value of the item for which you want equitable relief is under the small claims maximum (see the Appendix). Thus, you might describe the nature of your claim (see Chapter 11, Section B) as follows: "I want the delivery of a 'one-of-a-kind' antique jade ring worth approximately $700 according to my contract with defendant."

Conditional Judgments: In California and some other states, it's common for judges to issue conditional judgments in cases involving equitable relief. That is, they can order a party to perform, or stop, a certain act or else pay a money judgment. For example, you agree to sell your baby grand piano for $1,000. The buyer fails to pay, and you sue. The judge orders the buyer to either return the piano or fork over the $1,000. If the piano isn't returned within a short period, the money judgment may be enforced. (See Chapter 25.) ■

Is the Suit Brought Within the Proper Time Limit (Statute of Limitations)?

Each state has time limits within which lawsuits must be filed. These are called statutes of limitations. Time limits are different for different types of cases. If you wait too long, your right to sue will be barred by these statutes. Why have a statute of limitations? Because disputes are best settled relatively soon after they develop. Unlike wine, lawsuits don't improve with age. Memories fade and witnesses die or move away, and once-clear details tend to become blurred. Statutes of limitations are almost always at least one year, so if you file promptly, you should have little to worry about.

Act fast for claims against government entities. To sue a city, county, state, or governmental agency (for example, a school district), you first must promptly file a claim with the people in charge (the school board, county board of supervisors, city council). Once it's rejected—and it usually will be—you can file in small claims court. Often, your administrative claim must be filed within three to six months after your loss occurred, or you are out of luck.

Defendants usually don't need to worry about whether a case was filed on time. Typically, cases filed in small claims court are brought promptly, so the question of whether the person suing has waited too long usually doesn't come up. If your case is one of the rare ones in which the statute of limitations is, or may be, an issue, you will want to check out your state's time limit. Check your state's laws under the headings "Limitations" or "Statute of Limitations." Read the material carefully—the time periods within which a suit must be brought will vary, depending on the type of suit (for example, oral contract, written contract, personal injury, and so on).

A. Statute of Limitations Periods

I include here a table of statutes of limitation periods for four of the most common types of lawsuits. But you will probably need to do further legal research. Even the time limits on our table can be affected by things like the "Discovery Rule"—see "How the Discovery Rule Works," below. And the time limits on our table may not cover every situation. For example, claims involving medical malpractice, eviction, child or spousal support, fraud, product liability, consumer sales contracts, or faulty work by builders may all have different statutes of limitations. And some states distinguish between different types of property (usually real and personal property) when establishing statutes of limitations. You will find your state laws online at www.nolo.com and on your state's home page, and you will find a printed set at a law library or a large public library. (See Chapter 1, Section D, for more on how to do legal research.)

STATUTES OF LIMITATIONS FOR THE 50 STATES
(AND THE DISTRICT OF COLUMBIA)

State	Statute Citations	Contracts Written	Oral	Personal Injury	Property Damage
Alabama	Ala. Code § 6-2-30 et seq.*	6	6	2	6
Alaska	Alaska Stat. § 09.10.010 et seq.	3	3	2	6 (real property) 2 (personal property)
Arizona	Ariz. Rev. Stat. Ann. § 12-541 et seq.	6	3	2	2
Arkansas	Ark. Code Ann. § 16-56-101 et seq.	5	3	3	3
California	Cal. Civ. Proc. Code § 335 et seq.	4	2	2	3
Colorado	Colo. Rev. Stat. § 13-80-101 et seq.	6	6	2**	2
Connecticut	Conn. Gen. Stat. Ann. § 52-576 et seq.	6	3	2	2
Delaware	Del. Code Ann. tit. 10, § 8101 et seq.	3	3	2	2
D.C.	D.C. Code § 12-301 et seq.	3	3	3	3
Florida	Fla. Stat. Ann. § 95.11 et seq.	5	4	4	4
Georgia	Ga. Code Ann. § 9-3-20 et seq.	6	4	2	4
Hawaii	Haw. Rev. Stat. § 657-1 et seq.	6	6	2	2
Idaho	Idaho Code § 5-201 et seq.	5	4	2	3
Illinois	735 Ill. Comp. Stat. 5/13-201 et seq.	10	5	2	5
Indiana	Ind. Code Ann. § 34-11-2-1 et seq.	10	6	2	6 (real property) 2 (personal property)
Iowa	Iowa Code Ann. § 614.1 et seq.	10	5	2	5
Kansas	Kan. Stat. Ann. § 60-501 et seq.	5	3	2	2
Kentucky	Ky. Rev. Stat. Ann. § 413.080 et seq.	15	5	1	5 (real property) 2 (personal property)
Louisiana***	La. Civ. Code Art. 3492 et seq.	10	10	1	1
Maine	Me. Rev. Stat. Ann. tit. 14, § 751 et seq.	6	6	6	6
Maryland	Md. Code Ann. [Courts & Jud. Proc.] § 5-101 et seq.	3	3	3	3
Massachusetts	Mass. Ann. Laws ch. 260, § 1 et seq.	6	6	3	3
Michigan	Mich. Comp. Laws § 600.5801 et seq.	6	6	3	3

* et seq. means "and the next sections following in sequence"

** Colorado: 3 years if motor vehicle injury

*** Louisiana: Statute of limitations known as a "liberative prescription," personal injury known as "delictuel action"

State	Statute Citations	Contracts Written	Oral	Personal Injury	Property Damage
Minnesota	Minn. Stat. Ann. § 541.01 et seq.	6	6	2	6
Mississippi	Miss. Code. Ann. § 15-1-1 et seq.	3	3	3	3
Missouri	Mo. Rev. Stat. § 516.097 et seq.	5****	5****	5	5
Montana	Mont. Code Ann. § 27-2-201 et seq.	8	5	3	2
Nebraska	Neb. Rev. Stat. § 25-201 et seq.	5	4	4	4
Nevada	Nev. Rev. Stat. Ann. § 11.190 et seq.	6	4	2	3
New Hampshire	N.H. Rev. Stat. Ann. § 508:1 et seq.	3	3	3	3
New Jersey	N.J. Stat. Ann. § 2a:14-1 et seq.	6	6	2	6
New Mexico	N.M. Stat. Ann. § 37-1-1 et seq.	6	4	3	4
New York	N.Y. C.P.L.R. Law § 201 et seq.	6	6	3	3
North Carolina	N.C. Gen. Stat. § 1-46 et seq.	3	3	3	3
North Dakota	N.D. Cent. Code § 28-01-01 et seq.	6	6	6	6
Ohio	Ohio Rev. Code Ann. § 2305.03 et seq.	15	6	2	4 (real property) 2 (personal property)
Oklahoma	Okla. Stat. Ann. tit. 12, § 93 et seq.	5	3	2	2
Oregon	Or. Rev. Stat. § 12.010 et seq.	6	6	2	6
Pennsylvania	42 Pa. Cons. Stat. Ann. § 5521 et seq.	4	4	2	2
Rhode Island	R. I. Gen. Laws § 9-1-12 et seq.	10	10	3	10
South Carolina	S.C. Code Ann. § 15-3-510 et seq.	3	3	3	3
South Dakota	S.D. Codified Laws Ann. § 15-2-1 et seq.	6	6	3	6
Tennessee	Tenn. Code Ann. § 28-3-101 et seq.	6	6	1	3
Texas	Tex. Civ. Prac. & Rem. Code § 16.001 et. seq.	4	4	2	2
Utah	Utah Code Ann. § 78-12-22 et seq.	6	4	4	3
Vermont	Vt. Stat. Ann. tit. 12, § 506 et seq.	6	6	3	3
Virginia	Va. Code Ann. § 8.01-243 et seq.	5	3	2	5
Washington	Wash. Rev. Code Ann. § 4.16.005 et seq.	6	3	3	3
West Virginia	W. Va. Code § 55-2-6 et seq.	10	5	2	2
Wisconsin	Wis. Stat. Ann. § 893.40 et seq.	6	6	3	6
Wyoming	Wyo. Stat. § 1-3-102 et seq.	10	8	4	4

* et seq. means "and the next sections following in sequence"   Current as of March 2004
**** Missouri: 10 years for payment of debt

Most contracts are in writing. Some contracts that you assume to be oral may actually be written. People often forget that they signed papers when they first arranged for goods or services. For example, your charge accounts, telephone service, and insurance policies, as well as most major purchases of goods and services, involve a written contract, even though you haven't signed any papers for years. And another thing: To have a written contract, you need not have signed a document full of "whereases" and "therefores." Any signed writing can be a contract, even if it's written on toilet paper with lipstick. When you go to a car repair shop and they make out a work order and you sign it—that's a contract. (See Chapter 2, Section C, for more about contracts.)

How the Discovery Rule Works

With some types of cases, such as medical malpractice, the limitations period starts from the date the harm was discovered or reasonably should have been discovered. This rule protects people who don't know they have a problem until well after it has occurred.

Example: During an operation, a doctor leaves a small clamp in your abdomen. It isn't until a year later that you experience extreme pain and see a different doctor, who orders an x-ray that shows the clamp. In most states, the statute of limitations for suits based on medical malpractice (often three years) begins from the date you learn of the problem, not the date of the original operation. However, if you walked around in pain for several years before seeing a second doctor and getting an x-ray, chances are a court would rule that the limitations period would start before actual discovery, based on the theory that you should have discovered the problem sooner.

B. Computing the Statute of Limitations

Okay, now let's assume you have found out what the relevant limitations period is. How do you know what date to start your counting from? That's easy. Start with the day the injury to your person or property occurred, or, if a contract is involved, start with the day that someone failed to perform under the terms of the contract. Where a contract to pay in installments is involved, the limitations period for each installment is usually calculated from the date that payment was missed. (See "Tricky Rules for Installment Contracts," below.)

Example: Doolittle owes Crabapple $500, payable in five monthly installments of $100. Both live in San Jose, California. They never wrote down any of the terms of their agreement. Doolittle misses his third monthly payment, which was due on January 1, 2004. Crabapple should compute his statute of limitations period from that date, assuming, of course, that Doolittle doesn't later catch up on his payments. The statute of limitations for oral contracts in California is two years, so Crabapple has until December 31, 2006 to file his suit. If a written contract had been involved, Crabapple could file until December 31, 2008, as the statute of limitations on written contracts in California is four years.

Tricky Rules for Installment Contracts

When an installment contract is involved, the statute of limitations usually applies separately to each installment. To understand how this works, suppose you agree in writing to pay $5,000 in five installments commencing January 1, 2003, and continuing on January 1 of each succeeding year through 2007. Suppose also that the statute of limitations for written contracts in your state is four years. If you do not make the first payment, the creditor has until January 1, 2007 to sue. Or, looked at from your point of view, if the creditor fails to sue you by that date, you can claim that any subsequent lawsuit has been filed too late (in legalese, you would say that the lawsuit is "barred" by the statute of limitations). But because your second payment isn't due until January 1, 2004, your creditor's lawsuit for this installment will not be barred until January 2, 2008, and so on.

1. Voluntary Payment After Statute Has Run Out

I am frequently asked to explain the legal implications of the following situation: After the statute of limitations runs out (say after two years on an oral contract to pay for having a fence painted), the debtor voluntarily starts to make payments. Does the voluntary payment have the effect of creating a new two-year statute of limitations period, allowing the person who is owed the money to sue if the debtor again stops paying? In most states, including California, simply starting to pay on an obligation barred by the statute of limitations doesn't create a new period for suit. (Cal. Code of Civ. Proc. § 360.) All the creditor can do is keep his or her toes crossed and hope that the debtor's belated streak of honesty continues. However, if the debtor signs a written agreement promising to make the payments, this does create a new statute of limitations period. In legal slang, this is called "reaffirming the debt."

> **Example:** Back to the drama of Doolittle and Crabapple. Let's assume that in February 2006, Doolittle experiences a burst of energy, gets a job, and decides to pay off all of his old debts. He sends Crabapple $50. A week later, suffering terrible strain from getting up before noon, he quits his job and reverts to his old ways of sleeping in the sun when not reading the racing form. Is the statute of limitations allowing Crabapple to sue reinstated? No. Once the limitation period of two years has run out, it can't be revived by simply making a payment. However, if Doolittle had sent Crabapple the $50 and Crabapple had persuaded Doolittle to send him a letter saying that he would pay the remainder of the debt, Crabapple would again be able to sue and get a judgment if he failed to pay. Why? Because a written promise to pay a debt barred by the statute of limitations has the legal effect of reestablishing the debt.

⚠ **Debtors beware of waiving statute of limitations.** If a creditor and debtor discuss an unpaid bill and the debtor asks the creditor for more time to pay, lower payments, or some other accommodation, the creditor will almost always require that the debtor waive the statute of limitations in writing. This means that if the debtor fails to pay, the creditor will have more time to sue.

2. Suspending the Statute of Limitations

In a few situations, the statute of limitations is suspended for a period of time (lawyers say "tolled"). This occurs if the person sued is in prison, living out of state, insane, or a minor. If the statute of limitations is suspended (tolled) by one of these events, it means that it simply isn't counted until the event is over, at which point it starts up again.

> **Example 1:** Jack borrows money from Tim and signs a note promising repayment. Jack fails to pay the money back on the day required. Six months later, Jack is sentenced to a year in jail. The four-year statute of limitations would be tolled (suspended) during this period, and Tim would still have three-and-one-half years after Jack gets out of jail to file suit.

> **Example 2:** Ed, age 12, stars in a TV series. An accountant for the show tells Ed's family that Ed hasn't been paid all monies due under his contract. Neither Ed nor his family do anything about it. Eight years later, trying to figure out how to pay for college, Ed wonders if he can still sue the TV production company. The answer is probably yes, as most states would measure Ed's time to sue from his 18th birthday (that is, the statute of limitations period would be suspended or tolled while he was a minor). And because most states have four- or five-year statutes of limitation for disputes based on written contracts, Ed could file suit at least until his 22nd birthday.

C. Defendant Should Tell the Judge If the Statute of Limitations Has Run Out

A defendant who believes that the statute of limitations period on the plaintiff's lawsuit has run out should tell the judge. Do this in court as part of stating your defense, or, if your state is one of the few that requires a defendant to file a written request prior to the hearing date (see the Appendix), list your claim that the statute of limitations bars the plaintiff's lawsuit there. (Sometimes a judge will figure this out without a reminder, but you can't count on it.) ■

CHAPTER

6

How to Settle Your Dispute

Litigation should be a last, not a first, resort. In addition to being time-consuming, emotionally draining, and unpredictable, lawsuits—even the relatively efficient small claims variety—tend to polarize disagreements into win-all or lose-all propositions, in which face- (and money-) saving compromise is difficult. It's easy to understand how this happens. When forced to justify our actions in a public courtroom, most of us are likely to present an idealized version of our own conduct, while exaggerating the bad actions of our opponent. By contrast, many of us are willing to admit privately that we are less than perfect—especially if the other person does, too.

I am a strong advocate of small claims court, but it isn't the right way to resolve every problem—I have seen many otherwise sensible people litigate disputes that never should have been filed in the first place. In some instances, the amount of money was too small to justify the time and trouble of going to court. In others, the problem should have been talked out over the back fence. And I've seen more than a few situations in which the practical importance of maintaining civil personal or business relationships between the parties made it silly to go to court over a few hundred or even a few thousand dollars.

Let me emphasize this last point: It is almost always wise to look for a noncourt solution when your opponent is someone you'll inevitably deal with in the future, even if it means you pocket a few dollars less than you might win in court. For example, you should make an extra effort to settle when your spat is with a neighbor, a person who belongs to your swim club, or a relative. Similarly, a small business owner will almost always benefit from working out a compromise settlement (even one that is less than perfect) with another established local business, a long-term customer, or an influential client. For example, a dentist who depends on referrals for most new customers will want to think twice before suing a local patient who has angrily refused to pay a bill because the patient is genuinely—albeit wrongly—upset about the services provided. Even if the dentist prevails in court, he or she is likely to turn the former patient into a vocal enemy—one who may literally badmouth the dentist from one end of town to the other for years to come.

This chapter explains some basic strategies you can use to start the negotiations—and, hopefully, work out a settlement that will keep you out of court in the first place.

A. Demand Letters

I hope I've convinced you that, no matter how inconsiderate, unpleasant, or downright nasty your opponent has been, you should at least try to settle your dispute before filing it in court. But how do you begin a conversation with the other party about settlement? To start (or, if necessary, restart) your communications, it's usually best to send a polite letter outlining your demands.

Many courts require you to make a formal "demand" for settlement. But even where there is no such requirement, I highly recommend that you put your position in writing, for two good reasons: First, research has shown that in as many as one-third of all disputes, your "demand" letter will serve as the catalyst that eventually leads to a settlement. Second, even if your case doesn't settle, you will probably be able to show your letter to the judge in court, which gives you a valuable opportunity to lay out the facts of your case in a carefully organized way.

Example: Sunita purchases a designer dress from Maya on eBay. It arrives without the little jacket that was originally part of the outfit—and Sunita believes the dress is too skimpy to be worn alone. Maya refuses to provide the jacket or take the dress back, and she hangs up when Sunita calls. Sunita writes a demand letter outlining these facts. When Maya doesn't respond, Sunita files suit in small claims court. In court, Maya feigns complete surprise, claiming, "I had no idea you had a problem with the dress—why didn't you say something before?" In response, Sunita presents her demand letter to the judge, with its complete account of events. Not only does this show that Sunita made a sincere demand for payment, but her carefully written letter also provides the judge with an organized overview of the dispute—from Sunita's point of view, of course.

You might not think that a simple letter will be effective, especially if you have already argued, unsuccessfully, with your adversary in person or over the phone. But perhaps you'll change your mind about the power of the written word if you think about some of the consumer disputes that many of us have experienced. After angry words were exchanged—maybe even including a threat to file a lawsuit—what usually happens next? Often, nothing at all. For all sorts of reasons, from a death in the family or an impending vacation, to simply not having enough time or losing interest, most of us don't follow up our threat to sue. In fact, many potential defendants don't take such threats seriously precisely because so many people who verbally threaten to sue never carry out the threat.

But things change fast if you write a letter laying out the reasons why the other party owes you money and stating that you plan to file a lawsuit in small claims court right away if the other party refuses to pay. You and your dispute have just taken a giant step from the realm of remote possibility to the much more sobering world of impending probability. Not only must the other party confront the likelihood that you really do plan to have your day in court, but he or she must also face the fact that it will take time and energy to put up a defense. On top of those costs, the defendant will also have to consider the possibility that you might win. For all these reasons, the moment you make your case in writing, the chances that the other party will negotiate go way up.

A personal note is in order here. In the 25-plus years since I wrote the first edition of *Everybody's Guide to Small Claims Court*, readers have sent in hundreds of small claims success stories. One thing has consistently delighted me: Many self-described winners never stepped through the courthouse door. Instead, these readers took my advice and wrote the other party a clear, concise letter demanding payment. As a result of either the communication itself or the conversations it engendered, they received all or most of what they asked for.

Snail mail is better than email. It's a good idea to send your demand letter by first class mail, not email. Even if your opponent isn't impressed that you took the time to write a real letter, using paper and ink has another big advantage: You can more effectively produce a copy in court, which makes it harder for your opponent to claim that he or she didn't receive it. Incidentally, there is no need to send your letter certified mail with a return receipt—the judge will assume that properly addressed first class mail reached its destination.

1. Writing a Demand Letter

When composing your demand letter, keep these tips in mind:

- **Use a typewriter or computer.** A handwritten letter just doesn't have the same gravitas.

- **Start by concisely reviewing the facts of the dispute.** It may seem odd to outline all these details; after all, your opponent knows what happened. But remember: if you end up in court, your letter may be read by the judge, so you should clearly lay out the chronology of events as you see them.

- **Be polite.** Absolutely avoid personally attacking your adversary (even one who deserves it). The more annoying you are, the more you invite the other side to respond in a similarly angry vein. This is obviously counterproductive to your goal: getting your opponent to make a businesslike analysis of the dispute and seriously consider the risk of losing, the time and effort a defense could take, the possibility that the dispute could become public, and the wisdom of paying a reasonable amount to make the problem go away.

- **Ask for exactly what you want.** For example, if you want $2,000, don't beat around the bush by stating that the other party owes you "a significant amount of money." Come right out and say that you want $2,000, with a brief explanation of how you arrived at this figure.

- **Set a payment deadline.** Ten days to two weeks is usually a good time frame. If you give your opponent more time, he or she has less motivation to deal with you right away.

- **Remind the defendant that lawsuits and judgments are public records.** Many defendants are highly motivated to avoid having an adverse judgment appear on their credit record, particularly if they run a business. Remind the defendant that a private settlement avoids this.

- **Keep a copy of all correspondence.** Keep all of your letters and any written response you receive from the defendant; remember, you may need to present them in court.

2. Responding to a Demand Letter

Being on the receiving end of a demand letter can be an unpleasant experience. Depending on the circumstances, your reaction will probably be some variation of the following:

- The letter is completely bogus. I didn't pay all or part of the amount demanded because my opponent simply doesn't have a valid legal claim.

- In fairness, I probably owe something, but significantly less than the letter requests.

- True, I owe the amount demanded, but I simply can't afford to pay it right now.
- I'm the one with the valid legal claim. My opponent's demand is simply part of a cynical attempt to beat me to court and obscure what really happened.

If you are convinced that you owe nothing—or if you plan to sue for money you are owed—the chances of settling the dispute at this stage are probably slim. Your best bet is to write a polite return letter (see samples later in this chapter) that briefly reviews the facts from your point of view. If you believe the other party owes you money, say so and set a date for payment. (Follow the tips in Section A2, above, to write your own demand letter.)

But if you conclude that your opponent is at least partially in the right, your immediate goal should be to arrive at a compromise amount (or payment schedule) you can live with. When deciding what to offer, remember that if the case goes to court, you face exactly the same downsides as the plaintiff. Not only will your dispute require time and trouble to prepare, but it will also be aired and recorded in public. And despite the merits of your position, you may lose; even if you win, you may have trouble collecting the judgment.

In Section C of this chapter, I discuss a sensible way to arrive at a dollar amount for purposes of making a counteroffer. Once you have done this, your next task is to decide whether you'll reply by mail or simply give the other party a call and negotiate orally. Because it's quicker, easier, and less formal, I think it's usually better to talk. But in the following situations, it makes more sense to respond in writing:

- **Anger rules:** If for some reason, such as a recently ruptured romance or friendship, you and your opponent are so mad at each other that even the most business-like conversation is likely to result in a shouting match, your chances of success are better if you respond in writing.

- **No compromise is likely:** In this situation, you'll simply want to record your side of the story, so you'll have something to show the judge if your opponent presents his or her demand letter.

You could be sued without warning. Some people believe they can't be sued until they receive a demand letter asking for payment. However, this isn't necessarily true. Although sending a formal letter before filing a small claims case is good practice, it doesn't always happen and may not be required. For example, a bare-bones past due notice from a creditor, which states in the fine print that formal collection action will be taken if the account isn't paid promptly, satisfies any rule that a demand for payment must be made prior to initiating a lawsuit. And in many states, the law provides that an oral demand for payment is adequate. The upshot is that potential defendants shouldn't relax just because their mailbox is empty: If you know that you owe money and are likely to be sued, it usually makes sense to contact the other party to initiate settlement negotiations.

3. A Real Small Claims Case

To see how an effort to settle a potential small claims dispute might play out, let's consider a real case. The facts (with a little editorial license) were simple. Jennifer moved into Peter's house in August, agreeing to pay $850 per month rent. The house had four bedrooms, each occupied by one person. The kitchen and other common areas were shared. Things went well enough until one chilly evening in October when Jennifer turned on the heat. Peter was right behind her to turn it off, explaining that heat inflamed his allergies.

As the days passed and fall deepened, heat became more and more of an issue. One cold, late November night, Jennifer returned home from her waitress job to find her room "about the same temperature as the inside of an icicle." After a short cry, she started packing and moved out the next morning. She refused to pay Peter any additional rent, claiming she was within her rights to terminate her month-to-month tenancy without giving notice because the house was uninhabitable. It took Peter one month to find a suitable tenant and to have that person move in. Therefore, he lost $850 in rent.

After calling Jennifer several times and asking her to make good the $850 only to have her slam down the phone in disgust, Peter wrote her the following letter:

January 1, 20xx
61 Spring St.
Detroit, MI

Jennifer Tenant
111 Lake St.
Detroit, MI

Dear Jennifer:

You are a real idiot. Actually, you're worse than that: You're malicious—walking out on me before Christmas and leaving me with no tenant when you knew that I needed the money to pay my child support. You know that I promised to get you an electric room heater. Don't think I don't know that the real reason you moved out was to live with your boyfriend.

Please send me the $850 I lost because it took me a month to rerent the place. If you don't, I will sue you.

In aggravation,

Peter Landperson

To which Jennifer replied:

January 4, 20xx
111 Lake St.
Detroit, MI

Peter Landperson
61 Spring St.
Detroit, MI

Dear Mr. Landperson:

    You nearly froze me to death, you cheap bastard. I am surprised it only took a month to rent that iceberg of a room—you must have found a rich polar bear (ha ha). People like you should be locked up.

    I hope you choke on an ice cube.

Jennifer Tenant

    As you have no doubt guessed, both Peter and Jennifer made the same mistake. Instead of being businesslike, each deliberately set out to annoy the other, reducing any possible chance of compromise. In addition, they each assumed they were writing only to the other, forgetting that a judge might one day be privy to their sentiments. Thus, both lost a valuable chance to present the judge with a coherent summary of the facts as they saw them. As evidence in a subsequent court proceeding, both letters would be worthless.

    Now let's interrupt these proceedings and give Peter and Jennifer a chance to write more sensible letters.

January 1, 20xx
61 Spring St.
Detroit, MI

Jennifer Tenant
111 Lake St.
Detroit, MI

Dear Jennifer:

As you will recall, you moved into my house at 61 Spring St., Detroit, Michigan, on August 1, 20xx, agreeing to pay me $850 per month rent on the first of each month. On November 29, you suddenly moved out, having given me no advance notice whatsoever.

I realize that you were unhappy that the house was a little on the cool side, but I don't believe that this was a serious problem, as the temperature was at all times over 60 degrees and I had agreed to get you an electric heater for your room by December.

I was unable to get a tenant to replace you (although I tried every way I could and asked you for help) until January 1, 20xx. This means that I am short $850 rent for the room you occupied. Please pay this amount promptly, and no later than January 15th. If I don't hear from you by then, I will take this dispute to court because, as you know, I am on a very tight budget. I hope that this isn't necessary and we can arrive at a sensible compromise.

I am also willing to try to mediate this dispute using the local community mediation service, if you agree. I have tried to call you with no success. Perhaps you can give me a call in the next week to talk this over.

Sincerely,

Peter Landperson

To which our now enlightened Jennifer promptly replied:

January 4, 20xx
111 Lake St.
Detroit, MI

Peter Landperson
61 Spring St.
Detroit, MI

Dear Peter:

I just received your letter concerning the rent at 61 Spring St. and am sorry to say that I don't agree either with the facts as you have presented them or with your demand for back rent.

When I moved in August 1, 20xx, you never told me that you had an allergy and that there would be a problem keeping the house at a normal temperature. I would not have moved in had you informed me of this.

From early October, when we had the first cool evenings, all through November (almost two months), I asked that you provide heat. You didn't. Finally, it became unbearable to return from work in the middle of the night to a cold house, which was often below 60 degrees. It is true that I moved out suddenly, but I felt that I was within my rights under Michigan law, which clearly allows tenants to sue landlords for constructive eviction when the landlord fails to provide a necessity such as heat. In fact, you are lucky that I am not suing you for damages for constructive eviction.

You mentioned the nonexistent electric heater in your letter, so let me respond to that. You first promised to get the heater over a month before I moved out, but never produced it. Also, as I pointed out to you on several occasions, the heater was not a complete solution to the problem, as it would have heated only my room and not the kitchen, living room, and dining areas. You repeatedly told me that it would be impossible to heat these areas.

Peter, I sincerely regret the fact that you feel wronged, but I believe that I have been very fair with you. I am sure that you would have been able to rerent the room promptly if the house had been warm. Because I don't believe that any compromise is possible, mediation does not make sense. If you wish to go to court, I'll be there with several witnesses who will support my position.

Sincerely,

Jennifer Tenant

As you can see, the second round of letters, while less fun to read, are far more informative. In this case, the goal of reaching an acceptable compromise or agreeing to mediation was not met, but Peter and Jennifer have prepared a good outline of their positions for the judge. Of course, in court, they will testify and present witnesses and possibly other evidence that will tell much the same story as is set out in the letters. However, court proceedings are often rushed and confused, and it's nice to have a written statement for the judge to fall back on. Be sure the judge gets a copy of your demand letter when your case is presented. The judge won't be able to guess that you have it; you will have to let him or her know and hand it to the clerk. (For more about how to conduct yourself in court, see Chapters 14 through 16).

4. Sample Demand Letters

Below are letters a consumer might write to an auto repair shop after being victimized by a shoddy repair job and to a contractor who botched a remodeling contract. In both instances, I also include reply letters that attempt to begin a process that hopefully will lead to a compromise settlement. Incidentally, the repair shop owner and contractor might sensibly have chosen to negotiate by phone or in person rather than responding in writing, but as you can see, a polite letter can be very effective.

June 16, 20xx

Tucker's Fix-It-Quick Garage
9938 Main St.
Chicago, IL 61390

Dear Mr. Tucker,

On May 21, 2xxx, I took my car to your garage for servicing. Shortly after I picked the car up the next day, the engine caught fire because of your failure to properly reconnect the fuel line after repairing the fuel injection system. Fortunately, I was able to douse the fire without injury.

As a direct result of the engine fire, I paid the ABC Chevrolet $1,281 for necessary repair work. I enclose a copy of their invoice.

In addition, I was without the use of my car for three days and had to rent a car to get to work. I enclose a copy of an invoice showing the rental fee of $145.

In a recent phone conversation you claimed that the fire wasn't the result of your negligence and would have happened anyway because my car is old. You also said that even if it was your fault, I should have brought my car back to your garage so you could have fixed it at a lower cost.

As to the first issue, Peter Klein of the ABC Chevrolet is prepared to testify in court that the fire occurred because the fuel line was not properly connected to the fuel injector, the exact part of the car you were working on.

Second, I had no obligation to return the car to you for further repair. I had the damage you caused repaired at a commercially reasonable price and am prepared to prove this by presenting several higher estimates by other garages.

Please send me a check or money order for $1,425 on or before July 15. If I don't receive payment by that date, I'll promptly file this case in small claims court. And assuming I receive a judgment, which will be a part of the public record and available to credit agencies, I will promptly follow all legal avenues to collect it.

You may reach me during the day at 555-2857 or in the evenings until 10 p.m. at 555-8967.

Sincerely,

Marsha Rizzoli

June 21, 20xx

Marsha Rizzoli
907 Cambridge St. #2
Evanston, IL _____

Dear Ms. Rizzoli,

The 1998 Chevy Blazer you brought in for repair was in terrible condition. According to my records, the odometer showed that it had traveled 225,000 miles—surely far further than its reasonable road life. As I explained to you on May 21, there was no way to restore it to good condition for a reasonable price. But I did say that we could fix the fuel injection problem and get the vehicle back in operation.

Under the circumstances, I believe the repairs my garage made were reasonable and well done. The fact that you later suffered an engine fire is not proof of any negligence on my part; there are many other ways it could have come about, all of which I'll be happy to explain to a judge if we end up in court.

In addition, I do not think it was reasonable for you to have the problem fixed by the local Chevy dealership, surely one of the most expensive shops in town, particularly when I offered to fix all problems caused by the fire at no extra cost.

But in an effort to put this whole unfortunate event behind us, I'm willing to offer you $650 as a compromise settlement of all your claims. I do this without admitting any wrongdoing, but solely in the spirit of compromise.

Sincerely,

Ron Tucker

June 6, 20xx

Beyond Repair Construction
10 Delaney Avenue
Lincoln, Nebraska

Dear Sirs:

You recently did replacement tile work and other remodeling on my downstairs bathroom at 142 West Pine St., here in Lincoln. As per our written agreement, I paid you $4,175 upon completion of the job on May 17, 20xx.

Only two weeks later, on June 1, I noticed that the tile in the north portion of the shower (the side away from the door) had sunk almost half an inch, with the result that the shower floor was uneven and water pooled in the downhill corner before eventually going down the drain.

In our telephone conversations, you variously claimed that the problem:

- was in my imagination

- was my fault, because the floor was uneven to begin with, and

- was too minor to bother with.

Sorry, but I paid for a first-class remodeling job, and I expect to receive it or get my money back. Having water pool on one side of the shower, even for a short time, is not acceptable. Please contact me within 10 days to arrange to pay me $1,800 (the cost of redoing the work per the enclosed estimate from ABC Tile) or to arrange to redo the work yourself. If I don't hear from you by June 15, I will promptly file in small claims court. Assuming I receive a judgment, which of course will be part of the public record, I will promptly proceed to collect it.

Sincerely,

Ben Price

June 13, 20xx

Ben Price
142 West Pine St.
Lincoln, NE _____

Dear Mr. Price,

As you may remember, when I estimated your job, I pointed out that because your house is 90 years old, the original construction of the shower was far below current code requirements. At this point, we discussed doing a state of the art job would essentially involve stripping out and replacing your entire bathroom at great cost. When you indicated that you couldn't afford this approach, we opted for what I described to you as "a patch and hope for the best" approach.

From our recent telephone conversation, I gather that about 80% of the tile job has worked fine. As I told you at that time, I regret that a portion of the floor has subsided, and I offered to fix it free of charge. I renew this offer now. Given that I or any other reputable contractor could make the necessary repairs in four or five hours, I do not believe that the ABC estimate of $1,800 is reasonable. But in an effort to put this dispute behind us, I'm also willing to refund you $600 in full settlement of all claims between us.

Sincerely,

Alison Darnell

B. Try to Negotiate a Settlement

Once both parties have calmly laid out their positions in letters (or even if one or both of you has chosen to skip this step), your next job is to try to negotiate a compromise with the other party. Although the wisdom of talking about possible settlement scenarios, even to an unreasonable opponent, should be obvious, many people adamantly refuse to do it. There's no question that many of us have a strong psychological barrier to even speaking to people we are upset with, especially if we have already exchanged heated words. If you fall into this category, perhaps you'll find it easier to pick up the phone if you remind yourself that willingness to compromise is a sign of maturity and strength, not weakness. After all, it was Winston Churchill, one of the twentieth century's greatest warriors, who said, "I would rather jaw, jaw, jaw than war, war, war."

Settlement offers aren't binding. An offer of compromise (that is, an offer to settle a dispute), made either orally or in writing, does not legally obligate the person making it to sue for that amount if the compromise is rejected. Thus, you could make a written demand for $2,000, then offer to compromise for $1,500, and still sue for $2,000 should your compromise offer be spurned. Similarly, a defendant who offers to pay $1,200 to settle the $2,000 dispute can still contest the entire amount should the settlement be rejected. The judge is not legally permitted to even consider the existence of a compromise offer made as part of a failed settlement effort, so don't worry that your offer to compromise might affect how much you are awarded (or ordered to pay).

In an effort to help you arrive at a good compromise, here are a few of my personal dispute resolution rules, which, of course, I modify to fit the circumstances:

- If you are the potential plaintiff and have a strong case, respond to a defendant's low ball offer by proposing to shave about 15% to 20% off your original demand, in exchange for a quick settlement. Any less and you won't be taken seriously. Any more and you're giving away too much too soon.

- If you are the potential defendant and conclude that the plaintiff probably does have a decent case, it usually makes sense to start negotiations by offering about 50% of the amount demanded. This should be enough to keep the conversation going without conceding too much too soon. Many plaintiffs will ultimately agree to knock as much as one-third off their original demand just to save the time, trouble, and uncertainty of going to court.

- Money isn't always the root of the problem. If you pay close attention to the other party's concerns, you may find that the key to arriving at an agreement lies elsewhere. For example, a print shop might agree to refund a customer $2,000 on a disputed job in exchange for an agreement to continue to work together and speak well of each other in the future.

- Whether you are a potential plaintiff or defender, estimate how much money a compromise settlement is worth to you, given that it eliminates the time and aggravation of going to court. I do this by putting a dollar value on my time and then multiplying by the number of hours I think it will take to prepare my case and go to court. If I think I'll have trouble collecting a judgment, I add time for that.

- The patient negotiator has the edge. Many of us are in such a hurry to arrive at a solution that they will agree to a bad one. Take your time. If you make a lowball offer and the other person gets mad and hangs up, you can always wait a few days, call back, and offer more.

- Good negotiators rarely change their position quickly, even if the other side does. Instead, they raise or lower their offer in small increments (often 5 to 10%). For example, assume your opponent first offers $250 to settle your $1,000 demand, and you counter by asking for $800. Next, your opponent makes a big deal ("this is my final offer") of offering you $500. Your best move is not to immediately say yes, but instead to come down to $650 or $700. Following this gradualist negotiating approach, there is at least a decent chance your opponent will respond with a better offer. And even if he or she refuses to budge, you won't have lost anything; once the offer to settle for $500 is on the table, your opponent probably won't refuse to honor it just because you don't immediately accept.

Don't agree to split the difference. Often, one side will offer to split the remaining difference ("well, you offered to settle for $4,000, and I offered to pay $1,000, so why don't we meet halfway and settle this for $2,500?"). If you agree to this type of offer right away, you're missing a valuable bargaining opportunity—after all, an opponent who makes a "split the difference" offer has already conceded that he or she is willing to pay (or accept) the middle figure. Better to counter with an amount between your last offer and your opponent's "split the difference" offer.

- Based on the facts of your case, take into consideration the possibility that you might lose in court, or win less than you demand. To do this, you'll have to bend over backwards to see the dispute from your opponent's point of view (something that will prove valuable should you eventually need to present your case to a judge). In one study of 996 Small Claims cases that actually went to trial, the plaintiff received the entire amount claimed in only 32% of the cases; the plaintiff got between 50% and 100% of the amount claimed in 22% of the cases; the plaintiff got less than half in 20%; and in 26% of the cases, the plaintiff got nothing at all. ("Small Claims and Traffic Courts," by John Goerdt (National Center for State Courts).)

Example: In a dispute my business, Nolo, had with a phone company, Nolo originally asked for $5,000. The phone company admitted some liability and offered to compromise. After considering the value of the time and energy Nolo would have to spend to take the phone company to court, we were willing to settle for $3,500. And although we were sure we had a strong case, we had to admit that a judge might be troubled by our inability to quantify exactly how much business we lost when an inexperienced and negligent phone technician cut off our phones. As a result, we decided to subtract another $500 and were therefore willing to accept $3,000. Unfortunately, after several conversations and letters, the phone company wouldn't offer a dime more than $2,000. This was too low, and we decided to go to court. As it happened, the judge awarded us the entire $5,000. But then, unexpectedly, the phone company appealed and received a new trial (in California, a defendant who appeals can get a new trial). After the case was presented again, the second judge reduced our final award to $3,500. Considering that it was easier to prepare the case the second time, we still came out ahead, as compared to accepting the $2,000—but in truth, given the value of the time we spent preparing for two court presentations, it probably cost us about $1,000 to get the extra $1,500, so our net gain over the phone company's final offer was only about $500.

More information on negotiating. On several occasions when I have been involved in important negotiations, I've gotten help by rereading *Getting to Yes: Negotiating Agreements Without Giving In,* by Roger Fisher and William Ury (Penguin). I also like *Getting Past No: Negotiating Your Way From Confrontation to Cooperation*, by William Ury (Bantam).

C. Write Down the Settlement Terms

If you and the other party agree to a settlement, it's important to put it in writing. Lawyers often call a contract settling a dispute a "release," because in exchange for some act (often the payment of money), one person gives up or releases his or her legal claim against another. For instance, if John's building gets splattered when Joan, a neighboring property owner, uses a spray painter on a windy day, John might agree to release Joan from liability (that is, to not sue Joan) if Joan agrees to pay $2,000 to have the damaged area of John's building repainted.

As long as a written release is signed voluntarily by both parties, it is a valid contract. For example, if you and I agree, in writing, that you will pay me $500 if I promise not to sue you for shooting at my dog Rover and to keep Rover out of your yard in the future, we have a legally binding deal. Absent fraud, if either party later breaks the contract, the other can file a lawsuit solely based on breach of the contract and receive a court judgment for appropriate damages without ever having to prove the facts underlying the dispute.

A release is a powerful document. If you release someone who damaged your car for $500, only to find out later that the damage was more extensive, you'll be stuck with the $500 unless you can convincingly claim that the other party committed fraud or misrepresented key facts. Of course, if the details of a dispute are well known (as they are in many cases), you can comfortably sign a release, secure in the knowledge that the dispute will finally be laid to rest.

Below is a sample release adapted from Nolo's book *101 Law Forms for Personal Use*, by Robin Leonard and Ralph Warner. For a small fee, you can also complete and download a general release from legal claims from www.nolo.com. Both the book and the website also contain mutual release forms for use when both parties are giving up claims. You can also find release forms at office supply stores that carry legal documents and in lawyers' form books, available at law libraries.

No matter where you get your release, it should contain the following information:

- The names and addresses of the party being released and the party granting the release.

- A brief description of the "what," "when," and "where" of the dispute or issue to which the release pertains. (The release below provides several blank lines for you to briefly describe the events giving rise to the need for the release.)

- A statement of what the person giving up a claim is getting in return. For a release to be an enforceable contract, the person giving up the right to sue must receive something of value in exchange. Typically, this is money, but it could also be labor or goods. If money is involved, simply enter the amount. If the parties have reached a nonmonetary deal, describe it (for example, "Joan will repaint the garage at 210 Palmouth St." or "Rich will keep Zeke, the barking dog, inside at night").

- A statement that the release applies to all claims arising from the dispute or issue, both those known at the time the release is signed and those that may come along later. This provision is very common in releases; without it they wouldn't be worth much.

- A statement that the release binds all persons who might otherwise have a legal right to file a claim on behalf of the releasor (for example, the releasor's spouse or heirs).

- The date the release is signed.

- The signatures of the parties. Legally, only the person granting a release needs to sign it, but it is better practice for both parties to do so—after all, this important document contains statements that affect the rights of both. And, of course, in the case of a mutual release (where each party gives up any claims against the other), both must sign.

- The release below contains a place for the signatures of witnesses. There is no legal requirement that a release has to be witnessed, and it's ordinarily not necessary to do this. But if you don't trust the other person and think he or she may later claim "it's not my signature," a witness can be a good idea. If you decide to dispense with witnesses, put "N.A." on each of the lines.

GENERAL RELEASE

1. ___(Person signing release)___, Releasor, voluntarily and knowingly executes this release with the express intention of eliminating Releasee's liabilities and obligations as described below.

2. Releasor hereby releases ___(person being released)___, Releasee, from all claims, known or unknown, that have arisen or may arise from the following occurrence: ___(description of events giving rise to release, including location and date if appropriate; see box for sample language)___

Sample Language:

a. "Repair work incompletely done to Releasor's boat at the Fixemup shipyards on May 6, 2xxx."

b. "Agreement by Releasee made during the week of June 6, 2xxx to deliver the fully laid out and pasted-up manuscript for the book Do Your Own Brain Surgery to Releasor's address no later than July 6, 2xxx, which Releasee failed to keep."

c. "A tree growing on Releasee's property at 1011 Oak St. fell into Releasor's backyard at 1013 Oak St. on August 7, 2xxx. It damaged Releasor's fence, which had to be replaced. The tree itself had to be removed by ABC Tree Terminators."

3. In exchange for granting this release Releasor has received the following consideration: ___(amount of money, or description of something else of value that person signing release received from other party; see box for sample language)___

Sample Language:

a. "$150 cash."

b. "a SONY television set, #173B9."

c. "an agreement by (Releasee's name) to desist from further activities as described in Clause 2 of this release."

d. "an agreement by (Releasee's name) to repair Releasor's Apple Macintosh computer by January, 2xxx."

4.   In executing this release Releasor additionally intends to bind his or her spouse, heirs, legal representatives, assigns, and anyone else claiming under him or her. Releasor has not assigned any claim covered by this release to any other party. Releasor also intends that this release apply to the heirs, personal representatives, assigns, insurers, and successors of Releasee as well as to the Releasee.

This release was executed on _____, 2__ at   _(city and state)_____

_____   _____
Releasor's Signature   Releasee's Signature

_____   _____
Address   Address

_____   _____

_____   _____
Releasor's Spouse's Signature

Witnesses:

_____   _____
Name   Address

_____   _____
Name   Address

Reaching an Agreement on the Courthouse Steps

If the parties agree to mediate (see Chapter 7), last minute settlements are a frequent occurrence—especially because mediation is often held right before the parties are scheduled to present their case. But if your court doesn't require or offer mediation, it is perfectly proper to ask the other person if he or she wishes to step into the hall for a moment to talk the matter over. If you can agree on a last-minute compromise, you won't have time to prepare a settlement contract (a release). Instead, wait until your case is called by the courtroom clerk and then tell the judge that the two of you have agreed on a compromise settlement. At this point, the judge will probably order that the case be dismissed if one person pays the other the agreed-upon amount on the spot. If payment is to be made later or in installments, the judge may prefer to enter a judgment for the amount you have agreed upon, so the plaintiff will have some recourse if the defendant never pays up.

Another way to settle just before court is to schedule a mediation session. If no mediator is available right away, the judge will normally delay ("continue," in legalese) your case until the mediation session takes place. If mediation works and your case settles, the mediator will help you prepare an agreement (see Chapter 7).

■

Mediate Your Dispute

If, despite your letter writing and other settlement efforts, gridlock still reigns, it may be time to enlist the help of a third party. (And I don't mean the small claims court judge.) Mediation, a procedure in which the disputants meet with a neutral third party in an effort to resolve their dispute, is available in most small claims courts at no, or very low, cost. For a variety of reasons discussed in this chapter, mediation can be a good choice for many (if not most) plaintiffs and defendants.

In the majority of small claims courts that offer mediation, the decision to try to mediate a case is voluntary—in other words, you and the other party are free to try mediation or reject it, as you see fit. However, in an increasing number of cities and states, including Florida, Hawaii, Idaho, Maine, New Hampshire, and Washington, DC, parties generally must give mediation a try before their case can proceed to the courtroom. Even in areas where mediation is not mandatory, it may be built into the small claims process, often routinely scheduled to occur just before your planned court appearance.

In a small claims mediation meeting, which will typically last anywhere from 30 minutes to an hour, you and the other party sit down with a trained mediator whose role is to help you arrive at your own compromise solution. Unlike a judge, a mediator has no power to impose a judgment. As a result, mediation sessions tend to be more relaxed than court proceedings. And because mediators are often very effective at helping opponents surface and deal with hidden emotional issues, mediation can be a remarkably effective way to settle disputes. But it's also true that if you and your opponent can't agree on a settlement, there will be no resolution at the mediation stage. Instead, the dispute will be decided by a small claims judge, either on the same day as the mediation or at a future date.

A. Why Mediate?

In small claims courts that make mediation available but don't require it, people sometimes ask, "Why shouldn't I just tell my story to the judge and hope for the best instead of trying to compromise with someone I already know to be unreasonable?"

There are several good reasons to try mediation first, even when you and your opponent have exchanged harsh words. First, a number of studies have shown that when opposing parties voluntarily agree to mediate, as many as 70% of small claims disputes are settled. And even in court systems where everyone—including people who hate the idea—is forced to mediate as a mandatory precondition to going to court, over 50% of cases are resolved.

Settlement is especially likely when, deep down, one or both parties realize they have an interest in arriving at a solution that the other party can live with. For example, mediation tends to be an extremely effective way to settle disputes between neighbors or small business people who live or work in the same geographical area and really don't want the dispute to fester. One reason why mediation is so effective is that, unlike a small claims court proceeding, where a judge will try to focus solely on the facts, mediation gives the disputants a safe and appropriate way to express their anger or disappointment—often a key first step to discovering a compromise acceptable to both.

Because a mediated solution is more likely to be honored, mediation can also lead to higher long-term satisfaction than you might find in a courtroom. Several studies have shown that defendants who agree to a mediated solution are more likely to pay up promptly, often on the spot. If you are a plaintiff who is at least as worried about collecting your judgment as about winning it in the first place, mediation is clearly your best bet.

Example: The front left side of Latasha's Subaru was damaged when Rick's speeding pick-up truck skidded through a stop sign and banged into her fender. With three reliable witnesses, Latasha had little doubt she would win. But the fact that Rick was a self-employed handyman who worked out of a rented garage caused her to worry that she would never collect the resulting judgment. When the small claims clerk suggested that Latasha and Rick try mediation, she agreed. At the mediation session, she accepted Rick's claim that her Suburu could be fixed for $1,560, not the $2,000 she sued for. In exchange, Rick pulled out his wallet and counted out 78 $20 bills right on the mediation table.

The ability to control the result of your dispute is a third extremely practical reason to try mediation. Unlike small claims court, where the judge has the power to impose a result, your case can't be settled in mediation unless you agree. And based on my personal observations over the years, as well as the letters and emails I've received from hundreds of unhappy small claims litigants, judges—who spend an average of less than 15 minutes considering each case—don't always get it right. And because most states allow you to appeal only if the judge gets the law seriously wrong, there usually won't be much you can do if a bad judge renders an unfair judgment.

Is agreeing to mediate always a good idea? No. If you are absolutely determined to try to obtain 100% of the amount you are asking for, and especially if you are suing a large corporation, government agency, or anyone else with whom you'll have no ongoing relationship, proceeding directly to court (except in the few places where mediation is mandatory) can make sense.

> **Example:** John rented an apartment from Frontier Arms, Inc. When he moved out and left the unit undamaged and spotless, the Frontier Arms manager who had simply forgotten to return his $1,500 deposit made up a bogus "the apartment was filthy" story to justify his mistake to the building owners. Fortunately, John, had taken pictures of the apartment and had several reliable witnesses anxious to testify that it was immaculate. He was so sure the judge would award him his entire $1,500 plus the $700 penalty his state's law allows when a landlord improperly withholds deposits, that he saw absolutely no reason to compromise.

If you want to mediate but your court doesn't require it, how can you get a reluctant opponent to the table? Often, you can get help from your local court-sponsored or community mediation program. Typically, as soon as you notify the mediation staff or program that you would like to try mediation (the court may automatically provide this notification for court-sponsored programs), an employee or volunteer with the mediation program will contact the other party or parties and try to arrange a session. Because people with years of experience in the field of mediation know how to pitch its many advantages, they are often far more convincing than you would be. For example, staff will often explain to a reluctant defendant that a successful mediation is the best way to keep a dispute private—and make sure that no adverse judgment appears on his or her credit report.

Mediation Is Good for Defendants, Too

Suppose now that you are a defendant in a small claims case or have received a letter threatening you with a lawsuit. Should you ask for, or agree to, mediation? The answer is almost always a resounding "YES," especially if you have a partial defense to the plaintiff's claim or believe that, while the plaintiff may have a decent case, he or she is asking for too much money. Mediation will give you an opportunity to tell your side of the story and hopefully, with the help of the experienced mediator, arrive at an acceptable compromise.

Unlike court, where judges aren't allowed to consider extraneous issues, mediation also gives you a chance to bring up other issues that may be poisoning your relationship with the plaintiff and torpedoing any chance of settlement. Once these are acknowledged and dealt with, the chance of arriving at a compromise settlement goes way up.

Defendants: Put your checkbook on the table. If mediation fails, the plaintiff knows that it might be tough to collect any eventual judgment. Accordingly, if you offer to write a check on the spot, many plaintiffs will accept considerably less than they originally demanded. The plaintiff has far less incentive to compromise with a defendant who proposes to pay on an installment plan (although the plaintiff may accept if you are able to come up with a substantial first payment).

B. The Mediation Process

Because a mediator has no power to impose a decision, mediation is fundamentally different from small claims court. Instead of trying to convince a judge that the law is on your side, your job is to get the other party to agree to a compromise solution that you find at least minimally acceptable. In practice, this usually means that good psychology is more important than aggressive lawyering.

1. Preparing for the Mediation

Mediation is an informal procedure that is remarkably successful at helping people resolve disputes—but that doesn't mean you can just show up at the mediation session and expect a settlement to materialize. Taking a little time to prepare for the mediation will greatly increase your chances of reaching an agreement.

Getting ready for your mediation. Good mediation technique is a skill you can learn. One key to success is often to sit back and let your opponent vent without arguing every point. Another is to remember that achieving an acceptable result and bringing the dispute to a close is far more important than trying to establish that you are 100% in the right. The best source of information on how to mediate successfully is *Mediate, Don't Litigate,* by Peter Lovenheim and Lisa Guerin (Nolo). I can almost guarantee that reading it before you mediate will lead to better results than would otherwise have been possible.

Start by trying to figure out your opponent's key interests in the dispute. For example, the older affluent driver who rear-ended your car may care more about not having a court judgment on his record—and not being told he is an incompetent driver by someone half his age—than he does about paying to fix your car. As a result, a polite, respectful approach in which you are prepared to listen to a list of face-saving, but legally irrelevant, excuses, may pave the way to his writing you a check.

Once you have a handle on what is really fueling the dispute, think about what you'd be willing to settle for. Of course, settlement options that you hadn't considered may come up during the mediation, but it's a good idea to have a sense of your "bottom line"—the most you are willing to pay, or the least you are willing to accept—before you enter the mediation session. You probably won't want to reveal this to your opponent; just keep it in mind as you evaluate various settlement proposals.

Finally, take some time to prepare your presentation. A mediation is very different from a court proceeding, because your real audience is your opponent, not a third party decision maker. After all, you won't reach a settlement unless you and your opponent both agree to it. And if you do, it doesn't really matter what the mediator personally thinks is fair. For this reason, you should plan to state your side of the story in a way that will either be convincing to your opponent, or at least demonstrate that you will be able to prove your case in court. (For help figuring out what evidence will be most persuasive, see Chapters 17 through 23.)

2. At the Mediation Session

How your particular mediation will proceed will depend on a number of factors, from the style of the mediator, to the rules of the program, the time set aside for mediation, and whether mediation is voluntary or mandatory. Typically, the mediator will make some remarks about the process, then allow each of you to briefly state your version of events. If you have brought any evidence with you to the mediation, let the mediator know, and explain why you think the evidence is important. Again, the mediator can't make a decision, but if your case is very convincing, the mediator may be able to help the other party understand that settlement really is the best option.

Once you both have had an opportunity to speak, the mediator might ask some questions, start talking about settlement options, or ask you and your opponent how you think the dispute might be resolved. It's a good idea to stay open to the mediator's suggestions. It's also important that you listen carefully to your opponent without interruption. You might hear something that will help you figure out what is really motivating the other party—and therefore, how the dispute could be settled.

Example 1: A customer sues your dog grooming salon, claiming you caused physical and psychological harm to her twin poodles. In truth, your employee got mixed up and gave the poodles a crewcut instead of the requested trim. But even though you agree that the customer's nearly bald poodles look pretty silly, you regard her demand for $3,000 damages as ridiculous. After all, Mimi and Mona were treated well by your salon staff, and their hair will soon grow back. But you are definitely disposed to compromise with the irate dog owner if this will avoid your being bad-mouthed forever in the local poodle owner community.
At the mediation, you decide to bring your young employee who screwed up. As the dog owner expresses her anger in no uncertain terms—and even says a few unfair things—you calmly sit back and listen without interruption. Then, both you and your tearful employee apologize for the "serious mistake." Next, you briefly explain the new procedures you have implemented to guarantee that similar mistakes won't be made in the future. You then rely on the skilled mediator to help the somewhat mollified poodle parent to understand that she is asking for far too much money. Fortunately, once the owner sees how contrite your employee is, and how seriously you take the mishap, she agrees to settle the case for $400. Surprisingly, on the way out to the parking lot, the customer tells you how glad she is to have worked things out, because she knows you are the best dog groomer around and she wants to continue using your services.

Example 2: Tom's Print and Copy did regular printing work for Tara's restaurant for several years. Gradually Tara fell behind in her payments. One day, when she couldn't or wouldn't pay anything towards her $2,750 bill, Tom got disgusted and refused to print any more menus or ads. After writing a demand letter to which he got no response, Tom filed suit in small claims court. Worried that Tara might file for bankruptcy or close the restaurant and disappear, Tom was more interested in promptly collecting as much as possible than in getting every last dollar. When he learned that mediation was available, he quickly agreed to try it. At the mediation session, Tara said she was talking with a new investor to recapitalize her business—which is when Tom realized that Tara had a strong incentive to avoid having an adverse judgment on her credit record. Accordingly, he proposed that she pay $2,000 to settle the entire debt. When Tara proposed paying in monthly installments, Tom politely refused. When Tara then asked for a few days to try to raise the money, Tom and the mediator agreed to a week's continuance. When the mediation reconvened, Tara produced her dad's check for $1,800, which Tom accepted as payment in full.

The Defendant's Goals at a Mediation Session

It's not only the plaintiff who can gain by mediating a dispute. Defendants too can often use the mediation process to their advantage. Most defendants have one or more of the following three goals:

- **To explain the weaknesses in the plaintiff's case.** For example, a defendant tenant, whose landlord claims that he damaged a rental unit, might use the mediation session to show the plaintiff that some of the claimed damage existed before he moved in. Obviously, the tenant's goal is not to convince the mediator (who, after all, has no power to render a decision), but to shake the landlord's certainty in the strength of the case. A defendant who can convince a plaintiff that he or she might lose some or all of the lawsuit takes a huge step towards creating an environment where a reasonable compromise can take place.

- **To show that it may be hard for the plaintiff to prove his or her case.** By using the mediation forum to ask the plaintiff about evidence and witnesses, a savvy defendant—often with the help of an experienced mediator—may be able to show the plaintiff that proving his or her case may be easier said than done. For example, the defendant owner of a ski shop might ask an unhappy customer exactly which of his employees told her that a particular pair of "powder skis" were "the best choice for icy slopes." Assuming the plaintiff doesn't know the person's name and hasn't arranged for his or her testimony, the mediator will likely help the plaintiff understand that it will be hard to prove "a breach of warranty case" in court—and therefore, that it makes sense to accept the store owner's settlement offer of a generous merchandise credit.

- **To show plaintiff the money.** Which would you rather have—70 cents in your hand right now or the possibility of receiving a dollar six months from now (after going to court and then facing the uncertainties of collecting the judgment)? As I've emphasized throughout this chapter, lots of savvy plaintiffs will opt for the 70 cents now—which is why a wise defendant will emphasize his or her willingness to write a check for the entire settlement amount as soon as the dispute is resolved.

C.   After a Successful Mediation

If you are able to reach an agreement, the mediator will usually help you put it in writing, often using a court form. In a few states, the written agreement will be made part of a court judgment. But because many defendants settle their cases precisely to avoid a court judgment, mediation agreements usually take the form of a binding agreement (contract), not a court judgment.

Insist on prompt payment. Receiving cash on the barrelhead is one of the biggest benefits of settling a case in mediation. Usually, there is too little to be gained by agreeing to accept a compromise settlement, in which a financially unreliable defendant promises to pay $50 per month. While I rarely recommend that a plaintiff hold out for top dollar, I do advise holding out for full, or at least a very substantial, payment of any compromise settlement.

As long as the defendant pays on the spot, the form of the agreement shouldn't make much difference to the plaintiff. But if the defendant might not be able to promptly pay the full amount of the mediated settlement, the plaintiff will be better off pushing to have the settlement made part of official judgment. If a court order is not obeyed, collection procedures can begin immediately. In the case of a broken mediation agreement, on the other hand, you will have to take the extra step of going back to court to have the agreement turned into a judgment before you can start collecting. (This is usually no big deal, but it is an extra step.)

Plaintiffs—reserve your right to sue for the full amount. Most successful mediations result in a compromise. For example, John might sue Hank for $2,000 and agree to accept $1,500 in settlement. But if Hank fails to pay within the time allowed, John will undoubtedly feel twice wronged and want a judgment for the full $2,000. (After all, he wouldn't have compromised in the first place if he knew Hank wasn't going to keep his side of the bargain.) Unless your opponent pays you on the spot, try to add a sentence to your mediated agreement stating that if the other party doesn't meet his or her settlement obligations, you reserve the right to make your full, original claim in court. This approach may not be accepted in all courts, but it's worth a try.

Arbitration

In addition to mediation, a few states also offer binding arbitration before a volunteer lawyer as an alternative to having a case heard in small claims court. Typically, the lawyer and the parties sit down at a table and discuss the case. If the parties don't arrive at their own solution, the arbitrator renders a decision just as a judge would. The only advantage of arbitration over going before a small claims judge or a commissioner is that, in some areas, it's faster to meet with the arbitrator.

Unfortunately, arbitration also comes with a big built-in disadvantage: The arbitrator is likely to be a volunteer lawyer, who is far less knowledgeable than a judge about the broad range of laws that apply to consumers and small businesses. For this reason, I usually recommend against this procedure.

New York Note: In New York state, where volunteer lawyer arbitrators are routinely used, this disadvantage is compounded by the fact that you can't appeal from the decision of an arbitrator as you could from a judge's decision.

Nonbinding Arbitration: In a few areas, a procedure called nonbinding arbitration is available. This is much like mediation, in the sense that both parties must agree to any settlement. The only difference is that, unlike a mediator, who doesn't make a formal recommendation, the arbitrator will recommend—but not compel—a solution. Especially if it's more easily available than mediation, it's often a good idea to try nonbinding arbitration; the arbitrator's recommendation can be a pretty good indication of what will happen if the case ends up going to court.

■

CHAPTER

8

Who Can Sue?

Who can sue in small claims court? The answer is easy. *You* can, as long as you are an adult (18 in most states) or an emancipated minor and have not been declared mentally incompetent in a judicial proceeding. You must also be suing on your own claim (that is, you can't sue to vindicate or enforce someone else's rights—you must sue on your own behalf).

⚠ Special requirements for some plaintiffs. Some states do not let unlicensed contractors and other business people who work without required licenses to bring suit on claims related to their business. Prisoners are allowed to sue in some states, but not in others. In states where they can sue, their cases must usually be presented in writing. (In a few states, prisoners can name an adult representative to appear on their behalf.)

The way you refer to yourself on court papers depends on whether you are an individual or business. Your state's requirements may vary slightly, however, so you should check your state's guidelines.

- **Individuals:** If you are suing for yourself alone, simply list your full name as plaintiff.

- **Groups:** If more than one person is bringing suit, list all the names as plaintiffs. For married couples, list both spouses.

- **Individually owned businesses and sole proprietorships:** If you are filing a claim on behalf of your individually owned business, you (the owner of the business) must do the suing. You should list your name and the business name as plaintiffs, for example, "Jane Poe doing business as ABC Printing." Also, if the business uses a fictitious name (such as Tasty Donut Shop) instead of the owner's name, many states require you to complete a form stating that the fictitious business name has been properly registered.

- **Partnerships:** If you are a partner filing a claim on behalf of a partnership, list the partnership name as plaintiff (example, Jones & Wood Graphics). Only one of the partners need sign. If the partnership uses a fictitious name, list it and the partners' real names, such as "ABC Printing, a partnership, and Jane Poe and Phil Roe, partners."

- **Corporations:** If you are filing a claim on behalf of a corporation, whether profit or nonprofit, list the corporation as plaintiff. In most states, the form must be signed by either:

  a. an officer of the corporation, or

  b. a person authorized to file claims on behalf of the corporation by the corporation's board of directors. If a nonofficer of a corporation signs the forms, the court clerk may want to see some documentation that the person suing is properly authorized.

- **Limited Liability Companies:** If you are suing on behalf of a limited liability company (LLC), most states allow any member to sue. But check your local rules; LLCs are fairly new, so procedures are still in flux in many states.

- **Unincorporated Associations:** If you are filing on behalf of an unincorporated association, do so by listing the name of the association and the name of the officer by whom it is being represented (such as "ABC Society, by Philip Dog, president").

- **Motor Vehicle Claims:** When a claim arises out of damage to a motor vehicle, the registered owner(s) of the vehicle must file in small claims court. So, if you are driving someone else's car and get hit by a third party, you can't sue for damage done to the car. The registered owner must do the suing.

- **Public Entities:** If you are suing on behalf of a public entity such as a public library, city tax assessor's office, or county hospital, you must show the court clerk proper authorization to sue.

 **Defendants can sometimes challenge a plaintiff's right to sue.** As noted above, a person must meet certain legal requirements to sue in small claims court. For example, in some states, contractors must be licensed, and car repair dealers, structural pest control operators, and TV repair people must be registered with the appropriate state agency in order to sue in small claims court. And, in some states, anyone doing business under a fictitious name must file and maintain a fictitious business name statement as a precondition to using the courts. If you are being sued by someone who may not meet these requirements, check your state's rules by asking the court clerk or, better yet, looking up the law. (Your state's small claims statute numbers are listed in the Appendix, and Chapter 1, Section D, explains how to look them up.)

A. Participation by Attorneys and Bill Collectors

In the majority of states, attorneys are permitted to appear in small claims court. (See the chart below for your state's rules.) However, attorneys, or other people acting as representatives, cannot normally appear in small claims court in Arkansas (except in rural Justice of the Peace courts), California, Colorado, Idaho, Kansas, Michigan, Minnesota, Montana, Nebraska, Oregon, Virginia, and Washington. Minnesota, Oregon, and Washington allow attorneys only if the judge consents. Getting the advice of a lawyer before going to small claims court is perfectly legal in all states, however.

Many states, including Arkansas, California, Colorado, Kentucky, Michigan, Missouri, Montana, Nebraska, New Jersey (except by corporations), New York, Ohio, Oklahoma, and Texas forbid the use of small claims court by "assignees" (a fancy term that usually refers to collection agencies). In other words, in these states you cannot hire someone to sue for an unpaid debt. But the majority of states still allow suits by collection agencies. Texas and Kentucky seem to be unique in barring lenders of money at interest from using small claims court. See your state's entry in the Appendix under "Note" for details.

STATE SMALL CLAIMS LAWS ON ATTORNEY REPRESENTATION

State	Attorneys	Assignees
Alabama	Allowed. Required for collection agencies.	Allowed.
Alaska	Allowed. Required for collection agencies.	Allowed.
Arizona	Allowed if both parties agree in writing.	Not allowed.
Arkansas	Not allowed in small claims division; allowed in justice court.	Not allowed.
California	Not allowed.	Not allowed.
Colorado	Allowed only for partnership, corporation, or association. If one party has attorney, other party may also have one.	Not allowed.
Connecticut	Allowed. Required for corporations.	Allowed.
Delaware	Allowed.	Allowed.
D.C.	Allowed. Required for corporations.	Allowed.
Florida	Allowed. Court may require for collection agencies.	Allowed.
Georgia	Allowed.	Allowed.
Hawaii	Allowed (except in landlord-tenant security deposit cases).	Allowed.
Idaho	Not allowed.	Allowed.
Illinois	Allowed except in Cook County *Pro Se* court.	Allowed except for a corporation.
Indiana	Allowed.	Allowed.
Iowa	Allowed.	Allowed.
Kansas	Generally not allowed. If one party is permitted to have an attorney, all other parties may also have one.	Allowed.
Kentucky	Allowed.	Not allowed.
Louisiana	Allowed.	Allowed.
Maine	Allowed.	Allowed.
Maryland	Allowed.	Allowed.
Massachusetts	Allowed.	Allowed.
Michigan	Not allowed.	Not allowed.
Minnesota	Not allowed except with court approval.	Allowed.
Mississippi	Allowed.	Allowed.
Missouri	Allowed.	Not allowed.
Montana	Not allowed unless all parties have attorneys.	Not allowed.
Nebraska	Not allowed.	Not allowed.
Nevada	Allowed.	Allowed.
New Hampshire	Allowed.	Allowed.

STATE SMALL CLAIMS LAWS ON ATTORNEY REPRESENTATION (CONT.)

State	Attorneys	Assignees
New Jersey	Allowed. Required for corporation if claim over $3,000.	Not allowed
New Mexico	Allowed.	Allowed.
New York	Usually not allowed unless grounds exist for having attorney. If all parties have counsel, case may be transferred.	Not allowed.
North Carolina	Allowed.	Allowed.
North Dakota	Allowed.	Allowed.
Ohio	Allowed.	Not allowed.
Oklahoma	Allowed (fee restricted to 10% in uncontested cases).	Not allowed.
Oregon	Not allowed unless judge consents.	Allowed.
Pennsylvania	Allowed. Required for corporations if claim over $2,500.	Allowed.
Rhode Island	Allowed. Required for public corporations and private corporations with assets of $1 million or more.	Allowed.
South Carolina	Allowed.	Allowed.
South Dakota	Allowed.	Allowed.
Tennessee	Allowed. Required for corporations.	Allowed.
Texas	Allowed.	Not allowed.
Utah	Allowed.	Not allowed.
Vermont	Allowed.	Allowed.
Virginia	Not allowed.	Allowed.
Washington	Not allowed without court approval.	Allowed.
West Virginia	Allowed.	Allowed.
Wisconsin	Allowed.	Allowed.
Wyoming	Allowed. If one party has attorney, other party may have continuance to obtain one.	Allowed.

Attorneys can always bring suits on their own behalf. Even in states that don't allow attorneys to represent someone else in small claims court, attorneys are allowed to sue on or defend their own claims.

B. Suits by Minors

If you are a minor (in other words, you have not reached your 18th birthday), your parent or legal guardian must sue for you. The exception is that in some states, emancipated minors can sue on their own. When your parents or guardians are involved, a form must be filled out and signed by the judge appointing the person in question as your "Guardian Ad Litem." This simply means guardian for the purposes of the lawsuit. Ask the court clerk for the rules in your state.

C. Class Actions (Group Lawsuits)

In small claims court there is no such thing as a true class action in which a number of people in a similar situation ask a court's permission to join together in one lawsuit. However, a number of community groups have discovered that if a large number of people with a particular grievance (pollution, noise, drug sales) sue the same defendant at the same time, something remarkably like a class action suit is created. This technique was pioneered by a group of determined homeowners living near the San Francisco Airport who, several times, won over 100 small claims court judgments (for excessive noise) on the same day. They hired expert witnesses, did research, ran training workshops, and paid for legal advice when needed as part of a coordinated effort, to be sure they knew how to efficiently present their own cases. The City of San Francisco tried to fend off these cases by arguing that the homeowners were, in effect, involved in a class action lawsuit, and such suits are not permitted in small claims court. However, a California Court of Appeals disagreed, saying that "Numerous 'mass' actions against the City alleging that noise from the City airport constituted a continuing nuisance were neither too 'complex' nor had such 'broad social policy import' that they were outside the jurisdiction of small claims court ...." (*City and County of San Francisco v. Small Claims Div., San Mateo Co.* 190 Cal. Rptr. 340 (1983).)

A similar strategy has been used in many cities to shut down drug houses. Neighbors organize to sue landlords who rent to drug-selling tenants, claiming that the landlords had created a nuisance (that is, they had used their property so as to interfere with the rights of others—see Chapter 2, Section J; in these cases, the nuisance claimed was the emotional and mental distress that accompanied living near a drug house). Each neighbor sues for the small claims maximum. Thus, in a state where it's possible to sue for $7,500, 30 neighbors who coordinate their small claims filings can, together, bring what amounts to a $225,000 case. In a number of instances, cases such as these have resulted in large judgments against landlords who rent to dealers, with the result that problems that had dragged on for months or years were quickly cleaned up.

Small claims "class actions" are exciting; they show that people can change their neighborhood for the better, even in the face of overwhelming power on the other side. Successful lawsuits based on legal nuisance have also been brought against polluting refineries and factories. However, these suits also carry a negative message: They indicate that normal channels for change have broken down. For example, in the airport case, the residents only sued after prolonged inaction by officials. And in most drug house cases, residents had repeatedly informed police of illegal activities and housing code violations, but to no avail. Although small claims court is a good way to get action on local problems when all else fails, more flexible and effective solutions are needed.

D. Special Rules for Prisoners and Military Personnel Transferred Out of State

Some states have special procedures for prisoners who wish to sue in small claims court. In California, for example, a prisoner who wants to sue in small claims court must file papers by mail, and then either submit testimony in the form of written declarations *or* have another person (other than a lawyer) appear on his or her behalf in court (CCP § 116.540(g)).

In some states, military personnel who have been transferred out of state are also allowed to bring small claims court cases without having to appear in court personally. Check your state rules (using the index of your state code) for information on how to do this.

E. Employees May Appear on Behalf of a Business

States used to require the owner of a business to show up in small claims court personally. This discouraged the owners of many small unincorporated businesses from using small claims court. For example, a dentist who wished to sue on an overdue bill would have had to show up in court. But today, a number of states are more understanding of business time pressures. If a business (incorporated or unincorporated) wishes to sue on an unpaid bill, it can often send an employee to court to testify about the debt as it is reflected in the written records of the business. For instance, in many states, a landlord suing for unpaid rent can send the property manager to court to establish the fact that the rent was unpaid (but see cautions about bringing eviction cases in small claims court in Chapter 21). For a business owner to invoke this time-saving procedure, the employee sent to court must be familiar with the company's books and able to testify about how the debt was entered in them.

But make sure that anyone who goes to small claims court on behalf of your business has first-hand knowledge about the dispute. For example, if your rug store is suing a customer who refuses to pay because a carpet was improperly installed, you will probably lose if you send to court only your bookkeeper, who knows nothing about what happened on the particular job. In this situation, some judges may postpone (continue) the case for a few days to allow the business owner to show up with the carpet installer and present testimony about the quality of the repair, but don't count on it. ■

CHAPTER

9

Who Can Be Sued?

You can sue just about anybody (person, partnership, corporation, or state and local government) in small claims court. Under certain circumstances, you can even sue out-of-staters. Indeed, figuring out where to sue (see Chapter 10) is often more difficult that figuring out whom to sue.

⚠ **No suits against the federal government.** To sue the United States government, you must file in federal, not state, court. Contact the nearest federal district court clerk's office for information.

A. Suing One Person

If you are suing an individual, simply name him or her, using the most complete name that you have for that person. If the person calls himself J.R. Smith and you don't know what the J.R. stands for, simply sue him as J.R. Smith. However, if you can find out that J stands for James, it's better to sue him as James R. Smith.

What to do if a person has several names. Lots of people change their names by simply using a new name some or all of the time. Thus, Jason Graboskawitz may also use J.T. Grab. When in doubt, list the name the person uses most often for business purposes first, followed by the words "also known as" (or "aka") and any other names. Thus, you might sue "Jason Graboskawitz, a.k.a. J.T. Grab."

B. Suing Two or More People

If you are suing more than one person on a claim arising from the same incident or contract, you must list the names of all defendants. Then, you must "serve" each to bring them properly before the court. (See Chapter 12.) If you are suing a husband and wife, you must list both spouses. A problem may arise if you can sue a person only in the county or district where he or she lives. What happens when you sue two people who live in different counties or districts? In most states, including California, this type of situation is handled by allowing the plaintiff to sue in either place. But a few states don't make even this exception, so it might actually be impossible to sue both of these people in the same court. (See the Appendix for information on your state's rules.)

Example: J.R. and June Smith, who are married, borrow $1,200 from you to start an avocado pit polishing business. Unfortunately, in the middle of the polishing, the seeds begin to sprout. J.R. and June get so furious that they refuse to repay you. If you wish to sue them and get a judgment, you should list them as James R. Smith and June Smith—not Mr. and Mrs. Smith. But now suppose that J.R. borrowed $1,200 for the avocado pit business in January, June borrowed $1,000 to fix her motorcycle a month later and neither loan was repaid. In this situation, you would sue each in separate Small Claims Court actions.

Two defendants are better than one, and three are better than two. If two or more people are responsible for your loss (for example, three tenants damaged your apartment), sue them all. This will enable you to get judgments against several people. You'll be glad you did when you try to collect—if one of them turns out to be an artful dodger, you can go after the others.

C. Suing an Individually Owned Business

If you are suing a sole proprietorship (an individually owned business that is not a corporation or LLC), you list the name of the owner and the name of the business "Jim C. Smith—doing business as [d.b.a.] Smith's Texaco." Never assume that the name of the business is in fact the same as the name of the owner. For all you know, Ralph's Garage may be owned by Pablo Garcia Motors, Inc. (See Section E, below.) If you get a judgment against Ralph's Garage and there is no Ralph, you will find that it's worthless in many states—you can't collect from a nonexistent person. Take the trouble to learn the correct name of the owner of the business before you sue.

Fortunately California, New York, and a few other states have liberalized their rules and do not penalize plaintiffs who incorrectly state the business defendant's name. New York allows a plaintiff to sue a defendant under any name used in conducting business if it is impossible to find out the defendant's true name. California allows a plaintiff to correct a defendant's name at the time of the hearing and, in some cases, after judgment, when the defendant is a business person using a fictitious name.

How to find out who owns a business. Many states require that all people doing business using a name other than their own file a fictitious business name statement with the county clerk in the county or counties in which the business operates. This is public information, which you can get from the court clerk. Another way to figure out who owns a business is to check with the business tax and license office in the city in which the business is located. If the business is not in an incorporated area, try the county office. The tax and license office will have a list of the owners of all businesses paying taxes. They should be able to tell you, for example, that The Garden of Exotic Delights is owned by Rufus Clod. Once you find this out, you sue "Rufus Clod, d.b.a. The Garden of Exotic Delights."

If the tax and license office and the county clerk can't help, you may want to check with the state. Millions of people, from exterminators to embalmers, must register with one or another state office. So, if your beef is with a teacher, architect, smog control device installer, or holder of a beer or wine license, you will very likely be able to learn who and where he or she is with a letter or phone call. Find the phone book for the capital city of your state (usually available at public libraries, from the telephone company, or on the Internet) and look under the listings for state offices. When you find an agency that looks like it should have jurisdiction over the type of business you wish to sue, call its public information number and explain your problem. It may take a little persistence, but eventually you should get the help you need.

D. Suing Partnerships

All partners in a business are individually liable for the acts of the business. It follows that you should list the names of all the business partners, even if your dispute is only with one (Patricia Sun and Farah Moon, d.b.a. Sacramento Gardens). See Section C, above, for information on how to learn just who owns a particular business.

Example: You go to a local cleaners with your new sky blue suit. They apply too much cleaning fluid, which results in a small gray cloud settling on the right rear shoulder. After unsuccessfully trying to get the cleaners to take responsibility for improving the weather on the back of your suit, you start thinking about a different kind of suit. When you start filling out your court papers (see Chapter 10), you realize that you know only that the store says "Perfection Cleaners" on the front, and that the guy who has been so unpleasant to you is named Bob. You call the city business tax and license people, and they tell you that Perfection Cleaners is owned by Robert Johnson and Sal De Benno. You should sue both and also list the name of the business.

E. Suing a Corporation or Limited Liability Company (LLC)

Corporations and limited liability companies (LLCs) are legal people. This means that you can sue, and enforce a judgment against, the business entity itself. You should not sue the owners of the corporation or its officers or managers as individuals unless you have a personal claim against them that is separate from their role as part of the corporation. In most situations, the real people who own or operate the corporation aren't themselves liable to pay the corporation's debts. This concept is called "personal limited liability," and is one reason why many people choose to incorporate or form an LLC.

Be sure to list the full name of the corporation or LLC when you file suit (for example, John's Liquors, Inc., a Corporation). Here again, the name on the door or on the stationery may not be the real name, as corporations and LLCs occasionally use fictitious names. Check with the city or county business license people where the corporation or LLC is headquartered. Information is also usually available from either the secretary of state or the corporations commissioner's office, located in your state capital. You may sue a corporation or LLC in your state if it does business there, even if its headquarters is in another state. (See Chapter 10 for more on where you can sue.)

F. Suing on a Motor Vehicle Accident

Special rules apply in disputes over motor vehicle accidents. In most states, if your claim arises from an accident with an automobile, motorcycle, truck, or R.V., you should name both the driver of the vehicle and the registered owner as part of your suit. Most of the time, you will have obtained this information at the time of the accident. If a police accident report was made, it will also contain this information. You can get a copy of any police report from the police department for a modest fee. If there was no police report, but you got the license plate number of the offending vehicle, contact the Department of Motor Vehicles. In most states, for a small fee, they will tell you who owns the vehicle. In several states, the Department of Motor Vehicles will ask you why you want this information. Simply tell them, "To file a lawsuit based on a motor vehicle accident that occurred in (name of city or county) on (date) at (time), involving my vehicle and another vehicle with license plate number _____." This is a legitimate reason in most states, and you will get the information you need. However, in some states, the owner of the car will be notified of your request.

Remember, when you sue more than one person (in this case the driver and the owner, if they are different), you must serve papers on both. When a business owns a vehicle, sue both the driver and the owners of the business.

G. Special Procedures for Suits Against Minors

It is very difficult to successfully sue a minor for breach of contract in most states, because minors can disavow (back out of) any contract they sign as long as they do it before they become adults (unless the contract was for a necessity of life—for example, food—in which case the parents are probably responsible). The exception is for "emancipated minors" (16- and 17-year-olds who are legally treated as adults). Minors are treated as emancipated if they are on active duty in the armed forces, married, or have been freed from parental control by court order.

In theory, you can sue unemancipated minors for damage they cause to you or your property, but you must also list a parent or legal guardian on the court papers. Do it like this:

"John Jefferey, a minor, and William Jefferey, his father."

But it is usually not worthwhile to sue children, because it is very difficult to collect from most of them. Of course, there are exceptions to this rule, but most minors are, almost by definition, broke. But what about suing the offending kid's parents? Normally, a parent is not legally responsible to pay for damages negligently caused by his children, but there are some exceptions to this rule. In virtually all states, if a child is guilty of "malicious or willful misconduct," a parent may be liable up to a certain dollar amount per act for all property damage ($10,000 in some states; often a lot more if a gun is involved) and sometimes for personal injuries. Parents may also be liable for damage done by their minor children in auto accidents, if they authorized the child to drive. (Check the index to your state's laws under "Minors," "Children," or "Parent and Child" for your rules.)

Example 1: John Johnson, age 17, trips over his shoelace while delivering your newspaper and crashes through your glass door. Can you recover from John's parents? Probably not, as John is not guilty of "malicious or willful misconduct."

Example 2: John shoots out the same glass door with a slingshot after you have repeatedly asked his parents to disarm him. Can you recover from the parents? Probably.

H. Special Rules for Suits Against Government Agencies

As mentioned in Chapter 5, many states have special rules and procedures that must be followed before a suit can be brought against a state or local government entity. Often, you have to act very quickly or you lose your right to sue. Your local small claims court clerk will be able to advise you as to the procedures you must follow and time limits you must meet.

Let's look at the rules of a state we will call Typical. Before you can sue a city because your car was illegally towed away, a city employee illegally confiscated your pen knife, or for any other reason involving personal injury or property damage, you must first file a claim with the city and have it denied. To do this, get a claim form from the city clerk. Your claim must be filed within six months of the date of the incident (in a few states you have even less time to file your claim, so don't delay). The city attorney will review your claim and make a recommendation to the city council. Sometimes the recommendation will be to pay you—most often it will be to deny your claim, no matter how meritorious. Once the city council acts, you will receive a letter. If it's a denial, take it with you when you file your small claims action. The clerk will want to see it.

Typical rules for suits against counties and districts (for example, school districts) are basically the same. Get your complaint form from the clerk of the governing legislative body for the county (for example, county commissions or the board of supervisors). Complete and file it within six months of the incident. Within a month or so after filing, you will be told whether your claim is approved or denied. If your claim is denied, you can then file in small claims court. Claims against the state must also be filed within six months for personal injury and property damage.

⚠️ **No suits against the United States in state court.** As noted earlier, suits against the federal government, a federal agency, or even a federal employee acting within the scope of his or her employment must be brought in federal court.

I.   Special Procedures for Suits Against the Estates of Deceased People

Death does not prevent lawsuits from being brought and judgments collected against the deceased. However, it does present a number of technical legal hurdles that vary somewhat from one state to the next.

Assuming the defendant made a will (or died without a will or other estate planning device such as a living trust), a probate proceeding will be held. All claims against the estate should be promptly made, in writing, to the personal representative (called an executor or administrator in some states) of the deceased person's estate and directly to the probate court. If you don't know who the personal representative is (usually it's a surviving spouse, adult child, or other close relative), check probate filing records with the court in the county where the defendant lived at the time of death. If the personal representative doesn't honor your claim, you will need to promptly check your state's rules about where and how to sue.

These days, many people use living trusts and other devices to completely avoid probate. If this is the case, there will be no personal representative and no probate court proceeding; instead, the property of the deceased person is transferred directly to its inheritors. In this situation, you have the right to proceed against these people directly. In most states, you can do this in small claims court. Do it as soon as possible.

■

CHAPTER

10

Where Can You Sue?

Small claims courts are local. This makes sense, because the amounts involved aren't large enough to make it worthwhile to require people to travel great distances. A small claims court's judicial district might cover part of a city, an entire city, several cities, or a county. The next city or county will have its own small claims court. Normally, your dispute will be with a person or business located nearby. If so, all you really need to know is that you can sue in the judicial district where the defendant resides or, if a corporation is involved, where its main place of business is located.

Occasionally, however, the person or business you want to sue resides at a considerable distance from where you live. How you should proceed in this situation depends primarily on whether the defendant is located in your state or a different state.

A. When the Defendant Is Out of State

The rules about where you can sue an out-of-state defendant depend on whether your dispute is with an individual or a business.

1. Suits Against Out-of-State Individuals

The basic rule is that a state court—including small claims court—only has the power (lawyers call this jurisdiction) to hear cases against individuals who reside in that state or who are served with court papers while in that state. This means that if you want to sue someone who lives in another state and doesn't travel to your state, you will have to sue in the state where he or she lives, not in the one where you live. Often you can file papers by mail, but normally you'll need to show up in person on court day (a few states allow military persons transferred out of state to present their cases in writing).

Out-of-state drivers can be sued for traffic accidents that occur in your state. Special "motorist laws" allow you to sue residents of another state in the state where you live for injuries or property damage arising from a traffic accident that occurred on your state's highways. Contact your small claims court clerk for details.

2. Suits Against Out-of-State Businesses and Owners of Property

Rules for suing businesses are quite different. You may file suit in your state against any business that is organized (incorporated or established as an LLC) in your state or has an office, warehouse, retail establishment, restaurant, or other facility there, even if that business is headquartered or organized elsewhere. For example, if an airline lands at an airport in your state and has a ticketing office there, you can bring suit against the airline company in your state's small claims court even if the airline is incorporated elsewhere. Similarly, out-of-state landlords or property owners who own property in your state can normally be sued in small claims court.

Even if a business does not maintain a physical facility in your state, you can still sue there if the business has what lawyers refer to as "minimum contacts" with the state. This is a tricky and often litigated legal abstraction, but usually courts will find that "minimum contacts" exist if:

•   The business actively sells its goods or services in your state.

•   The business employs a sales rep who calls on you personally or by phone to solicit your business.

•   The business solicits business in your state—by sending you a catalogue, for example.

- The business solicits your business online, as would be the case with an online store. (It's not enough that the business has an informational website that you can access in your state—it must be trying to sell you something online to give your state courts jurisdiction.)
- The business places advertising in your state's media.
- The business has a franchise or dealership in your state. For example, you can sue Ford in any state where it has an authorized dealer.

What this amounts to is that most large national businesses can be sued in all 50 states, but smaller businesses that do business in one or two states and don't solicit business elsewhere can only be sued in the states where they operate.

Example 1: On vacation in Vermont, you are injured at a small local restaurant. When you return to Kansas, you file suit in small claims court there. Your case will be tossed out because Kansas courts do not have power (jurisdiction) to hear a case against a defendant that doesn't operate, advertise, or solicit business in that state. The only place you can sue is in Vermont.

Example 2: Same vacation, but this time you are injured at a discount store with branches in all 50 states. Now when you return to Kansas you can sue in small claims court. Because the store does business in Kansas, that state's courts have jurisdiction to hear your case.

B. When the Defendant Is in Your State

If the person or business you want to sue resides or does business in your state, you have to decide which small claims court should hear your suit.

Of all the aspects of small claims court that differ from state to state, the rules on where to sue seem to be the most variable. Some states let you sue only in the district or county where the defendant resides. Others also allow you to sue where an accident occurred, a contract was broken or originally signed, merchandise was purchased, a corporation does business, and so on.

On the very first page of the first chapter, I asked you to get a copy of the rules for your local small claims court. Refer to them now to determine where to sue (also look at your state's listing in the Appendix). The first thing you will want to look at is what type of political subdivisions (judicial district, precinct, city, county) your state uses to define the geographical boundaries of its small claims courts. Next, you will want to carefully study your local rules in order to understand the criteria used to define which district a particular lawsuit should be brought in (for example, suits can always be brought where a defendant lives). If this information is not set out in the information sheet, call the clerk of the court and ask. Often you may be eligible to sue in more than one judicial district (for example, where a defendant lives and where a traffic accident occurred). If you have a choice, you'll obviously want to pick the court that is most convenient to you.

In a few states you can sue for larger amounts in some areas. In some states, such as Indiana and Tennessee, you can sue for higher amounts in certain counties. Obviously, if yours is a larger claim, you'll want to see if you are eligible to sue in one of these locations. (The rules for all states are set out in the Appendix.)

General Rules on Where You Can Sue

Depending on the specific rules of your state, you can generally sue in any one of the following counties:

- The judicial district in which the defendant resides or has a place of business at the time you file your lawsuit.
- The judicial district in which the contract underlying your lawsuit was supposed to be carried out.
- The judicial district in which the injury underlying your lawsuit occurred.
- The judicial district in which the rental property is located (for landlord-tenant security deposit disputes or evictions).

Now let's consider some typical rules about where you can sue within a state.

1. You Can Sue Where a Person Resides or a Corporation or LLC Does Business

It makes good sense that a person can be sued where he or she resides, or a corporation where it does business, doesn't it? If a suit is brought where the defendant is located, he or she can't complain that it is unduly burdensome to appear. Still, books have been written about the technical definition of residence. Indeed, I remember with horror trying to sort out a problem on a law school exam in which a person with numerous homes and businesses had "contact" with six different judicial districts. The point of the examination was for us students to figure out where he could be sued. Thankfully, you don't have to worry about this sort of nonsense. If you believe that someone spends enough time within a particular judicial district so that it would not be a hardship for him or her to appear in court there, go ahead and file your suit. The worst that can happen—and this is highly unlikely—is that the judge or clerk will tell you to start over someplace else or transfer your case to another judicial district.

This will not be a big problem if you filed fairly promptly after the date of the incident that gave rise to your lawsuit; you will have plenty of time to refile before the statute of limitations period runs out (see Chapter 5).

Example: Downhill Skier lives in the city, but also owns a mountain cabin where he spends several months a year. Late one snowy afternoon, Downhill drives his new Porsche from the ski slopes to his ultra-modern, rustic cabin. Turning into his driveway, he skids and does a bad slalom turn right into Woodsey Carpenter's 1957 International Harvester pickup. Where can Woodsey sue? He can sue in the city where Downhill has his permanent address. He can probably also sue in the county where the cabin is located, on the theory that Downhill also lives there. But read on—as you will see below, it might not be necessary for Woodsey to even get into the residence question, because many states would allow Woodsey to sue in the mountain county because that is where the damage was done.

When you have multiple defendants living in different places. In California, Illinois, Minnesota, New Jersey, and the great majority of states, you can bring your suit in any judicial district in which one defendant resides, even though the other(s) live in another part of the state. But in a few states, including New York, you can sue only where the defendant resides or does business. This means that you can't sue defendants who reside in different judicial districts in a single lawsuit—you'll have to sue them separately. (Check with your court clerk and your state's small claims court website.)

2. You Can Sue Where a Contract Was Entered Into

Most states assume that the place where a written contract is signed is also where it will be carried out. Therefore, you can usually sue where the contract was signed, if a problem develops.

Arizona, California, Indiana, and a few other states are more thorough. (See the Appendix.) In these states, a suit can be brought either where the contract was signed or where the contract was to be performed. This is good common sense, as the law assumes that, if people enter into a contract to perform something at a certain location, it is probably reasonably convenient to both. If, for example, Downhill gets a telephone installed in his cabin, or has a cesspool put in, or agrees to sit for a portrait in the mountain county, he can be sued there if he fails to keep his part of the bargain, because the contract was (or was to be) performed in the mountain county. Of course, as we learned above, Downhill might also be sued in the city (judicial district) where he resides permanently, or where the contract was entered into.

Example: John Gravenstein lives in Sonoma County, California, where he owns an apple orchard. He signs a contract for spare parts with Acme Mechanical Apple Picker Co., an international corporation with offices in San Francisco, New York, Paris, and Guatemala City. John signs the contract in Sonoma County. The parts are sent to John from San Francisco via U.P.S. They turn out to be defective. After trying and failing to reach a settlement with Acme, John wants to know if he can sue them in Sonoma County. Yes. Even though Acme doesn't have a business office in Sonoma County, the contract was signed there. But what if John was from Bergen County, New Jersey, and signed the contract in New York City (with the goods going through New York City)? Could John sue in Bergen County? No. Acme doesn't reside in Bergen County and performed no action there in connection with their agreement to sell John the spare parts. John would have to bring his claim in New York City.

But now let's assume that John dealt with Acme's Bergen County representative, who came to his orchard to take the order and who later installed the defective machinery. In this case John can sue locally, because the contract was to be performed in Bergen County.

If you have a choice of judicial districts, it's fine to pick the most convenient one. As you should now understand, there may be two, three, or more judicial districts in which you can file your case. In this situation, simply choose the one most convenient to you, or the one where you can bring all the defendants (if there are more than one) into court. But check the Appendix and your local rules to find out which places are appropriate in your case. If you choose the wrong one, your action will either be transferred or dismissed. If it is dismissed, you can refile in the correct district, as long as the statute of limitations period hasn't run out in the meantime.

Where to sue in cases involving contracts. It isn't always easy to know where a contract has been "entered into" in a situation where the people making the contract are at different locations. If you enter a contract over the phone, for example, there could be an argument that the contract was entered into either where you are or where the other party is. Rather than trying to learn all the intricacies of contract law, your best bet is to sue in the place most convenient to you. On the other hand, if someone sues you at the wrong end of the state and you believe there is a good argument that the contract was formed where you live, write to the court as soon as you have been served and ask that the case be transferred to a court closer to you or dismissed.

3. In Most States, You Can Sue Where a Personal Injury or Damage to Property Occurred

California, Illinois, Indiana, and most other states allow you to sue in the district where the act or omission underlying the lawsuit occurred (see the Appendix). "Act or omission" is a shorthand term that lumps together things that lead to lawsuits like automobile accidents, warranty disputes, and landlord-tenant disputes, for the purpose of deciding where you're allowed to sue. This means that if you are in a car accident, a dog bites you, a tree falls on your noggin, or a neighbor floods your cactus garden, you can sue in the judicial district where the "act" or injury occurred, even if the defendant resides in a different district.

Example: Addison is returning to his home in Indianapolis from Bloomington, Indiana, following an Indiana University basketball game. At the same time, Lenore is rushing to Bloomington from her home in Brown County, Indiana, more than 40 miles west of Bloomington. Lenore runs a red light and demolishes Addison's Toyota near the Indiana University gym in downtown Bloomington, which is in Monroe County. After parking his car and taking a bus home, Addison tries to figure out where he can sue if he can't work out a fair settlement with Lenore. Unfortunately for him, he can't sue in Indianapolis, as Lenore doesn't reside there and the accident didn't happen there. Addison would have to sue either in Monroe County, where his property was damaged, or in Brown County, where Lenore lives. Luckily for Addison, Monroe County is just an hour from Indianapolis. ■

CHAPTER

11

Plaintiffs' and Defendants' Filing Fees, Court Papers, and Court Dates

A.   How Much Does It Cost?

Fees for filing a case in small claims court are very moderate—usually not much more than $50. In some states, people with very low incomes can ask to have court filing fees waived. Normally, a defendant doesn't have to pay anything unless he or she files a claim against the plaintiff (often called a counterclaim). There is usually an additional fee for serving papers on the opposing party, unless you are in a state that allows personal service to be carried out by a nonprofessional process server and you have a friend who will do it for you without charge. (See Chapter 12.) Most states allow service by certified or registered mail, which doesn't cost much. In a few situations, you may have to hire a professional process server. This will probably cost at least $25, but the fee will be higher if the person you are suing is hard to locate. You can get your filing fees and service costs added to the court judgment if you win. (See Chapter 16.)

B. Filling Out Your Court Papers and Getting Your Court Date

Now let's look at the initial court papers, to be sure that you don't trip over a detail. Again, I refer specifically to forms in use in California and also include some New York forms, but you will find that your local forms will require similar information. You should have little trouble filling out your papers by following the examples printed here, but, if you do, simply ask the clerk for help. Small claims court clerks are required by law in most states to give you as much help as possible, short of practicing law (whatever that is). A friendly, courteous approach to the clerk will often get you plenty of helpful information and advice. In a few small claims courts, such as those in New York City, trained legal advisors will be available to help you.

Step 1. Fill Out the Plaintiff's Statement

To start your case, obtain and complete the form entitled "Plaintiff's Statement." (In some states, slightly different terminology is used, such as "General Claim" or "Plaintiff's Claim.") All you need to do is properly name the defendant(s), as discussed in Chapter 9, and briefly state what happened, as outlined in Chapter 2, Section A. Some courts require that you fill this out at the courthouse, with the clerk's help.

Be sure you sue the correct defendant in the right place. In Chapter 9, I discuss how to properly name the defendant. In Chapter 10, you'll find the rules that establish the proper judicial district or districts in which to file your Small Claims case.

Step 2. Check It With the Court Clerk

When you have completed your plaintiff's statement, it's best to deliver it in person to the court clerk. If this is inconvenient for you, your state may allow filing online or by mail—but realize that you'll lose the advantage of having a live person review it for errors. In some states, the clerk will file your form as is, but often, he or she will type it in a slightly different format and assign it a case number. You will be asked to sign this second form under penalty of perjury. A copy of the "Claim of Plaintiff" will go to the judge, and another must be served on the defendant. (See Chapter 12.)

Step 3. Supplying Documentary Evidence

In most small claims courts, no written evidence need be provided until you get to court, but others, such as Washington, DC, require that certain types of evidence (such

PLAINTIFF'S CLAIM

Name and Address of Court:	**SC-100**

SMALL CLAIMS CASE NO.:

— NOTICE TO DEFENDANT — **YOU ARE BEING SUED BY PLAINTIFF**	— *AVISO AL DEMANDADO* — *A USTED LO ESTAN DEMANDANDO*
To protect your rights, you must appear in this court on the trial date shown in the table below. You may lose the case if you do not appear. The court may award the plaintiff the amount of the claim and the costs. Your wages, money, and property may be taken without further warning from the court.	*Para proteger sus derechos, usted debe presentarse ante esta corte en la fecha del juicio indicada en el cuadro que aparece a continuación. Si no se presenta, puede perder el caso. La corte puede decidir en favor del demandante por la cantidad del reclamo y los costos. A usted le pueden quitar su salario, su dinero, y otras cosas de su propiedad, sin aviso adicional por parte de esta corte.*

PLAINTIFF/*DEMANDANTE* *(Name, street address, mailing address, and telephone number of each)*:	DEFENDANT/*DEMANDADO* *(Name, street address, mailing address, and telephone number of each)*:
Andrew Printer 1800 Marilee St. Fremont, CA 94536 Telephone No.: 510-555-5555	Acme Illusions, Inc. 100 Primrose Path Oakland, CA 94602 Telephone No.: 510-555-1212
Telephone No.:	Telephone No.:
Fict. Bus. Name Stmt. No. Expires:	☐ See attached sheet for additional plaintiffs and defendants.

PLAINTIFF'S CLAIM

1. a. ☒ Defendant owes me the sum of: $ 950.00 , not including court costs, because *(describe claim and date)*:
   He failed to pay for a printing and typesetting job which was completed on March 15, 2004.

   b. ☐ I have had an **arbitration of an attorney-client fee dispute.** *(Attach Attorney-Client Fee Dispute form (see form SC-101).)*

2. ☐ This claim is against a government agency, and I filed a claim with the agency. My claim was denied by the agency, or the agency did not act on my claim before the legal deadline. *(See form SC-150.)*

3. a. ☒ I have asked defendant to pay this money, but it has not been paid.

   b. ☐ I have NOT asked defendant to pay this money because *(explain)*:

4. This court is the proper court for the trial because ☐ A *(In the box at the left, insert one of the letters from the list called "Venue Table" on page 3. If you select D, E, or F, specify additional facts in this space)*:

   If known, please give the zip code for the location of the letter you put in the box *(zip code)*:

5. I ☐ have ☒ have not filed more than one other small claims action anywhere in California during this calendar year in which the amount demanded is more than $2,500.

6. I ☐ have ☒ have not filed more than 12 small claims, including this claim, during the previous 12 months.

7. I understand that
   a. I may talk to an attorney about this claim, but I cannot be represented by an attorney at the trial in the small claims court.
   b. I must appear at the time and place of trial and bring all witnesses, books, receipts, and other papers or things to prove my case.
   c. **I have no right of appeal on my claim,** but I may appeal a claim filed by the defendant in this case.
   d. If I cannot afford to pay the fees for filing or service by a sheriff or marshal I may ask that the fees be waived.

8. I have received and read the information sheet (form SC-150) explaining some important rights of plaintiffs in the small claims court.

9. No defendant is in the military service ☐ except *(name)*:

I declare under penalty of perjury under the laws of the State of California that the foregoing is true and correct.

Date: April 27, 2004

Andrew Printer	▶ *Andrew Printer*
(TYPE OR PRINT NAME)	(SIGNATURE OF PLAINTIFF)

ORDER TO DEFENDANT

You must appear in this court on the trial date and at the time LAST SHOWN IN THE BOX BELOW if you do not agree with the plaintiff's claim. Bring all witnesses, books, receipts, and other papers or things with you to support your case.

TRIAL DATE *FECHA DEL JUICIO*	DATE	DAY	TIME	PLACE	COURT USE
1.					
2.					
3.					

Filed on *(date)*:   Clerk, by _____ , Deputy

— **The county provides small claims advisor services free of charge. Read the information on the reverse.** —

| Form Adopted for Mandatory Use Judicial Council of California SC-100 [Rev. July 1, 2003] | **PLAINTIFF'S CLAIM AND ORDER TO DEFENDANT** (Small Claims) | Page 1 of 3 Code of Civil Procedure, §§ 116.110 et seq., 116.220(c), 116.340(g) www.courtinfo.ca.gov |

as copies of unpaid bills, contracts, or other documents on which the claim is based) be provided at the time you file your first papers.

Whether your local rules require written documentation of certain types of claims or not, it is wise to spend a little time thinking about how you will prove your case. I discuss this in detail in the later chapters of this book. You should read ahead and figure out exactly what proof you will need and how you will present it, before you file your first court papers. Being right is one thing—proving it is another.

Step 4: Getting a Hearing Date

One of the great advantages of small claims court is that disputes are settled quickly. This is important. Many people avoid lawyers and the regular courts primarily because they can take forever to get a dispute settled. Business people, for example, increasingly rely on private mediation or arbitration, because they care more about resolving a dispute promptly than winning a complete victory. Anyone who has had to wait more than a year for a case to be heard in one or another constipated formal court knows, through bitter experience, the truth of the old cliché, "Justice delayed is justice denied."

In New York and some other states, an "early" hearing is required, but no maximum number of days is set. Many other states require that the case be set for trial within a certain number of days.

When you file your papers, you should also arrange with the clerk for a court date. Select a date that is convenient for you. You need not take the first date the clerk suggests. Be sure to leave yourself enough time to get a copy of the claim form served on the defendant(s). (See Chapter 12 for service information.) If you fail to properly serve your papers on the defendant in time, there is no big hassle—just notify the clerk, get a new court date, and try again.

Small claims court cases are most often heard beginning at 9:00 a.m. on working days. Some judicial districts are beginning to hold evening and Saturday sessions. (New York City's sessions are held in the evenings.) Ask the clerk for a schedule. If evening and Saturday sessions aren't available, ask why not.

C. The Defendant's Forms

In most states, a defendant doesn't have to file any papers to defend a case in small claims court unless the defendant wants the case transferred to formal court (see your state's transfer rules in the Appendix). However, in a few states, including Alabama and Arkansas, a defendant must respond in writing. (See the Appendix for your state's rules.) In the great majority of states, the defendant simply shows up on the date and at the time indicated, ready to tell his or her side of the story. (If you need to get the hearing delayed, see Section E, below.) It is proper, and advisable, for a defendant to call or write the plaintiff and see if a fair settlement can be reached without going to court. (See Chapter 6.)

Sometimes, someone you planned to sue sues you first (for example, over a traffic accident in which you each believe the other is at fault). As long as your grievance stems from the same incident, you can file a written "Defendant's Claim" for up to the small claims court maximum and have it heard by a judge at the same time that the plaintiff's claim against you is considered. However, if you believe that the plaintiff owes you money as the result of a different injury or breach of contract, you may have to file your own separate case.

Many states call a defendant's claim a "Claim of Defendant" or "Counterclaim." All states require you to file any defendant's claim (counterclaim) in writing within a certain time period after being served with the plaintiff's claim (usually ten to 30 days). When you file a defendant's claim, you become a plaintiff as far as this claim is concerned. In a few states, such as California, where only the defendant can appeal, this means that if you lose your defendant's claim, you can't appeal that part of the case. Of course, even in these states, if you lose on the original plaintiff's claim, you can normally appeal that portion of the judgment. Appeal rules vary a great deal from state to state and can be complicated. (See Chapter 24 and the Appendix.)

In most states, if a defendant's claim is for more than the small claims maximum, the case will be transferred to a formal court (some states allow this only at the discretion of a judge, who may inquire if the defendant's claim is made in good faith—check your court rules and your state's listing in the Appendix). A defendant who does not want to cope with a formal court may be wise to scale down his or her claim to fit under the small claims limit (see Chapter 4).

A defendant may be required to file a defendant's claim or lose the right to do so. A defendant who has a claim against a plaintiff arising out of the incident underlying the plaintiff's lawsuit will almost always want to promptly file it. Some states require defendants to file a counterclaim as part of the plaintiff's lawsuit; others allow defendants to file their own lawsuit later. If this is an issue for you, check your state's rules.

DEFENDANT'S CLAIM

Name and Address of Court:

Alameda County Small Claims Court
Oakland-Piedmont
600 Washington Street
Oakland, CA

SC-120

SMALL CLAIMS CASE NO.

— NOTICE TO PLAINTIFF — **YOU ARE BEING SUED BY DEFENDANT**	— *AVISO AL DEMANDANTE* — *A USTED LO ESTA DEMANDANDO EL*
To protect your rights, you must appear in this court on the trial date shown in the table below. You may lose the case if you do not appear. The court may award the defendant the amount of the claim and the costs. Your wages, money, and property may be taken without further warning from the court.	*Para proteger sus derechos, usted debe presentarse ante esta corte en la fecha del juicio indicada en el cuadro que aparece a continuación. Si no se presenta, puede perder el caso. La corte puede decidir en favor del deman- dado por la cantidad del reclamo y los costos. A usted le pueden quitar su salario, su dinero, y otras cosas de su propiedad, sin aviso adicional por parte de esta corte.*

PLAINTIFF/DEMANDANTE *(Name, address, and telephone number of each)*:

Andrew Printer
1800 Marilee St.
Fremont, CA 94536

Telephone No.: (510) 555-5555

DEFENDANT/DEMANDADO *(Name, address, and telephone number of each)*:

Acme Illusions, Inc.
100 Primrose Path
Oakland, CA 94602

Telephone No.: (510) 555-1212

Telephone No.:

Telephone No.:

Fict. Bus. Name Stmt. No.   Expires: ☐ See attached sheet for additional plaintiffs and defendants.

DEFENDANT'S CLAIM

1. Plaintiff owes me the sum of: $ 300   , not including court costs, because *(describe claim and date)*:
   of delays and poor workmanship in a printing job he performed for me in April of 2___.

2. a. ☐ I have asked plaintiff to pay this money, but it has not been paid.
   b. ☐ I have NOT asked plaintiff to pay this money because *(explain)*:

3. I ☐ have ☐ have not filed more than one other small claims action anywhere in California during this calendar year in which the amount demanded is more than $2,500.

4. I understand that
   a. I may talk to an attorney about this claim, but I cannot be represented by an attorney at the trial in the small claims court.
   b. I must appear at the time and place of trial and bring all witnesses, books, receipts, and other papers or things to prove my case.
   c. **I have no right of appeal on my claim,** but I may appeal a claim filed by the plaintiff in this case.
   d. If I cannot afford to pay the fees for filing or service by a sheriff or marshal, I may ask that the fees be waived.

5. I have received and read the information sheet explaining some important rights of defendants in the small claims court.

6. No plaintiff is in the military service ☐ except *(name)*:

I declare under penalty of perjury under the laws of the State of California that the foregoing is true and correct.

Date:

Waldo Fergus
(TYPE OR PRINT NAME)

▶ *Waldo Fergus, President*
(SIGNATURE OF DEFENDANT)

ORDER TO PLAINTIFF

You must appear in this court on the trial date and at the time LAST SHOWN IN THE BOX BELOW if you do not agree with the defendant's claim. Bring all witnesses, books, receipts, and other papers or things with you to support your case.

TRIAL DATE FECHA DEL JUICIO		DATE	DAY	TIME	PLACE	COURT USE
	1.					
	2.					
	3.					
	4.					

Filed on *(date)*:   Clerk, by _____ , Deputy

— The county provides small claims advisor services free of charge. (Advisor phone number: _____) —

Form Adopted for Mandatory Use
Judicial Council of California
SC-120 [Rev. July 1, 2000]

DEFENDANT'S CLAIM AND ORDER TO PLAINTIFF
(Small Claims)

Cal. Rules of Court, rule 982.7;
Code of Civil Procedure, § 116.110 et seq.

D. Jury Trials

Jury trials are not available in small claims court in the great majority of states, including California, Colorado, and Michigan. Plaintiffs know this when they file and can usually opt for a different court if they want trial by jury. Defendants, of course, don't have this upfront choice. To compensate, some states allow a defendant who wants a jury trial to transfer a case to a formal court no matter how small the claim. Others, including California and Ohio, only allow transfer when the defendant's claim exceeds the small claims court maximum. Normally, a defendant must request a jury trial (or a transfer to a court where a jury is permitted) promptly after being served with court papers. And "jury fees" (often ranging from $100 to $500) must typically be paid in advance. Fees are normally recoverable if you win. Asking for a jury trial also tends to delay proceedings, and some people will make the request for this reason.

E. Changing a Court Date

It is sometimes impossible for a defendant to be present on the day ordered by the court for the hearing. It can also happen that the plaintiff will pick a court date and get the defendant served only to find that an unexpected emergency makes it impossible for the plaintiff to be present.

It is normally not difficult to get a case postponed. To arrange this, call the other party and see if you can agree on a mutually convenient date. Don't call the clerk first—he or she doesn't know what days the other party has free. Yes, sometimes it is difficult to talk to someone with whom you are involved in a lawsuit, but try to swallow your pride and treat this as a routine business transaction. Once all parties have agreed to a new date, send the court clerk a notice in writing signed by both parties. Here is a sample:

11 South Street
Denver, CO
January 10, 20xx

Clerk of the Small Claims Court
Denver, CO
Re: SC 4117 Rodriguez v. McNally

Mr. Rodriguez and I agree to request that you postpone this case to a date after March 1, 20xx. If possible, we would prefer that it not be scheduled on March 27 or 28.

_____

JOHN MCNALLY

_____

JOHN RODRIGUEZ

If you can't reach the other party or he or she is completely uncooperative, put your request for a delay (continuance) in writing, along with the circumstances that make it impossible for you to keep the first date. Send your letter to the clerk of the small claims court.

Here is a sample:

37 Birdwalk Blvd.
Trenton, NJ
January 10, 20xx

Clerk
Small Claims Court
Trenton, NJ

Re: Small Claims No. 374–628

Dear Clerk:

I have been served with a complaint (No. 374–628) by John's Laundry, Inc. The date set for a hearing, February 15, falls on the day of my son's graduation from Nursing School in Oscaloosa, Oklahoma, which my husband and I plan to attend.

I called John's Laundry and asked to have the case delayed one week. They just laughed and said they would not give me any cooperation.

I feel that I have a good defense to this suit. Please delay this case until any date after February 22, except March 13, which is my day for a medical checkup.

Thank you,

Sally Wren

F. If One Party Doesn't Show Up

If one party to a case doesn't appear in court on the proper day, at the proper time, the case is normally decided in favor of the other. The terms the judge uses will depend on whether it is the plaintiff or defendant who fails to show up. If the plaintiff appears, but the defendant doesn't, a "default judgment" is normally entered in favor of the plaintiff. (See Chapters 13 and 16 for more information on defaults.) Occasionally, although it happens far less frequently, the plaintiff fails to show up. In this situation, the judge may normally either dismiss the case or decide it on the basis of the defendant's evidence. The defendant will usually prefer this second result, especially if a defendant's claim has been made. If the judge dismisses the case, depending on how it is done and the rules of the particular state, the plaintiff may or may not have the right to begin the case again. If you find yourself in this situation, check with the court clerk.

In some states, if neither party appears, a judge may simply take the case "off calendar," meaning that the plaintiff will get another chance to schedule it for a hearing.

If you are the person who failed to show up (whether defendant or plaintiff) and you still want a chance to argue the case on its merits, you must act immediately or forever hold your peace.

1. Setting Aside a Default (Defendant's Remedy)

Courts are not very sympathetic to setting aside or vacating a default judgment unless you can show that the original papers weren't properly served on you and that you didn't know about the hearing. In some states, this can happen if someone signs your name for a certified letter and then doesn't give it to you. In all states, it can occur when a dishonest process server doesn't serve you, but tells the court otherwise. As soon as you find out that a default judgment has been entered against you, call the court clerk. It doesn't make any difference if the hearing you missed was months before, as long as you move to set it aside immediately upon learning about it.

If you have had a default judgment entered against you after you were properly served, you will face an uphill struggle to get it set aside. A few judges will accept almost any hard luck story ("I forgot," "I was sick," "I got called out of town"). Generally, however, judges assume that you could have at least called, or had a friend call, no matter what the emergency, and will not vacate the judgment except for extremely good cause. However, if you act promptly and if you have a good excuse, you stand a reasonable chance of getting the judge to set the default aside.

⚠ You can't appeal from a default judgment unless you first try to get the default set aside. In most states, you can't appeal a default judgment even if you have a great case. Instead, you must promptly try to get the default set aside, or the judgment will be final. To try to set aside a default, go to the small claims court clerk's office and ask for the proper form, which will normally be titled something like "Notice of Motion to Vacate Judgment."

Sometimes the defendant files a motion to vacate (set aside) a default judgment only after a "writ of execution" to collect the Small Claims judgment has already been entered for the plaintiff. In this situation, in most states the writ of execution will be recalled (stayed) by the court until a decision on the motion to vacate the default judgment is made. If the writ of execution has already been served as part of an effort to collect, the defendant must file a motion to suspend the writ of execution (often called a Motion to Stay or Quash the Writ of Execution), pending the court's decision on whether or not to set aside the default judgment and reopen the case. For more information on how to do this, or to find out the exact rules for your state, consult your small claims court clerk.

SAMPLE NOTICE OF MOTION TO VACATE JUDGMENT

Name and Address of Court:

SMALL CLAIMS CASE NO.:

PLAINTIFF/DEMANDANTE *(Name, street address, and telephone number of each)*:

DEFENDANT/DEMANDADO *(Name, street address, and telephone number of each)*:

Telephone No.:

Telephone No.:

Telephone No.:

Telephone No.:

☐ See attached sheet for additional plaintiffs and defendants.

NOTICE TO *(Name)*:

One of the parties has asked the court to CANCEL the small claims judgment in your case. If you disagree with this request, you should appear in this court on the hearing date shown below. If the request is granted, ANOTHER TRIAL may immediately be held. Bring all witnesses, books, receipts, and other papers or things with you to support your case.

Una de las partes en el caso le ha solicitado a la corte que DEJE SIN EFECTO la decisión tomada en su caso por la corte para reclamos judiciales menores. Si usted está en desacuerdo con esta solicitud, debe presentarse en esta corte en la fecha de la audiencia indicada a continuación. Si se concede esta solicitud, es posible que se efectúe otro juicio inmediatamente. Traiga a todos sus testigos, libros, recibos, y otros documentos o cosas para presentarlos en apoyo de su caso.

NOTICE OF MOTION TO VACATE (CANCEL) JUDGMENT

1. A hearing will be held in this court at which I will ask the court to **cancel** the judgment entered against me in this case. If you wish to oppose the motion you should appear at the court on

HEARING DATE FECHA DEL JUICIO		DATE	DAY	TIME	PLACE	COURT USE
	1.					
	2.					
	3.					

2. I am asking the court to cancel the judgment for the reasons stated in item 5 below. My request is based on this notice of motion and declaration, the records on file with the court, and any evidence that may be presented at the hearing.

DECLARATION FOR MOTION TO VACATE (CANCEL) JUDGMENT

3. Judgment was entered against me in this case on *(date)*:
4. I first learned of the entry of judgment against me on *(date)*:
5. I am asking the court to cancel the judgment for the following reason:
   a. ☐ I did not appear at the trial of this claim because *(specify facts)*:

   b. ☐ Other *(specify facts)*:

6. I understand that I must bring with me to the hearing on this motion all witnesses, books, receipts, and other papers or things to support my case.

I declare under penalty of perjury under the laws of the State of California that the foregoing is true and correct.

Date:

▶

_____ (TYPE OR PRINT NAME)   _____ (SIGNATURE)

CLERK'S CERTIFICATE OF MAILING

I certify that I am not a party to this action. This Notice of Motion to Vacate Judgment and Declaration was mailed first class, postage prepaid, in a sealed envelope to the responding party at the address shown above. The mailing and this certification occurred at *(place)*: _____ , California,
on *(date)*:

Clerk, by _____ , Deputy

— The county provides small claims advisor services free of charge. —

Form Approved by the Judicial Council of California SC-135 [Rev. January 1, 1997*]

* NOTE: Continued use of form SC-135 (Rev. January 1, 1992) is authorized through December 31, 1997.
NOTICE OF MOTION TO VACATE JUDGMENT AND DECLARATION
(Small Claims)

Cal. Rules of Court, rule 982.7 Code of Civil Procedure, §§ 116.720, 116.730, 116.740

2. Vacating a Judgment of Dismissal (Plaintiff's Remedy)

If the plaintiff does not show up in court at the appointed time to pursue his or her own case, the judge will dismiss it. Generally, the plaintiff can refile the case as long as the statute of limitations period has not run out (see Chapter 5). Normally, you have to refile quickly (many states have a 30-day limit). However, there is an exception to this rule. If the judge dismisses the case "with prejudice," it can't be refiled unless the dismissal is vacated. In my view, it is improper to dismiss a case "with prejudice" just because the plaintiff doesn't show up, but occasionally a judge will do it on the theory that the plaintiff—who after all initiated the suit and arranged for the court date— should have at least written or phoned the court clerk to ask for a postponement.

However, now and then emergencies happen, or someone simply makes a mistake about the day. Judges can, and do, vacate dismissals if both of the following are true:

- The plaintiff moves to have the judgment vacated promptly upon learning of his or her mistake. "Promptly" usually means within 30 days after the day the dismissal was entered, and is thought by most judges to be a much shorter time.

- The plaintiff has a good explanation as to why he or she was unable to be present or call on the day the case was regularly scheduled. A judge might accept something like this: "I had a flu with a high fever and simply lost track of a couple of days. As soon as I felt better, which was two days after my case was dismissed, I came to the clerk's office to try to get the case rescheduled."

To get a dismissal vacated (when allowed), you must fill out a form similar to the one shown above. But what if the no-show plaintiff is also a defendant—in other words, the original defendant answered back with a defendant's claim? In that situation, the judge will very likely enter a default judgment on behalf of the original defendant. If this occurs, the judgment must be vacated before the plaintiff can schedule a court hearing to consider the merits of the case. Again, you would have to file a form similar to the one shown above.

After a motion to vacate is filed, the clerk will set a hearing before the judge to consider whether the plaintiff should get another chance. If the plaintiff's motion to vacate is granted, and all parties are present and agree to go forward, the actual case may be heard on the spot. Alternatively, the clerk may set a new hearing date.

If your motion to set aside the default judgment is denied, you may appeal to formal court, but only as to the decision not to grant the motion. ■

Serving Your Papers

After you have filed your plaintiff's claim form with the clerk, following the instructions in Chapter 11, Section B, a copy must be given to the person(s) or corporation you are suing. This is called "service of process." Your lawsuit is not complete without it. The reason that you must "serve" the other side is simple—whomever you are suing is entitled to be notified of the general nature of your claim and the day, time, and place of the hearing, so that he or she can show up and present a defense. The general rules of all states are similar, but details do differ. Refer to your local rules and to the Appendix to find out your state's requirements.

A. Who Must Be Served?

All defendants that you list on your claim should be served. It is not enough to serve one defendant and assume that he or she will tell the other(s). This is true even if the defendants are married or living together. If you don't serve a particular defendant, the court can't enter a judgment against that person. If you sue more than one person and can serve only one, a judge can only enter a judgment against the person served, in effect dismissing your action against the other defendant(s). (Some states will allow you to refile against these defendants if you wish.)

B. Where Can Papers Be Served?

Normally, papers must be served in the state where you filed your lawsuit. Thus, you can't sue someone in a Massachusetts court and serve papers on them in Oklahoma. An exception involves suits having to do with motor vehicle accidents. Many states allow out-of-state service on this type of claim. Your small claims court clerk will show you how this is handled in your state.

Now let's assume that the person you want to sue resides or does business in your state. In most states, papers can be served anyplace in the state as long as the suit is brought in the correct judicial district. (See Chapter 10.) But a few states, including New York, generally require that a defendant be served in the same county or judicial district where the suit was filed. (See the Appendix.)

C. How to Serve Papers on an Individual

There are several approved ways to serve papers on individual defendants. All depend on your knowing where the defendant is. If you can't find the defendant and do not know where he or she lives or works, you can't serve your papers, and it makes little sense to file a lawsuit.

Method 1: By Certified or Registered Mail

In California, New York, and the majority of states, you can serve papers by certified mail with return receipt. In some states, service by certified (or registered) mail is one option for the plaintiff, while others require you to try service by certified mail first, before any other method of service. (See the Appendix.) Normally, the court clerk does the mailing for you and charges a small fee. This is recoverable if you win. (See Chapter 16.) The mail method is both cheap and easy, but in most states the defendant must sign for the letter for this type of service to be effective. (In a few states, including Alaska, service is accomplished even if a certified letter is rejected by the defendant.) Most businesses and many individuals routinely sign to accept their mail. However, some people never do, knowing instinctively, or perhaps from past experience, that nothing good ever comes by certified mail. I have asked several court clerks for an estimate as to the percentage of certified mail services that are accepted. The consensus is 50%. If you try using the mail to serve your papers and fail, and you end up having to pay a process server, tell the judge about it as part of your presentation and chances are your costs will be added to the judgment.

Make sure service of process was accomplished. Never show up in court on the day of the hearing on the assumption that your certified mail service actually reached the defendant. If the defendant didn't sign for the paper, you will be wasting your time in all but a few states. Call the court clerk a couple of days in advance and find out if service of process has been completed. This means the certified letter has been signed for by the defendant, not by someone else at the same address.

Method 2: Personal Service

Personal service means that someone simply hands the defendant the relevant papers. You have various options regarding who performs this task. Of course, if you use someone who doesn't personally know the defendant, the server will need to be particularly careful to serve the right person.

- **Sheriff, Marshal, or Constable:** All states allow personal service to be made by law officers, although not all officers will serve civil subpoenas. Using this method is often valuable for its sobering effect. The fee can be added to your judgment if you win.

- **Private Process Servers:** Many states also allow service by private process servers, whom you will find listed in the Yellow Pages. Fees charged are usually based on how long the service takes. See your state's listing in the Appendix to find out whether your state allows service by private process servers.

How to Find the Best Process Server

Unfortunately, sheriff's offices in some states are getting out of the process-serving business. This means that if you can't talk a friend into serving process for you, you may have to hire a private person or company. Some of these are truly fly-by-night—they've figured out that process serving is a quick way to make a buck. You may even see them cruising around the courthouse looking for business. To make sure you're dealing with a business that backs up its promises, do a little research first. One indicator of trustworthiness is how long the process server has been in business—ask to see a business license, or look in the phone book for process servers who give the date of their business's founding.

- **Service by Disinterested Adult:** California, Colorado, Washington, and some other states (see the Appendix) allow service by any person who is at least 18 years old, except the person bringing a suit. Any person means just that—a relative or a friend is fine. However, many states require that this person be approved by the court.

 **A mailbox isn't personal enough.** No matter who serves the papers, if personal service is used, the claim and a summons must be handed to the defendant. You can't simply leave the paper at his or her job or home or in the mailbox. If the process server locates the right person, but he or she refuses to take the paper, acts hostile, or attempts to run away, the process server should simply put the paper down and leave. Valid service has been accomplished. The process server should never try to use force to get a defendant to take any papers.

Serving Someone With a Post Office Box

If you only know an individual defendant's post office box, you'll obviously need to get his or her street address in order to accomplish personal service. To do this, you must give the post office a written statement saying that you need the address solely to serve legal papers in a pending lawsuit. This should work, but if it doesn't, refer the post office employee to the Administrative Support Manual, § 352.44e(2).

Method 3:   By Regular First-Class Mail

A minority of states, including Connecticut and New York, allow papers to be served by first-class mail. The states differ, however, on what you must do if the defendant doesn't answer your complaint within the time limit. New York, for example, presumes that the defendant received the papers unless the envelope comes back as "undeliverable." Connecticut, on the other hand, requires you to back up unanswered regular mail service with personal service by the sheriff. Check with your court clerk to see if this method is available in your area.

Method 4:   Substituted Service (or "Nail and Mail")

It can be difficult to serve certain individuals. Some people have developed their skill at avoiding process servers into a high art. In some states, avoiding service no longer works, as there is now a procedure that allows "substituted service" if you try to serve a defendant and fail. Often the slang for this type of service is "nail and mail," because in several states, if you are unable to serve the defendant personally, you do not have to leave the claim with a live person, but can simply tack one copy to the defendant's door and mail the second copy.

In a typical state, substituted service works like this: If a person can't be served with "reasonable diligence," the papers may be served by leaving a copy at the person's dwelling place in the presence of a competent member of the household who is at least 18 years old and who is told what the papers are about, and afterwards by mailing a copy via first-class mail to the person served. Service is complete ten days after mailing. Be sure that all of these steps are carried out by an adult who is not named in the lawsuit. Because some small claims court clerks interpret the requirement for "reasonable diligence" differently, it is wise to check out the substituted service procedure with your local clerk before trying it. If your suit is against a corporation, the substituted service procedure is easier, as most states don't require you to try personal service before using it. Papers may be served by leaving them at the defendant's office with a person apparently in charge of the office during normal business hours, and then mailing another copy to the person to be served at the same address. Service is accomplished ten days after mailing.

After service is accomplished, you must return a "Proof of Service" form to the court clerk stating that all proper service steps have been completed. (See Section D, below.)

D. How to Serve Papers on a Business

When you sue a business, the same methods of service discussed just above can be used. However, if you use the personal service or certified mail service methods, the identity of the person you must serve will depend on how the business is legally organized (see Method 2, below) and in some states on whether a corporation or LLC has appointed a third party as its "Registered Agent for Service of Process." Again, as mentioned at the beginning of this chapter, it's crucial that you check your state's rules before attempting to serve your papers.

Method 1:   Personal and Certified Mail Service

Personal service or certified mail service (carried out by the small claims clerk) can usually be used to serve a business and will probably be your best choice if the business doesn't operate an office, store, or other physical location, or if your state doesn't allow substituted service as discussed just below.

Certified mail service will only work with reputable businesses. If a business has no physical location and you are having trouble locating its principals, serving your papers by certified mail probably won't work. Even if you find an address for an owner, chances are good that he or she won't sign to accept the court papers.

Who you must serve depends on how the business is organized:

- **Sole Proprietorship:** Serve the owner.
- **Partnership:** Serve at least one partner.
- **Limited Partnership:** Serve the Registered Agent for Service of Process or a partner who runs the business (the general partner).
- **Corporation (profit or nonprofit):** Serve the Registered Agent for Service of Process or a corporate officer (president, vice-president, secretary, or treasurer).
- **Limited Liability Company (LLC):** Serve the Registered Agent for Service of Process or an LLC officer (president, vice-president, secretary, or treasurer).

Sometimes it can be difficult to figure out who owns a business. One simple approach is to call the business and ask how it prefers to be served. Many will cooperate by voluntarily accepting the court papers. If they won't, the city or county business tax and license people where the business is located should be able to tell you who owns a sole proprietorship or partnership business (see Chapter 9). To serve a corporation or LLC, one good approach is to call the secretary of state or the commissioner of corporations at your state capital for information. Ask for the name of the person authorized to accept service for the company. This may be an officer of the corporation or a separate entity hired by the business as its Registered Agent for Service of Process.

Method 2:   Substituted Service

The substituted service method, available in many states, can be an excellent way to serve a business that has an office, store, or other physical location. If the business hasn't appointed a Registered Agent for Service of Process and you are having difficulty locating and serving the owner, check your state's rules regarding substituted service. If it is allowed, you can simply have an adult (other than you) leave the papers at the defendant's business during usual business hours with the person in charge, and then mail a copy of the summons and complaint to the person to be served at the same address. It's that easy.

E. How to Serve Papers on a Public Agency

As discussed in Chapter 9, before you can sue a city, county, or other government body, you often must first file an administrative (in-house) claim against that agency within a specified number of days after the incident that gave rise to your claim. Once your claim is denied, you can sue in small claims court. To serve your papers, call the governmental body in question and ask who should be served. Then proceed, following the rules set out in Method C1 or C2, above.

F. Notify the Court That Service Has Been Accomplished ("Proof of Service")

If service is accomplished through certified or registered mail, you don't have to tell the court about it. The court clerk sends out the certified mail for you, and the signed post office receipt comes back directly to the clerk if service is accomplished. It's as simple as that.

SAMPLE PROOF OF SERVICE

					FOR COURT USE ONLY

PARTY [X] PLAINTIFF [ ] DEFENDANT   (Name and Address):   TELEPHONE NO.:

Debbie Nakamura
200 West Hedding Street
San Jose, CA 95110

NAME AND ADDRESS OF COURT:

Santa Clara Small Claims Court
1095 Homestead Road
Santa Clara, CA 95050

PLAINTIFF(S): Debbie Nakamura

DEFENDANT(S): Sam Blue

PROOF OF SERVICE (Small Claims)	HEARING DATE: 12/22/__	DAY: Wed.	TIME: 9:00 a.m.	DEPT./DIVISION: 1	CASE NUMBER: 002001

1. At the time of service I was at least 18 years of age and not a party to this action, and **I served copies** of the following:

[ ] Plaintiff's Claim   [ ] Order of Examination   [X] Other (specify): Notice of Motion to Vacate Judgment
[ ] Defendant's Claim   [ ] Subpena Duces Tecum

2. a. Party served (specify name of party as shown on the documents served):

Sam Blue

   b. Person served: [X] party in item 2.a.   [ ] other (specify name and title or relationship to the party named in item 2.a.)

3. By delivery   [X] at home   [ ] at business
   a. date: December 3, 20xx
   b. time: 12:08 a.m.
   c. address: 191 North First Street, San Jose CA 95113

4. **Manner of service** (check proper box):
   a. [ ] **Personal service.** I personally delivered to and left copies with the party served. **(C.C.P. 415.10)**
   b. [ ] **Substituted service on corporation, unincorporated association (including partnership), or public entity.** By leaving, during usual office hours, copies in the office of the person served with the person who apparently was in charge and thereafter mailing (by first-class mail, postage prepaid) copies to the person to be served at the place where the copies were left. **(C.C.P. 415.20(a))**
   c. [ ] **Substituted service on natural person, minor, incompetent, or candidate.** By leaving copies at the dwelling house, usual place of abode, usual place of business, or usual mailing address other than a U. S. Postal Service post office box of the person served in the presence of a competent member of the household or a person apparently in charge of the office or place of business, at least 18 years of age, who was informed of the general nature of the papers, and thereafter mailing (by first-class mail, postage prepaid) copies to the person to be served at the place where the copies were left. **(C.C.P. 415.20(b))**
   d. [X] **Date of mailing:**   Dec. 4, 20xx   **From** (city):   Santa Clara, CA

> **Information regarding date and place of mailing is required for services effected in manner 4.b. and 4.c. above. Certified mail service may be performed only by the Clerk of the Court in small claims matters.**

5. **Person serving** (name, address, and telephone number):

Barbara Durent
200 W. Hedding St.
San Jose, CA 95110

   a. **Fee** for service: $
   b. [X] Not a registered California process server
   c. [ ] **Exempt** from registration under B&P Section 22350(b)
   d. [ ] **Registered** California process server
      1. [ ] Employee or independent contractor
      2. **Registration Number:**
      3. **County:**

6. [X] I declare under penalty of perjury under the laws of the State of California that the foregoing is true and correct.
7. [ ] I am a California sheriff, marshal, or constable and I certify that the foregoing is true and correct.

Date: December 3, 20xx   ▶   *Barbara Durent*
                                                 (SIGNATURE OF SERVER)

Form Approved by the Judicial Council of California SC-104 [New January 1, 1992]	**PROOF OF SERVICE** (Small Claims)	Code of Civil Procedure §§ 415.10, 415.20

However, a court has no way of knowing whether or not papers have been successfully served by personal service unless you tell the clerk. This is done by filing a piece of paper known as a "Proof of Service" with the court clerk after the service has been made. A proof of service is used when any legal documents are served by personal service (including by the plaintiff and by a defendant who files a defendant's claim). It is often a perforated tear-off form, or a separate form that you get from the court clerk. It must be signed by the person actually making the service and returned to the clerk's office before the trial.

Frequently, a defendant won't have enough time to properly complete service of a defendant's claim. If you're a defendant in this situation, you should simply file your claim and bring up the service problem in court. The plaintiff may well waive the time of service requirement and agree to proceed. Or, the plaintiff may request that the judge continue the case to a later date. The judge will normally grant the continuance if there is a good reason. If the papers are served by a law enforcement officer, he or she will prepare and file the proof of service automatically. Check your local rules for specific filing requirements.

G. How to Serve Subpoenas

In Chapter 15, I discuss subpoenaing witnesses and documents. Subpoenas can't be served by mail. They must be served by personal service. The rules as to who can do the serving and so forth are the same as those set forth above, in Method C2, with one important difference: Any person, including the person bringing the suit, can serve the subpoena. In addition, in many states, the person making the service must be ready to pay the person subpoenaed a witness fee on the spot if it is requested. This is often a flat fee (normally $40–$100), plus a mileage fee based on the distance to the courthouse. If you hire a sheriff or marshal to do the service, he or she will ask you to pay this fee, plus the service fee, in advance. In many states, if the witness doesn't ask for the fee, it will be returned to you.

H. How to Serve a Defendant's Claim

How to deal with improper service. If you are improperly served, because you are not given adequate time, the papers weren't handed to you personally, or you didn't sign for a certified letter, it is still wise for you to call the court clerk or show up in court on the day in question. Why should you have to do this if service was improper? Because the plaintiff may succeed in getting the case heard as a default if you fail to show up. While this is improper, the fact remains that it is often more trouble to get an improper default judgment set aside than to protect yourself from the start. But isn't this a Catch-22? You are entitled to proper service, but if you don't get it, you have to show up in court anyway? Perhaps, but as Catch-22s go, this one is mild. You can call the clerk or show up in court and request that the judge grant you a continuance (delay) to prepare your case. If the original service was in fact improper, your request will be honored. Of course, if you were improperly served and simply want to get the hearing out of the way, you can show up and go ahead with your case.

As you will remember from the discussion in Chapter 11, a defendant's claim or counterclaim is the form the defendant files to sue the plaintiff for money damages arising out of the same incident that forms the basis for the plaintiff's suit. A defendant's claim must be filed with the small claims court clerk and served on the plaintiff. Time limits vary from state to state, as do the technical requirements for service. In New York, for example, a defendant's claim should be filed and served at least five days prior to the date that the court has set for the hearing on the plaintiff's claim. Check your local rules. Often service can be accomplished by mail.

But even if personal service is required and you can't find the plaintiff to serve the papers, all is not lost. Explain your problem to the court clerk. In most states, the clerk will either arrange to have the hearing date delayed or will tell you to show up for the first hearing with your papers. You can serve them on the plaintiff in the hallway (not the courtroom). Then explain to the judge why it was impossible to locate the plaintiff earlier. The judge will either put the whole case over (delay the case) for a few days, or allow you to proceed with your claim that day. Either way, the judge will accept your claim as validly served.

I. How to Serve Papers on Someone in the Military

It is proper to serve someone who is on active duty in the armed forces. If he or she shows up, fine. If not, however, you have a problem. Although you can usually get a "default judgment" against a properly served defendant who fails to show up, this is not true if the person you are suing is in the military (unless he or she is in the reserves).

Default judgments cannot normally be taken against people on active duty in the armed forces, because Congress has given our military personnel special protections. To get a default judgment, you will probably have to file a statement under penalty of perjury that the defendant is not in the military. This declaration is available from the clerk. Clerks almost always accept a Declaration of Nonmilitary Service signed by the plaintiff, as long as the plaintiff reasonably believes that the defendant is not on active duty. This constitutes a lenient interpretation of the law by clerks, but no one seems to be complaining.

J. Costs of Personal Service

Professional process servers and law enforcement agencies commonly charge from $20–$75 per service, depending on the time and mileage involved. You can usually get your costs of service added to your judgment if you win, but be sure to remind the judge to do this when you conclude your court presentation. However, a few courts will not give the successful party an award of costs for a process server unless he or she first tried to have the papers served by the cheaper certified mail approach (Method C1, above). Other judicial districts prefer that you don't use the mail approach at all, because they feel that, too often, the mail isn't accepted. Ask the small claims court clerk in your district how you should accomplish service and how much the judge will allow as a service of process fee.

K. Time Limits for Serving

All states have a rule that the defendant is entitled to receive service of the claim form before the date of the court hearing. Rules as to how many days in advance of the hearing papers must be served vary considerably, with some states requiring as little as five and others requiring as many as 30. Check your local rules for details.

If the defendant is served too late (that is, fewer than the required number of days before the trial date), he or she can either go ahead with the trial anyway, or request that the case be delayed (continued). If a delay is granted, the hearing will be postponed anywhere from two weeks to a month. If you're the defendant and it is impossible for you to show up in person to ask for a delay, contact the court clerk and point out that you weren't served in the proper time and that you want the case put over (delayed). The clerk will see that a default judgment is not entered against you. (See Chapter 11, Section E.) But just to be sure, get the clerk's name.

To see if service has been accomplished by the time limit, most states do not count the day the service is accomplished, but do count the day of the court appearance (check your local rules). Weekends and holidays also count. Thus, if Jack served Julie on July 12 in Los Angeles County (where the limit is five days), for a July 17 court date in the same county, service would be proper. This is true even if Saturday and Sunday fell on July 14 and 15. To determine the number of days, you would not count July 12, the day of service, but you would count July 13, 14, 15, 16, and 17, for a total of five days. If you are unable to serve the defendant(s) within the proper time, simply ask the court clerk for a new court date and try again. ■

The Defendant's Options

This chapter is devoted to the concerns of the defendant. Most of this material has already been discussed in the first 12 chapters, but because the plaintiff, as the initiator of a lawsuit, gets more than half the space, let's even things up a little and use this chapter to look at a small claims case from the point of view of the person being sued.

How should a defendant approach a small claims case? There is no one correct course of action—it all depends on the facts of the dispute and your personal desires.

A. Claim Improper Service or Another Technical Defense

You may conclude that you were not properly (legally) served with the plaintiff's court papers. (See Chapter 12.) Perhaps the claim was left with your neighbors, you didn't have the correct number of days in which to respond, or you believe you were sued in the wrong district of your state. Figuring that the case can't be heard because you weren't served properly, you may even be tempted to not show up in court. This is not smart. The judge may be unaware of, or overlook, the technical problem and issue a default judgment against you. If this happens, you will have to go to the trouble of requesting that the default be vacated. (See Chapter 11.) Your better course of action is to contact the clerk, explain the problem, and ask that the case be dismissed, continued to a date that is convenient for you, or transferred to the correct court. If the clerk can't help promptly, show up on the day in question and make your request.

Out-of-state defendants. As discussed in Chapter 10, if you don't live—or do business—in a state where you are sued, the court normally doesn't have power ("jurisdiction," in legalese) to enter a valid judgment against you, unless you are served with court papers while you happen to be in that state. (Exceptions exist for people who live elsewhere but own land in the state where the small claims case was filed, or who got into a traffic accident in that state.) If you are an out-of-state resident and receive small claims papers via the mail, promptly write a letter to the court explaining that you do not believe you are subject to the court's jurisdiction. Stay in touch with the court until you are sure the case has been dismissed.

B. You Have a Partial Defense—Try to Compromise

If you feel that perhaps the plaintiff is partially in the right, but you are being sued for too much, contact the plaintiff and try to work out a compromise settlement. (See Chapter 6 for more on how to negotiate.) One good approach is to call or write the plaintiff and make an offer. How much to offer depends on the relative merits of your position as compared to that of the plaintiff's, and whether the plaintiff is asking for a dollar amount you think is more or less fair, or greatly inflated. Assuming the plaintiff has a pretty strong legal position (you probably are legally liable) and is asking the court for an amount that's, broadly speaking, reasonable, I recommend that you make an initial compromise offer to pay about half of the amount the plaintiff has requested. Even with a strong case, the plaintiff may be motivated to accept your lowball offer, if for no other reason than to save the time it takes to prepare for and appear in court. More likely, your offer will set in motion a little dance of offer and counteroffer, with an eventual compromise of somewhere between 65% and 80% of the plaintiff's original demand. Obviously, if the plaintiff is asking for way too much, or you are not sure that a judge would find that you are liable in the first place, you'll want to offer less.

Any settlement you make should be set down in writing along the lines outlined in Chapter 6.

Don't rely on being judgment proof. Some defendants who have at least a partial defense to the plaintiff's claim are tempted not to show up and defend a case in small claims court because they have no money and figure that, even if they lose, the plaintiff can't collect. If you have a decent defense, this is just plain dumb. Judgments are good for anywhere from five to 20 years, depending on the state (see chart in Chapter 25, Section F), and can usually be renewed for a longer period of time, if necessary. Hopefully, you'll get a job or otherwise put a few dollars together sometime in the future, and you probably won't want them immediately taken away to satisfy a small claims judgment that you believe shouldn't have been entered in the first place. So wake up and defend yourself while you can. One possible exception to this advice applies if you plan to declare Chapter 7 bankruptcy. Bankruptcy wipes out most debts, including those that have been turned into a small claims court judgment.

For more information on whether personal bankruptcy makes sense, see *Bankruptcy: Is It the Right Solution to Your Debt Problems?*, by Robin Leonard (Nolo).

C. You Have Absolutely No Defense

Now let's assume that the service of the plaintiff's papers was proper and you have no valid defense on the merits of the case. Perhaps you borrowed money under the terms of a written contract and haven't paid it back. You know you'll lose, so you may conclude that it makes little sense to fight back in court. Your decision not to show up will almost surely result in a default judgment being entered against you. The judgment will probably be for the dollar amount demanded by the plaintiff, plus the amount of the filing fee and any reasonable costs to serve the papers on you. I discuss default judgments and how you can try to set them aside if you take action immediately in Chapters 11 and 16.

In a number of states, if you do not dispute the plaintiff's claim but cannot afford to pay it all at once, the law allows you to request the right to make payments in installments. After checking with the small claims clerk to find out whether installment payments are allowed in your state, your best bet is to show up in court and explain your situation to the judge. If you can't be present, write a letter to the court prior to the court hearing (be sure to properly identify the case, using the case number from the plaintiff's claim form) explaining why it would be difficult or impossible to pay any judgment all at once. For example, if you are on a fixed income, have recently been unemployed, and have a lot of debts, or have a low or moderate income and a large family, explain this to the judge. Just state the facts; there is no need to tell a long sob story. Assuming your state's law allows it, when the judge enters a judgment against you, he or she will very likely order you to pay in reasonable monthly installments.

D. You Want to Avoid Conflict—Try to Mediate

In Chapter 7, I discuss mediation in some detail. Please reread this material and, as you do, consider that engaging in this process is almost always beneficial to the defendant, because the very process of mediation tends to encourage a compromise settlement for a lower amount than the plaintiff has demanded. In addition, mediation gives the defendant a chance to raise issues that are not officially part of the plaintiff's lawsuit. For example, in a dispute between neighbors, small business people, or relatives, it's often important to discuss and settle emotional (human) concerns in addition to sorting out how much is owed.

Ask the small claims clerk for help with mediation. Mediation of all small claims cases is mandatory or strongly encouraged in some areas of the country. In others, it is easily accessible on a voluntary basis, either right in the courthouse or at a nearby community mediation project. Ask the small claims court clerk where mediation is available in your area. Then contact the mediation project and enlist its help in bringing the plaintiff to the table.

E. Have Your Case Transferred to a Formal Court

Depending on state law and the facts of your case, you may be able to have your case transferred out of small claims court to a formal court. This may be called municipal, district, county, justice, circuit, city, or civil court. Whatever the name used in your state, this court will allow lawyers and require formal rules of evidence and procedure, including far more paperwork than is required in small claims court.

Transfer rules vary greatly from one state to the next. Some states allow any defendant to transfer any case, others allow it only if the defendant files his or her own claim (a counterclaim) over the small claims limit or makes a request for a jury trial. Still other states allow a case to be transferred only with the discretionary approval of a judge. And some states don't allow transfers at all.

If you are interested in transferring your case and you think this may be possible, after looking at the brief summary for your state in the Appendix, you absolutely need to consult your state's rules. But first it makes sense to ask yourself why you would want to transfer a case out of small claims court. My answer is that it is rarely a good idea. Because small claims court is cheaper, more user-friendly, and far less time-consuming than formal court, you'll usually want to defend your case right there, unless, of course, you want to file a defendant's claim (counterclaim) for an amount significantly over the small claims limit. Here are some other situations in which it might make sense to transfer your case:

- To get a jury trial (in states where transfer for this reason is allowed). In my view, nonlawyers are almost always better off trying a case before a judge under relaxed small claims rules than submitting to the extra level of formality a jury trial adds to the already fussy rules of formal court. But I know people who disagree, believing that there is no justice without a jury.

- Because you know how to navigate in formal court far better than the plaintiff—or are willing to hire a lawyer to represent you. Yes, this approach may be a tad cynical, but given the opportunistic nature of many plaintiffs, why not take full advantage of every possible edge you have.

F. Fight Back

Suppose you feel that you don't owe the plaintiff a dime and you want to actively fight the case filed against you. In this case, you must show up in court on the date stated in the papers served on you, unless you get the case delayed to a later date. (See Chapter 11.) In the majority of states, a defendant need not file any papers with the court clerk; showing up ready to present your side of the story is enough. However, a written response must be filed in several states, including Alabama, Alaska, Connecticut, Maryland, New Hampshire, Oregon, and Texas. In addition, some states require the defendant to make a pretrial appearance. To defend most types of cases successfully, you'll want to back up your oral presentation with as much evidence as possible.

Before you even think about the merits of the plaintiff's case, your first job is to make sure that the plaintiff filed suit within the time allowed by the statute of limitations (see Chapter 5). If not, tell the judge at the beginning of your presentation and request that the plaintiff's case be dismissed.

To successfully present your defense, be prepared to make a well-organized, convincing oral statement, backed up with as much evidence as possible. Good case presentation strategies, including how to present witnesses, estimates, diagrams, and other evidence, are discussed in Chapters 14 through 23 and apply to both defendants and plaintiffs. If the plaintiff has asked for too much money, you'll also want to be sure you tell the judge exactly why (see Chapter 4).

Here are some tips that should help you mount a powerful defense:

- **Take apart your opponent's case.** To do this, you will want to focus on any facts that show you are not legally liable (carefully reread Chapter 2 to see what plaintiffs must prove). Next, if you conclude that the plaintiff may have a winning case, focus on whether he or she has asked for the right dollar amount. If you can convince a judge that you only owe a couple of hundred, not several thousand dollars, you will have won a substantial victory (see Chapter 4).

Example 1: The plaintiff sues you for a breach of contract. You reread Chapter 2, Section C, to understand what the plaintiff must prove to win his or her case. Assuming the facts support your position, you might claim that no contract existed in the first place. Or that even if it did, the plaintiff violated its terms so thoroughly that you were justified in considering it to be void. And even if you have to admit that you broke a valid contract, you might claim the plaintiff is asking for far too much in damages.

Example 2: You are sued by someone claiming that your negligent (careless) conduct resulted in his or her property being damaged (as would be the case in a fender bender). To prevail, you would want to convince the court that you were not negligent, or if you were, that the plaintiff was far more at fault. And even if the judge decides that the incident was mostly your fault, you will probably want to claim that the other party was also negligent and that this should reduce the dollar amount of your liability. In addition, if you believe it to be true, you will want to claim that the plaintiff paid far more than was necessary to have his car fixed.

- **Gather evidence.** As emphasized in Chapters 14 and 15, the key to winning a small claims court case is to convince the judge that your version of the facts is correct. To do this, you need evidence to back up your oral presentation. One good approach is to present the testimony of eyewitnesses (if you are lucky enough to have any) and expert witnesses who can lend credence to your position (for example, a mechanic who can explain how the plaintiff ruined your engine). In addition, you will want to present any documentary evidence, such as contracts, canceled checks, and photos that support your position. For example, if you are a computer repair person sued by someone who claims you ruined her PC, you may want to get a written opinion from another repair shop that the current problem with the computer has nothing to do with what you fixed. In addition, you might want to present advertisements and trade pricing data to show that the plaintiff is placing an inflated value on her used computer. And don't forget that you can also bring along physical evidence that doesn't fit into the judge's file. Suppose, for example, you are sued for nonpayment on a handmade ceramic teapot that you commissioned from the plaintiff. If you can bring that teapot into court and show the judge that it doesn't pour, your defense may be in the bag. Don't, however, bring videotapes unless you're sure the court has a working VCR.

- **Practice your court presentation.** The plaintiff gets to present his or her case first. When it is your turn, be ready to make an incisive, logical presentation of why the plaintiff should receive little or nothing. Once you have your arguments thought out, practice them in front of a friend or family member until you are thoroughly comfortable. One trick here is not to repeat uncontested facts presented by the plaintiff, but to immediately focus on why the plaintiff's case is misguided.

Example: Tom, the landlord, listens patiently as Evie, the tenant, spends five minutes explaining the history of their landlord/tenant relations before claiming she should have gotten her security deposit back because she left the rental unit clean and undamaged. When it's Tom's turn, he ignores several small discrepancies in Evie's long rendition of her rental history. Instead, he focuses on the exact point of the dispute by saying, "Your Honor, the key to my defense is that the plaintiff left the rental at 127 Spring Street in a dirty and damaged condition. I have pictures to demonstrate this and a reliable witness to back it up. But first I would like to briefly list the worst problems."

You don't need a lawyer just because the plaintiff has one. In states where it's allowed, if the plaintiff has a lawyer, a question that defendants often ask is, "Am I at a disadvantage if I go it alone?" Considering the high costs of hiring a lawyer—and assuming you are willing to carefully prepare your case—my answer is "No." Start by understanding that because there are no technical legal procedures, rules of evidence, or legal jargon in small claims court, a lawyer has no inherent advantage. Then remember that no one knows the facts of your case as well as you do. Finally, consider that most small claims judges go out of their way to even the playing field if they see that a lawyer is trying to use professional tricks to gain an advantage.

G. File Your Own Claim

Some defendants will not only want to dispute the plaintiff's claim, but will also want to sue right back. Perhaps you are outraged that the plaintiff sued first, because you are the person who was wronged. To assert your own claim against the plaintiff, promptly file a defendant's claim (often called a counterclaim) in small claims court for up to the small claims court maximum, or, if you wish to sue for more, have the case transferred to the appropriate formal court. (For more on what to do if you wish to sue the plaintiff, see Chapter 11, Section C, and Chapter 12, Section H.)

Assuming your case stays in small claims court, both your claim and the plaintiff's will be heard together. You should prepare and present your case just as you would if you had filed first—that is, understand the legal basics that underlie your case, make a practical and convincing oral presentation, and back it up with as much hard evidence as you can find. ■

CHAPTER

14

Getting Ready for Court

Once you have filed your papers with the small claims clerk and the defendant(s) have been properly served, the preliminaries are over and you are ready for the main event—your day in court. Movies, and especially TV (yes, even "Court TV"), have done much to create false impressions of court proceedings. Ask yourself what a trial might have been like *before* every lawyer fancied himself Raymond Burr, Charles Laughton, or even Johnnie Cochran, and judges acted "parental," "stern," or "indignantly outraged" in the fashion of Judge Judy.

There are people whose lives revolve around courthouses, and who have been playing movie parts for so long that they have become caricatures of one screen star or another. Lawyers are particularly susceptible to this virus. All too often, they substitute posturing and theatrics for good, hard preparation. Thankfully, though, most people who work in our courts quickly recover from movieitis and realize that the majestic courtroom is, in truth, a large, drafty hall with a raised platform at one end; "His Honor" is only a lawyer dressed in a tacky black dress, who knew the right politician; and they, themselves, are not bit players in "L.A. Law," or even the murder trial of O. J. Simpson.

I mention movieitis because it's a common ailment in small claims court. Cases that should be won easily are sometimes lost because one party or the other goes marching around the courtroom antagonizing everyone with comic opera imitations of Marcia Clark. And don't assume you are immune. Movieitis is a subtle disease, with many people never realizing they have it. To find out if you are likely to be infected, ask yourself a few self-diagnostic questions:

• Have you watched courtroom scenes on TV or in the movies?

• Have you ever imagined that you were one of the lawyers?

• How many times have you been in a real courtroom in comparison to watching movie or TV courtrooms?

I'm sure you get the idea. Chances are good that, like most of us, your idea of what court is like comes mostly from the media. The best advice I can give you is to put all of this aside and just be yourself. To succeed in small claims court, you don't need fancy clothes, words, or attitudes. If you feel a little anxious about a first court appearance, drop by the court a few days before your case is heard and watch for an hour or two. You may not learn a great deal that will be helpful in your case, but you will be a lot more relaxed and comfortable when your turn comes.

Movieitis aside, most people I have watched in small claims court have done pretty well. Those who really stood out had prepared their evidence carefully and were ready to make a clear, concise verbal presentation. As I'll emphasize in the next few chapters, the best way to be sure you are in top form is to practice ahead of time. Do this by having a savvy friend or family member play at being the small claims judge while you present your case, just as you plan to do in the courtroom.

The rest of this chapter contains basic information about how small claims court works. I'll discuss how to prepare and present different types of cases in the next chapters.

A. Interpreter Services

In some states, small claims courts make an effort to have foreign language interpreter services available for those who need and ask for this help. Notify the court clerk well in advance if you or one of your witnesses will need an interpreter. However, in many courts, interpreters are not routinely made available by the court. Where this is true, it is normally permissible to bring your own. But check with the small claims clerk in advance to be sure you understand the rules. Many ethnic and cultural organizations offer interpreter services to low-income persons free of charge.

B. Free Legal Advice

If you are confused about any aspect of small claims court, be sure to ask the court clerk whether assistance is available. In most small claims courts, helpful "how-to" written pamphlets, videos, or easy-to-use computer tutorials are available free or at a low cost. Even better, many small claims courts—especially those in California—have free legal advisor programs. While there is no set approach, most court-sponsored legal advisor programs make it possible for people involved in small claims court actions, either as plaintiffs or defendants, to talk to a lawyer or a person with paralegal training, either in person or by phone, before going to court. The idea is that the legal advisor will help the person understand and prepare her case properly. More and more courts are putting small claims advice and information on the Web. Nolo's Small Claims Center, at www.nolo.com, and the websites listed in the Appendix of this book, will help you find free legal advice online (see also Chapter 1, Section D).

C. Private Lawyers

As noted several times, a number of states have, quite sensibly, banned lawyers from appearing in small claims court on behalf of either plaintiff or defendant. However, the majority of states do allow representation by an attorney. (See the Appendix.) In my view, this is a mistake—it is past time that the lawyers be banned from appearing in what really should be the people's court.

Suppose you live in a state that allows lawyers to appear in small claims court, and that your opponent has retained one. Does it make sense for you to hire one, too? Probably not. Given the high costs that are inevitably involved, you will almost always be better off handling the case yourself. As you will have gathered from this book, small claims court rules and procedures are quite simple—with a little study, you should be able to do a fine job of preparing and presenting your case. And you may actually have a psychological advantage—as a person without formal legal training going up against a lawyer, you can play David to the lawyer's Goliath. You may also be reassured to know that two studies sponsored by the National Center for State Courts have found that, broadly speaking, having an attorney represent a person in small claims court does not significantly enhance that person's chances of winning. (See specifically "Small Claims and Traffic Courts," by John Goerdt (National Center for State Courts).)

It can be cost-effective to hire a lawyer for advice only. If you are worried about some legal aspect of your case, it can be sensible to get legal advice on that particular point. This should not be expensive as long as you don't hire the attorney to handle the entire case. If no free legal advisor program is available through your small claims court and you are not a low-income person eligible for free legal assistance through a federally sponsored "legal aid" (often called "legal services") program, one good approach is to hire a lawyer for a short consultation. For $100–$250 or so, you should be able to find an attorney who will review your entire case and advise you on any tricky points. Also, you may wish to spend a few hours doing some of your own research. (See Chapter 1, Section D.)

D. Mediation and Arbitration

As discussed in more detail in Chapter 7, many courts utilize mediation techniques to provide an opportunity for the parties to settle their cases without actually going to court.

Mediation: In mediation, the parties sit down with a third person whose job it is to help them arrive at their own solution. In most areas, the mediator is either a volunteer, or a retired person who is paid a modest amount—often about $30–$50 per mediation. Most mediators have received a week or two of training in the art of helping disputing parties arrive at their own negotiated settlement. In some states, however, the mediator may be a local volunteer attorney. A mediator has no power to make a "decision." Rather, his or her job is to help the parties settle their dispute consensually. If this proves impossible, the case is referred to small claims court. If a mediation program is available in your area, I recommend that you give it a try, especially if the other party is a relative, neighbor, local business person, or anyone else with whom it's important to preserve or restore a decent personal relationship.

Arbitration: In a few states, including New York, arbitration is offered as an option. This usually consists of a volunteer lawyer listening to both sides and actually making a decision, just as a judge would. Although it's often possible to have a case heard sooner if you elect arbitration, I don't recommend it. Over the years, I have received more complaints from readers dissatisfied with the decisions of lawyer arbitrators and volunteer lawyer judges (often called "pro tem" judges) than with any other aspect of small claims court. I'm convinced this is because most lawyers specialize in fairly narrow areas of the law, and are simply not up to speed in many others; as a result, they are prone to make mistakes.

Be sure you know what you are agreeing to before you accept a noncourt alternative. The terms "mediation," "arbitration," and "conciliation" are often used so loosely you can't always be sure what they mean. For example, in a few courts, a hybrid process—nonbinding arbitration—is used, which allows an arbitrator to suggest a solution, but does not require the parties to accept it. So if anyone suggests you participate in any of these programs (sometimes called alternative dispute resolution or ADR), be sure you understand exactly what's involved before agreeing.

E. Getting to the Courthouse

Before you locate the right courtroom, you obviously have to get to the right building. Sometimes, doing this can be tricky, because small claims courts are often not in the main courthouse. Like a half-forgotten stepsister, many are housed wherever the city or county has an empty room. In short, don't assume you know where your small claims court is unless you've been there before. Plaintiffs have already had to find the clerk's office to file their papers, so they probably know where the courtroom is, but defendants should check this out in advance. Be sure, too, that your witnesses know exactly where and when to show up. And do plan to be a few minutes early—people who rush in flustered and late start with a strike against them.

F. Court Times

Small claims courts can schedule cases any time they wish on business days. The most user-friendly set five starting times (for example, 8:30 a.m., 10:30 a.m., 1:00 p.m., 3:00 p.m., and 7:00 p.m.), so no one has to wait long. Most commonly, however, court is scheduled at 9:00 a.m. or 1:00 p.m., with a considerable number of cases to be heard in turn. In other words, you may get to watch a few other cases before your own begins. In larger judicial districts, Saturday or evening sessions may also be held. If it is not convenient for you to go to court during business hours, request that your case be scheduled at one of these other sessions, if available.

Also, be aware that courts in many areas of the country use a "hurry-up-and-wait" technique that would make the Army blush. For example, you might be told to show up for court at 8:15 a.m. At this time, the judges are still home having coffee, because court doesn't really start until 9:00, with delays to 9:15 or 9:30 being common. To avoid cooling my heels, I always ask the small claims clerk what time the judge really begins court.

A few minutes before the judge arrives, it's common for the clerk to ask everyone to swear (or affirm, if you wish) to tell the truth, although in some areas, this is done later, just before each case is presented.

G. Understanding the Courtroom and Basic Procedure

Most small claims proceedings are conducted in standard courtrooms that are also used for regular trials. Indeed, sometimes you will have to sit through a few minutes of some other type of court proceeding before small claims court actually begins.

Most judges still sit on little elevated wooden throne boxes and wear depressing black dresses, both of which trace their history back over a thousand years to England, to a time when courts were largely controlled by kings, nobility, and clergy. In addition to the judge, a clerk and a bailiff will normally be present. They usually sit at tables immediately in front of the judge. The clerk's job is to keep the judge supplied with necessary files and papers, and to make sure that proceedings flow smoothly. The bailiff is there to keep order in the courtroom if tempers get out of hand.

To add to the sense of going back in time, many courtrooms are limited in their technological capacities. If your key piece of evidence is, for example, a bone-chilling videotape of the neighbor's dog snarling at small children in the same spot where it bit you, you'll want to call ahead and make sure that the court has, or can accommodate, a VCR.

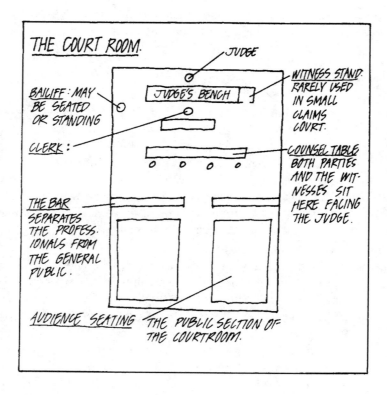

THE COURT ROOM.

JUDGE

JUDGE'S BENCH

BAILIFF: MAY BE SEATED OR STANDING

WITNESS STAND: RARELY USED IN SMALL CLAIMS COURT.

CLERK:

COUNSEL TABLE BOTH PARTIES AND THE WITNESSES SIT HERE FACING THE JUDGE.

THE BAR SEPARATES THE PROFESSIONALS FROM THE GENERAL PUBLIC.

AUDIENCE SEATING THE PUBLIC SECTION OF THE COURTROOM.

⚠ **No written record of court proceedings is kept.** A small claims clerk is not the same as a court reporter, who keeps a word-by-word record of proceedings. In most states, no such record is kept in small claims court, and no court reporter is present, although in a few areas, tape recordings or videotapes are made and used if a case is appealed.

Courtrooms are divided about two-thirds of the way toward the front by a little fence (known to initiates as the "bar"). The public must stay on the opposite side of the bar from the judge, clerk, bailiff, and attorneys, unless invited to cross. This invitation occurs when your case is called by name (*Smith vs. Jones Ford* or *Abercrombie vs. Lee*) by the clerk. At this point you, and any witnesses, will normally be asked to come forward and sit at a table (known as the "counsel table"). You will be facing the judge, with your back to the spectator section of the courtroom. However, in a few courtrooms, judges try to hurry things along by asking everyone to stand in front of the judge's bench. The idea seems to be that if people can't sit down, they will present their cases faster.

In the great majority of small claims courts, you, your opponent, and your witnesses will present the entire case from the counsel table. This means that neither you nor your witnesses sit in the witness box next to the judge. Many people (and judges) feel that it is polite to stand when addressing the judge, but you should do what feels most comfortable to you. The traditional way to refer to a judge is "Your Honor."

Normally, the plaintiff will be asked to present his or her case first and introduce any witnesses, who will also get a chance to have their say. When the plaintiff is done, it will be the defendant's turn to speak and present witnesses. Both sides should have any papers or other evidence that backs up their story carefully organized to present to the judge. This can include bills, receipts, estimates, photographs, contracts, letters to or from your opponent, and other types of documentation or physical evidence. At the appropriate place in your presentation, tell the judge you have materials you want him or her to see, and then hand them to the clerk, who in turn will give them to the judge. As I have said before, documentation is a great aid to your case, but don't go overboard. Judges are a little like donkeys—load them too heavily and they are likely to lie down and go to sleep.

H. Dealing With Your Opponent

Before you get to the courtroom, you should do a little thinking about your opponent. What sort of presentation will he or she make? How can you best counter these arguments? Take the negative energy you may feel (frustration, annoyance, anger) and turn it into creative planning and preparation. Always be polite when presenting your case. If you are hostile or sarcastic, you will gain nothing, and you may lose the respect of the judge. Never interrupt when your opponent is speaking—you will get your chance. When you do, lay out the key facts that support your position to the judge; don't get into an argument with the other side.

Cope with lies by presenting convincing evidence. I am often asked what to do if your opponent tells huge fibs. Although not an everyday occurrence, big lies definitely are told in small claims court and can be a big problem if you aren't prepared to poke holes in them. The best response to an opponent who tells whoppers is to wait calmly for your turn to speak and say something like this: "Your honor, almost everything defendant (or plaintiff) has said is simply not true. Please let me prove this to you with facts." Then present your evidence—or if you have already presented it, remind the judge of why it proves that your opponent's story is false. For example, if your opponent who has failed to return your cleaning deposit swears you left an apartment filthy, you should win if you show the judge photos of how clean you really left it. Fortunately, if you can demonstrate that your opponent has told one big lie, the judge will distrust and hopefully disbelieve the rest of what he or she says.

I. Dealing With the Judge or Commissioner

The person who hears your case may be a regular municipal court judge who also presides over other types of cases. But, increasingly, cities and counties are hiring full-time commissioners or referees to hear small claims cases. These are administrative positions designed to allow lawyers to be hired for lower salaries and benefits than are paid to judges (a bit like colleges hiring nontenured instructors instead of full professors). By and large, commissioners and referees—who usually hear small claims cases on a daily basis—do a very competent job, sometimes better than judges, who occasionally act as if they are too important to hear such small disputes.

In many states, volunteer lawyers are also routinely appointed as temporary judges when a judge, referee, or commissioner is ill or on vacation. The legal slang for a temporary judge is often "judge, pro tem" or "arbitrator." Especially if your case comes up on a day when only a pro tem judge or arbitrator is present, you usually will be given a choice as to whether you want to accept that judge or ask that your case be heard by a regular judge. Then again, you may not get to lay eyes on the pro tem judge before you make your choice. If your case is contested and you feel it involves fairly complicated legal issues, I recommend you ask that it be heard before a full-time judge or commissioner—unless you're in an area where all the full-time judges are known to be sub-par. Pro tem judges and arbitrators are not paid, are rarely trained, and often do not have much practical experience in the legal areas that are commonly heard in small claims court. While many are excellent, some are seriously substandard.

You have the right to reject a temporary judge. In some courtrooms, clerks simply ask you to sign or otherwise indicate your approval of a judge, without explaining the judge's temporary status and your right to say no. Don't fall for this. Whenever you are asked to approve a judge, you can be sure it's a substitute for the real judge, and you can say no.

You can't appeal from an arbitrator's decision in New York. To save time, residents of the Empire State are often encouraged to have their cases heard by a volunteer lawyer arbitrator instead of a small claims court judge. But beware of this alternative. In addition to getting a less experienced decision maker, there is no right to appeal from an arbitrator's decision, as there is from the decision of a regular small claims judge.

What if your case will be heard by a regular judge, commissioner, or referee whom you don't like, either because you know the person or because you have been put off by the way he or she has handled other cases? For example, you might live in a small town and be convinced a particular judge, whose reputation you know, is likely to be hard on you (perhaps you are a tenant and the judge owns a number of rental properties). Laws exist in nearly all states that allow you to "disqualify" a judge simply on your honest belief that he or she is "prejudiced" against you. (No one will ask you to prove it.) To disqualify a judge, in some states you can simply wait for your case name to be called and then stand up and say something like this: "Your Honor, I believe you are prejudiced against my interest, and I request a trial before another judge." Unfortunately, in other states, you need to put your disqualification request in writing and file it in advance. If you think you may want to take advantage of a disqualification procedure, check with the small claims clerk before your court date to be sure you understand the rules.

When thinking about presenting your case to a judge, referee, or commissioner, there is one constructive thing you can do: Imagine yourself in the decision maker's shoes. What would you value most from the people appearing before you? Before I ever sat as a judge, my answer to this question was "politeness, good organization of the material to be presented, and reasonable brevity." After experiencing small claims court from the judge's chair, I would add one word: "evidence." By this, I mean a presentation that consists of more than just your oral statement as to what happened. Witnesses, written statements, police accident reports, and photographs all give the judge the opportunity to make a decision based on something more than who tells the better story.

And two more points: First, remember that the person who is deciding your case has heard thousands of stories very much like yours, and will either cease paying attention or get annoyed if you are needlessly repetitive. Second, don't let the robe and other trappings of judicial office obscure the fact that you are dealing with a human being. The judge, like anyone else, is far more likely to be sympathetic to your point of view if you can show that you occupy the moral high ground (for example, you are honest, kind, and pay your debts) and that your opponent is the bad guy (tricky, hard-headed, and fails to keep promises).

J. Organizing Your Testimony and Evidence

As I've mentioned frequently, it's essential that you carefully organize what you have to say and the physical evidence that backs up each point. Do this by dividing your testimony into a list of the several main points you want to make. Under each heading, note any items of physical or documentary evidence (called exhibits in some states) you wish to show the judge. If your evidence consists of a number of items, make sure that you put them in order so you can find each item quickly.

Depending on the facts of your case, here is a brief outline of the main types of physical evidence you'll wish to bring to court:

- If your case is about a past due installment loan or unpaid bill, bring a copy of your business records, which should show the original charges and any payments of the current balance.

- If your case involves a defective product, bring any warranty papers.

- If your case involves a personal injury, bring receipts for any costs or expenses that you are asking the defendant to pay.

- If your case concerns damage to property, bring photographs that show the damage and receipts for repair costs. If you have not yet had the damage fixed, bring at least two estimates of the cost of the repairs.

- If your case involves destroyed or lost property, bring estimates of the value of the property at the time it was totaled. Receipts for the original cost of the property may also help establish its value, especially if it was purchased very recently. (See Chapter 4.)

- If your case involves lost wages, bring documentation from your employer that shows how much you lost—such as stubs that show your usual wage and the days or hours of work that you missed.

- If you case involves a car accident, it's wise to prepare a diagram or drawing showing how the accident occurred. (See Chapter 20.) If police were called to the accident, a copy of the police officer's report may be useful. (You may also want the officer to come to the hearing to testify as a witness. For information about witnesses, see Chapter 15.)

- If your case involves a bum check, bring the returned check. (See Chapter 4, Section C, for information about the procedures necessary to qualify for extra damages for bad checks.)
- If your evidence is in the form of a tape recording or video, call the court clerk's office before your hearing. Some courts have audio and video equipment available for your use. In others, you'll have to bring it.

Example (from the plaintiff's point of view): Let's assume your case is based on a hotel's failure to return your deposit when you canceled a wedding reception three months before the event was to be held. Your list of key points—and the evidence to back them up—might look like this:

- Valley View Hotel refused to return my $500 deposit when I canceled my wedding reception.
- This was true even though I canceled 83 days before the event.
- The contract I signed with the hotel allowed a full refund if cancellation occurred more than 60 days before the event. (Show contract to the judge.)
- When I canceled, Valley View told me (and claims they sent me a letter) stating that their cancellation policy had been changed the previous month to require 90-days' notice in order to get a refund.
- I never received a letter and had no idea of the policy change until I canceled and asked for my money back.
- Even if Valley View did send me a letter, the change should not affect my contract, which was signed prior to the policy change. The key point here is that I never signed a new contract, so the existing contract was still valid.
- In any event, the hotel has a duty to try to re-rent the banquet room to minimize (mitigate) any damages they suffered. And they had plenty of time (83 days) to do so. (See Chapter 4, Section C1, for a discussion of mitigation of damages.)
- 90 days is an unreasonably long cancellation policy.
- Here is a list of short cancellation policies of five other hotels in the area, all of which allow a full refund on much shorter notice than 83 days. (Give list to the judge.)

Example (from the defendant's point of view): Valley View goes second, so their representative can't know in advance what the plaintiff will say and what evidence it will present. It follows that Valley View will need to adopt a little more flexible approach. Still, chances are that Valley View reps have talked to the plaintiff or exchanged letters, so they probably have a pretty good idea of what to expect. Accordingly, Valley View's list might look something like this:

- True, we didn't refund the $500. The reason was we turned down two other receptions for that same day before plaintiff canceled. Since we ended up with no other function, we lost at least $500.
- Although it is true that the written contract allowed cancellation prior to 60 days before the event, plaintiff was notified that this policy had been changed to 90 days before the contract was signed in two ways:

- A sign on the reservations desk where the plaintiff sat to sign the contract. (Show sign to judge.)
- Testimony of Angie Ells, who booked the reservation. Angie will testify that she included written notice of the change with the contract package. (Show judge a copy of the notice.)

 Chapters 15 through 23 contain an extensive discussion about how to prepare for court and what to do once you get there. ■

Eye and Expert Witnesses

It is often extremely helpful to have someone in court with you who has firsthand knowledge of the facts of your case and supports your point of view. In many types of cases, such as car accidents or disputes concerning whether or not a tenant left an apartment clean, eyewitnesses are particularly valuable. However, in other fact situations, they aren't as necessary. For example, if a friend borrowed $500 and didn't pay it back, you don't need a witness to prove that your friend's signature on the promissory note is genuine, unless you expect the defense to be that the signature was forged.

An eyewitness should have firsthand knowledge of the facts in the dispute. This typically means that he or she saw something that helps establish your case (for example, the car accident, dog bite, or dirty apartment). A judge will not be interested in the testimony of a person who is repeating secondhand or generalized information such as "I know Joe is a good, safe driver and would never have done anything reckless," or "I didn't see Joe's apartment before he moved out, but both Joe and his mother, who couldn't be here today, told me that they worked like crazy cleaning it up."

An expert witness is usually someone you consult about an important aspect of your case after the damage occurs. For example, if you pay $1,000 to have your car's engine fixed only to have it immediately fail, you may want to consult an experienced mechanic to find out why your engine wasn't fixed properly by the first repair shop. This person may appear in court on your behalf as an expert witness—or, in most states, may submit a written opinion letter.

Above all, a good witness is believable. This isn't always an easy quality to define. For example, a police officer may be a symbol of honesty to some people, while others will automatically react to an officer with hostility and fear. But remember, it's the judge you are trying to convince, and judges tend to be fairly establishment folk. They make comfortable salaries, own their own homes, and generally tend to like the existing order of things. Most judges I know would instinctively believe a police officer.

In many situations, such as car accidents, you won't have much choice as to witnesses. You will be lucky to have one person who saw what happened. Unfortunately, in some types of disputes, close friends and family are your only eyewitnesses. There is no rule that says you can't have these people testify for you. Indeed, I have often seen a person's spouse or friend give very convincing testimony. But, given a choice, it is usually better to have a witness who is neither buddy nor kin. A judge may discount the testimony of people to whom you are close on the theory that they would naturally be biased in your favor. One little trick to dispel this judicial cynicism is to have a closely related witness bend over backwards to treat the other side as fairly as possible. Thus, if your brother is your only witness to the fact that ABC Painting splashed paint on your boat, he might point out to the judge not only that he saw them do it, but that it was a very windy day and ABC was having a hard time painting the breakwater.

In many types of disputes, whether your house was incompetently painted, your kitchen tile repairs botched, or your new dentures improperly fitted, you have an opportunity to plan ahead to locate an expert witness. Again, that's because the type of witness you need is not an eyewitness who saw the work in progress, but instead an expert in the field who can convincingly explain what went wrong. Obviously, these witnesses are only valuable if they really have good credentials, so that a judge is likely to believe what they say. Thus, in a dispute over whether car repairs were properly done, it's preferable to bring a working car mechanic with 20 years' experience who has completed a load of training courses rather than your neighbor "who knows a lot about cars."

I will talk more about witnesses as I go through the various case examples (Chapters 17 through 22), but let's outline a few basic rules here:

- Prepare your witness thoroughly about your legal and factual position, what your opponent is likely to say, and what you want the witness to say. In court, the witness will be on his or her own, and you want to be sure that the story comes out right. It is completely legal and ethical to thoroughly discuss the case with your witness beforehand, as long as you do not coach or encourage the witness to lie or exaggerate.

- Do not ask a witness to testify unless you know exactly what he or she will say. This sounds basic, but I have seen people lose cases because their witnesses got mixed up and, in one instance, the witness actually supported the other side.

- It's proper to pay an expert witness—say a car mechanic who has examined your engine—a reasonable fee in most small claims courts (check with yours). However, it may be unnecessary to bring the person to court, because most states allow the judge to accept written evidence. (See Chapter 18 for an example of an expert witness's written statement.)

- Never use a subpoena to require a witness to be present unless you make sure that it is okay with the witness. Some witnesses might actually prefer to be subpoenaed, so they can prove to their boss that they need to leave work for a few hours (see more about subpoenas in Section A, below). If the witness doesn't know a subpoena is coming, however, its arrival might end up making the witness so mad that he or she will testify against you.

- If an expert witness can't appear in person (or it's simply too expensive to pay for the expert's time), check your small claims rules to see if a letter from the expert can be used instead. The letter should state the expert's credentials, review the facts of the case, and then explain, for example, why the defendant's work didn't meet minimum acceptable standards. (See Section D, below, for a sample letter.)

- Do not offer to personally pay an eyewitness to testify on your behalf. If discovered, your payment will likely be seen as a bribe.

Don't act like a lawyer when asking your witnesses to testify. In the courtroom, your witness will normally sit next to you at the table facing the judge and give testimony from there (or in some courtrooms, the judge may ask all parties and witnesses to approach the judge's bench and stand there in a little group). It is fairly rare for the judge to ask a witness to take the witness stand in small claims court, but it happens in a few courts. Assuming your witness is seated at the counsel table, it is best for him or her to stand when it's time to speak and simply explain what happened. There is no need for you to pretend to be a lawyer and ask your witness a lot of leading questions. The judge is likely to ask the witness questions and may even interrupt while the witness is speaking. When the witness is done, if you feel something was left out, simply ask a question designed to produce the information you want.

A. Subpoenaing Witnesses

In most states, you can require that a witness with firsthand knowledge of what happened be present if that person resides within a certain distance from the courthouse. (The distance varies from state to state. It is often about 150 miles, but in some states subpoenas reach only within county boundaries.) To do this, go to the clerk's office and get a "subpoena" form. Fill it out and have it served on the person you wish to have present. But remember, you never want to subpoena a person unless you have talked to the witness first and gotten an okay. The very act of dragging someone into court involuntarily may set the witness against you. A subpoenaed witness is normally entitled to a modest fee upon demand. The person serving the subpoena must have this money ready to pay if it is requested. If you win your case, you will probably be able to recover your witness fees from the other side. The judge has discretion as to whether to grant you your witness fees. Some judges are strict about this, making the loser pay the winner's witness fees only if the subpoenaed witness was essential to the presentation of the case. This means that if your case is so strong that you don't need a witness but you subpoena one anyway, you may well have to pay the witness even if you win.

Expert witnesses cannot be subpoenaed. For this reason they often submit their opinions in writing, a practice that is allowed in most courts.

Below is the standard California subpoena form. The one in your state will probably look quite similar. You will probably need to prepare an original and two copies. Once prepared, take the subpoena form to the clerk, who will issue it. Service must be made personally, and the proof of service, which is probably on the back of the subpoena, returned to the clerk's office. Rules for service are discussed in Chapter 12.

B. Subpoenaing Police Officers

You can generally use your state's standard subpoena form to subpoena a police officer, firefighter, or other peace officer. Fill it out, then take it to the relevant department to comply with any additional procedures. You'll have to pay for the officer's time and give plenty of advance notice (five days in California). The deposit to subpoena an officer is usually at least $150. In some areas, this money must be paid to the clerk at the time the subpoena is issued; in others, the money must be paid directly to the agency or department employing the officer. Depending on the amount of the officer's time that is used, you may eventually get a refund of some of your deposit. Be sure to check your local rules.

CIVIL SUBPOENA

Name and Address of Court:
Municipal Court, County of Alameda
2000 Center St.
Berkeley, CA 94704

SC-107

SMALL CLAIMS CASE NO. [Fill in number]

PLAINTIFF/DEMANDANTE *(Name, address, and telephone number of each)*:

South Branch
1901 Russell St.
Berkeley, CA 94703

Telephone No.:

(510) 644-6860

DEFENDANT/DEMANDADO *(Name, address, and telephone number of each)*:

John O'Gara
15 Scenic St.
Albany, CA

Telephone No.:

(510) 555-1212

Telephone No.:

☐ See attached sheet for additional plaintiffs and defendants.

Telephone No.:

**SMALL CLAIMS SUBPOENA
FOR PERSONAL APPEARANCE AND PRODUCTION OF DOCUMENTS
AND THINGS AT TRIAL OR HEARING AND DECLARATION**

THE PEOPLE OF THE STATE OF CALIFORNIA, TO *(name, address, and telephone number of witness, if known)*:

Jane Doe, 1484 Bay Vista, Oakland, CA 94611; (510) 444-4444

1. **YOU ARE ORDERED TO APPEAR AS A WITNESS in this case at the date, time, and place shown in the box below UNLESS your appearance is excused as indicated in box 4b below or you make an agreement with the person named in item 2 below.**

   a. Date: Time: ☐ Dept.:   ☐ Div.:   ☐ Room:
   b. Address:

2. **IF YOU HAVE ANY QUESTIONS ABOUT THE TIME OR DATE YOU ARE TO APPEAR, OR IF YOU WANT TO BE CERTAIN THAT YOUR PRESENCE IS REQUIRED, CONTACT THE FOLLOWING PERSON BEFORE THE DATE ON WHICH YOU ARE TO APPEAR:**

   a. Name of subpoenaing party: Berkeley Public Library   b. Telephone number: 644-6860

3. **Witness Fees:** You are entitled to witness fees and mileage actually traveled both ways, as provided by law, if you request them at the time of service. You may request them before your scheduled appearance from the person named in item 2.

PRODUCTION OF DOCUMENTS AND THINGS

(Complete item 4 only if you want the witness to produce documents and things at the trial or hearing.)

4. YOU ARE *(item a or b must be checked)*:

   a. ☒ Ordered to appear in person and to produce the records described in the declaration on page two. The personal attendance of the custodian or other qualified witness and the production of the original records are required by this subpoena. The procedure authorized by Evidence Code sections 1560(b), 1561, and 1562 will not be deemed sufficient compliance with this subpoena.

   b. ☐ Not required to appear in person if you produce (i) the records described in the declaration on page two and (ii) a completed declaration of custodian of records in compliance with Evidence Code sections 1560, 1561, 1562, and 1271. (1) Place a copy of the records in an envelope (or other wrapper). Enclose the original declaration of the custodian with the records. Seal the envelope. (2) Attach a copy of this subpoena to the envelope or write on the envelope the case name and number; your name; and the date, time, and place from item 1 in the box above. (3) Place this first envelope in an outer envelope, seal it, and mail it to the clerk of the court at the address in item 1. (4) Mail a copy of your declaration to the attorney or party listed at the top of this form.

5. **IF YOU HAVE BEEN SERVED WITH THIS SUBPOENA AS A CUSTODIAN OF CONSUMER OR EMPLOYEE RECORDS UNDER CODE OF CIVIL PROCEDURE SECTION 1985.3 OR 1985.6 AND A MOTION TO QUASH OR AN OBJECTION HAS BEEN SERVED ON YOU, A COURT ORDER OR AGREEMENT OF THE PARTIES, WITNESSES, *AND* CONSUMER OR EMPLOYEE AFFECTED MUST BE OBTAINED BEFORE YOU ARE REQUIRED TO PRODUCE CONSUMER OR EMPLOYEE RECORDS.**

DISOBEDIENCE OF THIS SUBPOENA MAY BE PUNISHED AS CONTEMPT BY THIS COURT. YOU WILL ALSO BE LIABLE FOR THE SUM OF FIVE HUNDRED DOLLARS AND ALL DAMAGES RESULTING FROM YOUR FAILURE TO OBEY.

[SEAL]   Date issued:

Clerk, by _____, Deputy

(See reverse for declaration in support of subpoena)

Page one of three

Form Adopted for Mandatory Use
Judicial Council of California
SC-107 [Rev. January 1, 2000]

**SMALL CLAIMS SUBPOENA
AND DECLARATION**

Code of Civil Procedure,
§ 1985 et seq.

C. Subpoenaing Documents

In addition to witnesses, you can also subpoena documents. This is rarely done in small claims court, but there are times when it may be helpful. Someone (such as a police department, phone company, hospital, or corporation) may have certain books, ledgers, papers, or other documents that can help your case. To get the materials brought to court, many states require that you prepare a form called a subpoena duces tecum. This is very similar to the standard subpoena form, except that there is a space to describe the papers or other documents you want. To get a subpoena duces tecum issued, you must normally follow a procedure along the following lines: Attach an affidavit stating "under penalty of perjury" why you need the written material. Prepare three copies of all papers and, after you get the clerk to issue the subpoena, serve it on the witness using personal service, as described in Chapter 12. As with a regular subpoena, the witness is entitled to ask for a fee. The proof of service is on the back of the subpoena form; it must be filled out and returned to the clerk.

Rules for subpoenas vary from state to state. Technical rules on filing and serving papers, as well as paying witness fees, vary considerably from one state to the next. Make sure you know what will be required. Also, before subpoenaing documents, be sure to ask if the other side will simply give you photocopies in advance.

A subpoena duces tecum must be directed to the person who is in charge of the documents, books, or records you want produced in court. It may take a few phone calls to find out who this is. Be sure you get this information accurately. If you list someone on the subpoena duces tecum who has nothing to do with the documents, you won't get them. When dealing with a large corporation, public utility, municipal government, and so on, it is wise to list the person who is in overall charge of the department where the records are kept. Thus, if you want records having to do with library fines from a public library, or having to do with business license fees from the city tax and license department, you should not list the city manager or the mayor, but instead the head librarian or the director of the tax and license office.

Example: You are being sued by the city on behalf of the public library for $300 for eight rare books that they state you failed to return. You know that you did return the books, but can't seem to get that across to the library, which insists on treating you like a thief. You learn that each April the library takes a yearly inventory of all books on their shelves. You believe that if you can get access to that inventory, you may be able to figure out where the library misplaced the books, or at least show that a significant percentage of the library's other books are not accounted for, raising the implication that they, not you, lost the books.

Your first step is to ask the library officials to voluntarily open the inventory to you. If they refuse, you may well want to subpoena it. Here's how:

1. Check the "duces tecum" box on the subpoena form.

2. Prepare an affidavit using a form available from the court. It should be brief. Describe the documents you need and why they are necessary to prove issues involved in the case. If you want the custodian of the records to show up in person, give a reason. Don't argue the merits of your case on this form.

3. Have the subpoena issued by the small claims clerk. Then have the subpoena served, being sure that the proof of service (see Chapter 12) is properly filled out and returned to the clerk.

DECLARATION FOR SUBPOENA DUCES TECUM

PLAINTIFF/PETITIONER: Berkeley Public Library	CASE NUMBER:
DEFENDANT/RESPONDENT: John O'Gara	(Fill in number)

**DECLARATION IN SUPPORT OF
SMALL CLAIMS SUBPOENA FOR PERSONAL APPEARANCE
AND PRODUCTION OF DOCUMENT AND THINGS AT TRIAL OR HEARING**
(Code Civil Procedure sections 1985, 1987.5)

1. I, the undersigned, declare I am the ☐ plaintiff ☒ defendant ☐ judgment creditor ☐ other *(specify):* in the above entitled action.

2. The witness has possession or control of the following documents or other things and shall produce them at the time and place specified on the *Small Claims Subpoena* on the first page of this form.

   a. ☒ For trial or hearing *(specify the exact documents or other things to be produced by the witness)*:

      Book inventory information collected by the main branch of the public library during calendar year 20____.

   ☐ Continued on Attachment 2a.

   b. ☐ After trial to enforce a judgment *(specify the exact documents or other things to be produced by the party who is the judgment debtor or other witness possessing records relating to the judgment debtor)*:

      (1) ☐ Payroll receipts, stubs, and other records concerning employment of the party. Receipts, invoices, documents, and other papers or records concerning any and all accounts receivable of the party.

      (2) ☐ Bank account statements, canceled checks, and check registers from any and all bank accounts in which the party has an interest.

      (3) ☐ Savings account passbooks and statements, savings and loan account passbooks and statements, and credit union share account passbooks and statements of the party.

      (4) ☐ Stock certificates, bonds, money market certificates, and any other records, documents, or papers concerning all investments of the party.

      (5) ☐ California registration certificates and ownership certificates for all vehicles registered to the party.

      (6) ☐ Deeds to any and all real property owned or being purchased by the party.

      (7) ☐ Other *(specify):*

3. Good cause exists for the production of the documents or other things described in paragraph 2 for the following reasons:

   My contention is that I returned the books for which the library is suing me. The inventory should back me up on this.

   ☐ Continued on Attachment 3.

4. These documents are material to the issues involved in this case for the following reasons:

   The inventory should specifically include a listing of the books at issue in this case.

   ☐ Continued on Attachment 4.

I declare under penalty of perjury under the laws of the State of California that the foregoing is true and correct.

Date: October 31, 20xx

....
John O'Gara
(TYPE OR PRINT NAME)

▶   *John O'Gara*
           (SIGNATURE OF PARTY)

(See proof of service on page three)

Ask to examine documents prior to your court hearing. The documents you have subpoenaed will be mailed or presented to the court—not to you. You will probably want an opportunity to examine them, and should request it from the judge. The judge may well let you look at them right there in the courtroom while other cases go ahead. Or, if necessary, he or she may continue (delay) the case for a few days and arrange to let you examine the records where they are ordinarily kept (for example, at the library or a place of business).

D. Written Evidence

In most small claims courts, there are no formal rules of evidence requiring that a witness testify in person (but be sure to check your local rules). While it is best to have a witness appear in court, this isn't always possible. A judge will accept written statements from both eyewitnesses ("I was there and saw the filthy apartment") and expert witnesses ("I examined the transmission and found that a rebuilt part was installed improperly").

If you present the written statement of a witness, make sure the witness covers the following points:

For an eyewitness:

- Who the witness is.
- The date of the event.
- What the witness saw, heard, smelled, felt, or tasted, and where and how it happened.

For an expert witness:

- Who the witness is.
- The witness's work and education credentials, which demonstrate expertise in the field. (If credentials are lengthy, it's a good idea to include the person's resume or vita.)
- What the witness did to come up with an opinion, and when it was done. ("On November 2, 20xx, I examined the paint on Mr. Jones's 35-foot Cabin Cruiser and subjected it to the following test ....")

- The witness's conclusion ("the paint used was not suitable for salt water immersion").
- If possible, an estimate of the cost to redo the work properly.
- Any other facts that have a bearing on the dispute.

Make sure you establish your expert's experience and training. If your expert has a resume or vita listing educational and experiential credentials, attach it to the expert's letter. The more distinguished your expert, the more likely the judge is to respect his or her opinion.

Here are examples of letters an eyewitness and an expert witness might write (see Chapter 18 for another written statement by an expert witness):

---

37 Ogden Court
Kansas City, Kansas
September 30, 20xx

Presiding Judge
Small Claims Court
Kansas City, Kansas

Re: John Swift vs. Peter Petrakos
Small Claims Case No. 11478

Your Honor:

    On September 15, 20xx, I witnessed an auto accident a little after 7:30 a.m., involving John Swift and Peter Petrakos. I was about 50 feet away from the accident, parked at the corner of South Dora and 7th streets in Larchville, and could see what happened clearly.

    I clearly saw Mr. Petrakos' Toyota, which was heading north on South Dora, go through a red light and hit Mr. Swift's blue van, which was proceeding east on 7th, well inside the 25 MPH speed limit. I noticed that the traffic light facing Mr. Petrakos did not turn to green for ten seconds or so after the accident, so this was not a case of Mr. Petrakos just being a little early going through an intersection at a light change. It was obvious to me that Mr. Petrakos went through the light while it was fully red.

Sincerely,

Victor Van Cleve

Gail McClosky
47 Penrod Street
Helena, Montana

Sept. 30, 20xx

Judge
Small Claims Division
Helena, Montana

Re: James Dills vs. R&B Construction
Small Claims Case No. 54321

Dear Judge:

I am a fully licensed contractor with 20 years' experience here in Helena (Contractor's License 4021B). For the last ten years I've run my own five-person contracting company specializing in building enclosures and buildings to house horses and other large animals. I enclose a resume outlining my specialized training and experience in this field.

On April 23, 20xx, I was asked by James Dills to inspect several new stalls he had built in the main barn of his Lazy T Ranch by R&B Construction.

In my opinion these stalls are markedly below normal industry standards for three reasons:

1) They are too small for the animals intended to be kept in them. [Continue with details.]

2) Walls and doors are built of plywood too thin to safely contain an agitated animal. [Continue with details.]

3) Construction is so rough in several regards as to pose a danger of injury to an animal intended to be kept there. [Continue with details.]

In conclusion, I believe the stalls are so poorly constructed they can't reasonably be upgraded to provide safe habitable housing for horses. Were they mine, I would rip them out and start over.

Sincerely,

Gail McClosky

E. Judges as Witnesses

The conscientious small claims court judge has a fair amount of discretion to climb down off the bench and check out physical evidence. This can be a valuable technique. For example, in a dispute involving a defective automobile paint job, it would be silly to spend time waxing eloquent about the damage when you can just show the judge a photo. Better yet, ask the judge to walk down to the courthouse parking lot and look at your pigment-challenged steed. It makes sense to bring physical evidence if it meets these three criteria:

• showing it to the judge will help your case

• it will fit through the door, and

• bringing it into the courtroom is not dangerous or inappropriate, as would be the case with an animal, firearm, or something extremely dirty or smelly.

But what if your evidence is impossible to bring into the courtroom (a car with a poor paint job or a supposedly pedigreed puppy that grew up looking as if Lassie were the mother and Rin Tin Tin the father)? Why not ask the judge to accompany you outside the building to examine the car, the dog, or whatever else is important to your case? Many (but not all) judges are willing to do so if they feel it is necessary to better understand the dispute and won't take too long. For example, one excellent judge I know was disturbed one morning when two eyewitnesses gave seriously contradictory testimony about a traffic accident. He questioned both in detail and then took the case under submission. That evening, he drove over to the relevant corner. Once there, it was clear that one of the witnesses couldn't possibly have seen the accident from the spot on which she claimed to be standing (in front of a particular restaurant). The judge decided the case in favor of the other.

⚠ Don't waste a judge's time. Never ask a judge to leave the courtroom to view evidence if you can prove your case just as well by other means, such as witnesses and pictures. A good approach is to do as much as you can in court, and to ask the judge to view evidence outside of court only if it is essential. Sometimes it clearly is.

F. Testimony by Telephone

A surprising number of small claims court judges will take testimony over the phone if a witness cannot be present because he or she is ill, disabled, or out of state, or can't take time off from work. While procedures vary, some courts will set up conference calls so that the opposing party has the opportunity to hear what is being said and to respond.

Don't just assume that your local court will allow telephone testimony. Ask the clerk. If you get a negative response, don't give up—ask the judge when you get into the courtroom. It is also an extremely good idea to have a letter from the witness whom you want to reach by phone, explaining what he or she will testify to (for example, your opponent's car ran a red light and broadsided you) and why it is impossible for him or her to be in court. Such a letter might look like the one in Section D, above, except the witness should add:

"Mr. Swift has asked me to testify on his behalf, and normally I would be happy to do so—however, I will be in New York City on business during the months of October, November, and December 20xx and cannot be present.

"I have asked Mr. Swift to let me know the day and approximate time of the court hearing and have told him that I will give him a phone number where I can be reached. If you think it desirable, I will be pleased to give my testimony by phone."

■

CHAPTER

16

Presenting Your Case to the Judge

A. Uncontested Cases—Getting a Judgment by Default

You may get a pleasant surprise when you arrive at the courthouse for your hearing— your opponent may simply not show up. If this occurs, the judge will first check to see that the defendant was properly served with court papers. Then, in most states, you will be asked to briefly state the basic facts of your case and possibly to show the judge some documentary evidence, such as a copy of the written contract you claim the defendant broke. Once this is done you will be eligible to have a default judgment entered on your behalf. In the few states that require a defendant to file a written answer (see the Appendix), you should be able to find out before the court date whether the other side will appear. The next step is to ask what, if anything, you must do to get your default judgment.

Assuming you will be required to make an in-court presentation, you should be prepared to accomplish it in a few sentences.

Example: "Your Honor, I own the Racafrax Auto Repair Shop. On January 11, 2xxx, I repaired defendant's 2000 Ford Explorer. He paid me $500 and agreed to pay another $500 on March 1. He has not made the second payment. I have copies of the contract defendant signed and of several unpaid bills I sent him. I am asking for a judgment of $500 plus $55 for my court filing fee and the cost of having the papers served."

Don't make a longwinded presentation at the default hearing. If the other side doesn't show up, a judge only wants to hear the minimum facts necessary to support a judgment on your behalf. In the absence of your opponent, the judge will assume your version of what happened is true.

Assuming the judge is satisfied that there is no obvious defect in your case, he or she will enter a judgment for the amount of your request. A defendant who doesn't show up to argue his or her case usually can't appeal to a formal court (see Chapter 24) unless the default is first set aside. (See Chapter 11, Section F.)

In some small claims courts, such as those in Washington, DC, you won't even have to enter the courtroom if your case is for an unpaid debt and you have good documentation, such as a contract and copies of unpaid bills. A court clerk, not the judge, will enter the default judgment.

Occasionally, a person who has defaulted will show up in court a few days later with a good excuse. If the defaulting party makes a motion to set aside the default within a relatively short time (almost always 30 days or less), the judge in most states may—but does not have to—set it aside. The party who missed the first hearing has the job of convincing the judge that the reason he or she didn't show up or phone earlier is good enough to justify setting aside the default. (See Chapter 11 for more on setting aside a default.)

B. Contested Cases

Assume now that both sides show up and step forward when the case is called by the clerk. What happens next? First, the judge will establish everyone's identity. These will often be the principal people involved in the dispute, but in some states might include a collection agency or an attorney. Also, in many states, businesses can be represented by employees. Thus, a dentist or store owner could send a bookkeeper to establish that a bill wasn't paid.

Next, the judge will ask the plaintiff or his or her representative to briefly state his or her case; don't be thrown off if the judge does this casually, such as by asking, "What can I do for you today?" But before we focus on the plaintiff's and defendant's presentations, here are a few tips that both parties should find helpful. These are not rules written on golden tablets, only suggestions. Depending on the situation, you may want to follow some and ignore others.

- Stand when you make your initial presentation to the judge. This should give you a sense of confidence at a time when you may understandably be a little nervous. It's fine to sit while your opponent is talking. If the judge interrupts your opponent's presentation to ask you a quick question, there is no need to leap to your feet to answer it.

- Be as brief as you can while still explaining and documenting your case thoroughly.

- Start with the end of the story, not the beginning. That is, describe your loss and how much you are asking for. Then go back and tell your story chronologically.

- Don't read your statement. Reading in court is almost always a bore. But you may find it helpful to make a few notes on a card to serve as a reminder in case you get nervous or forget something. If you decide to do this, list the headings of the various points you want to make in an outline form. Be sure your list is easy to read at a glance and that the topics are in the correct order. (See Chapter 14, Section J for a sample list.)

- Never interrupt your opponent or any of the witnesses, no matter how outrageous their "lies." You will get your chance to respond.

- Try to present any portion of your case that is difficult to explain verbally in another way. This often means bringing to court your used car parts, damaged clothing, or other exhibits, such as photographs or canceled checks, and presenting them to the judge in an organized fashion. Short videos can be helpful, but call in advance to see whether the court will have a VCR.

- There will usually be a blackboard in court. If drawings will be helpful, as is almost always true in cases involving car accidents, be sure to ask the judge for permission to use the blackboard. You will want to draw clearly and legibly the first time, so it's wise to practice in advance.

- If you are the defendant, don't repeat uncontested facts already presented by the plaintiff (for example, that the two of you had a fender bender at a certain corner in a certain city at a certain time during certain weather conditions). Instead, focus on the point of your principal disagreement (like whether the light facing you was green or red) and introduce evidence to prove that point.

Practice your presentation early and often. As emphasized throughout this book, it pays to practice your oral presentation ahead of time. Have a tough-minded friend or family member play the part of judge and be ready to ask questions and try to poke holes in your best points. Use any evidence or visuals that you plan to present in court. Run through your presentation several times until you get it right.

1. From the Plaintiff's Side

If you are the plaintiff, you should clearly tell the judge what the dispute is about before you start describing the details of what happened. I call this starting with the end, not the beginning, of your story.

If your case involves a car accident, you might start by saying,

"This case involves a car accident at Cedar and Rose Streets in which my car suffered $872 worth of damage when the defendant ran a red light and hit my front fender,"

NOT

"It all started when I was driving down Rose Street after having two eggs and a bagel with cream cheese for breakfast."

Only occasionally have I seen a case where the plaintiff's initial presentation should take longer than five minutes. As part of your statement, you should present and explain the relevance of any papers, photos, or other documentary evidence. Hand these to the clerk, who will pass them on to the judge. You should also be sure to tell the judge if you have any witnesses to present.

If you have done legal research and believe that a statute or court decision supports your position, call it to the attention of the judge as part of your oral presentation. If possible, it's also a good idea to back this up with a brief written memo. Begin with the name and number of your case. Then list the official citation of the statute, ordinance, or court case you think helps your case, and briefly explain why. (See Chapter 1, Section D for an explanation of how statutes and cases are cited.) In court, give one copy of your memo to the clerk to hand to the judge and another to your opponent.

SAMPLE MEMO

MEMORANDUM

Lee vs. Yew

Small Claims #127654

To: Small Claims Judge

From: Robert Yew, Defendant

Re: California Law on boundary trees

This case involves Mr. Lee, my next-door neighbor, who is suing me because he claims my Monterey Pine tree drops debris on his roof and yard. Although he is asking for a judgment of $500 for clean-up costs, what he really wants is for me to pay several thousand dollars to remove the 80-foot tree.

There is only one problem with Mr. Lee's argument—because the tree touches our boundary line, the tree is half his. That's because California law, as set forth in Civil Code Section 834, clearly states that "Trees whose trunks stand partly on the land of two or more coterminous owners, belong to them in common."

Mr. Lee will argue that the tree was planted 100% on my property by the person who owned the house before I bought it and that the tree is still 90% on my side of the property line. Both contentions are true, but as you can see under Civil Code Section 834, it makes no difference. As long as the tree touches the boundary line—which the photographs I have presented to the court clearly prove—the tree belongs to both of us as co-owners (tenants in common) (*Anderson v. Weiland,* 12 CA 2d 730 (1936)).

I have offered to try to mediate the dispute, but so far Mr. Lee says, "No." I hope he will change his mind.

Respectfully submitted,

August 10, 20xx

Robert Yew

Your witnesses will usually be given a chance to speak after you complete your presentation. The witnesses should be well prepared to state their key information in an organized way (for example, that the witness inspected an apartment immediately after you did your final clean-up and found it to be clean). Too often, a witness either leaves out important points or is so disorganized that the force of the testimony is lost.

Just as is true with your presentation, the best way to be sure your witness really will be able to succinctly and concisely explain to the judge the key facts that support your case is to have the witness practice in advance. As long as the witness sticks to the truth, rehearsing the exact words he or she will say in court is completely legal. I suggest meeting with your witness and a friend you have asked to act as a mock judge. Start by presenting your case to the mock judge exactly as you plan to do it in court. Then ask your witness to stand and present his or her testimony.

If at first your witness is a little disorganized or unsure, work with him or her to develop a short convincing presentation that covers all key points. When the witness says something that sounds good, have the witness write it down—and practice it several times before your court date.

When the plaintiff and any witnesses are finished—or sometimes even before the plaintiff has made a decent start—the judge is likely to ask questions. Never put the judge off by saying you'll get to the point he or she is interested in later in your presentation. It is best to satisfy the judge's curiosity by answering the questions directly and concisely. Just be sure that you and your witnesses eventually get a chance to make all of your full presentation. If you feel rushed, say so. The judge will normally slow things down a little. If you appear before a volunteer lawyer (called an arbitrator in New York), you can expect the case to be heard even less formally, with the arbitrator taking an active role in questioning the parties and witnesses.

2. From the Defendant's Side

Sooner or later it will be your turn. Defendants often get so angry at something the plaintiff has said that when they finally get to speak, they attack angrily. This is usually counterproductive. Far better to calmly and clearly present your side of the dispute to the judge. Start with the key point of contention, and then fill in the details of what happened from your point of view. If the plaintiff has made false or misleading statements, you should definitely point them out. But to show the judge how calm and fair-minded you are, it is usually best to wait until the end of your presentation to point out your opponent's misstatements.

Example: "Your Honor, it's true that the bumper of my truck hit the defendant's fender and pushed it in slightly. But the key thing I want you to understand is that this happened because defendant's pickup entered the intersection before it was clear of the cars which were already there, including mine. Therefore the accident was his fault. Let me give you a little background. I was driving south on Cedar and entered the intersection just as the light first turned yellow. I slowed briefly near the center line behind a car that was turning left and then continued across, at which point defendant's car darted in front of me. Therefore when the defendant says the intersection was clear when he entered it—and that I ran a red light—he is not correct. Let me introduce you to Mr. Ed Jones, who witnessed what happened and will back up everything I've told you."

Like the plaintiff, the defendant should be prepared to present documentary evidence and, if possible, witnesses that will back up his or her story. And if any statutes or court decisions are relevant, call them to the judge's attention by preparing a brief memo as described in Section B1, just above.

3. A Sample Case

Now let's look at how a contested case might be presented from both the plaintiff's and defendant's perspectives.

Clerk: "The next case is *John Andrews v. Robertson Realty*. Will everyone please come forward?" (Four people come forward and sit at the table facing the judge.)

Judge: "Good morning. Which one of you is Mr. Andrews? Okay, will you begin, Mr. Andrews?"

John Andrews: (stands) "This is a case about a landlord's failure to return my $700 cleaning deposit, your Honor. I rented a house from Robertson Realty at 1611 Spruce Street in Rockford in March of 2xxx on a month-to-month tenancy. On January 10, 2xxx, I sent Mr. Robertson a written notice that I was planning to move on March 10. In fact, I moved out on March 8 and left the place extremely clean. I know it was clean because I spent eight hours, a lot of them on my hands and knees, cleaning it. In addition, all of my rent was properly paid. A few days after I moved out, I asked Mr. Robertson to return my $700 deposit. He wrote me a letter stating that the place was dirty and he was keeping my deposit.

"I have with me a copy of a letter I wrote to Mr. Robertson on March 15 setting out my position in more detail. I also have some photographs that my friend, Carol Spann, who is here as a witness, took on the day I moved out. I believe the pictures show pretty clearly that I did a thorough clean-up." (John Andrews hands the letter and pictures to the clerk, who hands them to the judge.)

"Your Honor, I am asking not only for the $700 deposit, but also for $500 in punitive damages, plus 2% monthly interest, which the law of this state allows a tenant when a landlord improperly refuses to return a deposit."

Judge: "Mr. Andrews, will you introduce your witness?"

Andrews: "Yes. This is Carol Spann. She helped me clean up and move on March 7 and 8."

Judge: (looking at the pictures) "Ms. Spann, were you in the house the day John Andrews moved out?"

Carol Spann: (standing) "Yes, your Honor, I was—and the day before, too. I helped clean up, and I can say that we did a good job. Not only did we do the normal washing and scrubbing, but we waxed the kitchen floor, cleaned the bathroom tile, and shampooed the rugs."

Judge: (turning to Mr. Robertson) "Okay, now it's your turn to tell me why the deposit wasn't returned."

Harry Robertson: (standing) "I don't know how they could have cleaned the place up, your Honor, because it was filthy when I inspected it on March 9. Let me give you a few specifics. There was mildew and mold around the bathtub, the windows were filthy, the refrigerator hadn't been defrosted, and there was dog—how shall I say it— dog manure in the basement. Your Honor, I have brought along Clem Houndstooth as a witness. Mr. Houndstooth is the tenant who moved in three days after Mr. Andrews moved out. Incidentally, your Honor, the place was so dirty that I only charged Mr. Houndstooth a $200 cleaning deposit, because he agreed to clean it up himself."

Judge: (looking at Clem Houndstooth) "Do you wish to say something?"

Clem Houndstooth: (standing) "Yes, I do. Mr. Robertson asked me to come down and back him up and I am glad to do it, because I put in two full days cleaning that place up. I like a clean house, your Honor, not a halfway clean, halfway dirty house. I just don't think that a house is clean if the oven is full of gunk, there is mold in the bathroom and the insides of the cupboards are grimy. All these conditions existed at 1611 Spruce St. when I moved in. I just don't believe that anyone could think that place was clean."

Judge: "Mr. Andrews, do you have anything to add?"

Andrews: (standing up) "Yes, I sure do. First, as to the mildew problem. The house is 40 years old and there is some dampness in the wall of the bathroom. Maybe there is a leaky pipe someplace behind the tile. I cleaned it a number of times, but it always came back. I talked to Mr. Fisk in Mr. Robertson's office about the problem about a month after I moved in, and he told me that I would have to do the best I could because they couldn't afford to tear the wall apart. As to the cupboards and stove, they are both old. The cabinets haven't been painted in 10 years, so, of course, they aren't perfect. And that old stove was a lot dirtier when I moved in than it is now, since I can tell you I personally worked on it with oven cleaner for over an hour."

Judge: "What about the refrigerator, Mr. Andrews? Was that defrosted?"

Andrews: "No, your Honor, it wasn't, but it had been defrosted about three weeks before I moved out, and I thought that it was good enough the way it was."

Judge: "Okay, if no one else has anything to add, I want to return your pictures and letters. You will receive my decision by mail in a few days."

Now, I have a little surprise for you. The case I just presented was a real case. As they used to say on *Dragnet*, "Only the names have been changed to protect the innocent." And I have another surprise for you. I spoke to the judge after the court session. Here is how he decided the case:

"This is a typical case in which both sides have some right on their side. What is clean to one person may be dirty to another. Based on what I heard, I would have to guess that the old tenant made a fairly conscientious effort to clean up and probably left the place about as clean as it was when he moved in, but that the new tenant, Houndstooth, had much higher standards, and convinced the landlord that it was filthy. The landlord may not have needed too much convincing, since he probably would just as well keep the deposit. But I did hear enough to convince me that Andrews, the old tenant, didn't do a perfect job cleaning up. My decision will be that Andrews gets a judgment for the return of $450 of the $700 deposit, with no extra damages. I believe that $250 is more than enough to compensate the landlord for any damages he suffered as a result of the apartment 'being a little dirty.' "

I then asked the judge if he felt the case was well presented. He replied substantially as follows:

"Better than average. I think I got a pretty good idea of what the problems were. The witnesses were helpful, and the pictures suggested that the place wasn't a total mess. Both sides could have done better, however. Andrews could have had a witness talk about the condition when he moved in if it was truly dirtier than when he left. Another witness to testify to the apartment's cleanliness when he moved out would have been good, too. His friend, Carol Spann, seemed to be a very close friend, and I wasn't sure that she was objective when it came to judging whether the place was clean. The landlord, Robertson, could also have done better. He could have presented a more disinterested witness, although I must say that Houndstooth's testimony was pretty convincing. Also, he could have had pictures documenting the dirty conditions and an estimate from a cleaning company for how much they would have charged to clean the place up. Without going to too much trouble, I think both sides could have probably done somewhat better with more thorough preparation."

C. Don't Forget to Ask for Your Costs

Both plaintiff and defendant are entitled to ask that a judgment in their favor include any recoverable costs, such as for filing and serving court papers or subpoenaing essential witnesses. Sometimes defendants have no costs, unless a necessary witness is subpoenaed. In most states, the winner can recover:

- The plaintiff's court filing fee (defendants pay no fee to appear unless they file a counterclaim).

- Service of process costs. A plaintiff must pay this fee unless a friend serves the papers, as is allowed in some states. Fees vary from a few dollars in states where certified mail is allowed, to considerably more if professional process service is required. A defendant will normally only pay to serve papers if she files a countersuit. (In some states, both parties must try and fail to serve papers by mail as a condition of the court awarding higher fees for a process server—see Chapter 12.)

- Subpoenaed witness fees. Both the plaintiff and defendant can incur this cost if a witness must be subpoenaed and claims a fee. (In some courts, witness fees must be approved by the judge ahead of time.) Generally, fees for subpoenaing witnesses and documents are only recoverable if the judge believes the person or documentary evidence was really necessary.

- The cost of obtaining necessary documents, such as verification of car ownership by the D.M.V. (Both plaintiffs and defendants can incur these costs.)

You can't recover for such personal expenses as taking time off from work to prepare for or attend court, paying a babysitter, parking your car, or making photocopies of evidence. For information on recovering collection costs incurred *after* judgment when your opponent won't voluntarily pay, see Chapter 25. ■

CHAPTER

17

Motor Vehicle Repair Cases

Most small claims court cases fall into a dozen or so broad categories, with perhaps another dozen subcategories. In the next six chapters, I look at the most common types of cases and discuss strategies to handle each. Even if your fact situation doesn't fit neatly into one of these categories, it makes sense to read them. By picking up a few hints here and a little information there, you should be able to piece together a good plan of action. For example, many of the suggestions I make to handle motor vehicle repair disputes can be applied to cases involving major appliances, such as televisions, washers, and expensive stereos.

Let's start by imagining that you go to the auto repair shop to pick up your trusty, but slightly graying, steed after a complete engine overhaul. The bill, as agreed to by you in advance, is $1,225. This always seemed a little steep, but the mechanic had talked you into it based on his claim that he would do a great job and that, when the work is done, the engine should last another 50,000 miles. At any rate, you write out a check and drive out of the garage in something approaching a cheerful mood. One of life's more disagreeable hassles has been taken care of, at least temporarily. Unfortunately, as most of us have learned through hard experience, "temporarily" can sometimes be a very short time. In this case, it lasts only until you head up the first hill. What's that funny noise, you think? Why don't I have more power? "Oh shit," you say (you rarely swear, but this is one of those times when nothing else will do). You turn around and drive back to the garage. Not only are you out $1,225, but your car runs worse than it did when you brought it in.

Funny, no one seems as pleasant as they did before. And no one appears to have time to listen to you. Finally, after a bit of foot stomping, you get someone to say they will look the car over. You take a bus home, trying not to be paranoid. The next day you call the garage. Nothing has been done. You yell at the garage owner and then call your bank to stop payment on the check. You are told it has already been cashed. The next day the garage owner tells you the problem is in a part of the engine they didn't work on. You only paid for a "short block job," he tells you. "Give us another $500 and we can surely solve this new problem," he adds.

In disgust, you go down and pick up your handicapped friend and drive it home—slowly. You are furious, and you decide to pursue every legal remedy, no matter what the trouble. How do you start?

First, park your car, take a shower, and have a glass of wine, milk, or whatever seems calming. Nothing gets decided well when you're mad. Now, following the approach presented in this book, ask yourself these two key questions:

A. Have You Suffered a Loss?

That's easy. Your car works worse than it did before, you shelled out a lot of money to have it fixed, and the garage wants more to fix it. Clearly, you have suffered a loss.

B. Can You Prove the Defendant's Negligence Caused Your Loss?

Ah ha, now we get to the nitty gritty. In this type of case, you can almost always expect the garage to claim they did their work properly and the car simply needs more work. For all the judge knows, this may even be true. It's your job to prove that the repair work was not up to a reasonable standard of competence. Doing so will make your case; failing to do so will break it. You'd better get to work.

Step 1. Collect Available Evidence

First, gather all the relevant evidence, pronto. In this situation, this means getting your used parts (it's a good idea to do this anytime you have major work done—some states require mechanics to give them to you). If the garage will not give them to you, make your request by letter, keeping a copy for your file. If you get the parts, fine—if you don't, you have evidence that the garage is badly run or has something to hide.

Step 2. Have the Car Checked by an Expert

Before you drive many miles, have your car checked by an established local mechanic or mechanics. Sometimes you can get a free estimate from a repair shop if the shop thinks it will get the job of fixing your car. In this situation, however, you may be better off paying for someone to look at the engine thoroughly, with the understanding that if the need arises, he or she will testify on your behalf in small claims court or, at the very least, write a convincing letter stating what's wrong with the engine. One way to try to accomplish this is to take your car to a garage that a friend patronizes and recommends. A few states require that you present three written estimates in small claims court. Whether this is required or not, it's a good idea to have them.

Step 3. Try to Settle Your Case

By now, you should have a pretty good idea of what the first garage did wrong. Call them and ask either that the job be redone, or that they give you a refund of part or all of your money. Often the repair shop will agree to do additional work to avoid a hassle. If they agree to take the car back, insist on a written agreement detailing what they will do and how long it will take. Also, talk to the mechanic who will actually work on the car to be sure he or she understands what needs to be done. Naturally, you may be a little paranoid about giving your car back to the garage that screwed it up, but unless they have been outrageously incompetent, this is probably your best approach—it's usually easier to get work redone than to get a big refund. Also, if you sue and the garage owner shows up in court and says he or she offered to work on the car again but you refused, it may weaken your case.

Step 4.   Write a Demand Letter

If the garage isn't cooperative, it's time to write a formal demand letter. Remember the discussion in Chapter 6. Your letter should be short, polite, and written with an eye to a judge reading it. In this situation, you could write something like the one below.

Jorge Sotomayor
15 Orange St.
Hamden, CT

Happy Days Motors
100 Speedway
New Haven, CT

Dear People:

On August 13, 20xx, I brought my 1993 Dodge to your garage. You agreed to do a complete engine rebuild job for $1,225. You told me, "Your car will be running like a watch when we're through with it." The car worked well when I brought it in, but was a little short on power. Two days later, when I picked up my car, it barely moved at all. The engine made such a clanging noise that I have been afraid to drive it.

I have repeatedly asked you to fix the car or to refund my money. You have refused. Shortly after the work was done, I asked for my used parts to be returned. You refused to give them to me, even though it is a violation of state law.

I have had two mechanics look my car over since you worked on it. They both agree that you did your job improperly and even installed some used parts instead of new ones. The work you did on the engine rings was particularly badly done.

After receiving no response from you, I had the work redone at a cost of $900. [Most small claims courts do not require that you actually have the work redone before going to court, but a few, such as New York City, require a repair bill marked "Paid."] My car now works well. Please refund my $1,225. Should you fail to do so, I will exhaust all my legal remedies, including complaining to interested state and local agencies and taking this dispute to small claims court. I hope to hear from you promptly.

Jorge Sotomayor

cc: Connecticut Dept. of Consumer Affairs
      Bureau of Automotive Repair
      Hartford, CT

 **Be sure to emphasize any promise (warranty) made by the garage.** Most small independent garages don't make any written warranty or guarantee of their work. However, if you were given any promises in writing, mention them here in your letter. Also, if you were told things orally about the quality of the work the garage planned to do and you relied on these statements as part of your decision to have the work done, you should call attention to this express verbal warranty. (See Chapter 2.)

Step 5. File Your Court Papers

If you still get no satisfactory response from the garage, file your papers at the small claims clerk's office of your local small claims court. Reread Chapters 8 through 11.

Step 6. Prepare for Court

If you want the judge to understand your case, you must understand it yourself. Sounds simple, doesn't it? It did to me, too, until I got involved with a case involving a botched car repair. All I really knew was that after I had paid to have the engine fixed, the darn thing was not supposed to belch black smoke and make a disgusting noise. I really wasn't interested in the details.

But, fortunately, I realized that for me to argue my case in small claims with this level of ignorance would likely end in a bad loss. To be able to convince a judge that the mechanic had ripped me off, I needed to do some homework. After all, I could expect the people from the garage to show up in court with a terrific-sounding story about the wonderful job they did. I clearly needed to be prepared to cope with their talk about pistons, bearings, and turning the cam shaft so as to convince the judge that they botched the job.

It turned out that 15 minutes' conversation with a knowledgeable mechanic was all I really needed to understand what the mechanic did wrong. (Also, my local library had several car manuals, complete with diagrams, which were a big help.) In court, armed with my new knowledge, I had no trouble explaining to the judge that the mechanic had done a substandard job and getting a judgment for the full amount I had paid.

Remember, the judge is probably not a mechanic. Pay attention to the person to whom you are presenting your case. Most small claims judges probably don't understand the insides of cars any better than you do. After all, people often become lawyers because they don't like to get their hands dirty. So be prepared to deal with a judge who nods wisely but doesn't really understand the difference between the drive shaft and the axle.

Step 7. Appearing in Court

When you appear in court, be sure you are well organized. Bring all the letters you have written, or received, about your car problem, as well as written warranties (if any), photographs if they are helpful, and your used parts if they aid in making your case. If you have a witness to any oral statements (warranties) made by the garage, be sure to bring that person with you to court. Also, be sure to present any letters written by independent garage people who have examined your car. A well-written letter from an expert saying that for the amount of money you paid, the engine should have been fixed, is likely to be particularly effective.

If you are well prepared, you should win the sort of case outlined here without difficulty. Judges drive cars and have to get them fixed, so they tend to be sympathetic to this type of consumer complaint. Simply present your story (see Chapter 16), your documentation, and your witnesses. If you feel your opponent is snowing the judge with a lot of technical lingo, get His or Her Honor back on track by asking that the technical terms be explained in ordinary English. This will be a relief to everyone in the courtroom except your opponent. You will likely find that, once the defendant's case is shorn of all the magic words, it will shrink from a tiger to a pussycat.

A good drawing can help. Several times in cases involving machinery, I have seen people give effective testimony by presenting a large drawing illustrating the screw-up. This approach is most effective when your expert appears in court and authoritatively points to the drawing to detail the problem.

Step 8: Ask for a Continuance in the Middle of Your Presentation If It Is Essential

The best-laid plans can occasionally go haywire. Perhaps a key witness doesn't show up, or maybe, despite careful preparation, you overlook some aspect of the case that the judge feels is crucial. If this occurs, you may want to ask the judge to reschedule the case on another day so that you can prepare better. It is perfectly proper to make this sort of request. Whether or not it will be granted is up to the judge. If he or she feels that more evidence isn't likely to change the result, or that you are making the request to stall, it will not be granted. If there is a good reason for a delay, however, it will usually be allowed. But if you want a delay, you have to ask for it—the judge isn't going to be able to read your mind. ■

Motor Vehicle Purchase Cases

Occasionally someone buys a vehicle and drives it a short way, only to have it fall apart. And all too often, the seller won't stand behind the product sold or work out some sort of fair adjustment. What can you do if you are the victim of this kind of rip-off? There are major differences between buying a new vehicle from a dealer, buying a used vehicle from a dealer, and buying a used vehicle from a private party, so let's look at each situation individually.

A. New Vehicles

A common problem with new vehicles occurs when you end up with a lemon—a car or truck with major manufacturing defects. Here is an example:

Example: You trade in your rusty '88 bomb that served you well for longer than you want to remember and fork over a ridiculously large pile of money on a shiny new car. Your new carriage runs fine for a few months, but then it begins to vibrate uncontrollably whenever you drive over 50 mph. You take it back to the dealer, who tries to fix it, but it still shakes. You take it back again, and again, but it's still not right. By now you're fed up. You paid for a new car that's supposed to work, and you feel you should either get a full refund or a replacement. How can you do this?

A large majority of states have enacted some sort of "lemon law" to protect consumers in your situation. Although the laws vary a little from state to state, most follow the same basic structure: If your new car has a substantial defect that cannot be repaired after repeated attempts or 30 days of service, you have a right to a refund or replacement vehicle from the manufacturer if you notify them of the problem and submit to arbitration. The arbitration is free, and you don't need a lawyer.

 For more information on lemon laws, see the following websites:

- www.autopedia.com/html/HotLinks_Lemon.html (includes individual summaries of each state's lemon laws)
- http://cartalk.cars.com/Got-A-Car/Lemon (yes, it's the guys you hear on the radio)
- www.autosafety.org/lemonlaws.html (includes information on defects common to particular car models)
- www.consumerlaw.org (by the National Consumer Law Center; for a reasonable price, you can order their book, *Return to Sender: Getting a Refund or Replacement for Your Lemon Car*, by Nancy Barron).

1. Enforcing Your Lemon Rights

To qualify for a refund or replacement under most lemon laws, you (or, rather, your car) must meet the following conditions:

- **Substantial Defect.** Your new car must have a defect within the first year. The defect must substantially impair the car's use, value, or safety (or some combination of the three). Unfortunately, many lemons have lots of little problems rather than one big one, and most lemon laws don't recognize this.

- **Opportunity to Repair.** The dealer or manufacturer gets three or four (depending on the state) chances to fix the defect within the first year, but can't keep the car in the shop for more than a total of 30 days. If the defect can't be fixed, the car is legally a lemon. (Note that the 30 total days during the year need not be consecutive; also, some states only count "business" days.) Most states treat each defect separately, and thus allow four repair attempts or 30 days for each one. A few states, however, allow the dealer only four repairs or 30 days to cure all the defects.

- **Notice to Manufacturer.** You must notify the manufacturer about the repairs as they are being done. In most states, this requirement is satisfied by simply taking the car to the dealer, because the dealer contacts the manufacturer for reimbursement for all repairs done under warranty. It's a good idea, however, to keep your own written chronology of repair attempts and not just rely on the dealer. You then have a document you can send to the manufacturer if you later request a refund or replacement, and you also have evidence for your small claims suit.

  If you've given the manufacturer three or four tries or 30 days to fix your car and it's still defective, it's time to ask for a refund or a replacement vehicle. This request must be made to the manufacturer in writing. Several states, including Alaska, Colorado, Florida, and Michigan, require this notice to be sent by certified mail. Even if your state has no such requirement, it makes sense to have proof that the manufacturer received your notice.

- **Arbitration.** After you've made your demand, most states require you to submit it to arbitration. In most states, you must use the manufacturer's arbitrator, if it has one (most major companies do). These arbitrators or arbitration boards must meet federal and/or state standards of impartiality. (The federal standards are at 16 C.F.R. § 703.) Arbitration must be free and designed to be conducted without a lawyer. You explain the problem to the arbitrator, either in person or in writing, and the arbitrator rules within 60 days whether your car is a lemon and whether you're entitled to a refund, replacement, or something less. The arbitrator, however, will not award consequential damages, such as the cost of a car you had to rent while your car was in the shop. For that you have to go to court.

In all likelihood, the manufacturer will try to settle before you ever get to arbitration. Manufacturers hate to buy back cars or give replacements, because they get stuck with a defective car that they have to resell as a used car, at a substantial loss. (One study showed that GM settled 90% of its cases before they reached arbitration. Of the 10% who did arbitrate, 60% got more than GM's final offer.)

If the arbitrator decides you don't qualify for a refund or a replacement, you can take your case to court. If you go to small claims court, you'll be limited by the maximum amount your state allows in recovery. If you go to a formal court and hire an attorney, the attorney's fees may exceed the cost of fixing the car, and your case may not be heard for several years.

2. If Your Car Doesn't Qualify as a Lemon

Unfortunately, many disputes involving new vehicles don't fall under the lemon law. This would be the situation if the same defect didn't recur four times, or if problems develop just after the warranty expires.

Sometimes it seems as though there is a little destruct switch set to flip 15 minutes after you hit the end of the warranty period. Often, too, a problem starts to surface while the car is still under warranty, and a dealer makes inadequate repairs that last scarcely longer than the remainder of the warranty term. When the same problem develops again after the warranty has run out, the dealer refuses to fix it.

Not long ago I saw a case involving this sort of problem. A man—let's call him Bruno—with a new, expensive European car was suing the local dealer and the parent car company's West Coast representative. Bruno claimed that he had repeatedly brought the car into the dealer's repair shop with transmission problems while it was still under the manufacturer's written warranty. Each time adjustments were made that seemed to eliminate the problem. But each time, after a month or so, the same problem would reappear. A few months after the written warranty ran out, the transmission died. Even though the car was only a little over a year old, and had gone less than 20,000 miles, both the dealer and the parent car company refused to repair it. Their refusals continued even though Bruno repeatedly wrote them, demanding action.

How did Bruno go about dealing with his problem? First, because he needed his car, he went ahead and had the repairs made. Then, although the repairs cost slightly more than the small claims limit, he decided that because it was too expensive to hire a lawyer and sue in a formal court, he would scale down his claim and sue for the small claims maximum. Because the dealer was located in the same city as Bruno, he sued locally. In this situation, it would have been adequate to sue only the local dealer and not the car company, but it didn't hurt to sue both, following the general rule, "When in doubt, sue all possible defendants."

In court, Bruno was well prepared and had a reasonably easy time. Both he and his wife testified as to their trials and tribulations with the car. They gave the judge copies of the several letters they had written the dealer, one of which included a list of the dates they had taken the car to the dealer's shop while it was still under warranty. They also produced a letter from the owner of the independent garage that finally fixed the transmission. The letter stated that, when the owner took the transmission apart, he discovered a defect in its original assembly. The new car dealer simply testified that his mechanics had done their best to fix the car under the written warranty. He then contended that, once the written warranty had run out, he was no longer responsible. The dealer made no effort to challenge the car owner's story, nor did he bring his own mechanics to testify as to what they had done while the car was still under warranty. Bruno won. He presented a convincing case that the defect had never been fixed when it should have been under the written warranty. The dealer did nothing to rebut it. As the judge noted to me after the hearing, an expensive car should come with a transmission that lasts a lot longer than this one did. Bruno would have had an even stronger case if he had brought the independent garage man to court, but the letters, along with his own testimony and that of his wife, were adequate in a situation where the dealer didn't put up much of a defense.

Document all attempts to have your vehicle repaired. Make sure the judge knows about all the trips you have made to the dealer's repair shop. You may be able to find copies of work orders you signed, or your canceled checks. If you don't have this sort of record, sit down with a calendar and do your best to make an accurate reconstruction of the dates you brought your car in for repair. Give the list to the judge in court. The judge will accept it as true unless the car dealer disputes it.

Even if your car is no longer covered by a written warranty when trouble develops, you may have a case. When a relatively new car falls apart for no good reason, many small claims court judges bend over backwards to give you protection over and above the actual written warranty period that comes with the vehicle. One reason for this is that many states have warranty laws that require a product to be reasonably fit for normal use. These laws have been interpreted to give the consumer more rights than the limited warranty that comes with the car. Thus, if the engine on your properly maintained car burns out after 25,000 miles, you will stand a good chance of recovering some money even if the written warranty has expired.

Investigate the possibility of a secret warranty. After a car has been in production for awhile, a pattern of problems or failures often develops. Manufacturers are extremely sensitive to complaints in "high problem" areas and may even have issued an internal memo telling dealers to fix certain types of problems upon request. One reason for this is that they want to avoid federal government-required recalls. How can knowing this benefit you? By giving you the opportunity to pressure the company where it is most vulnerable. If your car that is no longer covered by a written warranty develops a serious problem before it should, talk to people at independent garages that specialize in repairing this model. If they tell you the problem is widespread and the company has fixed it for some persistent customers, write a demand letter to the car dealer and manufacturer. (See Chapter 6.) Mention that if your problem is not taken care of, you will sue in small claims court and will subpoena all records having to do with this defect. (See Chapter 15.) This may well motivate the company to settle with you. If not, follow through on both threats.

B. Used Vehicle Dealers

Recovering from used vehicle dealers can be tricky, unless you live in Arizona, Hawaii, Maine, Massachusetts, Minnesota, New Jersey, New York, or Rhode Island, where at least some used cars are covered by the lemon law. Otherwise, recovering for a defective used car can be tough unless you deal with a reputable dealer who provides an adequate written warranty.

Traditionally, unlike new vehicle dealers, who are at least somewhat dependent upon their reputation in the community for honesty, many used vehicle dealers commonly have had no positive reputation to start with and have survived by becoming experts at self-protection. Also (and don't underestimate this one), judges almost never buy used vehicles and therefore aren't normally as sympathetic to the problems used vehicle owners encounter. Chances are a judge has had a problem getting her new car fixed under a warranty, but has never bought a 10-year-old Plymouth in "tip-top shape," only to have it die two blocks after leaving Honest Al's.

The principal self-protection device employed by used vehicle dealers is the "as is" designation in the written sales contract. The salesperson may promise the moon, but when you read the fine print of the contract, you will see it clearly stated that the seller takes absolutely no responsibility for the condition of the vehicle and that it is sold "as is."

Time and again I have sat in court and heard hard luck stories like this:

"I bought the car for $1,200 two months ago. The dealer at Lucky Larry's told me that the engine and transmission seemed solid. I drove the car less than 400 miles and it died. I mean really died—it didn't roll over and dig itself a hole, but it may as well have. I had it towed to an independent garage and they told me that, as far as they could see, no engine or transmission work had ever been done. They estimated that to put the car right would cost $800. I got one more estimate which was even higher, so I borrowed the $800 and had the work done. I feel I really got taken by Lucky Larry. I have with me the canceled check for the $800 in repairs, plus the mechanic who did the work, who will testify as to the condition of the car when he saw it."

Unfortunately, this plaintiff will probably lose. Why? Because going back to the sort of issues we discussed in Chapter 2, Section A, he has proven only half of his case. He has shown his loss (he bought a $1,200 car that wasn't worth $1,200), but he has not dealt with the issue of the defendant's responsibility to make the loss good ("liability"). Almost surely, the used car dealer will testify that he "had no way of knowing how long a 10-year-old Plymouth would last and that, for this very reason, he sold the car 'as is.' " He will then show the judge a written contract that not only has the "as is" designation, but that will say someplace in the fine print that "this written contract is the entire agreement between the parties and that no oral statements or representations made by the dealer or any salesperson are part of the contract."

How can you fight this sort of cynical semi-fraud? It's difficult to do after the fact. The time for self-protection is before you buy a vehicle, when you still have time to have it checked by an expert and can insist that any promises made by the salesperson as to the condition of the car or the availability of repairs be put in writing. Of course, good advice given after the damage has been done "isn't worth more than a passel of warm spit," as former Vice-President John Nance Garner so graphically put it. If you have just been cheated on a used car deal, you want to know what, if anything, you can do now. Here are some suggestions:

- If you reside in Arizona, Hawaii, Maine, Massachusetts, Minnesota, New Jersey, New York, or Rhode Island, your state's lemon law applies to used as well as new cars. Check to see if your situation is covered.

- If the car broke down almost immediately after you took it out of the used car lot, you can file in small claims court and argue that you were defrauded. Your theory is that, no matter what the written contract said, there was a clear implication that you purchased a car, not a junk heap. When the dealer produces the "as is" contract you signed, argue that it is no defense to fraud. I discuss fraud in more detail in Chapter 2.

- If the dealer made any promises, either in writing or orally, about the good condition of the vehicle, he or she may be required to live up to them. Why? Because, as noted in Chapter 2, statements about a product that you rely on as part of deciding whether to purchase may constitute an express warranty. This is true even if the seller had you sign an "as is" statement that disclaims all warranties. The key to winning this sort of case is to produce a witness to the dealer's laudatory statements about the vehicle, copies of ads that state the car is in good shape, plus anything else that will back up your story. Although not every state will let you make this argument (under the theory that the written agreement is the only thing that matters), try making it anyway. I have seen it succeed.

- You may also want to claim an implied warranty. One type—the implied warranty of fitness—means that the vehicle is warranteed to work for a particular purpose (say, consistency). The more common implied warranty is for merchantability. Here, if the car doesn't run at all, your basic claim is that because you haven't gotten a car worth anything at all, it isn't merchantable.

- You may want to consider having the car towed back to the lot and refusing to make future payments. This is a radical remedy and should only be considered in an extreme situation. It does have the beauty of shifting the burden of taking legal action to the other side, at which point you can defend on the basis of fraud. If you take this approach, be sure you have excellent documentation that the car was truly wretched. And be sure to set forth in writing the circumstances surrounding the difficulties, along with a convincing statement that, taken as a whole, the dealer's conduct amounts to consumer fraud. Send copies to the dealer and the bank or finance company to whom you pay your loan. Of course, you will probably have made some down payment, so even in this situation, you may wish to initiate action in small claims court.

- Have your car checked over by someone who knows cars and will be willing to testify, if need be. If this person can find affirmative evidence you were cheated, you will greatly improve your small claims case. It might turn out, for example, that the odometer had been tampered with in violation of federal or state law, or that a heavy grade of truck oil had been put in the crankcase so the car wouldn't belch smoke. Also, this is the sort of case where a subpoena duces tecum (subpoena for documents) might be of help. (See Chapter 15.) You might wish to subpoena records relating to the car dealer's purchase of the car or its condition when purchased. It might also be helpful to learn the name of the car's former owner, with the idea of contacting him or her. With a little digging, you may be able to uncover information that will enable you to convince a judge that you have been defrauded.

- Consider other remedies besides small claims court. These can include checking with your state department of consumer affairs, or the local department of motor vehicles, to see if used car lots are regulated. In many states, the department of motor vehicles licenses used car dealers and can be very helpful in getting disputes resolved, particularly where your complaint is one of many against the same dealer for similar practices. Also, contact your district attorney's office. Most now have a consumer fraud division, which can be of great help. If you can convince them that what happened to you smells rotten, or your complaint happens to be against someone they have already identified as a borderline criminal, they will likely call the used car dealer in for a chat. In theory, the D.A.'s only job is to bring a criminal action, which will be of no direct aid in getting your money back; but in practice, negotiations can often result in restitution. In plain words, this means that the car dealer may be told, "Look, buddy, you're right on the edge of the law here (or maybe over the edge). If you clean up your act, which means taking care of all complaints against you and seeing that there are no more, we will close your file. If you don't, I suggest you hire a good lawyer, because you are going to need one."

C. Used Vehicles From Private Parties

Normally, it is easier to win a case against a private party than against a used vehicle dealer. This runs counter to both common sense and fairness, as a private party is likely to be more honest than a dealer. But fair or not, the fact is that a nondealer is usually less sophisticated in legal self-protection than is a pro. Indeed, in most private party sales, the seller does no more than sign over the title slip in exchange for the agreed-upon price. No formal contract is signed that says the buyer takes the car "as is."

If trouble develops soon after you purchase the vehicle and you are out money for unexpected repairs, you may be able to recover. Again, the problem is usually not proving your loss, but convincing the judge that the seller of the vehicle is responsible ("liable") to make your loss good. To do this, you normally must prove that the seller claimed that the vehicle was in better shape than, in fact, it was, and that you relied on these promises when you made the deal.

Recently, I watched Barbara, a 20-year-old college student, succeed in proving just such a case. She sued John for $2,150, claiming that the BMW motorcycle she purchased from him was in far worse shape than he had advertised. In court, she ably and convincingly outlined her conversations with John about the purchase of the motorcycle, testifying that he repeatedly told her that the cycle was "hardly used." She hadn't gotten any of his promises in writing, but she did a creative job of developing and presenting what evidence she had. This included:

• A copy of her letter to John, which clearly outlined her position. Here's what her letter looked like:

                                          14 Harrison St.
                                          Moline, IL
                                          January 27, 20xx

John Malinosky
321 Adams St.
Moline, IL

Dear Mr. Malinosky:

   This letter is a follow-up to our recent phone conversation in which you refused to discuss the fact that the BMW motorcycle I purchased from you on January 15 is not in the "excellent condition" that you claimed.

   To review: On January 12, I saw your ad for a motorcycle that was "almost new—hardly used—excellent condition" in the local flea market newspaper. I called you and you told me that the cycle was a terrific bargain and you would never sell it except that you needed money for school. I told you I didn't know much about machinery.

   The next day, you took me for a ride on the cycle. You told me specifically that:

   1. The cycle had just been tuned up.

   2. The cycle had been driven less than 30,000 miles.

   3. The cycle had never been raced or used roughly.

   4. If anything went wrong with the cycle in the next month or two, you would see that it was fixed.

   I didn't have the cycle more than a week when the brakes went out. When I had them checked, the mechanic told me that the transmission also needed work (I confirmed this with another mechanic—see attached estimate). The mechanic also told me that the cycle had been driven at least 75,000 miles (perhaps a lot more) and that it needed a tune-up. In addition, he showed me caked mud and scratches under the cycle frame, which indicated to him that it had been driven extensively off the road in rough terrain and had probably been raced on dirt tracks.

   The low mechanic's estimate to do the repairs was $2,150. Before having the work done, I called you to explain the situation and to give you a chance to arrange for the repairs to be made, or to make them yourself. You laughed at me and said, "Sister, do what you need to do—you're not getting dime one from me."

   Again, I respectfully request that you make good on the promises (express warranty) you made to me on January 15. I relied on the truth of your statements (express warranty) when I decided to buy the bike. I enclose a copy of the mechanic's bill for $2,150, along with several higher estimates that I received from other repair shops.

                                          Sincerely,

                                          Barbara Parker

- Copies of repair bills (and three estimates) dated within two weeks of her purchase of the cycle, the lowest of which came to $2,150.
- A copy of John's newspaper ad that she answered. It read: "BMW 500, almost new—hardly used—excellent condition—$7,500."
- Finally, Barbara presented the judge with this note from the mechanic who fixed the cycle:

To Whom It May Concern:

It's hard for me to get off work, but if you need me, please ask the judge to delay the case a few days. All I have to say is this: The BMW that Barbara Parker brought to me was in *fair* shape at best. It's impossible to be exact, but I would conservatively guess that it had been driven at least 75,000 miles. Also, given the damage to the underside of the bike, I can say for sure that it was driven a lot of those miles on dirt.

Respectfully submitted,

Al "Honker" Green

February 3, 20xx

Barbara quickly outlined the whole story for the judge and emphasized that she had saved for six months to get the money to make the purchase. True, testimony about financial hardship isn't relevant, but a quick tug on the judge's heartstrings never hurts. As an old appeals court judge who had seen at least 75 summers told me when I graduated from law school and was proud of my technical mastery of the law, "Son, don't worry about the law—just convince the judge that truth and virtue are on your side and he will find some legal technicality to support you." No one ever gave me better advice.

Next, John had his turn. He helped Barbara make her case by acting like a weasel. His testimony consisted mostly of a lot of vague philosophy about machinery. He kept asking, "How could I know just when it would break?" When the judge asked him specific questions about the age, condition, and previous history of the cycle, he clammed up as if he was a mafioso called to testify by a Senate anti-racketeering committee. When the judge asked him if he had, in fact, made specific guarantees about the condition of the bike, John began a long explanation about how, when you sell things, you "puff them up a little," and that "women shouldn't be allowed to drive motorcycles anyway." Finally, the judge asked him to please sit down.

Even a little tangible evidence is better than none. In this type of case, absent a written warranty such as an ad that states the vehicle is in great shape, it's often one person's word against another's. Any shred of tangible evidence that the seller has made an express verbal warranty as to the condition of the goods can be enough to shift the balance to that side. Of course, if you have a friend who witnessed or heard any part of the transaction, his or her testimony will be extremely valuable. Getting a mechanic to check over a vehicle and then testify for you is also a good strategy. Sometimes you can get some help from publications such as Blue Books that list wholesale and retail prices for used cars. (The Blue Book is also available online, at www.kbb.com.) Several times I have seen people bring Blue Books (car dealers have them) into court and show the judge that they paid above the Blue Book price for a used car "because the car was represented to be in extra good shape." This doesn't constitute much in the way of real proof that you were ripped off, but it is helpful to at least show the judge that you paid a premium price for unsound goods. ■

Bad Debt Cases

Well over 60% of small claims cases involve a claim that the defendant has failed to pay the plaintiff a sum of money. Usually this means a bill for goods or services hasn't been paid, but it also can involve failure to pay a promissory note (for example, a loan from a friend or relative), or even a civil fine for something as simple as the failure to return a library book. In over 90% of these cases, the plaintiff wins (often because the defendant defaults). This makes small claims court a potentially very effective part of any business's bill collection strategy. But, paradoxically, small claims court can also work well for a defendant who believes that no money is owed or that the plaintiff is asking for too much. The defendant may, as a result, put up a spirited and successful defense. Unlike formal court, in small claims, a defendant doesn't have to jump through procedural hoops to show up and present his or her side of the story.

Some business people, especially professionals such as doctors, dentists, and lawyers, tend not to use small claims court to collect unpaid bills because they think it takes too much time, or is "undignified." You will have to worry about your "dignity" yourself, but small claims court actions can be handled with very little time and expense once you get the hang of it. And in many states, the job of actually appearing in court can be delegated. By contrast, business people who don't use small claims court as part of a self-help debt collection strategy must normally either write off the loss or turn the bill over to a collection agency.

I am indebted to the article by Sarah Klein in the August 16, 1999 issue of *American Medical News* ("Doctors Say: See You in Court") for an excellent illustration of just how effective filing a small claims case can be as part of a bill collection strategy. According to Klein, two New Mexico doctors filed suit against one of the state's leading health insurers when other efforts to get the medical plan to pay almost half a million dollars failed. The doctors, who had been reduced to charging office expenses on their personal credit cards, filed one small claims case for a mere $217.75. However, that one lawsuit finally got the attention of the medical insurers. Not only did a representative of the health plan visit the doctors to facilitate the payment of past due claims, but an employee of another delinquent insurer who had heard about the determined doctors' willingness to go to small claims court called with an offer to "get things straightened out."

As you might guess, the doctor's success wasn't lost on other area physicians. One family physician remarked, "It wouldn't surprise me if other people did it [filed small claims cases against health insurers]. It's a very effective tool."

A. Who Should Appear in Court?

Probably no aspect of small claims court practice varies more from state to state than who can sue to collect unpaid bills. As listed in the state-by-state Appendix, some states:

- allow bill collectors to use small claims court
- ban bill collectors, but let lawyers carry out much the same task by representing multiple creditors
- ban both bill collectors and lawyers, allowing only businesses to sue on their own behalf.

And even among the states where businesses can't hire third parties but must represent themselves to sue on bad debt claims, there are important differences. For example, a few states entirely prohibit corporations from suing in small claims court, while others make it difficult for unincorporated businesses to send anyone but an owner or partner to court. By contrast, most states allow corporations to sue and make it reasonably easy for both incorporated and unincorporated businesses to designate a bookkeeper or other employee to handle court appearances. (See Chapter 8 for more on who can sue in small claims court.)

After first checking the summary of rules in the Appendix and on your state's website, contact your small claims court clerk and find out exactly what rules govern bill collection activities in your state. Then talk to other small business people (or business associations, such as the chamber of commerce) to learn practical strategies to cope with any rules that hinder using small claims as part of a cost-efficient bill collection strategy. Also, if you are in a state where bill collectors or lawyers do small claims collection work, you will want to find out how much they charge and how efficient they are, and then compare this to the time and energy it would take for you to do it yourself. Because bill collectors and lawyers typically charge from 30% to 50% of any money they collect, you'll probably conclude that you can do this work cheaper yourself.

A bookkeeper or other representative is often, but not always, a good choice to appear in small claims court. In many states, a business owner does not have to personally appear in court, but can send an employee. Where money is owed, a bookkeeper or financial manager is normally a good choice, because he or she can testify that a valid contract existed and the defendant has not paid the promised amount. However, if the defendant shows up and defends on the basis that the goods or services were defective, delivered late, or otherwise not acceptable, the bookkeeper is likely to be at a serious disadvantage; he or she probably has no firsthand knowledge of anything except that the check was not in the mail. For example, if you own a graphics business and are suing on an unpaid bill in a situation where you expect the defendant may show up in court and falsely claim you did lousy work, you will obviously need to have someone in court who knows the details of the particular job. Typically, this should be the employee(s) who dealt with the customer and did the work.

B. Debt Cases From the Plaintiff's Point of View

The job of the plaintiff in a case where he or she is suing for nonpayment of a debt is usually pretty easy—in the majority of cases, the debtor doesn't even show up (defaults, in legalese). In the absence of a defendant, the plaintiff need only prove that a valid debt exists and has not been paid. In a few small claims courts, this is done by showing your documentation to the court clerk, who enters the default order. But in most courts the plaintiff must make a very brief court presentation, showing the judge proof of the debt in the form of a contract, work order, promissory note, or purchase order signed by the defendant. At this point, the court will issue a judgment—which, of course, is necessary if you wish to collect from a debtor who refuses to pay voluntarily.

Here are a few suggestions for plaintiffs.

1. Don't Bother Suing on Some Types of Debts

Although using small claims court as part of your debt collection process often makes sense, there are exceptions. Here are the principal ones:

- **When there isn't enough money at stake.** For disputes involving a few hundred dollars or less, your costs of filing, preparing, and presenting a small claims case are likely to be unacceptably high relative to what you are likely to receive. Even if the defendant defaults, a small claims case will typically take up at least five hours of your time, so you'll want to go forward only if the amount you are likely to recover is worth it.

- **When the defendant is a deadbeat.** As discussed in more detail in Chapter 3, most court judgments are fairly easy to collect, because the defendant has a job, a bank account, investments, or real property. However, it's also true that some people are judgment proof and are likely to stay that way. Although they probably make up only between 10%–20% of the U.S. population, people who have so little money or property that they can effectively thumb their noses at creditors undoubtedly run up a disproportionate share of bad debts. One thing is sure: As a sensible business person, you don't want to spend your time and energy chasing people who are never likely to have enough money to pay you. Better to write off the debt and tighten up your credit-granting procedures.

- **When you want to get along with the person in the future.** Any court action, even a small claims case, tends to polarize disputes and make the parties angrier at one another. This isn't a problem when dealing with people or businesses with whom you don't plan to have future contact or, as in the case of the New Mexico doctors, your real goal is to get the other party's attention. But in other circumstances, such as when a former friend or local business owes you money, it's possible that your ongoing relationship with a debtor may be more important than collecting all that you are owed. In these situations, you may sensibly try to minimize conflict by trying to work out your dispute through negotiation or court-sponsored mediation. (See Chapters 6 and 7.)

Extra damages for bad checks. Every business is stuck with a rubber check now and then. Until recently, it usually didn't pay to take a bad check writer to court, especially for smaller checks. Today, however, many states permit a person holding a bad check to obtain a judgment for additional money—sometimes three or four times the amount of the check. I discuss how to take advantage of these laws in Chapter 4, Section C1.

2. Ask for Your Money Before You Sue

In Chapter 6, I discuss techniques for settling your case without going to court. Because writing an effective letter demanding payment will often produce a check by return mail, you should always do this before filing in small claims court. Unfortunately, many businesses rely on fill-in-the-blanks past due notices and dun letters purchased from commercial sources. While these may be better than nothing, it's usually much more effective to write your own, more personal, demand letter (see the sample in Chapter 6) and modify it slightly to fit the circumstances. But realize that whenever you are demanding payment of a bill, a number of laws protect debtors from overzealous bill collection practices, including conduct defined as harassing or threatening. For do's and don'ts in collecting bills, check out the Debt and Bankruptcy section of Nolo's free online legal encyclopedia at www.nolo.com.

Plan in advance to counter any claim that your bill wasn't paid for a good reason. If you provide goods or services, it's wise to include a statement on all your bills and collection letters requesting that the debtor notify you if the goods are defective or services substandard. Bring copies of these notices to court. Then, if the debtor shows up and, for the first time, claims he or she didn't pay you because of some problem or defect, you can show the judge that you consistently asked to be informed about any problems with your product or service. The fact that the debtor made no complaints will normally go far toward convincing the judge that he or she is fabricating, or at least exaggerating, the current complaint in an effort to avoid paying you.

3. Bring Debt Collection Cases Promptly

For maximum success in collecting on bad debts, file suit as soon as you conclude that informal collection methods are unlikely to work. For starters, you'll be pleasantly surprised that a small but significant number of debtors will quickly pay up—or call you to work out a payment plan—to avoid having a court judgment appear in their credit records. But fast action is also advisable for other reasons, the most important being that people who owe you money are likely to have other debts as well, and may be considering bankruptcy. The quicker you act, the faster you'll get a judgment and be eligible to start collection activities, such as a wage garnishment or property attachment.

In addition, if you file promptly, you will avoid having to worry about whether you are within the legal filing deadline, called the "statute of limitations." Depending on the state and the type of debt, this can be anywhere from one to four years. (You will find a discussion of the statutes of limitations applicable to different sorts of debts in Chapter 5.) Even when there is no danger that your limitations period will run out, it makes sense to get to court as soon as is reasonably possible. One good reason for this advice is that judges tend to be skeptical of old claims. For example, several times when I served as a pro tem (temporary) small claims judge, I wondered why someone waited three years to sue for $500. Was it because he or she wasn't honestly convinced that the suit was valid? Was it because the plaintiff and the defendant got into a spat about something else and the plaintiff was trying to get even? You could end up answering a lot of questions you weren't prepared for.

4. Special Rules Apply to Installment Debts

If you lend money or sell an item with payments to be made in installments, and a payment is missed, you are entitled to sue only for the amount of the missed payment, not the whole debt. Before you can sue for the entire amount, you must wait until all payments are missed. But there is a major exception to this rule: You can immediately sue for 100% of the debt—plus any interest—if your contract contains an "acceleration clause." This is legal jargon contained in the underlying written contract stating that if one payment is missed, the whole debt is due. Read your written installment contract carefully to see if this type of language is included.

5. Written Contracts—Bring Documentation to Court

Most debts are based on a written contract. This may be a purchase order, credit agreement, lease, or formal contract. It makes no difference what your document is called, as long as you have something in writing with the defendant's signature. A few courts require you to submit a copy of a purchase contract, signed work order, or any other written evidence of indebtedness when you file your action. (Check your local rules.) In most states, however, there is no need to file anything in advance. Simply bring your written documentation to court on the day your case is heard, both as proof of the debt and so that, in some states, the court can mark it canceled when a judgment in your favor is entered. Also, bring any ledger sheets, computer printouts, or other business records documenting any payments that have been missed.

Being organized wins cases. Take your responsibility to put your paperwork in order seriously. Too often I have seen otherwise sensible business people show up with botched records—then become flustered when closely questioned by the judge. The courtroom is not the place to straighten out a poor accounting system.

6. How to Prove Debts Covered by Oral Contracts

Generally, a debt based on an oral contract is legal as long as the contract was (or could have been) carried out in one year, and is not for the sale of real estate or for goods (personal property) worth more than $500. (See Chapter 23 for more on written documentation rules for the sale of goods.) Of course, proving that the debt exists may become challenging if the defendant flat out denies borrowing the money or buying the goods or services.

Your best bet is to attempt to come up with some written documentation showing that your version of what occurred is true. For example, even if there is no written agreement, the defendant may have written you a down payment check or a letter asking for more time to pay. Either would be a huge help in convincing the judge that a debt exists. If you can't come up with anything in writing, try to think of a person who has firsthand knowledge of the debt and who is willing to testify. For example, if the defendant told you, in the presence of a friend, "I know I owe you $1,000. I'll pay you next month," or even, "Too bad you will never get your money back," or anything similar to indicate that a loan existed, bring your friend as a witness or have him or her write a letter explaining what the defendant said.

Unfortunately, in many oral contract situations, there is no direct written or verbal evidence sufficient to prove its existence. If so, you will have to try to establish the existence of the contract by reference to the conduct of the parties. Fortunately, it can be fairly easy to do this in one common commercial context: where one person provides goods or services that no one normally gives away for free and the other person knowingly accepts them.

> **Example:** Jane is a commercial illustrator who works as a freelancer for a variety of ad agencies, publishers and other clients. One day she got a call from Harold, a dress designer, asking her to do a series of drawings of his new line of evening wear. Jane did the drawings and submitted her bill for $2,000. Harold refused to pay, alternately claiming that payment was conditional on the drawings being published in a fashion magazine (they weren't) and that Jane was charging too much. Jane filed in small claims court. The judge had no trouble finding the existence of an oral contract based on Harold's admission that he asked Jane to do the work. However, the judge only awarded Jane $1,400, because she could not document her claim that she was to be paid $100 an hour, and Harold made a convincing presentation that illustrators customarily charge no more than $70 per hour. (See Chapter 2, Section C, for more on oral and implied contracts.)

C. Debt Cases From the Debtor's Point of View

When I first observed debt collection cases, I did so with scant attention. I assumed that individuals being pursued by businesses were likely to lose, especially because I guessed they mostly did owe the money. I even wondered why a lot of folks bothered to show up—knowing in advance they had no realistic defense.

But then a curious thing happened. As I sat in on more small claims court sessions, I saw that many debtors refused to play the stereotyped deadbeat role I had assigned them. Instead of shuffling in with heads down, saying "I'm short of money right now," they often presented well-thought-out, convincing defenses, with the result that the judge reduced or sometimes even eliminated the debt. My observation has been corroborated by a prominent study of small claims court cases, which concludes that when a defendant shows up to contest a case, the plaintiff's chance of winning 100% of the amount asked for declines substantially ("Small Claims and Traffic Courts," by John Goerdt (National Center for State Courts)). In fact, defendants win outright in 26% of debt cases and pay half or less of what the plaintiff asked for in an additional 20%.

Here are some examples of cases in which I have observed defendants succeed in whole or part:

- A local hospital sued an unemployed man for failure to pay an emergency room bill for $678. It seemed an open-and-shut case—the person from the hospital had all the proper records, and the defendant hadn't paid. Then the defendant told his side of it. He was taken to the emergency room suffering from a superficial but painful gunshot wound. Because it was a busy night and he was not in critical condition, he was kept waiting four hours for treatment. When treatment was given, it was minimal—and he suffered later complications he claimed might have been avoided if he had been treated more promptly and thoroughly. He said he didn't mind paying a fair amount, but that he didn't feel he got $678 worth of care in the 20 minutes the doctor spent with him. The judge agreed and awarded judgment to the hospital for $250, plus court and service of process costs. After the defendant explained that he had only his unemployment check, the judge took advantage of a state law that allowed payments over time and ordered that he pay the judgment at the rate of $25 per month.

• A large local tire retailer sued a woman for not paying the balance on a tire bill. She had purchased eight light truck tires manufactured by a major tire company and still owed $512. The tire company presented the judge with the original copy of a written contract, along with the woman's deficient payment record, and then waited for judgment. It is still waiting. In her defense, the woman, who ran a small neighborhood gardening and landscaping business, produced several advertising flyers from the tire company that strongly implied the tires would last at least 40,000 miles. She then testified and presented a witness to the fact that the tires had gone less than 25,000 miles before wearing out. The defendant also had copies of four letters written over the past year to the headquarters of the tire company in the Midwest complaining about the tires. Both in the letters and in court, she repeatedly stated that the salesperson at the tire company told her several times that the tires were guaranteed for 40,000 miles. Putting this all together, the judge declared the total price of the tires should be pro-rated on the basis of 25,000 miles and, after figuring what the defendant had already paid, gave the tire company a judgment for only $150. The woman wrote out a check on the spot and departed feeling vindicated.

• A rug company sued a customer for $686 and produced all the necessary documentation showing that carpet had been installed and that no payment had been received. The defendant testified that the rug had been poorly installed, with a seam running down the center of the room. He brought photographs that left little doubt that the rug installer was either drunk, blind, or both. The defendant also presented drawings that illustrated that there were obviously several better ways to cut the carpet to fit the room. The rug company received nothing.

The point of these examples is not the facts of the individual situations—yours will surely differ—but to say that if you feel goods or services you received were worth less than the amount for which you are being sued, there are several possible defenses, and it often makes good sense to fight back.

1. Kinds of Defenses Common to Debt Cases

As discussed in more detail in Chapter 2, defenses can include:

- **Breach of contract:** The other party failed to live up to (perform) the terms of the contract within the correct period of time. For example, you contracted to have your kitchen counter remodeled using white ceramic tile, and ended up with beige plastic tile. Or, you ordered concert tickets from a website and they weren't mailed until the day after the concert.

> ⚠ **Trivial defects won't void a contract.** To succeed with a breach of contract defense, you must show that the breach was significant (lawyers say "material")—that it prevented you from receiving all or a substantial amount of the product (or benefit) you entered into the contract to obtain. For example, if you order light yellow flowers for a wedding and cream-colored flowers are delivered, you can be pretty sure the judge will decide in favor of the florists, especially if you used the flowers. By contrast, if you had ordered yellow flowers and received dark red ones, which clashed with your color scheme, your chances of winning would be much better.

- **Fraud:** The other party intentionally lied to you about a key fact in a transaction. For example, you buy a used car from a car lot with 25,000 miles on the odometer. Later, you meet the first owner, who says it went 100,000 miles and that the odometer had reflected that when the lot bought it.

- **Breach of warranty:** An express written or implied warranty (statement or guarantee) made by the seller of goods turned out to be bogus. For example, a roofer claims in writing that your new roof will last five years. In fact, it leaks in the first big storm.

- **Violation of statute:** Many federal and state laws require the seller of a particular type of goods or service to comply with specific rules. For example, the Federal Trade Commission provides that a seller of door-to-door goods and services for more than $25 must give you notice of your right to cancel within three days, along with a cancellation form. If he or she fails to do so, your right to cancel continues forever.

Example: TopHat Models, a New York modeling agency, sued Mary P., claiming she had not paid its $1,000 fee for creating a portfolio of "professional quality photographs." The photos were designed to help Mary obtain employment as a model. In her defense, Mary claimed that TopHat had violated New York State's employment agency licensing law (N.Y. Gen. Bus. L. § 170 and following) by falsely claiming it would help her find modeling jobs but that TopHat in fact made no effort to do so. After concluding that TopHat was primarily a scheme designed to get consumers to overpay for photographs and that it had not attempted to find Mary modeling work, the Court agreed and ruled that Mary owed nothing.

2. Evidence to Defend Your Case

To successfully defend a suit claiming you owe money, you'll need to show a very good reason why the goods or services you received were inadequate or why you are otherwise not legally required to pay for them. Sorry, but this almost always means you'll need to do more than tell the judge a sad story. If shoddy goods are involved, show them to the judge, or bring a picture or written report from an expert. (See Chapter 15, Section D.) If you received truly bad service, bring a witness (see Chapter 15) or other supporting evidence to court. For example, suppose the new paint on your recently refinished boat immediately began to chip and peel and, as a result, you notified the boat yard that you would not pay for the job. In case you are later sued, you will want to take pictures clearly showing the problem, and get a written opinion from another boat refinisher stating the work was substandard, as well as an estimate to fix or redo the job.

3. Appearing in Court

There is often a tactical advantage for the debtor if the person who appears in court on behalf of the creditor is not the same person with whom you had dealings. If, for example, you state that a salesperson told you X, Y, and Z, that person probably won't be present to state otherwise. This may tilt a closely balanced case to you. It is perfectly appropriate for you to point out to the judge that your opponent has only books and ledgers, not firsthand knowledge of the situation. The judge may sometimes delay (continue) the case until another day to allow the creditor to bring in the employee(s) with whom you dealt, but often this is impossible because the employee in question will have left the job, or will be otherwise unavailable.

You can ask the judge for a little more time to pay. In some states, the judge can order that a judgment be paid in monthly installments. Time payments can be particularly helpful if you really can't come up with all the money at once because they will prevent the creditor from initiating a wage attachment or other intrusive collection activity. Don't be afraid to ask the judge for time payments—he or she won't know that you want them if you don't ask for them. And even if you forget, some courts allow you to file a request to pay a judgment in installments after the hearing. ■

CHAPTER

20

Vehicle Accident Cases

It is a rare small claims court session that does not include at least one fender bender. Unfortunately, these cases are often badly prepared and presented. The judge commonly makes a decision at least partially by guess. I know from personal experience when I sat as a "pro tem" judge that it sometimes wouldn't take much additional evidence for me to completely reverse my decision.

The average vehicle accident case that ends up in small claims court doesn't involve personal injury, but is concerned with damage to one, or both, parties' car, cycle, RV, moped, or whatever. Because of some quirk of character that seems to be deeply embedded in our overgrown monkey brains, it is almost impossible for most of us to admit that we are bad drivers, or were at fault in a car accident. We will cheerfully acknowledge that we aren't terrific looking or geniuses, but we all believe that we drive like angels. Out of fantasies such as these are lawsuits made.

In Chapter 2, I discuss the concept of negligence. Please reread this material. Except in states that follow no-fault rules (see below), to recover in a vehicle accident case you have to prove either that the other person was negligent and you were driving safely or, if both of you were negligent, that you were less so. Normally, dealing with concepts of negligence in a vehicle accident is a matter of common sense; you probably have a fairly good idea of the rules of the road and whether you or the other driver screwed up. One key is often whether either you or the other party was cited for breaking a law having to do with highway safety (see Section D, below). When a safety-related law is broken, negligence is usually presumed.

File personal injury cases in formal court. Cases involving all but very minor personal injuries don't belong in small claims court, as they will involve claims for far more money than the small claims maximum. And in states that have no-fault insurance, personal injury cases may not be allowed in court at all unless you've first complied with the requirements of your state's no-fault insurance law.

Check rules in no-fault states. States with no-fault insurance laws generally require that auto accident disputes—especially those involving less serious injuries—be submitted to the no-fault administrative system, not to the court. Check your state's rules.

A. Who Can Sue Whom?

The owner of a vehicle is the person who should file a claim for damage done to the vehicle, even if he or she wasn't driving when the damage occurred. Your lawsuit should be brought against the negligent driver and, if the driver is not also the registered owner, against the owner as well. To find out who owns a car, contact the department of motor vehicles. As long as you can tell them the license number, they can tell you the registered owner. (Some states require that you provide a good reason in order to get this information—telling them you are filing a lawsuit based on a vehicle accident should do it.)

B. Witnesses

Because the judge wasn't there when your accident occurred, a good witness can make or break your case. It is better to have a disinterested witness than a close friend or family member, but any witness is better than none. If your opponent is likely to have a witness who supports his or her point of view (even though it's wrong) and you have none, you will have to work extra hard to develop other evidence to overcome this disadvantage. Reread Chapter 15 for more information on witnesses. If you do have an eyewitness but can't get that person to show up in court voluntarily, bring a written statement from the witness describing what he or she saw.

C. Police Accident Reports

When you have an accident and believe the other person was more at fault than you were, it is almost always wise to call the police so that a police report can be prepared. A police report is admissible as evidence in small claims court in most states. The theory is that an officer investigating the circumstances of the accident at the scene is in a better position to figure out what happened than is any other third party. So, if there was an accident report, buy a copy for a few dollars from the police station. If it supports you, bring it to court. If it doesn't, be prepared to refute what it says. This can best be done with the testimony of an eyewitness. If both an eyewitness and a police report are against you, try prayer.

Of course, many of you will be reading this book some considerable period of time after your accident. Obviously, my advice to call the police and have an accident report prepared will be of no use. Unfortunately, if the police are not called at the time of the accident, it's too late.

D. Determining Fault

In Chapter 2, I discuss the general concept of negligence. While that discussion is fully applicable to motor vehicle cases (go back and read it if you haven't already), negligence can also be determined in these types of cases by showing that the other driver caused the accident (in whole or in part) as a result of a vehicle code violation or other similar statutory violation. For instance, if Tommy runs a red light (prohibited by state law) and hits a car crossing the intersection, Tommy is negligent (unless he can offer a sufficient excuse for his action). On the other hand, if Tommy is driving without his seatbelt on (also prohibited by most states) and has an accident, the violation cannot be said to have caused the accident and therefore can't be used to determine negligence.

If there is a police report, the reporting officer may have noted any vehicle code violations that occurred relative to the accident. The report may even conclude that a code violation caused the accident. If there is no police report, or the report does not specify any violations, you may wish to do a little research on your own. Your state's vehicle code is available in most large public libraries, at all law libraries, online and sometimes at the department of motor vehicles. You can use its index to very quickly review dozens of driving rules that may have been violated by the other driver. If you discover any violations that can fairly be said to have contributed to the accident, call them to the attention of the judge.

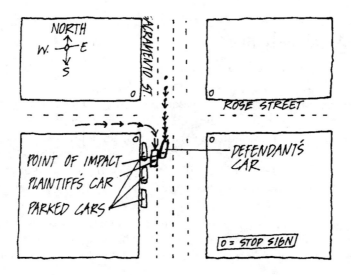

E. Diagrams

With the exception of witnesses and police accident reports, the most effective evidence is a good diagram. I have seen many a good case lost because the judge never properly visualized what happened. All courtrooms have blackboards, and it is an excellent idea to draw a diagram of what happened as part of your presentation. If you are nervous about your ability to do this, you may want to prepare your diagram in advance and bring it to court. Use crayons or magic markers and draw on a large piece of paper about three feet square. Do a good job, with attention to detail.

Above is a sample drawing that you might prepare to aid your testimony if you were going eastbound on Rose St. and making a right-hand turn on Sacramento St. when you were hit by a car that ran a stop sign on Sacramento. Of course, the diagram doesn't tell the whole story—you have to do that.

F. Photos

Photographs can sometimes be helpful in fender bender cases. They can serve to back up your story about how an accident occurred. For example, if you claimed that you were sideswiped while you were parked, a photo showing a long series of scratches down the side of your car would be helpful. It is also a good idea to have pictures of the defendant's car if you can manage to get them, as well as photos of the scene of the accident.

G. Estimates

In a few courts, you must have the repairs completed and paid for before you are eligible for a small claims court judgment (bring your canceled check or a receipt marked "paid"). But in most states, you can prove your property loss by bringing estimates from repair shops to court.

You should obtain several estimates for the cost of repairing your vehicle. Three is usually a good number. Be sure to get your estimates from reputable shops. If, for some reason, you get an estimate from someone you later think isn't competent, simply ignore it and get another. You have no responsibility to get your car fixed by anyone suggested to you by the person who caused the damage. Common sense normally dictates that you don't. Unfortunately, you can't recover money from the other party to cover the time you put in to get estimates, take your car to the repair shop, or appear in court.

In addition to damage to your car, you can also recover for the fair market value of anything in your car that was destroyed. You must be prepared to establish not only the fact of the damage, but also the dollar amount of the loss. You can also recover for alternate transportation while your car is disabled. However, you can only recover for the minimum reasonable time it should take to get your car fixed. Thus, if you could arrange to get a fender fixed in two days, you are only entitled to rent a car for two days, even if an overworked mechanic takes four days to get around to it.

If you think the plaintiff's repair bill is too high. Some plaintiffs dishonestly try to get already existing damage to their car fixed as part of getting the legitimate accident work done. If you think the repair bill is high, try developing your own evidence that this is so. If you have a picture of the plaintiff's car showing the damage, this can be a big help. Also, remember that the plaintiff is only entitled to get repairs made up to the total value of the car before the accident. If the car was worth only $500 and the repairs would cost $750, the plaintiff is only entitled to $500. (See Chapter 4.)

H. Your Demand Letter

Here again, as in almost every other type of small claims court case, you should write a letter to your opponent (with an eye to the judge reading it). See the example letters in Chapter 6. Here is another:

---

18 Channing Way
Eugene, OR
August 27, 20xx

R. Rigsby Rugg
27 Miramar Crescent
Eugene, OR

Dear Mr. Rugg:

On August 15, 20xx I was driving eastbound on Rose Street in Eugene, Oregon, at about 3:30 p.m. on a sunny afternoon. I stopped at the stop sign at the corner of Rose and Sacramento and then proceeded to turn right (south) on Sacramento. As I was making my turn, I saw your car going southbound on Sacramento. You were about 20 feet north of the corner of Rose. Instead of stopping at the stop sign, you proceeded across the intersection and struck my car on the front left fender. By the time I realized that you were coming through the stop sign, there was nothing I could do to get out of your way.

As you remember, after the accident the Eugene police were called and cited you for failure to stop at a stop sign. I have gotten a copy of the police report, which confirms the facts as I have stated them here.

I have obtained three estimates for the work needed on my car. The lowest is $612. I am proceeding to get this work done, as I routinely need my car in the course of my employment.

I will appreciate receiving a check from you as soon as possible. If you wish to talk about any aspect of this situation, please don't hesitate to call me, evenings, at 486–1482.

Sincerely,

Sandy McClatchy

I. Appearing in Court

In court, Sandy would present her case like this:

Clerk: "Next case, *McClatchy v. Rugg*. Please come forward."

Judge: "Please tell me what happened, Ms. McClatchy."

Sandy McClatchy: "Good morning. This dispute involves an auto accident that occurred at Rose and Sacramento Streets on the afternoon of August 15, 20xx. I was coming uphill on Rose (that's east) and stopped at the corner. There is a four-way stop sign at the corner. I turned right, or south, on Sacramento Street, and as I was doing so, Mr. Rugg ran the stop sign on Sacramento and crashed into my front fender. Your Honor, may I use the blackboard to make a quick diagram?"

Judge: "Please do. I was about to ask you if you would."

Sandy McClatchy: (makes drawing like the one on page 20/4, points out the movement of the cars in detail, and answers several questions from the judge) "Your Honor, before I sit down, I would like to give you several items of evidence. First, I have a copy of the police accident report from the Eugene police, which states that Mr. Rugg got a citation for failing to stop at the stop sign. Second, I have some photos that show the damage to the front fender of my car. Third, I have my letter to Mr. Rugg, trying to settle this case, and finally I have several estimates as to the cost of repairing the damage to my car. As you can see from my canceled check, I took the lowest one."

Judge: "Thank you, Ms. McClatchy. Now, Mr. Rugg, it's your turn."

R. Rigsby Rugg: "Your Honor, my case rests on one basic fact. Ms. McClatchy was negligent because she made a wide turn into Sacramento Street. Instead of going from the right-hand lane of Rose to the right-hand, or inside lane, on Sacramento Street, she turned into the center lane on Sacramento Street. (Mr. Rugg moves to the blackboard and points out what he says happened.) Now it might be true that I made a rolling stop at the corner. You know, I really stopped, but maybe not quite all the way—but I never would have hit anybody if she had kept to her own side of the road. Also, your Honor, I would like to say this—she darted out; she has one of those little foreign cars, and instead of easing out slow, like I do with my Lincoln, she jumped out like a rabbit being chased by a red fox."

Judge: "Do you have anything else to say, Ms. McClatchy?"

Sandy McClatchy: "I am not going to even try to argue about whether Mr. Rugg can be rolling and stopped at the same time. I think the policeman who cited him answered that question. I want to answer his point about my turning into the center lane on Sacramento St., instead of the inside lane. It is true that, after stopping, I had to make a slightly wider turn than usual. If you will look again at the diagram I drew, you will see that a car was parked almost to the corner of Sacramento and Rose on Sacramento. To get around this car, I had to drive a little farther into Sacramento before starting my turn than would have been necessary otherwise. I didn't turn into the center lane, but as I made the turn, my outside fender crossed into the center lane slightly. This is when Mr. Rugg hit me. I feel that since I had the right of way and I had to do what I did to make the turn, I wasn't negligent."

Judge: "Thank you both—you will get my decision in the mail."

(The judge decided in favor of Sandy McClatchy and awarded her $612 plus service of process and filing costs.)

Don't assume you will lose if you were partially at fault. You can win, or partially win, a case involving negligence in most states even if you were not completely in the right. If the other person was more at fault than you were, you have a case. This concept of "comparative" negligence is a new one in many states. It used to be that if you were even a little at fault, you couldn't recover because of a legal doctrine known as "contributory negligence."

Professional drivers have an added incentive to bend the truth. Be particularly wary when you are opposing a bus or truck driver. Many of them will land in trouble with their employer if they are found to be at fault in too many accidents. As a result, they deny fault almost automatically. Judges usually know this and are often unsympathetic when a bus driver says that there has never been a time when "I didn't look both ways twice, count to ten, and say the Lord's Prayer" before pulling out from a bus stop. Still, it never hurts to question the driver in court as to whether his or her employer has any demerit system or other penalty for being at fault in an accident. ■

Landlord-Tenant Cases

For tenants in most states, small claims court can be a useful avenue to gain money damages for a whole array of landlord violations: failure to return a cleaning or damage deposit, invasion of the tenant's privacy, violation of the duty to provide habitable premises, or rent control violations.

While the majority of cases are initiated by tenants, landlords can and do use small claims court as well—for example, to sue a tenant or former tenant for unpaid rent or damage done to the rental property. In some states, it is also possible for a landlord to use small claims court to evict a tenant. (See the Appendix for state-by-state information.) This is an exception to the general rule that only money damage cases can be handed down by small claims court—but it's an exception landlords may find hard to take advantage of, as discussed below in Section E.

There is much more to know about your rights and responsibilities as a landlord or tenant than we could possibly fit in this chapter. Two excellent resources are *Every Landlord's Legal Guide*, by Marcia Stewart, Ralph Warner, and Janet Portman (Nolo), and *Every Tenant's Legal Guide*, by Janet Portman and Marcia Stewart (Nolo). Also check our website, www.nolo.com, for free updates, articles, and further guidance.

A. Security Deposit Cases

The most common landlord-tenant disputes concern the landlord's failure to return a tenant's cleaning and damage deposits after the tenant moves out. These days, deposits can add up to many hundreds of dollars, and tenants understandably want this money back.

Problems involving security deposits often arise like this:

- The tenant moves out, making what he or she considers to be a reasonable effort to clean the place.
- The landlord keeps all or part of the deposit, stating that the place was left damaged or dirty.
- The tenant is furious, claiming the landlord is illegally withholding the deposit.

If the tenant and landlord can't reach a compromise, the tenant's best remedy is to sue the landlord for the money withheld, leaving it up to the small claims court judge to decide who is telling the truth.

1. Deposit Cases From the Tenant's Point of View

How should a tenant prepare a case involving failure to return deposits? Ideally, preparation should start when the tenant moves in. Any damage or dirty conditions should be noted as part of the lease or rental agreement. The tenant should also take photographs of substandard conditions and have neighbors or friends look the place over. When the tenant moves out and cleans up, he or she should do much the same thing—take photos, have friends and neighbors (preferably disinterested ones) check the place over, keep receipts for cleaning materials, and try to get the landlord to agree in writing that it's in satisfactory condition. Ideally, the tenant and landlord (or manager) should tour the apartment together and check for any damage or dirty conditions (comparing it to the inventory sheet at move-in, if one was made). Landlord and tenant then have a chance to work out any disputes on the spot. If they can't and the dispute ends up in small claims court, the tenant will at least have witnesses and evidence at the ready.

Check your state law regarding return of security deposits. State law often dictates how large a deposit a landlord can require, how it must be used, when and how it must be returned, and more. In most states, it is up to the landlord to prove that dirty or damaged conditions justified keeping all or part of a deposit. Often state law also provides that if a deposit is not returned within a short time after the tenant moves out (usually somewhere between 14 and 30 days, depending on the state), and if the landlord acted in bad faith in retaining the deposit, the tenant may be entitled to extra ("punitive") damages over and above the actual amount of the withheld deposit. Whether or not the tenant actually gets these extra damages is a matter of judicial discretion, but after checking your state's rule (which you can do using our website at www.nolo.com), it never hurts to bring your small claims suit for an amount that includes these extra damages.

Now let's assume you are a tenant and have not gotten $900 in cleaning and damage deposits returned even though you moved out of an apartment three weeks ago, having paid all your rent and given proper notice. Start by writing the landlord a letter like this:

750 Lampost Lane
Costa Mesa, CA
October 15, 20xx

Anderson Realty Co.
10 Rose St.
Costa Mesa, California

Dear People:

As you know, until September 30, 20xx, I resided in apartment #4 at 300 Oak Street in Costa Mesa and regularly paid my rent to your office. When I moved out, I left the unit cleaner than it was when I moved in.

As of today, I have received neither my $450 cleaning deposit nor my $450 damage deposit. Indeed, I have never received any accounting from you for any of my money. Please be aware that I know my rights under California Civil Code § 1950.5. If I do not receive my money within the next week, I will regard the retention of these deposits as showing "bad faith" on your part and will sue you, not only for the $900 deposit, but also for the $600 punitive damages allowed by § 1950.5 of the California Civil Code.

May I hear from you soon?

Sincerely,

Farah Shields

Be specific when requesting the return of a deposit. If your landlord has returned only part of your security deposit, having deducted more for cleaning or damages than you thought was reasonable, your demand letter should detail exactly why you believe the deductions were improper. For example, if the landlord says a door was damaged and cost $200 to fix, you might claim that the work could have been done competently for $75. If you get no satisfactory response from your landlord, file your lawsuit.

Whom Should Tenants Sue?

A tenant who knows who owns the building should sue this person or business. Sometimes, however, it is hard to know whom to sue, because rent is often paid to a manager or other agent instead of the owner. In most states, multiple occupancy buildings with two or more units must have ownership information posted on the premises, or list the name of the owner (or the owner's agent for purposes of suit) on the rental agreement. If you are in doubt as to who owns your unit, you are probably safe if you sue both the person to whom you pay your rent and the person who signed the rental agreement, unless you have received notice that the building has been transferred to a new owner, in which case you would sue that person.

On court day, a well-prepared tenant would show up in court with as many of the following pieces of evidence as possible:

- Photos of the apartment on moving in, which show any dirt or damage that already existed.
- Photos of the apartment on moving out, which show clean conditions.
- A copy of an inventory of conditions when moving in and moving out, signed by the landlord and tenant (if one was prepared).
- Receipts for cleaning supplies used in the final clean-up.
- A copy of the written lease or rental agreement.
- A copy of a demand letter to the landlord, such as the one set out above.
- One, or preferably two, witnesses who were familiar with the property and saw it after it was cleaned up, and who will testify that it was in good shape. Incidentally, the testimony or written statements of people who actually scrubbed an oven or toilet are particularly effective. If a witness saw the place when the tenant moved in and will say that it wasn't so clean (or that damage already existed), so much the better.

Proceedings in court should go something like this:

Clerk: "*Shields v. Anderson Realty.* Please step forward."

Judge: "Good morning. Please tell me your version of the facts, Ms. Shields."

Farah Shields: "I moved into the apartment at 300 Oak St. in Costa Mesa, in the spring of 2___. I paid Mr. Anderson, here, my first and last months' rent, which totaled $800. I also paid him a $450 damage security deposit and a $450 cleaning deposit. I moved out on September 30 of this year. Three weeks after I moved out, Mr. Anderson had not yet returned my $900 total deposit, so I wrote him a letter asking for my money back. I have yet to hear from him. As I believe this constitutes a willful denial of my rights under California Civil Code Section 1950.5, I am asking for not only the

$900 Mr. Anderson owes me, but also the $600 in punitive damages (the maximum statutory amount) allowed under the Code, plus my court costs. Here is a copy of my rental agreement, which specifically states my deposit is to be returned to me if the apartment is left clean and undamaged.

"When I moved into #4 at 300 Oak, it was a mess. It's a nice little apartment, but the people who lived there before me were sloppy. The stove was filthy, as were the bathroom, the refrigerator, the floors, and just about everything else. In addition, the walls hadn't been painted in years. But I needed a place and this was the best available, so I moved in despite the mess. I painted the whole place—everything. Mr. Anderson's office paid me for the paint, but I did all of the work. And I cleaned the place thoroughly, too. It took me three days. I like to live in a clean place.

"Here are some pictures of what the place looked like when I moved in *(hands photos to clerk, who gives them to the judge)*. Here is a second set of photos that were taken after I moved out and cleaned up *(again hands photos to clerk)*. Your Honor, I think these pictures tell the story—the place was clean when I moved out. I also have receipts *(hands to clerk)* for cleaning supplies and a rug shampooer that I used during the clean-up. They total $45.25. I have also brought with me two people who saw the place on the day I left and can tell you what it looked like."

Judge: (looking at one of the witnesses) "Do you have some personal knowledge of what this apartment looked like?"

John DeBono: "Yes, I helped Farah move in and move out. I simply don't understand what the landlord is fussing about. The place was a smelly mess when she moved in, and it was spotless when Farah moved out."

Judge: (addressing the second witness) "Do you have something to add?"

Puna Polaski: "I never saw 300 Oak when Farah moved in because I didn't know her then. But I did help her pack and clean up when she moved out. I can tell you that the windows were washed, the floor waxed, and the oven cleaned, because I did it. And I can tell you that the rest of the apartment was clean, too, because I saw it."

Judge: "Mr. Anderson, do you want to present your case?"

Adam Anderson: "Your Honor, I am not here to argue about whether the place was clean or not. Maybe it was cleaner when Miss Shields moved out than when she moved in. The reason I withheld the deposits is that the walls were all painted odd, bright colors, and I have had to paint them all over. Here are some color pictures of the walls taken just after Miss Shields moved out. They show pink and purple walls, two of which are adorned with rainbows. And in one of the bedrooms, there were even animals painted on the walls. I ask you, your Honor, how was I going to rent that place with a purple bulldog painted on the wall? It cost me more than $300 to have the place painted over white."

Judge: (looks at the pictures and gives up trying to keep a straight face, which is okay, as everyone in the courtroom is laughing—except Mr. Anderson) "Let me ask a few questions. Was it true that the place needed a new coat of paint when you moved in, Ms. Shields?"

Farah Shields: "Yes."

Judge: "Do you agree, Mr. Anderson?"

Adam Anderson: "Yes, that's why my office paid her paint bills, although we never would have if we had known about that bulldog, not to mention the rainbows."

Judge: "How much did the paint cost?"

Adam Anderson: "$125."

Judge: "I normally send decisions by mail, but today I am going to explain what I have decided. First, the apartment needed repainting anyway, Mr. Anderson, so I am not going to give you any credit for paying to have the work redone. However, Ms. Shields, even though the place looked quite—shall I say, cheerful—when you moved out, Mr. Anderson does have a point, in that you went beyond what is reasonable. Therefore, I feel it's unfair to make Anderson Realty pay for paint twice. My judgment is this: The $125 for the paint that was given to Ms. Shields will be subtracted from the $900 deposit. This means that Anderson Realty owes Farah Shields $775 plus $11 for costs (the filing fee plus service by certified mail). I am not awarding any punitive damages because I do not believe that Anderson Realty acted in bad faith by retaining the deposit."

2. Deposit Cases From the Landlord's Point of View

Your best protection against spending hours haggling over security deposits is to follow the law scrupulously when a tenant moves out. It is your responsibility to return the deposit within the number of days legally required, or explain why you are withholding some or all of it. But no matter how meticulous you are, sooner or later you may be sued by a tenant who disagrees with your assessment of the cost of cleaning or repairs.

This section shows landlords how to defend themselves in tenant-initiated small claims court cases. The following section covers the occasional necessity of taking a tenant to small claims court for unpaid rent, damage, or cleaning bills not covered by the deposit. After inspecting the premises and documenting the dirty or damaged conditions, send the tenant a written itemization of deductions for repairs, cleaning, and unpaid rent within three weeks or the time limit set out by law in your state. Include details on the costs of any cleaning or damage repair, including a reasonable hourly charge if you or your employees do any necessary cleaning or repainting and an itemization of work done by an outside firm. Be sure to keep receipts for costs of damage repair such as new carpets or repainting. If you use an outside cleaning service, ask the service if they will testify in small claims court if necessary, or if they will at least write a letter describing what they did in detail if the tenant contests your deposit deductions.

Before your court hearing, you (or, if allowed in your state, your properly authorized property manager) should gather all evidence that the premises needed cleaning or were damaged. It's important to understand that the landlord normally has the legal burden of proving one or both of these facts. If you fail to do that, the tenant will win. In other words, all a former tenant needs to prove to win is that a residential tenancy existed, he or she paid you a deposit, and you didn't return all of it.

To make a winning case, a landlord or authorized manager should show up in court with as many of the following items of evidence as possible:

- Photos of the premises before the tenant moved showing how clean and undamaged the place was.
- Photos taken after the tenant left showing a mess or damage.
- Copies of inventory sheets (if prepared) detailing the condition of the rental unit when the tenant moved in and out, signed by the landlord and tenant. (These are particularly valuable if they show that an item that is now broken was in good shape when the tenant moved in.)
- An itemization of hours spent to clean or repair the unit, complete with the hourly costs for the work.
- A copy of the written security deposit itemization the landlord sent to the tenant detailing deductions.
- Any damaged items appropriate to be brought into the courtroom (for example, a curtain with a cigarette hole would be effective evidence).
- Receipts for professional cleaning or repair services.
- One, or preferably two, witnesses who were familiar with the property, saw it just after the tenant left, and will testify that the place was dirty or that certain items were damaged. People who helped in the subsequent cleaning or repair or the new tenant who saw the place before it was cleaned are likely to be particularly effective witnesses. Written statements or declarations under penalty of perjury can be used, but they are not as effective as live testimony. A sample written statement is shown below.

SAMPLE DECLARATION

DECLARATION OF PAUL STALLONE

I, Paul Stallone, declare:

1. I am employed at A&B Maintenance Company, a contract cleaning and maintenance service located at 123 Washington Street, Champaign, Illinois. Gina Cabarga, the owner of an apartment complex at 456 Seventh Street, Champaign, Illinois, is one of our accounts.

2. On May 1, 20xx, I was requested to go to the premises at 456 Seventh Street, Apartment 8, to shampoo the carpets. When I entered the premises, I noticed a strong odor, part of which seemed like stale cigarette smoke. An odor also seemed to come from the carpet.

3. When I began using a steam carpet cleaner on the living room carpet, I noticed a strong smell of urine. I stopped the steam cleaner, moved to a dry corner of the carpet, and pulled it from the floor. I then saw a yellow color on the normally white foam-rubber pad beneath the carpet, and I smelled a strong urine odor. It looked and smelled like other places I have seen where a pet (most likely a cat) urinated on the carpet. On further examination, I noticed similar stains and odors all over the carpet and pad.

4. In my opinion, the living room carpet and foam-rubber pad underneath need to be removed and replaced and the floor should be sanded and sealed. I declare under penalty of perjury under the laws of the state of Illinois that the foregoing is true and correct to the best of my knowledge.

DATED: June 15, 20xx

SIGNATURE: _____
                    PAUL STALLONE

B. Unpaid Rent, Rent Withholding, and Other Money Damage Cases

In most states, landlords can initiate small claims actions to sue for unpaid rent. Typically, the tenant will have broken the lease early or skipped out on a month-to-month tenancy without providing adequate notice—and the security deposit (if any) doesn't cover the unpaid rent. In an alternate scenario, the tenant may still be residing on the premises, but may claim that the premises are uninhabitable or that their condition violates housing standards. However, in cases where the tenant is still residing on the premises, it's usually better to request damages as part of an unlawful detainer (eviction) action in formal court.

If you are a landlord who decides that it is worthwhile to go after your tenant for money owed, your first step is to write a letter asking the tenant to pay the amount of your claim. Assuming the tenant has already moved out, a written statement itemizing how you applied the tenant's security deposit to the charges for cleaning and damage repair and requesting payment of the balance is legally considered to be such a demand.

1. No Defense by Tenant

A tenant who has already moved out often doesn't bother to show up in court. If this happens, in most states the landlord briefly states his or her case, and, assuming it's credible, will win by default. (In a few states, the court clerk will enter the judgment in favor of the landlord with no court appearance needed). Sometimes the tenant does show up but presents no real defense (often the tenant is there only to ask permission to make payments over time). Again, the landlord should easily prevail.

The landlord (or manager, if you're in a state that allows authorized representatives to appear on behalf of landlords—see Chapter 8, Section E) should bring the lease or rental agreement to court and simply state the time periods for which rent is due but unpaid. Nothing else is required unless the tenant presents a defense, as discussed below.

If the tenant fails to pay rent but stays in the rental unit, the landlord may, if the lease or rental agreement so provides, sue for three times the amount of rent owed (triple damages). Doing this will almost guarantee that the tenant will put up a fight. In my experience, landlords are rarely awarded more than their actual out-of-pocket loss, so it makes little sense to request more.

2. When a Tenant Breaks a Lease

A tenant who leaves before the expiration of a fixed-term lease (with or without notice) and refuses to pay the remainder of the rent due under the lease is said to have "broken the lease." This means the tenant is liable for the entire rent for the remainder of the lease term (except where the landlord breaches an important lease provision first). However, in most states, the tenant's liability is limited by the landlord's duty to "mitigate damages." Stated in plain English, the landlord has a legal duty to try to find a new tenant as soon as reasonably possible.

What all this adds up to is that, in most states, a landlord whose tenant breaks a lease with no good reason is entitled to:

1. the remaining rent due under the lease,

MINUS

2. any portion of this amount that was or could have been reasonably recovered by obtaining a new tenant,

PLUS

3. any reasonable expenses incurred in finding a new tenant (such as advertising costs).

A landlord can deduct the total of these items, plus necessary repair and cleaning charges, from the tenant's security deposit (see Section A, above) and sue for the remainder in small claims court. (See Chapter 4, Section C1, for a discussion of mitigation of damages; also see the resources listed under "Recommended Reading" in the introduction to this chapter for further detail, particularly regarding those states that don't allow mitigation of damages.)

3. Lawsuits Regarding Defective Conditions or Damage to the Premises

Now let's look at small claims suits in which a tenant stops paying rent based on a claim that the rental unit is seriously defective (uninhabitable). Although this issue most often comes up in the context of an eviction (unlawful detainer) lawsuit, which can't be filed in small claims court (see Section G, below), occasionally a landlord brings a separate small claims suit for unpaid rent.

a. From the tenant's point of view

There are several valid defenses to a suit claiming you failed to pay rent. The principal one is that the condition of the premises was so bad that it was "uninhabitable" or "untenantable." This amounts to the tenant saying to the landlord, "I won't pay my rent until you make essential repairs." Assuming the rental unit really does have major problems, it is legal to withhold rent for this reason in most states. In addition, in some states a tenant may pay withheld rent to a contractor and have essential repairs made directly.

State and local laws often set housing standards for residential real property. These laws require landlords to put their rental apartments and houses in good condition before renting them and keep them that way while people live there. If a landlord doesn't meet these requirements—for example, if the property has a leaky roof—a tenant may well be excused from paying all or part of the rent.

The important thing for a tenant to understand, however, is that rent withholding is not legal where the landlord refuses to fix some minor defect. For rent to be legally withheld (whether or not the tenant actually hires someone to make the repairs), the problem must be sufficiently serious so as to make the home "uninhabitable," un-healthy, or unsafe. In addition, the landlord must have been given reasonable notice to correct the problem. Thus, a broken furnace that a landlord refuses to fix in February would qualify as a condition making a unit uninhabitable, but lack of heat in the summer probably wouldn't.

If you are involved in a rent withholding case as a tenant, your job is to prove (using pictures, witnesses, and other evidence) that the condition that caused you to withhold rent is indeed serious. Thus, you might call the building inspector or an electrician to testify that the wiring was in a dangerous state of decay. The landlord, of course, will probably testify that the rental unit is in fundamentally sound shape, even though there may be some minor problems. A landlord has the right to inspect the property, as long as he or she gives the tenant reasonable notice. In many states, 24 hours' notice is presumed by the law to be reasonable in the absence of an emergency.

Don't Overplay Your Victim Role:
Tenants Have Responsibilities, Too

Tenants are usually assigned certain responsibilities under state and local housing laws. For example, tenants must normally keep their rental unit as clean and safe as possible, dispose of garbage appropriately, and pay to fix things that they break or damage (beyond ordinary wear and tear). Lease and rental agreements commonly make the tenant financially responsible for repair of damage caused by the tenant's negligence or misuse. For example, if the oven no longer works because the tenant kept it on broil while away for a two-week vacation, it's the tenant's responsibility to pay for the repairs. If a tenant refuses to repair or pay for the damage, the landlord can sue the tenant in small claims court.

Assuming your landlord is at fault in failing to maintain the premises, how much will the judge let you get away with in unpaid rent? Theoretically, a tenant can withhold an amount of rent equal to the dollar amount by which the unfixed defect lowers the value of the property. As a practical matter, however, the tenant can withhold as much rent as the landlord—or a judge, if the matter gets to court—will allow under the circumstances. A judge will make a decision based on what he or she thinks is the rental value of the premises, in light of the seriousness of the defect.

On top of your right to withhold rent, you may have a separate claim or counterclaim against your landlord. A landlord who fails to maintain property can, in almost every state, be sued by a tenant for failing to provide a habitable dwelling. The tenant, whether or not he or she remains in the property, can normally sue the landlord for the following:

- partial or total refund of rent paid while conditions were substandard

- the value, or repair costs, of property lost or damaged as a result of the defect— for example, furniture ruined by water leaking through the roof, and

- compensation for personal injuries—including pain and suffering—caused by the defect. These may be physical injuries caused by faulty premises, such as a broken step, inadequate lighting, or substandard wiring. Don't forget to add the costs of your medical bills and lost earnings. (See Chapter 2, Sections E and F, and Chapter 4, Section C4, for more on this.) A landlord is not protected from liability by a provision in a lease or rental agreement in which the tenant purports to give up the right to sue the landlord. These clauses are illegal and will not be enforced by courts.

Many states forbid your landlord from retaliating against you—for example, by raising the rent or terminating your tenancy—if you complain to authorities about conditions in the property or file a lawsuit and stay in the property. Unfortunately, some states offer no such protections.

Laws concerning habitability, repairs, and other landlord-tenant issues are slightly different in every state. See Chapter 1, Section D, for tips on legal research, or go straight to our website at www.nolo.com. You'll also find excellent and extensive material on these subjects in:

- *Every Landlord's Legal Guide*, by Marcia Stewart, Ralph Warner, and Janet Portman (Nolo).
- *Every Tenant's Legal Guide*, by Janet Portman and Marcia Stewart (Nolo).

b. From the landlord's point of view

If you are a landlord involved in a rent withholding case, you're probably either responding to a tenant's suit based on claimed substandard conditions or, more likely, suing the tenant for the portion of the rent the tenant withheld based on his or her claim that the rental unit was uninhabitable. Either way, be prepared to prove the following:

- The defect was not so serious or substantial as to make the property uninhabitable. One good way to do this is to have the repair person who eventually corrected the problem write a letter or testify in person (saying, for example, that the hot water heater was indeed noisy, but still functioning).

OR

- Even if the defect was substantial, the tenant didn't give you adequate notice and a chance to fix it. Especially if you regularly solicit and respond quickly to tenant complaints about potential safety problems, you install and maintain basic security features, and you have a detailed complaint procedure for tenants to report potential safety hazards or maintenance problems, you'll want to explain your system to the judge. Show him that if the tenant had made a timely complaint, the problem surely would have been attended to.

OR

- Assuming there was a substantial defect that you didn't fix within a reasonable time, this defect justifies only the withholding of a small amount of rent (not the amount the tenant withheld) because it didn't inconvenience the tenant much.

4. Tenants Suing Co-tenants for Unpaid Rent

When two or more people rent property together, and all sign the same rental agreement or lease, they are co-tenants, unless otherwise agreed in writing. Each co-tenant shares the same rights and responsibilities under the lease or rental agreement. Therefore all co-tenants, regardless of agreements they make among themselves, are liable for the entire amount of the rent, and a co-tenant who fails to meet this responsibility may be sued by the other co-tenants in small claims court.

Example: James and Helen sign a month-to-month rental agreement for an $800 apartment. They agree between themselves to each pay half of the rent. After three months, James moves out without notifying Helen or the owner, Laura. As one of the two co-tenants, Helen is still legally obligated to pay all the rent and may be able to recover James's share by suing him in small claims court. In the same way, Laura, the owner, may sue Helen, the tenant, for the full amount of the rent in small claims court.

5. Rent Control Cases

In the few areas with rent control laws, landlords who charge illegally high rent can be sued by the tenant not only for the excess rent charged, but for a punitive amount as well (often three times the overcharge).

C. Obnoxious Behavior

Occasionally, a particular landlord or tenant can get pretty obnoxious. This is also true of plumbers, physics teachers, and hair stylists, but this chapter is about landlord-tenant disputes, so I will concentrate on these folks.

From the start, there is a major difference between how landlords and tenants handle problems. This is because landlords have two advantages tenants don't have. First, they can charge deposits, and if a tenant fails to pay rent or damages the place, a landlord can often recoup the loss by subtracting the amount in question from the deposit. In addition, the landlord usually has the right to ask a tenant to move out. (If the tenant has a lease or the unit is located in a city requiring just cause for eviction, this right is restricted.) Tenants, on the other hand, have neither of these rights and, as a result, are much more likely to sue for money damages in small claims court when they are seriously aggrieved.

Typically, tenants have problems with landlords who cannot stop fidgeting and fussing over their property. Smaller landlords tend to develop this problem to a greater extent than do the larger, more commercial ones. Nosy landlords are always hanging around or coming by, trying to invite themselves in to look around or tinker with their half-baked home-repair jobs. In addition, a tenant may also run into a manager who sexually harasses tenants or is on a power trip.

A landlord or manager who is difficult or unpleasant to deal with can make a tenant's life miserable. There is no law that protects a tenant from a landlord's disagreeable personality; tenants without a lease are especially unprotected from all but the most outrageous invasions of privacy, sexual harassment, or trespass. However, if the landlord's conduct is truly obnoxious, courts in some states recognize that tenants have a right to sue for the intentional infliction of emotional distress. (See Chapter 4, Section C5, for advice on determining the dollar amount of a suit for emotional or mental distress.)

D. The Landlord's Right of Entry and the Tenant's Right of Privacy

One area where tenants are easily and understandably upset is when they feel their privacy has been invaded. Landlords, on the other hand, have a legal right to enter their rental units in certain situations. Sometimes a tenant's need to be left alone and a landlord's need to enter conflict. If they do, it is extremely important that both parties understand their rights.

About half the states have access laws specifying when and/or under what circumstances landlords may enter tenants' premises. Typically, there are only four broad situations in which a landlord may legally enter while a tenant is still in residence. They are:

- to deal with an emergency
- to make needed repairs (or assess the need for them)
- to show the property to prospective new tenants or purchasers, and
- when the tenant invites the landlord in.

In most instances (emergencies and tenant invitations excepted), a landlord can enter only during "normal business hours" (9:00 a.m. to 5:00 p.m.) and then only after "reasonable notice," presumed to be 24 hours.

If a landlord ignores these rules, a tenant's first step is to politely ask him or her to follow them. If violations persist, a letter is in order. If this doesn't help, it is possible to sue in small claims court for invasion of privacy if the landlord's conduct is persistently outrageous.

One difficulty faced by a tenant who sues the landlord for entering the unit without permission (lawyers call this "trespass") is that it is hard to prove much in the way of money damages. A judge will want to know why the landlord's improper entry justifies a good-sized monetary award. However, if a tenant can show a repeated pattern of trespass (and the fact that he or she asked the landlord to stop it) or even one clear example of outrageous conduct, it may tip the scales in the tenant's favor. Indeed, the landlord's conduct may rise to the level of a "tort" (legal wrongdoing) such as not only trespass, but invasion of privacy, breach of the tenant's implied covenant of quiet enjoyment, harassment, intentional infliction of emotional distress, or negligent infliction of emotional distress.

As a tenant who feels you've been trespassed upon, how much do you sue for? There is no easy answer, but one approach is to keep or reconstruct a list (or diary) of each incident, complete with a fair amount of detail about the distress it caused you. Then read it over and assign a reasonable dollar value to each hour of distress. For example, if a landlord's repeated illegal entries into your home caused you 75 hours of serious upset, and you value your time at $25 per hour, you would sue for $1,875.

If you are a landlord being sued, but believe that your entry or conduct was legal, you should be able to document this. For example, if a tenant claims that you entered the apartment without 24-hour notice, to prove your case, you should be able to show a copy of the formal 24-hour notification of your intended entry to make needed repairs that you sent the tenant (any notes of related phone conversations would also be useful). Additionally helpful would be testimony by a repair person or other witness confirming that entry was made 24 hours later. Or, you may be able to explain that the urgent nature of the repair required less than 24-hours' notice. Also, if there is a good reason—for example, a repair person is available to make urgently needed repairs on a few hours' notice—you may legally be able to give a reasonable but shorter notice.

But what if you are a landlord whose tenant repeatedly refuses to let you or your employees enter during normal business hours for one of the legitimate reasons cited above? In such a situation, you can probably legally enter anyway, provided you do so in a peaceful manner. (You don't have to arrive bearing flowers, but try not to imitate a television SWAT team.) A wise landlord should bring someone along who can later act as a witness in case the tenant claims that property is missing or damaged.

E. Evictions

In some states, it is legal to do some types of evictions (known technically as "unlaw-ful detainer," "summary dispossess," or "forcible entry and detainer," depending on the state) in small claims court. A few, even have, in their larger cities, separate "landlord-tenant" courts that amount to small claims courts for this one specific purpose. Without question, landlords should have a simple and cheap way to free themselves of tenants who don't pay their rent. But in many states, if a landlord wants to be sure to get a tenant out without ridiculous delays, the only practical method is to file an "unlawful detainer" action in formal court. Traditionally this has required the expense of a lawyer, but more and more landlords are learning to handle their own eviction actions.

Formal court is more practical because the small claims court rules, even in those states where evictions are allowed, tend to limit a landlord's rights when it comes to getting the tenant out in the minimum time and getting a judgment for the maximum amount of rent and other damages. In a few states, a small claims defendant even has an automatic right to appeal the eviction judgment and to remain living in the rental unit while the appeal is pending, despite the fact that no rent is being paid and no bond has been posted.

So before you bring an eviction action in small claims court, check out the answers to the following questions in your state rules:

- If you win an eviction order, can you get the sheriff or marshal to enforce it immediately?

- If the defendant appeals, can he or she stay in the dwelling while the appeal is pending?

- Can you sue for enough damages to fully or at least mostly cover your legitimate claim for back rent and damages to the premises?

- If the defendant can stay in the dwelling during an appeal, is there a requirement that he or she must post some money in the form of a bond that will go to you to cover lost rent if the appeal fails?

If you decide to go ahead with an eviction in small claims court, you must prove that the rent was not paid and that a correct notice was properly served. Bring a copy of this notice to court and an appropriately completed proof of service form. The fact that a tenant is suffering from some hardship, such as illness, poverty, birth of a child, and so on, is not a defense to failure to pay rent. Possible tenant defenses are discussed above, in Section B of this chapter. In most states, the tenant may claim, as a defense, that the rental property was uninhabitable. But remember, a tenant cannot legally raise the existence of a defect for the first time on the day of the court hearing. The landlord must be given reasonable notice that a defect exists before rent is withheld or repairs are made by the tenant.

F. Discrimination

It is illegal for a landlord to refuse to rent to a tenant, or to engage in any other kind of discrimination (such as requiring higher rent or larger deposits), on the basis of any group characteristic such as nationality, race, religion, sex, physical disability, sexual orientation, being on public assistance, or being a family with children. A landlord who attempts to or who actually terminates someone's tenancy for a discriminatory reason, or who discriminates in providing services such as the use of a pool or other common area, is also acting illegally. A tenant who has been discriminated against may use this as a defense to an eviction lawsuit, or sue the landlord for damages.

Because most discrimination cases involve amounts over the small claims maximum, I do not discuss them in detail here. Your most effective remedy is to sue the offending landlord in formal court. For more information on how to spot and prove discrimination, see *Every Tenant's Legal Guide*, by Janet Portman and Marcia Stewart (Nolo). To find a lawyer who handles this type of lawsuit, contact an organization in your area dedicated to civil rights and fighting discrimination.

Drug dealing and neighborhood nuisance cases are discussed elsewhere. See Chapter 8, Section C, for a discussion of how tenants can group together and use small claims courts to hold landlords accountable for security and other issues that impact a number of tenants and neighbors. Group lawsuits may be useful, for example, where the landlord's property is inhabited or frequented by drug dealers, local gangs, or tenants who create excessive noise, run an illegal business, or throw trash into common areas. ■

Miscellaneous Cases

By now you should have a pretty clear idea of how a small claims case should be researched and presented. The facts of each situation will vary, but the general approach will not. Here I will very briefly discuss a few of the common types of cases not covered in the previous chapters. If I don't cover your situation in detail, simply make your own outline of steps to be taken, and adapt the general approaches I have suggested.

A. Clothing (Alteration and Cleaning)

One morning when I stopped by small claims court, the case being presented involved an elderly German-American gentleman with a strong accent suing an equally aged Armenian-born tailor, who was also seriously uncomfortable with the English language. The dispute centered on whether a suitcoat that the tailor had made for the plaintiff should have had two or three buttons. After ten minutes of almost incomprehensible testimony, I understood only that the plaintiff had never owned a suit with two buttons, and the tailor had never made one with three. The two men ended by standing and facing each other—each pulling a sleeve of the suitcoat and yelling as loud as he could in his own language, apparently about how many buttons a suit ought to have. Much to her credit, the judge just sat and listened. What happened? I don't know. I was still actively practicing law then and had to bustle off to argue before another judge that my client thought the two pounds of marijuana he was carrying in a money belt was really oregano. You can probably guess how that argument ended.

While I have never seen another clothing case quite as colorful as that of the two-button suit, I am amazed at how often I have encountered people in small claims court clutching, and waxing poetic about, an injured garment. We humans must really view our clothing as an extension of ourselves, because so many of us react with an indignation out of proportion to our monetary loss when some favorite item is damaged.

Winning a significant victory in a case involving clothing is often difficult. Why? Not because of liability issues—it's usually easy to prove, for example, that the seamstress cut off the collar instead of the cuff. But what brought the person into court, namely the sentimental value of the item or its initial cost, isn't likely to be reflected in the damages award. Courts are supposed to award a plaintiff only the fair market value of a damaged item, not its replacement cost. The judge has to reckon with the fact that used clothing has little actual market value. But because this rule of law commonly works a severe injustice in clothing cases (a $400 suit bought last week may be worth only $100 this week), many judges tend to bend it a little in favor of the person who has suffered the loss.

I've seen judges do this by allowing an amount pretty close to the original purchase price when the clothing involved was almost new, even though its fair market value for resale would be much less. Thus, the owner of a $300 dress that had been ruined by a seamstress after only one wearing might recover $250. Remember, judges are not required to take this approach, but many do. With older clothing, I have also seen some judges take a flexible approach. They do this by making a rough estimate of the percentage of total use that remains in a garment and then awarding the plaintiff this percentage of the original purchase price. Thus, if a cleaner ruined a $300 suit that had been worn about 50 percent of its useful life, the plaintiff might recover $150.

Here are some hints to engage the sympathies of the judge:

• Bring the damaged clothing to court. It's hard for a tailor to muster an effective defense when confronted with a coat two sizes too big or featuring three sleeves.

• Be ready to prove the original purchase price with a canceled check, newspaper ad, or credit card statement. If the item was purchased at a pricey store, let the judge know where. Most judges at least occasionally shop at stores like Nordstrom, Saks, or Macy's, and may be sympathetic if an item you just paid top dollar for was destroyed.

• If you only wore the damaged or destroyed item a few times, make sure the judge knows it and values it close to its original price.

• Be sure that the person you are suing (tailor, cleaner, seamstress, and so on) caused the problem. As noted in the example of the suede coat in Chapter 2, some problems that develop during cleaning or alterations may be the responsibility of the manufacturer.

Don't let the laundry take you to the cleaners! Dry cleaning shops are particularly apt to offer "proof" from "independent testing laboratories" that damage caused to your garment during cleaning was really the fault of the manufacturer. Because these labs work almost exclusively for the dry cleaning industry, the idea that they are independent is pretty suspect. If you are faced with one of these reports, ask the defendant:

• How much the cleaner paid the testing lab for the report
• How many times the same cleaner used the same testing lab before
• How did the cleaner know about the testing lab. (For example, does it place ads in dry cleaners' trade journals that say, 'Let us help you win in court'?)

B. Dog-Related Cases

There's no question that dogs can be frustrating, especially to non-dog owners. As a result, many dog-related cases end up in small claims court. Because many of these involve neighbors who will benefit by maintaining (or establishing) a pleasant relationship, trying to work out the dispute through mediation is often a good first step. (See Chapter 7).

1. Dog Bites

Many states have dog-bite statutes that make dog owners completely liable for injuries their dogs cause—no ifs, ands, or buts. Some statutes cover only injuries occurring off the owner's property. Also, some statutes cover only bites, while others apply to any injury (for example, the dog jumps on you, scratches you, and knocks you over) or property damage (for example, the dog digs up your rose garden). Do some legal research (see Chapter 1, Section D) to find out if your state has a dog-bite statute. If it does, your task in court could be a lot easier.

If your state doesn't have a dog-bite statute, the old "common law" rule probably applies. This means you'll have to prove that the owner was aware of, or should have been aware of, the fact that the dog was vicious. So, if you're bitten by a dog and can show that the dog had snarled, snapped, and lunged at people before and the owner knew about it but let the dog run free anyway, the owner is probably liable (unless you provoked the dog or offered the dog your hand). If the dog is mean-looking, a photo will be a great help in court; a video is even better, if possible.

Also be ready to prove the extent of the injury, the location where it occurred, and the amount of your money damages. As discussed in Chapter 4, Section C4, this consists of the value of any uncompensated time you took off from work, out-of-pocket medical expenses, resultant property damage (your chewed-up coat), and the value of your pain and suffering.

Dog Law, by Mary Randolph (Nolo), answers common legal questions about biting, barking, leash laws, problems with veterinarians, and other common dog-related problems. You will also find a lot of interesting dog law-related articles on our website, www.nolo.com; try doing a keyword search for "dog."

C. Damage to Real Property (Land, Buildings, and So On)

There is no typical case involving damage to real property, because individual fact situations vary greatly. So instead of trying to set down general rules, I'll explain how one person (let's call her Babette) coped with a property damage problem. Hopefully some of the lessons Babette learned will apply to your fact situation.

Babette owns a cinderblock building that houses two stores. One morning, when she came to work, she noticed water pouring in through the back of her building. Because the building was set into a hill, it abutted about eight feet of her uphill neighbor's land (let's call her neighbor Boris). After three days of investigation involving the use of green dye in Boris's plumbing system, it was discovered that the water came from an underground leak in Boris's sewer pipe. By this point, Babette had spent considerable effort and some money to pay helpers to get the water mopped up before it damaged anything in the stores.

Instead of fixing the leak promptly, Boris delayed for four days. All of this time, Babette and her helpers were mopping frantically. Finally, when Boris did get to work, he insisted on digging the pipe out himself, which took another four days. (A plumber with the right equipment could have done it in one.) In the middle of Boris's digging, when his yard looked as though it was being attacked by a herd of giant gophers, it rained. The water filled the holes and trenches instead of running off, as it normally would have. Much of it ran though the ground into Babette's building, bringing a pile of mud with it.

When the flood was finally over, Babette figured out her costs as follows:

First three days *(before the source of the water was discovered)*	$148 *(for help with mopping and cleaning)*
Next four days *(while Boris refused to cooperate)*	$188 *(for help with mopping and cleaning)*
Final four days *(including day it rained)*	$262 *(for help with mopping and cleaning)*
One secondhand water vacuum purchased during rain storm	$200
Babette's own time, valued at $8.00 per hour	$600

Assuming that Boris is unwilling to pay Babette's costs, for what amount should she sue, and how much is she likely to recover? Remembering the lessons taught in Chapter 2: Before Babette can recover for her very real loss, she must show that Boris was negligent or caused her loss intentionally. She probably can't do this for the first three days, when no one knew where the water was coming from, and it's probably impossible to show that Boris was negligent for failing to replace a pipe that, up until then, had worked fine. (But Babette might try to show that the pipe was so old that it was likely to break, and Boris should have anticipated this by replacing it.)

However, once the problem was discovered and Boris didn't take immediate steps to fix it, he was clearly negligent, and Babette can recover at least her out-of-pocket loss ($450 for her labor and $200 for the water vacuum). Can Babette also recover for the value of her own time? Maybe. It would depend on the state and the judge. If Babette could show she had to close her store or take time off from a job to stem the flood, she probably could recover. But if she was retired and lost no pay as a result of her efforts to stem the flood, it would be more difficult. If I were Babette, I would sue for about $1,250 ($450 for labor she paid for, $200 for the vacuum and $600 for the value of her own labor) and count on getting most of it.

D. Police Brutality/False Arrest Cases

Now and then someone sues the police in small claims court—and more often than not, the plaintiff loses. Why? Because the police and jailers have excellent legal advice and aren't afraid to bend the truth to back each other up. It's no secret that the unwritten rule in any law enforcement agency is to protect your own derriere first and to protect your buddies' derrieres right after that. Or put another way, few police officers are going to tell the whole truth if doing so means collecting black marks on their (or a buddy's) service record. Add to this the fact that most law enforcement people have testified many times, and know how to handle themselves in court.

The reason many plaintiffs must use small claims court to sue law enforcement personnel pretty much tells the story. Private lawyers normally won't invest their time and money in this sort of case, because they find them almost impossible to win. Does this mean I believe that bringing false arrest, police brutality, and similar types of cases is a waste of your time? If you're going it alone, and your primary goal is monetary compensation, then the answer is, "Yes."

But given the attention police misconduct is currently receiving, you may get some form of justice by linking up with other groups or individuals. A simple Web search for "police brutality" or "police misconduct" should bring up the names of organizations in your area that keep watch on, or help victims of, police brutality. Some will even recruit free lawyers to take such cases to court, usually in groups—and small claims court may be their first stop. However, these lawyers say that the police will invariably appeal the case to a higher court, so the plaintiffs would have had to get lawyers at some point. There doesn't seem to be a spate of success stories out there yet—but even if you don't get a big win yourself, you may find satisfaction in helping draw attention to the ways that certain public employees abuse their power.

If, despite the above, you are still brave enough to individually drag a police officer, jailer, or anyone else with a badge into small claims court, be sure that you have several witnesses or other evidence to back you up. Never, never rely on one officer to testify against another. You would also be wise to spend a few dollars and talk to a lawyer who specializes in criminal cases, or, again, find a nonprofit organization that can give you free or low-cost advice.

Sue the city and county as well as the officer. In most cases alleging police misconduct, you will want to sue the city, county, or state government that employs the officer, as well as the individual involved. But remember, in most states, before you can sue a government entity, you must file an administrative claim. (See Chapter 9.)

E. Defamation (Including Libel and Slander)

In California, libel and slander cases may be brought in small claims court. However, many states have placed an outright bar on bringing libel, slander, and other defamation cases in small claims court.

Think twice before bringing a libel or slander case. Even in states that allow defamation cases to be brought in small claims court, these lawsuits are hard to win. A big reason is that it's usually tough to show that your reputation was really damaged by a false statement or article. (For example, if your brain-dead neighbor refers to you as an idiot in a flyer he or she circulates around the neighborhood, your reputation may not be damaged one bit.) If you wish to learn more about the many intricacies of defamation law, a good place to start is with a law student course outline on torts (negligent or intentional "wrongs" that result in damage). These are carried by all law bookstores (usually located near law schools).

F. Suits Against Airlines or Hotels

Because of overbooking, it is not uncommon for an airline or a hotel to refuse to honor your reservation. In some situations, this can cause considerable financial loss, especially if, as in the case of an airline bumping, you miss work or an important meeting. Airlines are governed by federal regulation, which requires them to follow certain rules (see "Your Rights as an Air Passsenger," below).

Your Rights as an Air Passenger

Here is a brief summary of the rules to which airlines are subject, governing ticket purchases, check-in, and more. For more information, see the Department of Transportation website at www.dot.gov, or go straight to the following page and look for a publication called *Fly Rights*: http://airconsumer.ost.dot.gov/publications/sources.htm.

- Bumping: Airlines must seek out passengers who will voluntarily give up their seats in exchange for compensation before bumping a passenger who wants to take the flight. However, if an airline must substitute a smaller plane for the one originally scheduled, bumped passengers are not entitled to compensation.
- Passengers are not entitled to compensation if they are rescheduled but will still arrive at their destination within an hour of the originally scheduled time.
- All passengers who are bumped involuntarily must be given a written statement describing their rights, one of which may be on-the-spot payment.
- If the airline arranges substitute transportation scheduled to get a passenger to his or her destination no more than two hours late (four hours internationally), the airline must pay the passenger the amount of the fare up to $200.
- If the airline schedules a passenger to arrive at a destination more than two hours late (four hours internationally), the passenger is entitled to compensation of 200% of the fare up to $400.

If you feel that one of your rights as a passenger has been violated, contact the airline's consumer complaints office. If this doesn't result in your receiving appropriate redress, you may want to sue in small claims court. To prepare your case, do as much of the following as possible:

- Understand the rules.
- At the airline gate when you are being bumped, tell the airline personnel you will suffer financial loss if you don't get to your destination promptly, and ask that they find another passenger to take a later flight. Try to make your complaint in the presence of another passenger who will later confirm in writing that you did so.
- Find out the name of the local airline manager, and put him or her on notice that you will sue if you are bumped.
- Note down all out-of-pocket expenses the delay causes you.
- Compute any loss of wages, commissions, or paid vacation time the delay causes.
- Write to the airline requesting payment of your loss, and inform them you will file in small claims court if they don't pay up.
- File your case in small claims court for the amount of your out-of-pocket expenses and lost business. If your claim appears reasonable, the airline may pay voluntarily or allow you to win on a default judgment. ■

CHAPTER

Disputes Between Small Businesses

More and more people who own or manage small businesses are turning to small claims court to settle disputes with other businesses when they have been otherwise unable to negotiate or mediate an acceptable compromise. They have learned that small claims court is a relatively fast and cost-efficient way to resolve intractable problems. In several states, business-friendly changes in the law are making it easier for businesses to use the court efficiently. For example, New York state has established a separate commercial small claims court in Manhattan and other areas.

This chapter focuses on how to handle substantive disputes between businesses in small claims court. Typically, these center on a claim that one party's work for the other was done poorly, late, or not at all. (Cases involving the simple failure to pay a bill are covered in Chapter 19.)

I have been asked for advice on preparing small claims court cases by a surprising variety of business people. They include:

- a dentist who was furious at a dental equipment wholesaler who passed off slightly used equipment as new

- an architect who wasn't paid for drawing preliminary plans for a small retail complex when the development failed to get financing

- a phototypesetter who refused to pay its former accountant in a dispute involving the value of the latter's services

- a landscape designer who tried to enforce a verbal agreement, which he claimed allowed him to increase his fee when a client asked for changes to the final design plans

- an author who claimed that her publisher had taken too long to publish her book.

- a client who claimed that his lawyer's incompetence was a prime reason he had to pay too much to settle a case

- an importer whose excellent credit history was incorrectly reported by a credit reporting agency, with the result that she suddenly had difficulty arranging financing for several shipments.

A. Remember: You Didn't Always Hate Your Opponent

Although the disputes set out above seem very different, most have one thing in common: The disputing parties had previously enjoyed a friendly business or personal relationship. And, at least part of the reason the plaintiff brought the dispute to court was that he or she was just plain mad at the defendant.

In short, disappointment is often a significant factor driving many small business disputes. Unfortunately, feeling let down by the other party doesn't help you evaluate whether you have a good case. Nor does it help you prepare for court or collect your money should you win. In fact, aside from their value as a goad to taking action in the first place, your personal feelings may get in the way of the clear thinking necessary to make good decisions. It follows that your first job is to try to cool your emotions. If you are having trouble doing this, enlist another small business person as your mentor. First, explain both sides of the dispute as carefully as you can. Then ask your mentor for a frank evaluation both of the merits of the argument and whether there is enough at stake to warrant taking the case to court.

B. Try Negotiation and Mediation Before Suing

As discussed in Chapter 6, trying to settle your case before going to court almost always makes sense—even if you have to accept a compromise. And this is doubly true for business disputes, where time really can equate literally to money. Not only does settling a case save valuable hours, but it helps preserve relationships and, more important, reputations—two of the cornerstones of all successful enterprises.

So before filing any court action, consider writing a firm but reasonable demand letter. This is especially useful in a breach of contract case, because in many states the law requires you to give the other party a reasonable opportunity to complete the contract (called curing the breach of contract in legal lingo). You will find several sample demand letters in Chapter 6. Here is another sample letter written in a business-to-business context:

Roger's Marine Services
10 Water Street
Rockport, Maine
August 10, 20xx

John Top, President
TipTop Builders
20 Maple Street
Rockport, Maine

Dear Mr. Top,

As you will recall, on May 13, 20xx, Roger's Marine signed a contract with TipTop Builders to repair our wooden dock and boat slip (a copy of the contract is attached). Under section 3B of this agreement you agreed to do the work in 30 days for a total payment of $20,000, with $10,000 paid upon signing and the additional $10,000 when 50% of the work was satisfactorily completed.

Although it took your business six weeks to complete the first half of the contract (true, a couple of days of the delay was caused by our not being ready), we paid you the second $10,000 installment on July 7, 20xx, at which time we reminded you that because of the summer boating season your prompt completion of the job was a priority. Under the terms of our agreement, which clearly contemplated that each half of the job be finished in two weeks, we expected work to be completed by August 1, 20xx. Except for a couple of days of additional work in mid July, the remainder of the job has not been completed and is not now in progress.

Although we understand that several of your workers have quit or are ill, it is imperative that repairs to our dock and boat slip be completed as soon as possible. Accordingly we hereby request that TipTop Builders resume work on our job in the next 45 hours and complete it within 14 business days as per our contract or that TipTop immediately refund 80% of our second payment or $8,000 (this fully credits TipTop for work done on July 10–July 12).

Because we are losing revenue every day that our dock can't be used, time is clearly of the essence in resolving this problem. Accordingly, I will call you this Wednesday morning at 10:00 a.m. to learn of your plans.

Sincerely,

Ed Rogers,
President

Despite your best efforts, you may be unable to negotiate a settlement of your dispute with another business. In that case, I recommend you next consider mediation as an alternative to filing in small claims court. Especially if your business may benefit from working with, or at least maintaining civil relations with, the other business in the future, resolving your dispute without litigation should be a priority. Although going to small claims court can be a reasonably efficient and effective way to resolve disputes in a small business context, it has the huge downside of greatly deepening enmity.

In Chapter 7, I discuss mediation, including how to get started and bargain effectively. As you'll see, in many areas of the country reasonably priced mediation services are widely available with no need to file a lawsuit. But in other communities where free mediation is provided directly by the small claims court, it may make more sense to file your case with the court clerk and make use of these mediation services. If you go this route, I recommend that you make it clear to the other party from the start that you wish to mediate. (In a few states, mediation is mandatory before going to court.)

C. Organizing Your Case

If negotiation and mediation fail to resolve your dispute, your next step is to file your court papers and serve them on the defendant. Follow the instructions in Chapters 9 through 12 and the information provided by your court.

Once you have filed, it is time to plot your strategy. Small business people normally have two advantages over run-of-the-herd mortals when it comes to preparing for court: First, as a matter of course, they maintain a record-keeping system. Depending on the type of business, this typically includes a good filing system to maintain bids, contracts, and customer correspondence, as well as a bookkeeping system that tracks payables and receivables. Taken together, these resources contain considerable raw material helpful to successfully proving a small claims case. The second advantage is more subtle, but no less real. It involves the average small business person's organizational skill—that is, his or her ability to take a confused mess of facts and organize them into a coherent and convincing narrative. Of course, when one business person sues another, those advantages often cancel out, meaning that both sides are more likely to be well organized and prepared.

Throughout this book I talk about how to decide if you have a good case (Chapter 2) and, if so, how to prepare and present it in court (Chapters 14 through 16). I don't attempt to repeat this information here. Instead, I'll supplement it in this chapter with material of particular interest in small business disputes.

1. Most Business Disputes Involve Contracts

The majority of business cases involve one business claiming that the other has broken a contract. (See Chapter 2, Section C, for more on contract law.) Start by taking a close look at any contract involved in your case. Specifically, think about your obligations under the contract—and how you expected to benefit from it. Similarly, consider what the other person was supposed to do, and what he or she expected to get out of the deal.

Oral contracts are usually legal. Most oral contracts—except those that involve the sale of real estate or the sale of goods (tangible property) worth $500 or more, or those that can't be carried out in one year—are legal and enforceable in all states. Of course, the oral contract's existence must be proven before anyone can collect on it. But when nothing has been written down, proving that a contract existed can be difficult. An exception to this general rule occurs in a situation where you were hired to work for someone on the basis of an oral promise of payment but weren't compensated. For example, if you are a commercial photographer and spent a day taking pictures of a hat designer's new creations, a judge is likely to agree with your contention that you wouldn't have done the work unless you had a deal with the designer. It isn't reasonable to assume that a business person provided services for free in this situation.

You should also remember that, as discussed in Chapter 2, a written contract need not be a formal negotiated document with both parties' signatures at the end. Under the Uniform Commercial Code (UCC)—which has been adopted in all states and applies to the sale of goods, but not services—a letter or other document qualifies as a contract if it says that the parties agree on the sale of goods and the quantity of goods sold, even if it doesn't state the price or time of delivery. If it meets this modest requirement, any letter, fax, or other writing can constitute a contract. (See "The Sale of Goods," below.)

Example: Hubert, a pest control operator, sends a fax to Josephine, the business manager of a company that manufactures rodent traps, saying, "I would like to order 1,000 gopher traps at $14 per trap." Josephine faxes back, saying, "Thank you for your order. The traps will be sent next week." There is a contract. In fact, even if Josephine didn't write back at all but simply sent the traps in a reasonable period of time, a contract would be formed based on the circumstances of the transaction.

You should also be aware that the business usage and practices in a particular field are commonly viewed as being part of a contract and can be introduced as evidence in small claims court to support or thwart your case. Thus, if Hubert ordered rodent traps in February and Josephine didn't send them until September, Hubert could present evidence in court that everyone in the rodent control business knows that traps are only salable in the spring and summer, when rodents attack crops, and that Josephine's failure to deliver the traps in the correct season constituted a breach of contract.

Finally, keep in mind that contracts can be, and often are, changed many times as negotiations go back and forth and circumstances change. The agreement that counts is the most recent one.

The Sale of Goods

The Uniform Commercial Code (UCC), adopted by all states, contains special rules affecting contracts for the sale of goods. While it requires that you produce something in writing if you want to enforce a contract for a sale of goods for $500 or more, this writing can be very brief—briefer than a normal written contract. Under the UCC, the writing need only:

• indicate that the parties have agreed on the sale of the goods, and

• state the quantity of goods being sold.

If terms such as price, time and place of delivery, or quality of goods are missing, the UCC fills them in based on customs and practices in the particular industry. And if specially manufactured goods are ordered, the UCC doesn't require any writing at all once a party makes a significant effort towards carrying out the terms of the contract.

Example: A restaurant calls and orders 500 sets of dishes from a restaurant supply company. The dishes are to feature the restaurant's logo. If the supply company makes a substantial beginning on manufacturing the dishes and applying the logo, the restaurant can't avoid liability on the contract simply because it was oral.

If work that was supposed to be done according to a contract has not yet been completed, you may have a legal duty to ask the other party to finish the job before suing. The sample letter from Roger's Marine to TipTop Builders earlier in this chapter illustrates how to do this.

But what if the other party has done such poor work that you are convinced he or she doesn't have the ability to complete the job correctly? If you are sure you can demonstrate this in court (see Chapter 15 for information on how to use the written opinion of an expert witness to help do this), it's fine to skip this "please finish the job" step. After all, the law does not require you to work with incompetents. But if there is any reasonable scenario under which the other party could complete the work, I suggest you specify in writing exactly what needs to be done and ask the contractor for a detailed schedule, including time and materials estimates, for getting it done. In my experience, poorly organized businesses will not be able to do this—a fact that will buttress your court case, because you'll now be able to show that you asked the other party to finish the job (cure the contract breach), but he or she failed to do so in a reasonable manner.

2. Presenting Your Evidence in Court

In addition to the general techniques of presenting evidence efficiently in court, here are a few more suggestions of special interest to small business people.

In business disputes, the problem is often having too much evidence, rather than too little. If this is your situation, your job is to separate the material that is essential to proving your case from that which is less important. The best approach is to organize both your verbal presentation and the backup evidence around the heart of the dispute, rather than trying to first fill in all the background information.

> **Example:** Ted, an interior decorator, was hired by Alice, the owner of Ames Country Inn, to freshen up the decor of her bed and breakfast. Ted submitted an estimate, which Alice verbally accepted on the telephone. Later, Alice stopped by Ted's office and dropped off a set of detailed architectural drawings. Ted had worked for three days on the new decor plan when Alice, quite suddenly, called and canceled the deal because, on second thought, she didn't like the colors Ted was proposing. Ted's bills were not paid, and his demand letter was ignored.
>
> Ted filed in small claims court, asking for three days' pay plus the money he was out of pocket for supplies. In court, Ted very sensibly began his presentation like this: "Your Honor, the defendant hired me to prepare a detailed plan to redecorate the Ames Country Inn. I had worked on the job for three days and bought $200 worth of supplies when she canceled. Today, I'm asking for a judgment for my normal rate of pay of $80 per hour for the 24 hours I worked, plus the $200 for supplies. The total is $2,120."
>
> Of course, there is a lot more to Ted's story, and, after stating the crux of his claims, he will need to fill in the key points. Were I Ted, I would next make these points:
> - He and Alice had worked together before and his work had always been acceptable and paid for.
> - He really did the 24 hours of work he claimed, as documented by drawings and worksheets presented as evidence.
> - He had a list of the supplies purchased for the job, plus canceled checks.
>
> This should be enough to make Ted a winner. But it is always a good idea for any litigant to anticipate and deflect the other side's key points. For example, in this instance, if Ted was pretty sure Alice was going to claim she canceled because Ted was using a theme and colors she had specifically rejected, he would be wise to make it clear that no such restrictions were contained in their contract.

Many business people have employees, partners, or business associates who have intimate knowledge of the dispute. By all means, bring them to court as witnesses. A witness who is knowledgeable about the transaction is almost always worth more than a stack of documentary evidence.

> **Example:** Assume Ted's assistant, Doris, attended a preliminary meeting with Alice at which Ted asked for a list of Alice's suggestions. Great! Doris can testify that when the subject of color came up, Alice just waved her hand and said, "You know I don't like purple too much, but it's really up to you—you're the designer."

In some situations, having a witness testify as to the normal business practices in a particular field can also be helpful. For example, if in your field goods are normally shipped within five to 15 days after an order is received (unless written notice of a delay is sent), but the person you are having a dispute with is claiming you must pay for goods that were shipped 90 days after your order was received, it would be a good idea to present an "expert" witness—or a letter from someone knowledgeable about relevant business practices—who could testify that unfilled orders are never good for more than 30 days.

D. The Drama of the Distraught Designer

Now let's review a typical small business case, with an eye to identifying winning strategies. As you'll see from Don Dimaggio's story, good preparation, including developing and presenting convincing evidence, and making a short, fact-filled, and well-organized oral presentation in court, are the keys to success.

Don Dimaggio is a successful architect and industrial designer who heads his own small company, specializing in designing small manufacturing buildings. He has offices in a converted factory building and prides himself on doing highly innovative and creative work. Recently Don did some preliminary design work for an outfit that wanted to build a small candle factory. When they didn't pay, he was out $6,500. In Don's view, the dispute developed like this:

"Ben McDonald, who makes custom candles, had a good year and wanted to expand. He called me and asked me to rough out a preliminary design. McDonald claims now that we never had a contract, but that's simply not true. What really happened is that McDonald authorized me to do some preliminary work before his company got their financing locked down. When interest rates went through the roof,

the whole deal collapsed. I had already completed my work, but they got uptight and refused to pay. My next step was to get Stephanie Carlin, a lawyer who has done some work for me, to write McDonald a letter demanding payment. When that didn't do any good, I took Stephanie's advice and filed a small claims court suit against McDonald. To do it, I had to scale my claim back to $5,000, the small claims maximum in my state. I couldn't afford to pay Stephanie $200 an hour to file in District Court, so this was really my only option."

Don's immediate problem was that he had never used small claims court before. He wasn't sure how he needed to prepare, but knew, at the very least, he had to develop a coherent plan—if for no other reason than to overcome his anxiety. Here is how I coached him to do this:

RW: "Your first job is to establish why McDonald owed you money. Presumably it's because you claim he broke a contract with you that called for him to pay you for your work."

DD: "True, but unfortunately, nothing was written down."

RW: "Oral contracts to provide service are perfectly legal if they can be proven, and judges typically bend over backwards to see that freelancers get paid. But don't be so sure you have nothing in writing. Tell me, how did McDonald contact you?"

DD: "Mutual friends recommended me to him. He phoned me and we talked a couple of times. There was some back and forth about how much I would charge for the whole job and how much for parts of it. After a little garden-variety confusion, we decided that I would start with the preliminary drawings and be paid $6,500. If the whole job came through, and we felt good about one another, I would do the entire thing. On big jobs, I always insist on a written contract, but this one was tiny and I couldn't see wasting the time. They just stopped by the next day, and we hashed out the whole thing in person."

RW: "Did you make notes?"

DD: "Sure. In fact, I made a few sketches, and then they gave me specifications and sketches they had made."

RW: "Do you still have those?"

DD: "Of course, in a file along with a couple of letters they sent later thanking me for my good ideas and making a few suggestions for changes. And, of course, I have copies of the detailed drawings I made and sent them."

RW: "Well, that's it."

DD: "What do you mean, that's it?"

RW: "You've just told me that you can prove a contract exists. The combination of the sketches they provided and the letters McDonald's company wrote you pretty convincingly proves they asked you to do the work. Of course, it helps that legally there is a strong presumption in law that when a person is asked to do work in a situation where compensation is normally expected, he must be paid when the work is completed." (Lawyers call this legal doctrine "quantum meruit.")

DD: "That all the evidence I need? I just tell the judge what happened, bring the letters and my notes, and I win?"

RW: "Not so fast. First, let me ask a basic question—are you positive you can present your case convincingly? Most people do a poor job unless they prepare an outline and practice. After you make your opening statement, you need to back it up with the key facts showing that McDonald hired you, you did the work, and he broke the contract by failing to pay you. Pick a friend who has a critical mind and appoint him or her your pretend judge. Then present your case as if you were in court. Encourage your friend to interrupt and ask questions; that's what a judge will likely do. Finally, be sure you have organized all your evidence, especially the plans and letters, so you are ready to present them to the judge at the appropriate time."

DD: "What about McDonald? Is he likely to show up?"

RW: "Many cases involving money being owed result in defaults, meaning the person being sued ignores the whole proceeding and a judgment is entered after you present written documents or orally outline your case. (See Chapter 16.) But you know that McDonald claims he doesn't owe you the money, so it's my guess he will probably show up and claim that no contract existed. You should be prepared to counter the points he is likely to make."

DD: "You're right. Although it's a total crock, he will probably claim I agreed to do the work on speculation that he would get financing and hire me for the rest of the job."

RW: "And if your case is typical, McDonald will also probably try to claim your work was substandard in some way. That way, even if you prove that a contract existed, the judge may award you less than you asked for."

DD: "But they wrote me that my design was of excellent quality."

RW: "Great, now your job is to use this evidence to play offense, not wait to present it later after the defendant criticizes your work. Because you can be pretty sure this point will come up, you should emphasize how pleased McDonald was with your work as a key part of your opening statement. And talking about going on the offensive, let's think about how to deal with McDonald's argument that there was no contract in the first place. Do you ever do preliminary work on spec, with no expectation of being paid unless the deal goes through? And is that a common way to operate in your business?"

DD: "Me? Never! I don't have to. I suppose some designers do, or at least prepare fairly detailed bid proposals without pay, but I have so much work coming my way these days, I'm turning jobs down right and left, so when I do submit a bid, I make it clear to all potential clients that I charge for preliminary drawings. In this situation, as I said, we agreed on the price in advance."

RW: "Were there any witnesses to that conversation?"

DD: "Well, Jim, my partner, sat in on one of the early discussions. We hadn't agreed on the final price yet, but we weren't too far apart."

RW: "Was it clear to Jim that you intended to charge for your work and that McDonald knew you did?"

DD: "Yes, absolutely."

RW: "Great, bring Jim to court with you as a witness. Here is how I would proceed. Organize your statement outlining what happened so it takes you no longer than five minutes to present it to the judge. Remember, start with the end of the story—that you did excellent work under the terms of a contract and were never paid. Bring your sketches and, most important, the sketch that McDonald made, along with the letters they sent you, and show them to the judge. (See Chapter 16.) Then introduce your partner and have him state that he was present when payment was discussed."

This little scenario is a simplified version of a real case. What happened? Don was given a judgment for the entire amount he requested, and McDonald paid it.

E. Old Friends Fall Out

Finally, let's review another typical small business dispute from a somewhat different perspective. Here I emphasize the steps each party can take to develop and present their legal position. Your goal will be to adopt a similarly organized approach. Try to break down your story into bite-sized pieces that can be convincingly explained in court.

Toni, a true artist when it comes to graphics, is an ignoramus when it comes to dollars and cents. Recognizing this, she never prepares her own tax returns. For the past several years, she has turned all of her tax affairs over to Phillip, a local C.P.A. Price was discussed the first year, but after that, Toni just paid Phillip's bill when the job was done. One spring, things went wrong. As usual, Toni's records weren't in great shape, and she was late in getting them to Phillip. Phillip was busy and put Toni's tax return together quickly, without discussing it with her in detail. When Toni saw the return, she was shocked by the bottom line. She was sure she was being asked to pay way too much to Uncle Sam.

She called Phillip and reminded him of a number of deductions she felt had been overlooked. There was some discussion of whether Phillip should have known about these items or not. Things began to get a little edgy when Phillip complained about Toni's sloppy records and her delay in making them available, and Toni countered by accusing Phillip of doing a hurried and substandard job. But after some grumpy talk back and forth, Phillip agreed to make the necessary corrections. In a week this was done, and the return was again sent to Toni. While her tax liability was now less, Toni was still annoyed, feeling that not all of the oversights had been corrected. Toni called Phillip again, and this time they quickly got into a shouting match. It ended with Phillip very reluctantly agreeing to look at the return a third time, but Toni saying, "Hell, no," she was taking her business to an accountant who could add.

True to her word, Toni did hire another accountant, who made several modifications that resulted in a slightly lower tax liability. The second accountant claimed that, because he needed to check all of Phillip's work to satisfy himself that it was correct, he ended up doing almost as much work as if he had started from scratch. As a result, he billed Toni for $2,300, saying that this was only $500 less than if he had not had the benefit of Phillip's work. Toni paid the bill, but wasn't happy about it.

When Phillip then billed Toni $3,000, Toni went ballistic and refused to pay. Phillip next sent Toni a demand letter stating that most of the problems were created by Toni's bad records. He added that he had already made a number of requested changes and had offered to make relatively minor final changes at no additional charge. Phillip also suggested in his letter that he was willing to try to mediate the claim using a local mediator who specialized in small business disputes. When Toni didn't answer the letter, Phillip filed suit.

Now comes the fun part, where I first pretend to be Phillip and organize his case, and then turn around and climb into Toni's shoes and structure her defense.

Phillip's Case

Step 1: Write a demand letter. Phillip has already written a clear, concise demand letter (see Chapter 6 for a discussion of how to do this). In the letter, he suggested mediation—a good idea, as both he and Toni work in the same area and Phillip has an obvious interest in not turning Toni into a vocal enemy. Unfortunately, Phillip's suggestion of mediation didn't interest Toni.

Step 2: Make sure Toni is solvent. As discussed in Chapter 3, it makes no sense for Phillip to sue if he can't collect. Fortunately, in this instance Phillip knows that Toni's business makes money, so he is pretty sure he can collect if he wins.

Step 3: Prepare evidence. In court, Phillip's main job will be to prove that he did work that was worth $3,000 and to refute Toni's likely contention that his work was so bad it amounted to a breach of their contract. Bringing copies of the tax returns he prepared for Toni as well as his own worksheets is the simplest way for Phillip to accomplish this. The returns should not be presented to the judge page by page, but as a package. The purpose is to indicate that a lot of work has been done, not go into details. In addition, Phillip will want to present as evidence the sloppy records Toni gave him.

Step 4: Rehearse the court presentation. Phillip should then be prepared to make a concise, well-organized statement of his case. If he is wise he will rehearse this in advance, as discussed in Chapter 16. Phillip's presentation should include his normal hourly rate and how many hours he worked. He should emphasize that he had to spend extra hours on Toni's return because she did not have the raw data well organized. To illustrate his point, Phillip should present to the judge Toni's raw data (for example, a shoebox full of messy receipts). If he no longer has Toni's material, he might create something that looks like it, carefully pointing out to the judge that this is a simulation of Toni's data, not the real thing. Phillip should also emphasize that he offered to redo the return a third time to make any needed additional changes, but that Toni refused to let him work on it.

Step 5: Anticipate Toni's case. Phillip has now presented his basic breach of contract case, by testifying that he was hired to do a job, he did it, and he wasn't paid. However, Phillip would be wise to go beyond this and anticipate at least some of Toni's defenses, which will almost surely involve the claim that Phillip broke the contract by doing poor quality work and doing it late. In addition, Phillip should anticipate Toni's backup claim that he charged too much and that the judge should award him far less. To accomplish this, Phillip should attempt to take the sting out of Toni's likely presentation by saying something along these lines:

"Your Honor, when I finished my work, my client pointed out that several deductions had been overlooked. I believed then and believe now that this was because the data she provided me with was disorganized and inadequate, but I did rework the return and correct several items that were left out. When my client told me that she felt the revised draft needed additional changes, I again told her that I would work with her to make any necessary modifications. It was at this point that she refused to let me see the returns and hired another accountant. In my professional opinion, very little work remained to be done at this stage—certainly nothing that couldn't be accomplished in an hour or two.

"Now, as to the amount charged—it took me ten hours to reconstruct what went on in the defendant's business from the mess of incomplete and incoherent records I was given. At $90 per hour, this means that $900 of my bill involved work that had to be done prior to actually preparing the return, meaning that I charged $2100 to actually prepare the return. This fee is very reasonable given the fees charged by other local tax preparers for similar work. Taking into consideration the difficult circumstances, I believe I charged fairly for the work I did, and that I did my work well."

Toni's Case

Okay, so much for getting into the head of an indignant accountant. Now let me help Toni, the upset graphic artist, present her case.

Step 1: Negotiate, don't litigate. For starters, I think Toni made a mistake by refusing to negotiate or mediate with Phillip. Because this is a dispute over the quality of work, a judge is likely to enter a compromise judgment. It would have saved time and anxiety for Toni and Phillip to settle outside of court and put the matter behind them. (See Chapter 6.)

Step 2: Prepare a written statement. Once Toni decided not to try to settle the case, it became time for her to write a letter of her own, rebutting Phillip's demand letter point by point. (See Chapter 6.) She should bring a copy of this letter to court and give it to the judge as part of her presentation. In some states, the judge doesn't have to accept it (it's not really evidence of anything except the fact that Phillip's request for payment was rejected). More often than not, however, the judge will look at all the demand letters submitted. The key in convincing the judge to read Toni's statement is for her to put it in the form of a letter she actually sends to Phillip.

Step 3: Prepare evidence. To have any chance of winning, Toni will need to convince the judge that Phillip did an incompetent job. The tax return as correctly prepared by the new accountant will be of some help, because it presumably includes deductions Phillip overlooked, with the result that Toni owed less tax. But it will be far better to have the second accountant or some other tax expert come to court to testify about the details of Phillip's substandard work. Unfortunately for Toni, professionals are commonly reluctant to testify against one another, so this may be difficult to arrange. Anyway, Toni may conclude it's too expensive to pay an expert to appear in court. But following the instructions in Chapter 15, Toni should at the very least get a letter from her new accountant—or some other tax expert—outlining the things Phillip missed. Most, though not all, small claims courts will accept written letters from experts—carefully check your state's rules on this point (see the Appendix for your state's website).

Step 4: Prepare a convincing court presentation. Toni should prepare to testify that she refused to pay the bill because she felt that Phillip's work was so poorly done that she didn't trust Phillip to finish the job. (And, of course, she should practice her presentation.) To make this point effectively, Toni should testify as to the details of several of the tax issues that Phillip overlooked. Thus, if Toni provided Phillip with information concerning the purchase of several items of expensive equipment and Phillip forgot to claim depreciation, this would be important evidence of poor work. But Toni should be careful to make her points about tax law relatively brief and understandable. She won't gain anything from a long and boring rehash of her entire return. One good approach might be for Toni to submit pertinent sections of IRS publications or a privately published tax guide outlining the rules that require equipment to be depreciated.

Step 5: Rebutting Phillip's points in advance. Toni should also present to the court her canceled checks, to establish the amounts she paid Phillip for the last several years' returns. (This strategy assumes, of course, that Phillip's previous bills were substantially less.) For example, if Toni had been billed $1,700 and $1,900 in the two previous years, it would raise some questions as to whether Phillip's bill of $3,000 for the current year was reasonable.

If Toni can convince the judge that Phillip padded his bill because he was mad about being fired, she should at the very least succeed in reducing the amount Phillip is awarded.

 Both Toni and Phillip should be prepared to answer questions. Especially in a case like this one involving technical matters, the judge is almost sure to interrupt both Toni's and Phillip's presentations and ask for explanation and details. So in addition to preparing and practicing presenting their cases before a critical friend, both Phillip and Toni should be prepared to answer any questions and to then smoothly return to presenting their cases.

What Happened?

Phillip was given a judgment for $1,800. The judge didn't explain his reasoning, but apparently felt that there was some right on each side. So the judge split the difference with a little edge to Phillip, probably because Toni hired him in the first place and had worked with him for several years, so she was on somewhat shaky ground claiming he was incompetent. This sort of compromise decision, where each side is given something, is common in small claims court. It again illustrates the wisdom of working out or mediating compromise out of court. Even if Toni and Phillip had arrived at a solution where one or the other gave up a little more than the judge ordered, their savings in time and aggravation probably would have more than made up the difference. ■

Judgment and Appeal

A. The Judgment

In most states, including California, the decision in your case will be mailed to the address on record with the clerk any time from a few days to a few weeks after your case is heard. Default judgments are normally announced in the courtroom. The truth is that, in the vast majority of contested cases, the judge has already made up his or her mind at the time the case is heard, and notes down the decision before the parties leave the courtroom. Decisions are sent by mail because the court didn't want to deal with angry, unhappy losers, especially those few who might get violent. More recently, however, some judges have begun explaining their decisions in court, on the theory that both parties are entitled to know why a particular decision was reached. One progressive judge explained his policy in this regard as follows: "The only time I don't announce in court is when I have phoning or research to do or if I feel the losing party will be unnecessarily embarrassed in front of the audience."

Legal Jargon Note: Now that a judgment has been entered, we need to expand our vocabulary slightly. The person who wins the case (gets the judgment) now becomes "the judgment creditor," and the loser is known as "the judgment debtor."

Often, the person who lost feels the judge would surely have made a different decision if he or she hadn't gotten mixed up or overlooked some crucial fact, or had properly understood an argument. On the basis of my experience on the bench, I can tell you that, in the vast majority of small claims cases, there is little likelihood the judge would change a decision even if you had a chance to argue the whole case over. In any event, you don't. You have had your chance and the decision has gone against you. It won't help you to call or visit the judge, or to send him or her documents through the mail. (See Section E, below, for appeal rights.)

If you sued more than one person, the judgment should indicate who the judgment is against and for how much. Some defendants may not owe anything, or their financial liability may be limited to a stated amount. If so, this is the maximum you can collect from them. However, in most instances where a judgment is against two or more defendants, they will be "jointly and severally liable." This means that each defendant is 100% liable to pay you the entire amount. For example, if you receive a $1,000 judgment against two defendants, you may collect in any proportion from either defendant (for example, you could collect $800 from one defendant and $200 from another). If you collect a disproportionate amount from one defendant, he or she is left with the task of evening things out. (In this example, the defendant who paid the $800 could sue the other for $300 so that each ends up having paid $500.)

The words "joint and several liability" may not appear on the judgment. A judgment against two or more defendants will often simply list the names of the judgment debtors. This means they are jointly and severally liable for the entire amount. If the judge intended for one defendant's judgment debt liability to be limited (say to $200), then the written judgment will make that clear.

B. Installment Payments

In a great many states, a judge may order that the loser be allowed to pay the winner over a period of time, rather than all at once. But the judge normally won't make this sort of order unless you request it. If you are in a state in which the judge announces decisions in court, this is not a problem—you'll be able to ask for time payments if you lose. If you're in a state in which decisions are sent by mail, and you have no real defense to a claim or you have a fairly good case but aren't sure which way the judge will go, plan ahead. Tell the judge that, if the judgment goes against you, you wish to pay in installments. You might put your request this way:

- "In closing my presentation, I would like to say that I believe I have a convincing case and should be awarded the judgment, but in the event that you rule for my opponent, I would like you to allow me to make time payments of no more than (whatever amount is convenient to you) per month."

Or, if you have no real defense:

- "Your Honor, I request that you enter the judgment against me for no more than (an amount convenient to you) per month."

If you neglect to ask for time payments in court and wish to make this request after you receive the judgment, first contact the other party to see if he or she will voluntarily agree to accept the money on a schedule under which you can afford to pay. If the other party agrees, it is wise to write your agreement down and each sign it. Some courts also have a form for you to fill out, as in the sample below. If your opponent is an all-or-nothing sort of person and refuses payments, promptly contact the court clerk and ask that the case again be brought before the judge—not as to the facts, but only to set up a payment schedule you can live with. The clerk should arrange things for you, but if there is a problem, write a letter like this one to the judge:

---

47 West Adams St.
Brooklyn, NY
October 17, 20xx

Honorable Felix Hamburg
Judge of the Small Claims Court
111 Center St.
New York, NY

Re: *Elliot v. Toller*
Index No. __

Dear Judge Hamburg:

I recently appeared before you in the case of *Elliot v. Toller* (Index No. _____). Mr. Elliot was awarded a judgment in the amount of $526. Paying this amount all at once would be nearly impossible because of (*lack of employment, illness or whatever*). I can pay $25 per month.

Please change the order in this case to allow for a $25 per month payment. If it is necessary for me to make this request in court, please inform me of the time I should be present.

Sincerely,

John Toller

REQUEST TO PAY JUDGMENT IN INSTALLMENTS

Name and Address of Court: Ventura County Municipal Court
Small Claims Div.
800 So. Victoria Ave
Ventura, CA 93009

SMALL CLAIMS CASE NO.

PLAINTIFF/DEMANDANTE *(Name, address, and telephone number of each)*:

Don Gonzalez
P. O. Box 6489
Ventura CA 93006
805-654-2610
Telephone No.:

DEFENDANT/DEMANDADO *(Name, address, and telephone number of each)*:

Luke Smith
10 N. Main St.
Ventura, CA 93006
805-654-2609
Telephone No.:

Telephone No.:   Telephone No.:

☐ See attached sheet for additional plaintiffs and defendants.

REQUEST TO PAY JUDGMENT IN INSTALLMENTS

1. I request the court to allow me to make installment payments on the judgment entered against me in this case in the amount and manner stated below.
2. My request is based on this declaration, the court records, my completed financial declaration (Form EJ-165 — *obtain from court clerk*) attached to this declaration, and any other evidence that may be presented.
   NOTE: YOU MUST ATTACH A COMPLETED FINANCIAL DECLARATION WITH THIS REQUEST TO MAKE INSTALLMENT PAYMENTS.
3. Judgment was entered against me in this matter on *(date)*: 8/31/___ in the amount of *(specify)*: $1,004.91
4. Payment of the entire amount of the judgment at one time will be a hardship on me because *(specify)*:

   I am currently unemployed

5. I can and will make payments toward the judgment in the amount of *(specify)*: $ 40.00   per ☐ week ☒ month.
6. I request the court to order that I make payments as specified in item 5 and that execution on the judgment be stayed as long as I make payments according to this schedule.

I declare under penalty of perjury under the laws of the State of California that the foregoing is true and correct.

Date: 10/12/___

...Luke Smith..........................   ▶ *Luke Smith*
(TYPE OR PRINT NAME)   (SIGNATURE OF JUDGMENT DEBTOR)

NOTICE TO JUDGMENT CREDITOR

The judgment debtor has requested the court to allow payment of the judgment in installments. Complete the following and return this form to the court within 10 days. You will be notified of the court's order, or, if a hearing is necessary, the date of the hearing.

1. I am the judgment creditor, and I have read and considered the judgment debtor's request to make installment payments on the judgment.
2. a. ☐ I am willing to accept the payment schedule the judgment debtor has requested.
   b. ☐ I am willing to accept payments in the amount of *(specify)*: $ per ☐ week ☐ month.
   c. ☐ I am opposed to accepting installment payments because *(specify)*:

I declare under penalty of perjury under the laws of the State of California that the foregoing is true and correct.

Date:

....   ▶
(TYPE OR PRINT NAME)   (SIGNATURE OF JUDGMENT CREDITOR)

SEE REVERSE FOR HEARING DATE, IF ANY.
(Continued on reverse)

Form Approved by the
Judicial Council of California
SC-106 [New January 1, 1992]

REQUEST TO PAY JUDGMENT IN INSTALLMENTS
(Small Claims)

Code of Civil Procedure, § 116.620(b)

C. Paying the Judgment Directly to the Court

In some states the judgment debtor may pay the amount of the judgment directly to the small claims court, which will then notify the judgment creditor. This procedure is helpful for a judgment debtor who doesn't want to deal directly with the prevailing party or doesn't know his or her current address. Contact your small claims clerk to find out whether your court has a direct pay procedure.

D. The Satisfaction of Judgment

In all states, once a judgment is fully paid, a judgment creditor (the person who won the case, remember) must acknowledge the receipt of payment by filing a "Satisfaction of Judgment" form with the court clerk. Doing so makes it clear to the world (and especially credit rating agencies) that the person who lost the case (the judgment debtor) has met his or her obligation. If the judgment creditor also recorded a lien on the judgment debtor's real property (see Chapter 25), he or she must make sure the lien is removed. Ask the small claims clerk for more information.

If a judgment creditor receives payment in full on a judgment but fails to file a satisfaction of judgment, the judgment debtor will want to send a written demand that this be done. A first-class letter is adequate. If, after written demand, the judgment creditor still doesn't file within the required number of days of the request (usually between 15 and 30—check your local rules) and without just cause, many states allow the judgment debtor to recover all actual damages he or she may sustain by reason of such failure (for example, denial of a credit application). In addition, some states will penalize the judgment creditor by requiring him or her to pay a set amount of money to the judgment debtor.

Here is a sample satisfaction of judgment form used in California. Again, it should be signed by the judgment creditor when the judgment is paid, and then filed with the court clerk. Don't forget to do this; otherwise, you may have to track down the other party later.

ACKNOWLEDGMENT OF SATISFACTION OF JUDGMENT

EJ-100

ATTORNEY OR PARTY WITHOUT ATTORNEY *(Name, state bar number, and address):*

After recording return to:

    Phillip Yee
    150 Elm Street
    Martinez, CA 94553

TELEPHONE NO.:   510-555-1234
FAX NO. *(Optional)*:
E-MAIL ADDRESS *(Optional)*:
ATTORNEY FOR *(Name)*:

SUPERIOR COURT OF CALIFORNIA, COUNTY OF   Contra Costa
STREET ADDRESS:
MAILING ADDRESS: 1020 Ward Street
CITY AND ZIP CODE: Martinez, CA 94553
BRANCH NAME:

FOR RECORDER'S OR SECRETARY OF STATE'S USE ONLY

PLAINTIFF: Phillip Yee

DEFENDANT: Eric Smith Motors, Inc.

CASE NUMBER:

ACKNOWLEDGMENT OF SATISFACTION OF JUDGMENT	FOR COURT USE ONLY
[X] **FULL** [ ] **PARTIAL** [ ] **MATURED INSTALLMENT**	

1. Satisfaction of the judgment is acknowledged as follows:
   a. [X] Full satisfaction
       (1) [X] Judgment is satisfied in full.
       (2) [ ] The judgment creditor has accepted payment or performance other than that specified in the judgment in full satisfaction of the judgment.
   b. [ ] Partial satisfaction
       The amount received in partial satisfaction of the judgment is $
   c. [ ] Matured installment
       All matured installments under the installment judgment have been satisfied as of *(date)*:

2. Full name and address of judgment creditor:*
   Eric Smith Motors, Inc.
   1000 Main Street
   Lafayette, CA 94549

3. Full name and address of assignee of record, if any:

4. Full name and address of judgment debtor being fully or partially released:*
   Phillip Yee
   150 Elm Street
   Martinez, CA 94553

5. a. Judgment entered on *(date)*:   7/21/03
   b. [ ] Renewal entered on *(date)*:

6. [X] An [X] abstract of judgment [ ] certified copy of the judgment has been recorded as follows *(complete all information for each county where recorded)*:

COUNTY	DATE OF RECORDING	INSTRUMENT NUMBER
Contra Costa	8/14/03	21

7. [ ] A notice of judgment lien has been filed in the office of the Secretary of State as file number *(specify)*:

NOTICE TO JUDGMENT DEBTOR: If this is an acknowledgment of full satisfaction of judgment, it will have to be recorded in each county shown in item 6 above, if any, in order to release the judgment lien, and will have to be filed in the office of the Secretary of State to terminate any judgment lien on personal property.

Date: 3/24/04

▶ *Phillip Yee*

*(SIGNATURE OF JUDGMENT CREDITOR OR ASSIGNEE OF CREDITOR OR ATTORNEY**)*

Page 1 of 1

*The names of the judgment creditor and judgment debtor must be stated as shown in any Abstract of Judgment which was recorded and is being released by this satisfaction. ** A separate notary acknowledgment must be attached for each signature.

Form Approved for Optional Use
Judicial Council of California
EJ-100 [Rev. January 1, 2003]

ACKNOWLEDGMENT OF SATISFACTION OF JUDGMENT

Code of Civ. Proc., §§ 724, 060,
724, 120, 724, 250

Sometimes judgment debtors forget to make sure the satisfaction of judgment form is signed when they paid a judgment, only to find that they can't locate the judgment creditor later. If this happens and you need a satisfaction of judgment to clean up your credit record or for some other reason, you can usually get one if you present the court with proof the judgment was paid. The following documents will help you:

- your canceled check or money order for the full amount of the judgment, or a cash receipt for the full amount of the judgment, signed by the judgment creditor after the date the court awarded judgment, and

- a statement by you, signed under penalty of perjury, stating all of the following:

  - The judgment creditor has been paid the full amount of the judgment and costs.

  - The judgment creditor has been asked to file a satisfaction of judgment and refuses to do so or can't be located.

  - The documents attached (such as the check or money order) constitute evidence of the judgment creditor's receipt of the payment.

See "Sample Statement," below. Check with the clerk of your state for your local rules.

It's easy to get a copy of a satisfaction of judgment. If either party ever needs it (for example, to correct an out-of-date credit report), the court clerk will, for a small fee, provide a certified copy of a filed satisfaction of judgment.

Sample Statement

My name is John Elliot. On January 11, 20xx a judgment was awarded against me in small claims court in Ithaca, New York (Case # 1234). On March 20, 20xx I paid Beatrice Small, the prevailing party, $1,200, the full amount of this judgment [or, if payments were made in installments—"I paid Beatrice Small, the prevailing party in this action, the final installment necessary to pay this judgment in full."]

I attach to this statement a canceled check [or other proof that the judgment was paid] for the full amount of the judgment endorsed by Beatrice Small.

Beatrice Small did not voluntarily file a satisfaction of judgment. When I tried to contact her, I learned that she had moved and had left no forwarding address.

DATED: June 5, 20xx.   _____

                                            John Elliot

E. The Appeal

Unlike small claims court itself, where rules and procedures are remarkably the same throughout the United States, the rules that cover appeals from small claims court judgments vary greatly from one state to the next. A few, such as Connecticut, Hawaii, Michigan, North Dakota, and South Dakota, allow no appeal. New York allows an appeal of a judge's decision, but not an attorney-arbitrator's. California, Massachusetts, and a few other states allow a losing defendant to appeal, but do not permit the person who brought the suit (the plaintiff) to do so, except to appeal from counter-claims initiated by the defendant. In the Appendix you will find a very brief summary of the appeal procedures of every state.

Determining whether you are eligible to appeal is important, but it is only part of the information you need. It is just as important to determine what kind of appeal is permitted in your state. While it may be true, as Gertrude Stein suggested, that "a rose is a rose is a rose," small claims appeals are not nearly so consistent. Some states allow an appeal only on questions of law, while others allow the whole case to be replayed from scratch. Let's pause for a moment and look at some of the differences.

You can't appeal if you didn't show up in small claims court. Appeal rights are almost always restricted to those who showed up in small claims court, argued their case and lost. If you defaulted (didn't show up), you normally can't appeal unless and until you get the default set aside. Normally you must file paperwork to do this almost immediately, or the small claims judgment will become final and unappealable. (See Chapter 10, Section F.)

1. New Trial on Appeal

In several states, including Pennsylvania and Texas, either party can appeal and have the case heard over from scratch. In other states, including California and Massachusetts, only the defendant can appeal (in most cases), but if he or she does, the whole case is also presented again by both sides, as if the first hearing hadn't occurred. When a whole new hearing is allowed on appeal (it's called a trial "de novo," in legalese), you simply argue the case over, presenting all necessary witnesses, documents and testimony. Starting from scratch is required because records usually aren't kept at small claims court hearings. However, in a few courts, judges now tape record hearings, and these recordings are available to the judge who considers the appeal as part of the reargument of the case.

On appeal, both sides should give careful thought to how their presentation can be improved. This is particularly true if you are the person who lost. Ask yourself: Did the judge decide against me because I presented my case poorly or because I didn't support my statements with evidence? Or did the judge simply misapply the law? To answer these questions, you may have to do some additional legal research. (See Chapter 1, Section D, for some tips on how to do this.) Once you have decided how to improve your case, practice presenting it to an objective friend. When you are done, ask your friend which parts of your presentation were convincing and which need more work.

In some states, small claims appeals can be presented to the judge just as informally as any small claims court case. At the other extreme, however, some states' small claims court appeal rules require that an appeal be conducted with all the pomp and circumstance of a regular trial court. Because procedures can differ even within the same state, I can't tell you exactly what type of hearing you will face. So, again, it is important to take the time to check out exactly what type of appeal hearing rules you will encounter. For example, you may learn you'll need to be prepared to present your testimony while sitting in the witness box. You may also have to question your witnesses using the formal lawyer style you have seen so often on TV, and introduce evidence according to a strict, step-by-step script.

What should you do if you see that your appeal will be conducted in a style you find intimidating?

- Read *Represent Yourself in Court*, by Paul Bergman and Sara J. Berman-Barrett (Nolo). This book beautifully explains how to conduct a contested civil trial in a formal courtroom setting, including how to present testimony and cross-examine witnesses. It should quickly increase your comfort level.

- Ask the judge, in advance, to conduct your appeal as informally as possible. You can do this on the day of your hearing or, better yet, by writing a brief, polite letter to the court ahead of time. Explain that, as a nonlawyer, you are thoroughly prepared to present the facts of your case, but because you are unfamiliar with formal rules of evidence and procedure, you would appreciate it if your small claims appeal could be conducted so that a citizen who has not spent three years at law school is given a fair opportunity to be heard.

• During your small claims appeal, if there is some procedure you don't understand, politely ask the judge for an explanation. If necessary, remind the judge that, as a taxpayer and a citizen, you are entitled to understand the rules and procedures that control the presentation of your case.

Don't assume the deck is stacked against you just because you lost in small claims court. You may have heard scuttlebutt to the effect that some higher court judges consider small claims appeals to be a nuisance, and try to discourage them by routinely upholding the original judgment. If there is any truth to this urban legend, it's very little. My experience is that most judges will give you a fair hearing on appeal if you are well prepared and able to present a convincing case. So, if you believe you were victimized by a bad decision in small claims court and your case involves enough money to make a further investment of time and energy worthwhile, go ahead and appeal.

2. Appeal on Questions of Law Only

In many states, including Alaska, Colorado, Wisconsin, and Vermont, appeals can be based only on questions of law, not on the facts of the case. (See the Appendix for the other states.) This is the sort of appeal that the United States Supreme Court and the other formal appellate courts normally hear.

Example 1: You sue your mechanic in small claims court, claiming that he botched a repair job on your car. After listening to both sides, the judge rules for the mechanic, concluding that the repairs were made properly and something else was wrong with your car. You disagree, contending that the repairperson really did mess up the job. Too bad—you are not eligible to appeal, because this is a factual dispute.

Example 2: You are a tenant suing for the return of a cleaning deposit withheld by the landlord. The court agrees with you and awards you the amount of the deposit plus $500 in punitive damages. The landlord appeals, claiming that under the law of your state, the judge only has the power to award punitive damages in the amount of $250. Because this appeal claims a mistake was made in applying the law, it is proper and will be considered.

In most states, appeals made on the basis of a mistake of law must be backed up by a written outline of what the claimed mistakes are. This can put nonlawyers at a disadvantage, because they are unfamiliar with legal research and legal writing techniques. Start by contacting the court clerk and requesting all forms and rules governing appeals. While you should take these seriously and do your best to comply, the good news is that most appellate judges will consider any well-reasoned written statement you submit claiming the small claims judge made a legal error.

Here is a brief example of appropriate paperwork:

Appeal from Small Claims Judgment #___, Based on Legal Error: Under the laws of the state of
_____.

A small claims judgment may be set aside if it is based on a legal error or mistake. In my personal injury case, the court incorrectly applied the statute of limitations, because it did not take into consideration the fact that I was a minor when the accident occurred.

My case is based on a personal injury I suffered on January 23, 2001, when I was 17 years and two months old. The Small Claims judge dismissed my case because it was not filed within one year after my injury, as is required by the statute of limitations. This was an incorrect application of the law.

It's true that under the terms of Code of Civil Procedure Sec. 340, a personal injury case must normally be filed within one year of the date of the injury, which in my case occurred on January 23, 2001. However, Sec. 352 of the Code of Civil Procedure also states: "If a person entitled to bring an action, mentioned in Chapter 3 of this title, be, at the time the cause of action occurred, ... under the age of majority ... the time of such disability is not a part of the time limited for the commencement of the action."

Because I was still a minor until November 23, 2002 (when I turned 18), under the terms of CCP Sec. 352, it was from this date (not from January 23, 2001) that the court should have begun counting the one-year statute of limitations for personal injury actions. Therefore, I was entitled to file my case until November 22, 2003. In fact, because I filed on June 27, 2003, I was well within the allowed time.

In conclusion, I request that the judgment in this case be vacated and that I be granted a new small claims court hearing.

F. Filing Your Appeal

If you haven't already done so, it is absolutely essential that you obtain and study a copy of your state's small claims appeal rules. They vary considerably, especially between those states where you can only appeal questions of law and those where you are entitled to a completely new trial.

1. File Your Appeal Promptly

In all states, appeals must be filed promptly (usually within 10 to 30 days), so wherever you are, don't delay. In California, New York, Ohio, and many other states, you must file a notice of appeal within 30 days after the court clerk mails the judgment to the parties (or hands it over, if a decision is made in the courtroom). This means that if the decision was mailed, there will be less than 30 days to file an appeal from the day that the defendant receives the judgment. In a number of other states, including Massachusetts, Texas, and Virginia, appeals must be filed within 10 days.

> ⚠️ **Don't oversleep in Washington, DC or Rhode Island!** You'll have only two days to appeal your small claims court decision in Rhode Island, and three days in Washington, DC. Luckily, weekends and holidays don't count.

You'll need to consult your state statute to find out when to start counting your time to appeal. Because many states start counting from the date the judgment was mailed, this date, which should appear on the judgment, is critical. If for some reason attributable to the magic of the U.S. Postal Service your judgment doesn't show up within the number of days in which you are allowed to appeal, call the small claims clerk immediately and request help in getting an extension of time to file your appeal.

Appeals must usually be filed using a form supplied by the small claims court.

2. Appeal Fees

The appeal fee is often higher than the original filing fee. If you ultimately win your appeal (that is, get the original decision turned around in your favor), you can add these court costs to the judgment. In many states, the party filing an appeal must post a cash bond (or written guarantee by financially solvent adults) to cover the amount of the judgment if he or she loses.

G. Arguing Your Appeal Without a Lawyer

You are entitled to have an attorney in formal court, where small claims court appeals are heard. By definition, your small claims case is not worth big bucks, so you will probably decide it is not wise to hire one. Indeed, there should be little practical reason for an attorney, as you probably have an excellent grasp of the issues by this time.

But what if your opponent hires a lawyer? Aren't you at a disadvantage if you represent yourself? Not necessarily. As noted in Section D, above, in many states, the appeals court must follow informal rules similar to those used in small claims court. This puts you on a relatively equal footing, even if your opponent has a lawyer. If you have prepared carefully, you may even have an advantage: You carry with you the honest conviction that you are right, while a lawyer arguing a small claims appeal always seems a bit pathetic. If, despite this commonsense view of the situation, you still feel a little intimidated, the best cure is to go watch a few small claims appeals. Ask the court clerk when they are scheduled.

Jury Trial Note: A few states, including Massachusetts, Minnesota, North Carolina, and Virginia, permit jury trials on appeal. Most states don't. Check with your court clerk and the Appendix.

Discovery Note: Most states allow you to subpoena documents for your original hearing. (See Chapter 15, Section C.) Other formal discovery techniques, such as taking the deposition of your opponent and witnesses or requesting that your opponent answer a series of written questions, are normally prohibited in small claims court. Unfortunately, in a few states, some of these discovery techniques are allowed for appeals. This is a mistake, because these techniques are expensive and time-consuming (and they favor lawyers, who know all the tricks). I look forward to the day when these have been eliminated in all states.

H. Further Appeals

If a defendant loses the appeal, there is usually no right to file a second appeal. However, it is sometimes possible to file an "extraordinary writ" (a special request for review based on extraordinary circumstances) to a court of appeal claiming that either the small claims court or first appeals court has made a serious legal mistake in their handling of the case (for example, had no power to consider the issues involved in your case). In some states, the lower court judge may have the power to recommend that the court of appeal hear your case. But because of the relatively small amounts of money involved, extraordinary writs based on small claims judgments are almost never filed. And when they are, they are seldom granted. For these reasons, I do not cover this procedure here. ■

Collecting Your Money

You won. You undoubtedly want to collect every penny from the opposing party or parties pronto, but slow down a bit. You need to be patient for a short while longer. Here's why.

A.   When You Can Start Collection Efforts

When you can collect depends in part upon whether or not the defendant was in court for the hearing.

1.   Contested Cases

If the other party appeared in court and fought the case, you must wait to see if he or she files an appeal. Depending on your state's rules, an appeal must normally be filed within 10 to 30 days.

   Exception: In a few states, no appeals are allowed, and in several more, only a losing defendant can appeal. (See the Appendix.) If the other party can't appeal, you can begin collection activities immediately.

2.   Default Judgments

If you got your judgment because the defendant defaulted (that is, didn't show up), the defendant usually can't appeal until he or she first asks the court to set aside the default. Most defendants who didn't show up in the first place don't bother to do this. Nevertheless, in some states, such as California, you must wait out the time period during which the losing party is allowed to ask the court to set aside the default judgment. (See Chapter 11.) And even if waiting isn't required, it's always a good idea if you are in a state that allows defendants a certain number of days in which to petition the court to set aside the default judgment. The reason is simple: If you move to collect your judgment immediately, you may alert the defendant to try to set it aside.

Let sleeping defendants lie. If you face a short waiting period before you can initiate official collections procedures (such as a wage attachment), is it a good idea to use this time to ask the losing party to pay up voluntarily? No. While it is not illegal to ask for your money during these waiting periods, it is unwise. If you make your request for money, you may remind the defendant to take advantage of his or her right to appeal or set aside a default judgment.

3. After the waiting period

Once any waiting period is up, what should you do? Try asking politely for your money. This works in many cases, especially if you have sued a responsible person or business. If you don't have personal contact with the person who owes you money, try a note like the one below. Notice that the note mentions the possibility of making payments directly to the court—use this if you think there is a chance that the judgment debtor is unwilling to deal with you directly (after checking that this payment option is available in your state).

P.O. Box 66
Byron, CA
February 15, 20xx

Mildred Edwards
11 Milvia Street
Byron, CA

Dear Mrs. Edwards:

As you know, a judgment was entered against you in small claims court on January 15 in the amount of $1,457.86. As the judgment creditor, I would appreciate your paying this amount to me within 10 days. If you would prefer to pay the small claims court and have them transfer payments to me, you can do so. I believe there is a charge for this service, however.

Thank you for your consideration.

Very truly yours,

David Osaki

If you receive no payment after sending your polite note, you will have to get serious about collecting your money—or forget it. The emphasis in the previous sentence should be on the word "you." Much to many people's surprise, the court does not enforce its judgments and collect money for you—you have to do it yourself.

Don't harass the debtor. Now that you are a creditor, you are subject to the laws that protect debtors from abusive or unfair conduct. At a minimum, they require that you don't call the debtor at odd hours or badmouth him or her in the community (of course, it's fine to talk about the judgment to officials who are helping with the collection process).

Fortunately, a few of the ways to collect money from a debtor are relatively easy. I mentioned these briefly in Chapter 3. Hopefully, you gave some thought to collection before you brought your case. Should you only now realize that your opponent doesn't have the money to buy a toothbrush, and probably never will, you are better off not wasting more time and money trying to get your money, at least for the present. If the deadbeat debtor nevertheless owns real property, you'll want to establish a lien on it, as detailed in Section C, below.

But if the debtor doesn't even own any real property, your only sensible course of action is to sit on your judgment, with the hope that your judgment debtor will show a few signs of life in the future. Remember, a judgment is valid for many years (between ten and 20 years in most states) and can be renewed for an additional number of years if you can show you have tried to collect it but failed.

Collection rules are getting tighter. A few states, such as New York, are putting teeth into their collection rules. In New York, if a judgment debtor who has the ability to do so doesn't pay three or more small claims court judgments, a judgment creditor can get triple the judgment as damages, plus attorney fees. If you are in New York, contact the small claims court clerk for details.

When the Debtor Pays by Check

Always make copies of checks written by the debtor to pay the judgment. Should you receive only partial payment and later want to collect the rest, you'll have information on where the debtor has been banking. If the debtor's check bounces, you may, depending on your state's law, be entitled to:

• Sue in small claims court for the original amount of the bounced check plus damages. First, you must follow your state's detailed procedures, usually including sending a demand letter to the debtor (often by certified mail).

• See if your county's district attorney's office will prosecute the debtor or refer the debtor to a bad check diversion program. These generally allow the person who wrote the bad check to avoid prosecution by making the check good and complying with other rules. Usually, you cannot seek damages if you enlist the district attorney's help—but you'll be spared the hassle of another lawsuit.

B. Finding the Debtor's Assets

Collecting on your small claims judgment usually isn't difficult if the judgment debtor has some money or property and you know where it is. But what do you do when you suspect that money or other assets exist, but have no idea how to find them? For example, you may know a person works, but not where, or that he has money in the bank, but not which one. Wouldn't it be nice to simply ask the judgment debtor and have the right to insist on an answer?

Well, you often can. In a number of states, when a small claims court judgment is entered against a person (or business), the loser (judgment debtor) must fill out a "Statement of Assets" form. This form must be sent by the judgment debtor to the person who won the case (the judgment creditor) within a required number of days after the judgment is mailed out by the clerk, *unless* the judgment debtor pays off the judgment, appeals, or makes a motion to set aside or vacate the judgment.

If a judgment debtor does not fill out this statement of assets form when required to do so (or if no such form exists), the judgment creditor can ask the court clerk to issue an order requiring the judgment debtor to appear in court in person to be questioned. In some states, this is called an order of examination or judgment debtor's examination. This order, which must be properly served on the judgment debtor, requires the debtor to show up in court and provide the information personally. If the debtor fails to show up, the judge can issue a bench warrant for his or her arrest. Oh, and one hint—in many states, at the order of examination hearing, the judgment creditor can ask if the debtor has any cash in his or her possession. If so, this can be taken to satisfy at least a portion of the debt right on the spot.

Collecting Judgments Across State Lines

What if your judgment debtor moves to another state, or you discover that he or she owns property or assets elsewhere? Collecting on the judgment will become less convenient, but it is still possible. The majority of U.S. states have enacted what's called the Uniform Enforcement of Foreign Judgments Act, creating standard procedures for going after a debtor's assets or property across state lines.

Here's how it ordinarily works: Say you file your small claims case in Illinois and get a judgment for $2,500. When you try to collect, you discover that the debtor has moved to Florida. In order to start your collection efforts, you will need to file your judgment in Florida, the new state. The procedure there, as in most states, is that you mail a certified copy of the original judgment to the Florida court clerk, along with an affidavit showing your and the judgment debtor's names and addresses. (Some states vary this routine, so check with the court clerk first.)

Once the court receives the certified copy and affidavit, your filing becomes a valid part of the court record. The court will also notify the judgment debtor of your filing. Now you can proceed with your collection efforts, following the collection laws of the new state.

C. Creating Property Liens

One important collection device used by judgment creditors is the property lien. In just under half of the states, the entry of a court judgment automatically creates a lien on any real property the debtor owns in the county where the judgment was obtained. In the rest of the states, you must record the judgment with the county to create a lien on the debtor's real property. Also, in some states where you do not get a lien on personal property after the judgment is entered or recorded, you may be able to get a lien on the debtor's personal property by filing the judgment with the Secretary of State. See *Money Troubles: Legal Strategies to Cope With Your Debts,* by Robin Leonard (Nolo), for a comprehensive listing of different states' lien laws.

Once you have a lien on the judgment debtor's property, especially real property, there is a good chance you'll eventually be paid. It usually works like this: When the debtor sells or refinances the property, the buyer will see your lien on the property. In the case of a sale, you will be notified and paid out of the proceeds. If property is refinanced, the lender will probably insist that the existing liens be paid off.

Instead of waiting for the debtor to sell the property, you may be able to execute on the lien—that is, have the sheriff seize the property (typically a house) and arrange for a public sale from which you are paid out of the proceeds. This is unusual, however, because arranging a public sale is time-consuming and expensive. Furthermore, you may not get much money by selling property at this kind of sale, called a distress sale. Any mortgage holder, government taxing authority, or other creditor who has placed a lien on the debtor's property before you is paid first. In addition, in most states, a portion of the debtor's equity is protected from being used to pay debts by "homestead laws." Only if the debtor has money over and above the mortgage and whatever he or she already owes on the real property—plus the amount of any homestead exemption—can you collect anything.

> **Example:** A married California judgment debtor owns a house worth $300,000, subject to a $250,000 mortgage. This means her equity is only $50,000—the bank owns the rest. As $75,000 is exempt under California's homestead law, you would end up with nothing.

In many states, here's how to record your judgment against real property: First get an "Abstract of Judgment" from the small claims clerk's office. The clerk will prepare this paper for you. Then take the abstract of judgment to the county recorder's office in the county where the property is located, pay a fee, and give the recorder the mailing address of the judgment debtor so he or she can be notified. Check with your small claims court for the exact procedures.

Note: In some states, you have to specifically identify the property you're putting the lien on.

D. Levying on Wages, Bank Accounts, Business Assets, Real Property, and More

In this section, I discuss a number of ways to collect a court judgment. One or more may work easily and quickly. However, some judgment debtors hide assets or are otherwise difficult to collect from. If you face this situation, and believe the judgment debtor may own or buy real property, your best bet may be to establish a lien against the property. Sooner or later the judgment debtor will sell or refinance, and chances are good your judgment will be paid, with interest. (See Section C, above, for details.)

Think twice before using a collection agency. It is also possible to turn your debt over to a collection agency. However, this probably doesn't make too much sense, as the agency usually takes up to 50% of what it collects. Unless you are a regular customer, the agency probably won't treat your debt with much priority unless it believes it is easy to collect. If it is easy for the agency to collect, it probably won't be hard for you to do it yourself and save the fee.

If you know where the judgment debtor works, you are in good shape. In most states, you can get up to 25% of a person's net wages to satisfy a debt unless that person has a very low income, in which case the amount you can recover may be considerably less than 25%. Wage garnishments are not allowed in Texas and are limited to 10% of a debtor's wages in New York. Some other states make it difficult to garnish the wages of a head of family if the family has a low income and needs all of it to survive. The sheriff's or marshal's office in your area can supply you with the rules in your state.

As mentioned, knowing where a judgment debtor banks can also be extremely valuable, as you can order a sheriff, marshal, or constable to levy on a bank account and get whatever it contains at the time of the levy. Of course, a bank account levy will only work one time at any given bank, as the debtor is pretty sure to move the account when he or she realizes you have access to it.

⚠️ **Rules restrict some types of bank account levies.** Bank account levies are subject to your state's exempt property laws. In most states, approximately 75% of wages placed in a bank account are exempt from being taken to pay debts (100% if there has been a previous wage attachment involving the same money) for 30 days after payment. Social Security money and deposits from other public benefits, such as AFDC, unemployment insurance, and veteran's benefits, are totally exempt from attachment (unless you happen to be a federal government agency; see 31 U.S.C. § 3716(c)(3)(A)(i)).

Stocks, bonds, mutual funds, and other securities are usually not difficult to levy on if you know where they are held.

Other types of property can be much more difficult to grab. Why? Because all states have a number of "exemption" laws that say that, even though a person owes money, certain types of property can't be taken to satisfy the debt. Items protected typically include a portion of or all equity in a family house, furniture, clothes, and much more. (*Money Troubles: Legal Strategies to Cope With Your Debts*, by Robin Leonard (Nolo), includes a list of the exempt property laws of all 50 states.) Practically speaking, the only assets other than wages, bank accounts, and securities that are normally worth going after to satisfy a small claims judgment are the receipts of an operating business (Section 4, below) and a motor vehicle (Section 5, below) in which the judgment debtor has an equity considerably in excess of the exemption amount in your state. Theoretically, there are many other assets you could reach. However, in most cases, they are not worth the time and expense involved, considering your judgment is for a fairly modest amount.

1. The Writ of Execution

Before you can levy on a person's wages or other property, you must get court permission, usually in the form of a writ of execution, writ of garnishment, writ of attachment, or similarly titled document. Some courts also require that you complete a short application for the writ. If you have a small claims judgment, you are entitled to this writ. In most states, you get your writ from the small claims court clerk, who will help you fill it in. There is often a small fee, which is a recoverable cost. (See Section E, below.)

2. The Sheriff (or Marshal or Constable)

Once you obtain your writ from the court, the procedure to collect your money will be as follows in most states: Take or send the writ to the sheriff, marshal, or constable in the county in which the assets are located. The small claims court clerk will direct you. Give the sheriff, marshal, or constable the following:

- The writ (original) and one to three or more copies, depending on the asset to be collected. Remember to keep a copy of the writ for your files.

- The required fees for collecting (this will vary as to the type of asset); call ahead to inquire.

- Instructions on what type of asset to collect and where it is located. The sheriff, marshal, constable, or small claims clerk may have a form they wish you to use when providing these instructions. Or the instructions might be a part of the writ form itself. Normally, however, they will accept a letter if it contains all the necessary information.

Don't delay in serving a writ of execution. A writ of execution expires within a certain period (often 60 to 180 days) if it is not served by the sheriff or marshal. If this time runs out, you will have to go back to the small claims court clerk and get another writ issued.

3. How to Levy on Wages and Bank Accounts

To seize a person's wages or bank account, you will probably have to provide an official copy of the writ of execution to the sheriff, marshal, or constable, and a letter of instruction like that shown below. If a bank account is in the name of the defendant and someone else, you may have to post a bond, depending on your state's laws. If your state has a special wage garnishment form, use that—your small claims court clerk should know.

P.O. Box 66-D
Jackson, Wyoming 83001
March 1, 20xx

Sheriff (Civil Division)
Mapleville, Wyoming
Re: Carol Lamp vs. Frank Post
Small Claims Court No. 81-52

To Whom It May Concern:

Enclosed you will find the original and one copy of a Writ of Execution (Garnishment or Attachment) issued by the small claims court in the amount of $___(fill in total due)___. I also enclose a check for your fee in the amount of $_____.

I hereby instruct you to levy on the wages of Frank Post, who works at the Graphite Oil Co., 1341 Chester St., Mapleville, Wyoming. Please serve the Writ on or before March 15, 20xx.

or

I hereby instruct you to levy on all monies in all accounts of Frank Post, located at the Bank of Trade, 11 City St., Mapleville, Wyoming.

Very truly yours,

Carol Lamp

---

4. Business Assets

In many states, it is possible to send someone from the sheriff's, marshal's, or constable's office to the business of a person who owes you money to collect it from the cash on hand. You will want to ask your court clerk about your local rules. In many states, this can be done by authorizing the sheriff or marshal to initiate a "till tap" or a "keeper."

A till tap consists of a one-time removal of all cash receipts from the business. The fees for this service are usually reasonable. For a keeper, a deputy goes to the place of business, takes all the money in the cash register, and then stays there for a set period of time (an "8-hour keeper," a "24-hour keeper," or a "48-hour keeper") to take more money as it comes in. Keepers' fees are high; a 48-hour keeper can cost as much as $400. It is also possible for the business's property to be seized and sold. But costs of doing so are often prohibitive.

Talk to the sheriff, marshal, or constable in your area to get more details. He or she will want an original and copies of your writ, as well as instructions about where and when to go. Fees are recoverable from the judgment debtor if enough money comes in to cover them, plus the judgment.

5. Levying on Motor Vehicles (Including Planes, Boats, and RVs)

Selling a person's motor vehicle tends to be difficult for several reasons:

* A portion of the equity in a car is exempt from your levy in many, but not all, states. The exempt amount ranges widely between states, from $1,000 to $20,000.

Example: A judgment debtor in Oregon has a car worth $4,000 on which he owes $3,000 to a bank. This means his equity is $1,000—the bank owns the rest. As equity of up to $1,700 is exempt under Oregon law, you would end up with nothing.

- You may not be able to instruct the sheriff to pick up the car from a garage or other private place unless you first go to court and obtain a judge's permission.
- The judgment debtor may not own the car he or she drives. It may be in someone else's name or belong to an employer, or the debtor may owe a bank or finance company as much or more than the car is worth.

To find out if a judgment debtor owns the car he or she drives, go to the department of motor vehicles. In most states, for a small fee, they will tell you who owns the car, including whether or not a bank or finance company is involved. Once you have this information, you can determine whether selling the car is likely to yield enough to pay off any loan you discover, provide the debtor with the exemption amount, cover the costs of sale, and still leave enough to pay off all, or at least a substantial part, of your judgment. If you are convinced the vehicle is worth enough to cover these costs, as would be the case if it is relatively new and owned by the debtor free and clear, have the sheriff pick up the car and sell it. But remember, the sheriff's fees to do this are relatively high (usually $400 or more) and must be paid in advance. Also, the sale price at a public auction will fetch far less than at a private sale. Your costs are recoverable when the vehicle is sold.

Call the sheriff, marshal, or constable of the county in which the car is located to find out how much money he or she requires as a deposit with your writ and how many copies of the writ you need. Then write a letter such as this:

P.O. Box 66-D
Jackson, WY 83001
March 1, 20xx

Sheriff (Civil Division)
Cheyenne, Wyoming
Re: Carol Lamp v. Frank Post
Small Claims Court
No. SC 81-52

To Whom It May Concern:

You are hereby instructed, under the authority of the enclosed writ, to levy upon and sell all of the right, title, and interest of Frank Post, judgment debtor, in the following motor vehicle:

[Type the description of the car as it appears on your D.M.V. report, including the license number.]

The vehicle is registered in the name(s) of Frank Post, and is regularly found at the following address(es):

[List home and work addresses of owner. Remember that the car might have to be parked in a public place.]

Enclosed is my check for $_____ to cover your costs of levy and sale.

Very truly yours,

Carol Lamp

⚠️ **Some states have no exemption for motor vehicles, and some exempt a higher amount of equity.** Check your state legal codes, call your local sheriff's or marshal's office, or consult *Money Troubles: Legal Strategies to Cope With Your Debts*, by Robin Leonard (Nolo), which contains an up-to-date list of all states' exemptions.

6. Stocks, Bonds, Mutual Funds, and Other Securities

If the judgment debtor owns stock or other securities, your collection method will depend on how the ownership is physically represented.

If ownership is manifested in certificates held by the judgment debtor, you can levy against the certificates themselves as tangible personal property. However, you will first need to get a court order allowing you to reach property in a private home.

If, as is common, the certificates are held for the judgment debtor by a broker, you can initiate a third-party levy against the branch office of the stock brokerage firm. The sheriff, marshal, or constable will require a writ, written instructions, and a fee to handle the levy.

Sometimes stock or mutual fund ownership is not manifested in certificates, but is recorded in the computers of the company issuing the securities. In this case, it is possible to make a third-party levy at a company's in-state headquarters. If the company's headquarters are out of state, you will need to obtain a court order assigning you the right to the securities.

7. Other Personal Property

As mentioned, it isn't usually worth the trouble to try to levy on small items of personal property, such as furniture or appliances, because they are commonly covered by one or another of the state exemption laws that protect certain possessions from being taken to satisfy debts. Even if property isn't exempt, you would need a court order to allow a levying officer access to property in a private home.

8. Pensions and Retirement Benefits

In many states, you can get at money in individual or self-employment retirement plans held in banks or savings institutions. You'll need to check your state laws to find out if retirement accounts are fair game. If you're entitled to go after this money, you can do so just as you would with any other money kept in a bank. Of course, you need to know where the money is.

Private company retirement plans and state or local government retirement plans generally can't be touched until the money is paid over to the employee. Even then, the judgment debtor might claim those amounts as exempt.

Federal government pension and retirement benefits may not be garnished to satisfy any debts, except those for alimony and child support.

E. Recovering Collection Costs and Interest

Costs (including the filing fee, costs of service, and so on) incurred prior to recovering a judgment should be included in the judgment total when it is entered by the judge. I discuss this in Chapter 16, Section C.

Here I am concerned with costs incurred after judgment. These are the costs that result when the judgment debtor doesn't pay voluntarily and you have to levy on his or her assets. This can be expensive, and you will want to make the judgment debtor pay, if possible. Many costs of collecting a judgment are recoverable; a few are not. Generally speaking, you can recover your direct costs of collecting, which include such things as sheriff, marshal, or constable fees, costs to get copies of required papers issued by the court (such as a writ of execution or abstract of judgment), and recording fees. Indirect costs, such as babysitting costs, time off work, postage, photocopying, gasoline, and so on, can't be recovered. Check with your clerk for rules on what costs are recoverable and how to collect.

You can also recover interest on the judgment. The interest rate depends on your state's laws; 8% to 12% per year is usual.

F. Renew Your Judgment

Judgments expire after a certain number of years—usually between five and 20, depending on the state. To find out your state's rule, see the chart at the end of this chapter. Be aware that the expiration periods may differ if you are collecting on a judgment that was originally entered in another state.

Fortunately, most states allow you to renew your judgment—and any liens based on it—if you do so before the expiration date. For information on how to renew a judgment, contact your small claims court clerk's office.

TIME LIMITS TO COLLECT COURT JUDGMENTS

State	Code Citation	Time Limit
Alabama	Ala. Code § 6-2-32	20 years
Alaska	Alaska Stat. § 09.10.040	10 years
Arizona	Ariz. Rev. Stat. § 12-1551	5 years
Arkansas	Ark. Code Ann. § 16-56-114	10 years (5 years in justice of peace courts
California	Cal. Civ. Proc. Code § 683.020	10 years
Colorado	Colo. Rev. Stat. § 13-52-102	6 years
Connecticut	Conn. Gen. Stat. Ann. § 52-598	20 years (10 years if small claims court judgment)
Delaware	Del. Code Ann. tit. 10, § 4711	10 years
District of Columbia	D.C. Code Ann. § 15-101	12 years
Florida	Fla. Stat. Ann. § 95.11(1)	20 years
Georgia	Ga. Code Ann. § 9-12-60	7 years
Hawaii	Haw. Rev. Stat. § 657-5	10 years
Idaho	Idaho Code § 5-215	6 years
Illinois	735 Ill. Comp. Stat. § 5/12-108	7 years
Indiana	Ind. Code Ann. § 34-11-2-11	10 years
Iowa	Iowa Code § 614.1(6)	20 years
Kansas	Kan. Stat. Ann. § 60-2403	5 years
Kentucky	Ky. Rev. Stat. Ann. § 413.090	15 years
Louisiana	La. Civ. Code art. 3501	10 years
Maine	Me. Rev. Stat. Ann. tit. 14, § 864	20 years
Maryland	Md. Code Ann., [Cts. & Jud. Proc.] § 5-102(a)(3)	12 years
Massachusetts	Mass. Gen. Laws ch. 260, § 20	20 years
Michigan	Mich. Comp. Laws § 600.5809(3)	10 years
Minnesota	Minn. Stat. Ann. § 541.04	10 years

State	Code Citation	Time Limit
Mississippi	Miss. Code Ann. § 15-1-43	7 years
Missouri	Mo. Rev. Stat. § 511.360	10 years
Montana	Mont. Code Ann. § 27-2-201	10 years
Nebraska	Neb. Rev. Stat. § 25-1515	5 years
Nevada	Nev. Rev. Stat. Ann. § 11.190(1)(a)	6 years
New Hampshire	N.H. Rev. Stat. Ann. § 508:4	20 years
New Jersey	N.J. Stat. Ann. § 2a:14-5	20 years
New Mexico	N.M. Stat. Ann. § 37-1-2	14 years
New York	N.Y. C.P.L.R. Law § 211(b)	20 years
North Carolina	N.C. Gen. Stat. § 1-47	10 years
North Dakota	N.D. Cent. Code § 28-01-15(1)	10 years
Ohio	Ohio Rev. Code Ann. § 2325.18	10 years
Oklahoma	Okla. Stat. Ann. tit. 12, § 735	5 years
Oregon	Or. Rev. Stat. § 12.070	10 years
Pennsylvania	42 Pa. Cons. Stat. Ann. § 5525(5)	4 years
Rhode Island	R.I. Gen. Laws § 9-1-17	20 years
South Carolina	S.C. Code Ann. § 15-35-810	10 years
South Dakota	S.D. Codified Laws Ann. § 15-2-6	20 years
Tennessee	Tenn. Code Ann. § 28-3-110(2)	10 years
Texas	Tex. Civ. Prac. & Rem. Code Ann. § 34.001	10 years
Utah	Utah Code Ann. § 78-12-22	8 years
Vermont	Vt. Stat. Ann. tit. 12, § 506	8 years
Virginia	Va. Code Ann. § 8.01-251	20 years
Washington	Wash. Rev. Code Ann. § 4.16.020(2)	10 years
West Virginia	W. Va. Code § 38-3-18	10 years
Wisconsin	Wis. Stat. Ann. § 893.40	20 years
Wyoming	Wyo. Stat. § 1-17-307	5 years

Appendix

Small Claims Court Rules for the 50 States
(and the District of Columbia)

PLEASE READ THIS

The following summary of state-by-state small claims rules is for general reference only. Because laws may have changed after this book went to press and local court rules may vary from one county to the next, be sure to check your local small claims court rules before making any legal decisions. Whether you are a plaintiff or a defendant, you should either call your local small claims court clerk or see if the information you need is on the Web. This Appendix lists websites for each state's small claims information. (All links are accurate at the time of publication, but as you know, websites are subject to frequent change. Be sure to check the "Legal Research" section in Chapter 1 for tips on using the Web.) You will also find links to small claims courts at Nolo's Small Claims Center, www.nolo.com.

ALABAMA

Court: Small Claims Docket (district court).
Statutes: Ala. Code §§ 12-12-31, 12-12-70, 12-12-71.
Court Rules: Alabama Small Claims Rules, Rule A to N and Alabama Small Claims Forms, 1 to 5.
Court Information: *www.alacourt.org/publications/sc_questions.htm*
Dollar Limit: $3,000.
Where to Sue: County or district where any defendant resides, or injury or property damage occurred. Corporation, wherever it does business.
Service of Process: Sheriff, adult approved by court or certified mail.
Defendant's Response: Defendant must file a written answer within 14 days of service to avoid default.
Transfer: No provision.
Attorneys: Allowed; required for assignees (collection agencies).
Appeals: Allowed by either party within 14 days. Heard in circuit court as a new trial.
Evictions: No; must go on regular district court docket.
Notes: Equitable relief is available.

ALASKA

Court: Small Claims Procedure (district court or magistrate).
Statutes: Alaska Stat. § 22.15.040.
Court Rules: District Court Rules of Civil Procedure, Rule 8 to 22.
Court Information: *www.state.ak.us/courts/forms.htm#sc*
Dollar Limit: $7,500.
Where to Sue: Court nearest to the defendant's residence or place of employment, district in which injury or property damage occurred, or district where defendant does business.
Defendant's Response: The defendant must file a written answer within 20 days of service to avoid default.

Service of Process: Peace officer or registered or certified mail. Certified or registered mail service is binding on defendant who refuses to accept and sign for the letter. If defendant refuses service, clerk will send by regular first-class mail, and service is assumed.

Transfer: Defendant (or plaintiff against whom a counterclaim has been filed) or judge may transfer case to regular district court.

Attorneys: Allowed; required for assignees (collection agencies). Includes legal interns.

Appeals: For claims over $50, allowed by either party, on law, not facts.

Evictions: No.

Notes: Magistrates and court clerks authorized to assist public in preparing small claims documents.

ARIZONA

Court: Justice of the Peace Court (Small Claims Division) and Justice Court.

Statutes: Ariz. Rev. Stat. Ann. §§ 22-201 to 22-284 (justice court); 22-501 to 22-524 (small claims division).

Court Information: *www.supreme.state.az.us/info/brochures/smclaims.htm*
www.jp.co.pima.az.us/www/iserv.html#small_claims

Dollar Limit: $2,500 (small claims division); $5,000 (justice court).

Where to Sue: Precinct where any defendant resides, act or omission occurred, or obligation was to be performed. Corporation, wherever it does business.

Service of Process: Sheriff, adult approved by court, or registered or certified mail with return receipt requested.

Defendant's Response: Defendant must answer within 20 days in writing to avoid default.

Transfer: To justice court, if defendant in small claims division counterclaims over $2,500 or objects at least 10 days before hearing (for right of appeal and jury). For counterclaims over $5,000, transfer is allowed to superior court.

Attorneys: Allowed in small claims division only if both parties agree in writing.

Appeals: Not allowed in small claims division. Allowed in justice court.

Evictions: In justice court, but not in small claims division.

Jury Trials: Not allowed in small claims division. Allowed in justice court.

ARKANSAS

Court: Small Claims Division (district court); Justice of the Peace (in towns without district or county court).

Statutes: Ark. Code Ann. §§ 16-17-701 to 16-17-706; 16-19-401 to 16-19-1108.

Court Information: *www.arkbar.com/publications/publication_public.html#small*

Dollar Limit: $5,000.

Where to Sue: County where a defendant resides, act or omission occurred, or obligation was to be performed. Corporation, wherever it is doing business.

Service of Process: Sheriff, constable (justice of the peace court only); certified mail (small claims division only).

Defendant's Response: Defendant must file written answer within 20 days of service if within the state, within 30 days if outside the state.

Transfer: In the small claims division, if the judge learns that any party is represented by an attorney, case will be transferred to regular district court; no transfer provision in justice of the peace courts.

Attorneys: Not allowed (small claims division); allowed (justice of the peace).

Appeals: Allowed by either party within 30 days. Heard in circuit court as a new trial.

Jury Trials: Not allowed in small claims division. Allowed in justice of the peace court.

CALIFORNIA

Court: Small Claims Division (superior court).

Statutes: Cal. Civ. Proc. Code §§ 116.110 to 116.950.

Court Information: *www.courtinfo.ca.gov/selfhelp/smallclaims*

Dollar Limit: $5,000, except that a plaintiff may not file a claim over $2,500 more than twice a year. $4,000 is the limit for suits involving a surety company or a licensed contractor.

Where to Sue: Judicial district where any defendant resides (or resided when promise or obligation was made), act or omission occurred, or obligation was to be performed. Corporation, wherever it is doing business.

Service of Process: Certified or registered mail, return receipt, by court clerk; sheriff or disinterested adult.

Defendant's Response: No written answer required.

Transfer: If defendant counterclaims over $5,000, case will be heard in higher court if the small claims court agrees to the transfer.

Attorneys: Not allowed.

Appeals: Allowed by defendant (or plaintiff who lost on a counterclaim) within 30 days. Heard in superior court as a new trial. Plaintiff may not appeal on a judgment, but may make a motion to correct a clerical error or a decision that is based on a legal mistake.

Evictions: No.

Jury Trials: Not allowed.

Notes: (1) Equitable relief is available.

(2) Small claims advisory service available at no cost.

(3) Judge may make a "conditional judgment" to order the performance or cessation of actions by a party.

COLORADO

Court: County Court (Small Claims Division).

Statutes: Colo. Rev. Stat. §§ 13-6-401 to 13-6-417.

Court Rules: Rules of County Court Civil Procedure, Rule 411; Rules of Civil Procedure for Small Claims Courts Rule 501 to 521.

Court Information: *www.courts.state.co.us/chs/court/forms/smallclaims/smallclaims.html*

Dollar Limit: $7,500.

Where to Sue: County in which any defendant resides, is regularly employed, is a student at an institution of higher education, or has an office for the transaction of business.

Service of Process: Sheriff, disinterested adult, or certified mail.

Defendant's Response: Defendant must file a written and signed response on or before the trial date.

Transfer: Allowed by defendant who has a counterclaim over $5,000.

Attorneys: Allowed only if attorney is a full-time employee or a general partner (partnership), an officer (corporation), or an active member (association). If an attorney does appear as permitted above, the other party may have one also.

Appeals: Allowed by either party within 15 days. Heard in district court on law, not facts. Parties may agree before or at trial that there will be no appeal.

Evictions: No.

Jury Trials: Not allowed.

Notes: No plaintiff may file more than 2 claims per month or more than 18 claims per year in the small claims court of any county.

CONNECTICUT

Court: Small Claims (superior court).

Statutes: Conn. Gen. Stat. Ann. §§ 51-15; 52-259; 52-549a to 549d.

Court Information: *www.jud.state.ct.us/faq/smallclaims.html*
  www.jud2.state.ct.us/webforms/forms/smallclaims.pdf

Dollar Limit: $3,500 (except in landlord-tenant security deposit claims).

Where to Sue: County or geographical area where the defendant resides or does business, where act or omission took place, or where obligation arose.

Service of Process: Peace officer, disinterested adult, registered mail, or regular first-class mail.

Defendant's Response: Must file an answer on or before the "Answer Date" that appears on the "Notice of Suit."

Transfer: Allowed by defendant to regular superior court procedure upon counterclaim over $3,500.

Attorneys: Allowed; required for corporations.

Appeals: Not allowed.

Evictions: No.

DELAWARE

Court: Justice of the Peace Court (no small claims system).

Statutes: Del. Code Ann. tit. 10, §§ 9301 to 9640; 9801.

Court Rules: Delaware Rules, Justice of the Peace Courts, Rule 1 to 72.1.

Court Information: *http://courts.state.de.us/courts/justice%20of%20the%20peace%20court*

Dollar Limit: $15,000.

Where to Sue: Anywhere in the state.

Service of Process: Court serves by certified mail, sheriff, or constable.

Defendant's Response: In all debt or trespass claims, defendant must file written answer within 15 days after service is made to avoid default.

Transfer: No provision.

Attorneys: Allowed.

Appeals: Allowed by either party within 15 days. Heard in superior court as a new trial.

Evictions: Yes.

Jury Trials: Generally not allowed.

Notes: (1) Interest due on any cause of action may be added to the claim, even if adding it will make the amount exceed $15,000.

(2) If defendant's counterclaim exceeds $15,000, can still pursue the counterclaim in justice of the peace court. (There is no provision for transfer to higher court.) If defendant wins counterclaim, there are two options: (1) the court will note the outcome on the record and defendant may take the case to a higher court, or (2) defendant may waive the excess over $15,000 and accept $15,000 as the judgment.

DISTRICT OF COLUMBIA

Court: Small Claims and Conciliation Branch (superior court).

Statutes: D.C. Code Ann. §§ 11-1301 to 11-1323; 16-3901 to 16-3910; 17-301 to 17-307.

Court Rules: Superior Court Rules of Procedure for Small Claims and Conciliation Branch, Rule 1 to 19.

Court Information: *www.dcbar.org/for_lawyers/courts/superior_court/civil_division/smclaimconcil.cfm*
www.dcbar.org/for_lawyers/courts/superior_court/forms.cfm

Dollar Limit: $5,000.

Where to Sue: District of Columbia Superior Court.

Service of Process: U.S. Marshal, adult approved by court, or certified (with return receipt) or registered mail. Certified or registered mail is binding on defendant who refuses to accept letter.

Defendant's Response: No written response required.

Transfer: Transferable to regular superior court if justice requires, if defendant's counterclaim affects interest in real property (land or housing), or if either party demands a jury trial.

Attorneys: Allowed; required for corporations. Normally attorney fees may not exceed 15% of judgment. (Certified law students may also appear.)

Appeals: To court of appeals by either party within 3 days.

Evictions: No.

Jury Trials: Either party may demand one, but then case will transfer to regular branch of superior court.

Notes: Judges have power to refer cases to mediation.

FLORIDA

Court: Small Claims Procedure or Summary Procedure (county court).

Court Rules: Florida Small Claims Rules 7.010 to 7.345; Florida Rules of Appellate Procedure, Rule 9.110.

Court Information: *www.clerk.leon.fl.us/wrapper.php3?node=general&page=/general_info/faq/small-claimshtml#1*

http://orangeclerk.onetgov.net/faq/faq-smallclaims.htm

Dollar Limit: $5,000.

Where to Sue: County where a defendant resides, act or omission occurred, or contract entered into. Corporation, where it customarily does business.

Service of Process: Peace officer, adult approved by court, or (for Florida residents only) certified mail, return receipt.

Defendant's Response: Must appear at pretrial conference. Must file counterclaim in writing at least 5 days before initial appearance date (which is the pretrial conference).

Transfer: Allowed to regular county court procedure only if defendant counterclaims over $5,000.

Attorneys: Allowed; if attorneys are involved, parties are subject to discovery.

Appeals: Motion for new trial within 10 days after return of verdict or filing of judgment. Appeals may be filed by either party within 30 days. Heard in circuit court on law, not facts.

Evictions: Yes.

Jury Trials: Either party may demand jury trial; plaintiff must make demand when filing suit; defendant must make demand within 5 days after service or notice of suit or at pretrial conference.

GEORGIA

Court: Magistrate Court.

Statutes: Ga. Code Ann. §§ 15-10-1, 15-10-2, 15-10-40 to 15-10-53, 15-10-80, 15-10-87.

Court Information: *www.georgiacourts.org/councils/magistrate/faq.html*

www.ncourt.com/navigation.aspx?juris=GACherokee

Dollar Limit: $15,000 (no limit in landlord-tenant cases).

Where to Sue: County where defendant resides.

Service of Process: Sheriff or person authorized by judge. Personal service only, no mail.

Defendant's Response: Defendant must answer within 30 days (either in writing or in person—no phone calls) to avoid default.

Transfer: To appropriate court if defendant's counterclaim over $15,000.

Attorneys: Allowed.

Appeals: To county superior court for new trial.
Evictions: Yes.
Jury Trials: Not allowed.

HAWAII

Court: Small Claims Division (district court).
Statutes: Haw. Rev. Stat. §§ 633-27 to 633-36.
Court Rules: Hawaii District Court Rules, Small Claims Division, Rule 1 to 13.
Court Information: *www.courts.state.hi.us/page_server/SelfHelp/SmallClaims/ 695F88B9A961B33EAB295F3B7.html*
Dollar Limit: $3,500; no limit in landlord-tenant residential deposit cases. For return of leased or rented personal property, the property must not be worth more than $3,500.
Where to Sue: Judicial district in which the defendant resides, where act or omission occurred or, in security deposit cases, where rental property is located.
Service of Process: Certified or registered mail (return receipt requested); sheriff, disinterested adult, or by either party personally.
Defendant's Response: No formal written answer required.
Transfer: If either party demands jury trial. Otherwise, only if plaintiff agrees.
Attorneys: Allowed (except in landlord-tenant security deposit cases). Generally, attorney's fees are not awarded unless required by law.
Appeals: Not allowed.
Evictions: No.
Jury Trials: Not allowed. Cases will be transferred to circuit court.
Notes: (1) Cases limited to recovering money, recovering rented or leased personal property, and landlord-tenant security deposit disputes.
(2) No punitive damages.
(3) Equitable relief available in landlord-tenant cases.
(4) Counterclaims up to $20,000 are allowed.

IDAHO

Court: Small Claims Department of Magistrate's Division.
Statutes: Idaho Code §§ 1-2301 to 1-2315.
Court Information: *www.isc.gov/material.htm#claim www2.state.id.us/cao/forms.asp?cat_id=24*
Dollar Limit: $4,000.
Where to Sue: County where the defendant resides or where claim arose. Corporation, wherever it is doing business.
Service of Process: Sheriff, disinterested adult, or certified or registered mail, return receipt.
Defendant's Response: Must file written answer within 20 days and sign it in front of court clerk or notary public to avoid default.
Transfer: No provision.
Attorneys: Not allowed.
Appeals: Allowed by either party within 30 days. Heard by attorney magistrate as a new trial.
Evictions: No.
Jury Trials: Not allowed.
Notes: No claims for punitive damages; no claims for damages for pain and suffering.

ILLINOIS

Court: Small Claims (circuit court); *Pro Se* Court (Cook County).
Statutes: 735 Ill. Comp. Stat. §§ 5/2-101 to 5/2-208; 5/2-416; 705 Ill. Comp. Stat. § 205/11
Court Rules: Illinois Supreme Court Rules 281 to 289, Cook County Circuit Court Rules 1.6, 18.3.
Court Information: *www.cookcountyclerkofcourt.org/Community_Resources/pro_se_count/ pro_se_count.htm*
www.19thcircuitcourt.state.il.us/self-help/s_claims/index.htm [Lake County]
www.illinoissecondcircuit.info/html/small_claims.html [Jefferson County]
Dollar Limit: $5,000 (small claims); $1,500 (Cook County *Pro Se*).
Where to Sue: County in which any defendant resides, or act or omission occurred. Corporation, where it is doing business.
Service of Process: Sheriff, other law enforcement officer, licensed detective, or court-approved adult, certified or registered mail, return receipt.
Defendant's Response: No formal written answer required. Must appear by date on court summons.
Transfer: If claim or counterclaim is over $5,000.
Attorneys: Allowed except in Cook County *Pro Se* Court.
Appeals: Allowed by either party within 30 days. Heard in appellate court on law, not facts.
Evictions: No.
Jury Trials: Either party may demand a jury trial. (If jury trial is demanded in Cook County *Pro Se* Court case is transferred to small claims.)

INDIANA

Court: Small Claims Docket (circuit court, superior court, and county court); Marion County Small Claims Court.
Statutes: Ind. Code Ann. §§ 33-4-3-5 to 33-4-3-13 (circuit court); 33-5-2-2 to 33-5-2-10 (superior court); 33-10.5-7-1 to 33-10.5-7-10 (county court); 33-11.6-4-1 to 33-11.6-4-24 (Marion County Small Claims Court).
Court Information: *www.county.tippecanoe.in.us/departments/cc1/manual.htm*
www.small-claims-court.com/infomenu.html [Marion County]
Dollar Limit: $3,000 ($6,000 in Marion and Allen counties).
Where to Sue: County in which any defendant resides or is employed, where act or omission occurred, or where obligation arose or was to be performed by defendant. For landlord-tenant disputes, in county or town where property is located.
Service of Process: Personal service first; if unable to serve papers, then registered or certified mail.
Defendant's Response: No formal written answer required.
Attorneys: Allowed.
Appeals: From small claims docket of other courts within 60 days by either party for a new trial.
Evictions: Yes, if total rent due does not exceed $3,000 ($6,000 in Marion and Allen counties).
Jury Trials: Defendant may request jury trial within 10 days following service of complaint upon submitting an affidavit stating questions of fact that require a jury trial. Marion County Small Claims Court: no jury trials; case will be transferred to superior court if defendant requests jury trial at least 3 days before trial date.
Notes: Dollar limit will increase to $6,000 throughout the state, July 1, 2005.

IOWA

Court: Small Claims Docket (district court).
Statutes: Iowa Code §§ 631.1 to 631.17.
Court Information: *www.judicial.state.ia.us/faq/representing.asp*
Dollar Limit: $5,000.

Where to Sue: County in which any defendant resides, act or omission occurred, or obligation was to be performed.

Service of Process: Peace officer, disinterested adult, or certified mail, return receipt requested.

Defendant's Response: The defendant must appear within 20 days after service is made in order to avoid default.

Transfer: At judge's discretion if defendant counterclaims over the dollar limit.

Attorneys: Allowed.

Appeals: Allowed by either party upon oral notice at end of hearing or by written notice within 20 days of judgment. Heard in district court; no new evidence on appeal.

Evictions: Yes.

Notes: (1) *Replevin* (an action to recover a specific item of property) may be granted if value of property is $5,000 or less.

(2) The small claims docket has jurisdiction over orders and motions to collect judgments from personal property, including garnishments, where the amount involved does not exceed $5,000.

KANSAS

Court: Small Claims (district court).

Statutes: Kan. Stat. Ann. §§ 61-2701 to 61-2714.

Court Information: *www.kscourts.org/dstcts/*
www.kscourts.org/dstcts/4claims.htm

Dollar Limit: $4,000.

Where to Sue: County in which defendant lives, or county where plaintiff resides if defendant is served there, or defendant's place of doing business or employment.

Service of Process: Personal service by sheriff or adult approved by court; certified mail.

Defendant's Response: No formal written answer required.

Transfer: If the defendant counterclaims over $1,800 but still within the dollar limit of the regular district court, judge may either decide claim or allow defendant to bring claim in court of competent jurisdiction.

Attorneys: Generally not allowed, but if one party has an attorney, all other parties are entitled to have an attorney.

Appeals: Allowed by either party within 10 days. Heard in district court as a new trial.

Evictions: No.

Notes: (1) *Replevin* (an action to recover a specific item of property) may be granted if value of property is $1,800 or less.

(2) No person may file more than 10 claims in the same court during any calendar year.

KENTUCKY

Court: Small Claims Division (district court).

Statutes: Ky. Rev. Stat. Ann. §§ 24A.200 to 24A.360.

Court Information: *www.kycourts.net/resources/small_claims.pdf*

Dollar Limit: $1,500.

Where to Sue: Judicial district in which the defendant resides or does business, or if corporation, county of corporate headquarters.

Service of Process: Certified or registered mail first; if that fails, then by sheriff or constable.

Defendant's Response: Must appear for hearing (20 to 40 days from service of process). Must file counterclaim within 5 days of hearing.

Transfer: Allowed to regular district court or circuit court if defendant's counterclaim is over $1,500, if defendant demands a jury trial, or if judge decides the case is too complex for small claims division.

Attorneys: Allowed.
Appeals: Allowed by either party within 10 days. Heard in circuit court on law, not facts.
Evictions: Yes.
Jury trials: Only if defendant makes a written request within at least 7 days before hearing date. Case is then transferred to regular court.
Notes: (1) Lenders of money at interest cannot sue in small claims court.
(2) No person may file more than 25 claims in one calendar year in any district court.

LOUISIANA

Court: Rural: Justice of the Peace; Urban: Small Claims Division (city court).
Statutes: La. Rev. Stat. Ann. §§ 13:5200 to 13:5211 (city court); La. Code Civ. Proc., Art. 4831, 4832, 4845, 4901 to 4925, and Art. 42 (justice of the peace court).
Court Information: *http://brgov.com/dept/citycourt/smclaims.htm* [Baton Rouge]
Dollar Limit: $3,000.
Where to Sue: Parish in which the defendant resides. A corporation or partnership may be sued in a parish or district in which a business office is located.
Service of Process: Certified mail with return receipt, or sheriff, marshal, or constable, if certified mail is unclaimed or refused.
Defendant's Response: Must file written answer within 10 days of service (15 days if served by secretary of state) in order to avoid default.
Transfer: Small claims may be transferred to regular city court procedure if defendant files written request within 10 days of service of process, or if counterclaim ("reconventional demand") is over the dollar limit. In justice of the peace court, if demand in amended or supplemental pleading ("incidental demand") exceeds jurisdictional amount, case will be transferred to court of appropriate jurisdiction.
Attorneys: Allowed.
Appeals: In justice of the peace courts, allowed by either party within 15 days; heard in district court as a new trial. No appeal from small claims division of city court.
Evictions: Yes. Monthly rental may not exceed $3,000, but no limit on claim to recover overdue rent.
Jury Trials: Not allowed.
Notes: (1) Equitable relief is available in either court.
(2) Either party may request arbitration.

MAINE

Court: Small Claims Proceeding (district court).
Statutes: Me. Rev. Stat. Ann. tit. 14, §§ 1901; 7481 to 7487.
Court Rules: Maine Rules of Small Claims Procedure, Rule 1 to 18.
Court Information: *www.courts.state.me.us/mainecourts/smallclaims/index.html*
Dollar Limit: $4,500 (Reviewed every 4 years; next review 1/1/2005).
Where to Sue: District court division in which the defendant resides or has place of business, where the transaction occurred, or where registered agent resides if corporation.
Service of Process: Registered or certified mail, or personal service.
Defendant's Response: No formal written answer required.
Transfer: Allowed.
Attorneys: Allowed.
Appeals: Allowed by either party within 30 days. Heard in superior court. Plaintiff's appeal on questions of law only; defendant may request a new trial.
Evictions: Yes.

Jury Trials: Not allowed.

Notes: (1) Equitable relief available but limited to orders to return, reform, refund, repair, or rescind.

(2) Judges have power to refer cases to mediation.

MARYLAND

Court: Small Claims Court (district court).

Statutes: Md. Code Ann. [Cts. & Jud. Proc.] §§ 4-405; 6-403.

Court Rules: Maryland Court Rules, Rule 3-701, 7-104, 7-112.

Court Information: *www.courts.state.md.us/district/smallclaims.html*

Dollar Limit: $5,000.

Where to Sue: County in which any defendant resides, is employed, or does business, or where injury to person or property occurred. Corporation may be sued where it maintains principal office.

Service of Process: Sheriff, constable, or disinterested adult, personally or by certified mail. If service or mail refused, clerk remails and service is presumed.

Defendant's Response: Defendant has 15 days from receipt of summons to file "Notice of Intention to Defend" in order to avoid default (out-of-state defendant has 60 days).

Transfer: To regular civil docket if counterclaim exceeds $2,500 or if defendant demands jury trial.

Attorneys: Allowed.

Appeals: Allowed by either party within 30 days. Heard in circuit court as a new trial.

Evictions: Yes, as long as the rent claimed does not exceed $2,500, exclusive of interest and costs.

Jury Trials: Not allowed.

Notes: May sue for money only.

MASSACHUSETTS

Court: Small Claims Division, Boston Municipal Court; elsewhere, Small Claims Section (district court).

Statutes: Mass. Gen. Laws ch. 214, §§ 1A, 2; ch. 218, §§ 21 to 25; ch. 93A, § 9 (consumer complaints).

Court Information: *www.state.ma.us/courts/admin/legal/courtrules2.html*

Dollar Limit: $2,000; no limit for property damage caused by a motor vehicle.

Where to Sue: Judicial district in which the plaintiff or defendant resides, is employed, or does business. Actions against landlords can also be brought in the district in which the property is located.

Service of Process: Sheriff, constable, or registered mail.

Defendant's Response: Written answer is optional, not required.

Transfer: Allowed only at court's discretion to regular civil docket.

Attorneys: Allowed.

Appeals: Allowed by defendant within 10 days. Heard in superior court as a new trial; jury allowed on appeal.

Evictions: No.

Jury Trials: Not allowed except on appeal.

Notes: (a) General small claims:

(1) Equitable relief is available.

(2) Mediation is available at request of either party and with agreement of both parties.

(b) Consumer complaint small claims:

(1) Plaintiff must make written demand for relief at least 30 days before filing suit.

(2) Attorney's fees available.

(3) Triple damages available.

MICHIGAN

Court: Small Claims Division (district court).
Statutes: Mich. Comp. Laws §§ 600.8401 to 600.8427.
Court Information: *www.courts.michigan.gov/scao/services/selfhelp/smallclaims.htm*
Dollar Limit: $3,000 ($500 limit on motor vehicle damages in no-fault traffic accident).
Where to Sue: County where defendant resides or where act or omission occurred.
Service of Process: Certified mail, return receipt requested; personal service by court officer or disinterested adult (required if certified mail is unclaimed).
Defendant's Response: No formal written answer required.
Transfer: Either party may transfer to regular district court. If defendant's counterclaim is over $3,000 or if defendant wants to be represented by an attorney, case will be transferred.
Attorneys: Not allowed.
Appeals: Not allowed. Exception: If action is heard by district court magistrate, parties can appeal to small claims division for new trial within 7 days.
Evictions: No.
Jury Trials: Not allowed.
Notes: May not file more than 5 claims in one week.

MINNESOTA

Court: Conciliation Court (district court).
Statutes: Minn. Stat. Ann. §§ 491A.01 to 491A.02.
Court Rules: Minnesota General Practice Rules 501 to 525.
Court Information: *www.courts.state.mn.us/ctforms/conciliation_index.asp*
www.courts.state.mn.us./districts/fourth/conect/ccmain.htm [Minneapolis]
www.ramsey.courts.state.mn.us/ramsey_conciliation.htm [St. Paul]
Dollar Limit: $7,500 ($4,000 for claims based on a personal or household consumer credit transaction).
Where to Sue: County in which any defendant resides or automobile accident occurred. A corporation may be sued in any county in which it has a resident agent, a place of business, or an office. For landlord-tenant disputes (other than evictions), county where rental property is located.
Service of Process: First-class mail or, if claim is over $2,500, certified mail or personal service by court clerk.
Defendant's Response: No formal written answer required. Must file counterclaim within 5 days of the trial date.
Transfer: To county court on demand for a jury trial or defendant's counterclaim above jurisdictional limit.
Attorneys: Not allowed except with court's approval.
Appeals: Filed within 20 days. Heard in district court as a new trial; jury trial permitted upon appeal.
Evictions: No.
Jury Trials: Not allowed. If demanded, case will be transferred.
Notes: (1) If defendant counterclaims over jurisdictional limit and files in another court, clerk will strike the small claims case from calendar; plaintiff who is not served with counterclaim may reinstate small claims action after 30 days.
(2) Equitable remedy to recover a specific item of property (*replevin*) is available as long as the value of the property is not over $7,500.
(3) Educational institution may bring actions to recover student loans, if loans were originally awarded in the county in which it has administrative offices, even though the defendant is not a county resident.

(4) Uniform court forms must be accepted in all counties. Upon request, clerk or judge will help with filling them out.

MISSISSIPPI

Court: Justice Court.
Statutes: Miss. Code Ann. §§ 9-11-9 to 9-11-15; 11-9-101 to 11-9-143, 11-51-85.
Court Information: *www.co.hinds.ms.us/pgs/ctydivision/justicecourt.asp*
Dollar Limit: $2,500.
Where to Sue: County in which any defendant resides; if nonresident, where act or omission occurred, or obligation entered into. Corporation, where its registered office is located.
Service of Process: Sheriff, constable, or disinterested adult (only in emergency with court's permission).
Defendant's Response: No formal written answer required.
Transfer: No provision.
Attorneys: Allowed.
Appeals: Allowed by either party within 10 days. Heard in county court as a new trial.
Evictions: No.
Jury Trials: Either party may demand a jury trial.
Notes: Equitable remedy to recover a specific item of property (*replevin*) is available.

MISSOURI

Court: Small Claims Division (circuit court)
Statutes: Mo. Rev. Stat. §§ 482.300 to 482.365.
Court Rules: Missouri Supreme Court Rules of the Small Claims Division of Circuit Court, Rule 140.01 to 152.
Court Information: *www.mobar.org/pamphlet/smllclam.htm*
www.osca.state.mo.us/circuits/index.nsf
Dollar Limit: $3,000.
Where to Sue: County in which at least one defendant resides, or in which one plaintiff resides and at least one defendant may be found, or where act or omission occurred.
Service of Process: Certified mail, return receipt. May be served personally by court if plaintiff requests.
Defendant's Response: No formal written answer required. Must file counterclaim in person within 10 days after service of process and any time before the hearing.
Transfers: Allowed to regular circuit court if defendant counterclaims over $3,000, unless all parties agree to stay in small claims court. (Parties must be informed of right to consult an attorney before giving consent.)
Attorneys: Allowed.
Appeals: Allowed by either party within 10 days for new trial before regular circuit court judge.
Evictions: No.
Jury Trials: Not allowed.
Notes:(1) Only 8 claims allowed per plaintiff per calendar year.
(2) Court clerks required to assist parties with filling out forms and pleadings.

MONTANA

Court: Small Claims Court (district court); Small Claims Division (justice court).
Statutes: Mont. Code Ann. §§ 3-12-101 to 3-12-107 (district court); 25-33-101 to 25-33-306 (appeals); 25-35-501 to 25-35-807; 3-10-1001 to 3-10-1004 (justice court).

Court Information: *www.montanabar.org/forthepublic/smallclaimscourt.html*
www.lawlibrary.state.mt.us/dscgi/ds.py/Get/File-7927/Small_Claims_Court_Guide.pdf
Dollar Limit: $3,000.
Where to Sue: County or judicial district in which any defendant can be served.
Service of Process: Sheriff, constable. (justice court only: disinterested adult.)
Defendant's Response: No formal written answer required. Defendant must serve counterclaim on plaintiff at least 72 hours before the hearing date.
Transfer: Allowed by defendant to justice court if request filed within 10 days of receipt of complaint.
Attorneys: Not allowed, unless all parties have attorneys.
Appeals: Allowed by either party within 30 days (from justice or city court to district court) for new trial. Within 10 days (from small claims court to justice or district court) on law, not facts.
Evictions: No.
Jury Trials: Not allowed. Defendant may request transfer to regular justice court for jury trial.
Notes: (1) Small claims suits must be based on contract, express or implied.
(2) May not file more than 10 claims per calendar year.
(3) The justice or court clerk must assist any party in preparing a complaint.

NEBRASKA

Court: Small Claims Court (county court).
Statutes: Neb. Rev. Stat. §§ 25-2801 to 25-2807; 25-2728 to 25-2737 (appeals).
Court Information: *http://court.nol.org/publications/smallclaims.htm*
Dollar Limit: $2,400 (adjusted every 5 years based on Consumer Price Index; next change 7/1/05).
Where to Sue: County in which any defendant resides or works, or where injury or property damage occurred. Corporation, wherever it regularly conducts business.
Service of Process: Sheriff or by certified mail sent according to court instructions.
Defendant's Response: Written answer not required. Counterclaim: must file and deliver to plaintiff at least 2 days prior to trial.
Transfer: Transferable to regular civil court on defendant's request or counterclaim over $2,400.
Attorneys: Not allowed.
Appeals: Allowed by either party within 30 days. Heard in district court as a new trial; attorneys are allowed, but jury trial not permitted.
Evictions: No.
Jury Trials: Not allowed in small claims court. Defendant may request transfer to regular docket of county court and demand a jury trial by giving notice at least 2 days before the hearing.
Notes: (1) Equitable relief available.
(2) Plaintiff may bring no more than 2 claims per calendar week and no more than 10 per calendar year.

NEVADA

Court: Small Claims Action (justice court).
Statutes: Nev. Rev. Stat. Ann. §§ 73.010 to 73.060.
Court Rules: Justices' Courts' Rules of Civil Procedure, Rule 88 to 100.
Court Information: *www.accessclarkcounty.com/justicecourt_lv/smallclaim.htm* [Las Vegas]
www.co.washoe.nv.us/rjc/civil/sc_faqs.htm [Reno]
Dollar Limit: $5,000.
Where to Sue: City or township in which defendant resides, does business, or is employed.
Service of Process: Court determines method. Either registered or certified mail, return receipt, or personal service by sheriff, constable, disinterested adult, or other person approved by court.

Defendant's Response: No formal written answer required.

Transfer: No provision.

Attorneys: Allowed. No awards for attorney fees except in claims against shoplifters.

Appeals: Allowed by either party within 5 days. Heard in district court on law, not facts; at court's discretion there may be a new trial.

Evictions: No.

Jury Trials: No provision.

Notes: Claims must be for recovery of money only.

NEW HAMPSHIRE

Court: Small Claims Actions (district court).

Statutes: N.H. Rev. Stat. Ann. §§ 503:1 to 503:11.

Court Rules: District and Municipal Court Rules, Rule 4.1 to 4.28.

Court Information: *www.courts.state.nh.us/district/claims.htm*

Dollar Limit: $5,000.

Where to Sue: Town or district in which defendant or plaintiff resides, defendant does business or owns property, or act or omission occurred.

Service of Process: Certified mail sent by court, return receipt; if not delivered, then personal service as instructed by court.

Defendant's Response: Must respond to claim in writing within 30 days of return date that is given on summons to avoid default.

Transfer: To superior court if amount claimed exceeds $5,000. May also transfer if either party requests a jury trial (claim must be more than $1,500).

Attorneys: Allowed.

Appeals: Allowed by either party within 30 days. Heard in supreme court on law, not facts.

Evictions: No.

Jury Trials: Not allowed, must transfer to superior court. Defendant must file request for jury trial within 5 days of plaintiff's claim.

Notes: Any party may request that sound recording be made of proceedings; request must be made at least 5 business days before trial, and party making request must pay.

NEW JERSEY

Court: Small Claims Section or Special Civil Part (superior court).

Court Rules: New Jersey Superior Court Rules, Law Division, Special Civil Part, Rule 6:1 to 6:12-2; N.J. Court Rules, Rule 2:4-1.

Court Information: *www.judiciary.state.nj.us/civil/civ-02.htm*
www.judiciary.state.nj.us/civil/civ-03.htm

Dollar Limit: $3,000 (small claims section); $15,000 (special civil part, superior court).

Where to Sue: County in which any defendant resides or, if defendants do not reside in New Jersey, county where act or omission occurred. For security deposit claims, county where property is located. Corporation, wherever it is actually doing business.

Service of Process: Certified and regular mail by the court; if service not made, court officer or other adult approved by the court.

Defendant's Response: Defendant must file written answer within 35 days of service (special civil part); no written answer, appearance only (*pro se* defendants and small claims section).

Transfer: Allowed from special civil part to law division of superior court if plaintiff submits affidavit that recovery will cost more than $15,000, or if defendant's counterclaim is more than $15,000. Allowed from small claims section to special civil part if defendant's counterclaim is more than $3,000 or if defendant demands a jury trial.

Attorneys: Allowed. Required for corporations if claim is more than $3,000.

Appeals: Allowed by either party within 45 days. Heard in appellate division of superior court on law, not facts.

Evictions: In special civil part only.

Jury Trials: In special civil part either party may demand jury trial no more than 10 days after time defendant required to answer. In small claims section defendant must submit demand at least 5 days before return of summons (case is then transferred to special civil part).

Notes: Small claims court has jurisdiction over landlord-tenant security deposit and other disputes (except eviction).

NEW MEXICO

Court: Metropolitan Court (Bernalillo County); Magistrate Court.

Statutes: N.M. Stat. Ann. §§ 34-8A-1 to 34-8A-10 (metropolitan court); 35-3-1 to 35-3-6, 35-8-1 and 35-8-2 (magistrate court); 35-13-1 to 35-13-3 (appeals).

Court Rules: Rules of Civil Procedure for the Magistrate Courts, Rule 2-101 to 2-804; Rules of Civil Procedure for the Metropolitan Court, Rule 3-101 to 3-804.

Court Information: *www.metrocourt.state.nm.us/civil/civil%20brochure.htm*

Dollar Limit: $10,000.

Where to Sue: County in which the defendant resides or may be found, or where the act or omission occurred.

Service of Process: By mail. If no response, personal service by sheriff or disinterested adult. May also serve papers electronically or by fax.

Defendant's Response: Must file answer on or before appearance date in summons.

Transfer: No provision.

Attorneys: Allowed.

Appeals: Allowed by either party within 15 days. Heard in district court as a new trial.

Evictions: Yes.

Jury Trials: Allowed at either party's request. Plaintiff must make jury trial request in the complaint, and defendant must make request in the answer.

Notes: (1) Voluntary mediation programs available in metropolitan court.
(2) Court papers may be filed or served electronically or by fax.

NEW YORK

Court: Small Claims Part (civil court, cities—including New York City; district court, Nassau and Suffolk counties; justice court, rural areas). Commercial Small Claims (city courts and district courts).

Statutes: N.Y. Unif. Cty. Ct. Act §§ 1801 to 1815, 1801-A to 1814-A (commercial claims); N.Y. Unif. Dist. Ct. Act §§ 1801 to 1815, 1801-A to 1814-A (commercial claims); N.Y. Unif. Just. Ct. Act §§ 1801 to 1815; N.Y. NYC Civ. Ct. Act §§ 1801 to 1815; 1801-A to 1814-A (commercial claims).

Court Rules: N.Y. Uniform Trial Court Rules, Rule 208.41, 208.41-A, 210.41, 210.41-A, 212.41, 212.41-A, 214.10.

Court Information: *www.courts.state.ny.us/courthelp/faqs/smallclaims.html*
www.courts.state.ny.us/litigants/courtguides/index.shtml

Dollar Limit: $5,000 (town and village justice courts, $3,000).

Where to Sue: Political subdivision in which the defendant resides, is employed, or has a business office.

Service of Process: Certified mail (binding on defendant who refuses mail) or ordinary first-class mail. If after 21 days not returned as undeliverable, then notice presumed.

Defendant's Response: Defendant to file counterclaim within 5 days of receiving plaintiff's claim.

Transfer: Allowed by court's discretion.

Attorneys: Generally not allowed unless either party has grounds for needing an attorney. If all parties are represented, case may be transferred..

Appeals: Allowed only on the ground that "substantial justice" was not done. Must file appeal within 30 days. Heard in county court or appellate division of supreme court (for NYC) on law, not facts. There is no appeal from an arbitrator's decision.

Evictions: No.

Jury Trials: Defendant may request jury trial at least one day prior to hearing. Must file affidavit stating the issues that require a jury trial.

Notes: (1) Arbitration is available; ruling may not be appealed.

(2) Corporations and partnerships cannot sue in small claims court, although they may appear as defendants. (Does not apply to municipal and public benefit corporations and school districts.)

Commercial Claims

(1) Same limits and procedures as regular small claims except claim is brought by corporation, partnership, or association.

(2) Business must have principal office in NY state.

(3) Defendant must reside, be employed, or have a business office in the county where suit is brought.

(4) Claim can be for money only.

(5) There is a limit of 5 claims per month.

NORTH CAROLINA

Court: Small Claims Court (district court, heard by magistrate).

Statutes: N. C. Gen. Stat. §§ 7A-210 to 7A-232.

Court Information: *www.nccourts.org/courts/trial/sclaims/default.asp*
www.aoc.state.nc.us/www/public/html/cvmforms.html

Dollar Limit: $4,000.

Where to Sue: County in which the defendant resides. Corporation, where it maintains a place of business.

Service of Process: Sheriff, registered or certified mail.

Defendant's Response: Defendant has option to file written answer any time before trial; no particular form required. If an answer is not filed, general denial of all claims is assumed.

Transfer: No provision unless question of land title. However, if district court judge does not assign case to magistrate within 5 days of complaint, then trial will take place according to regular district court procedure.

Attorneys: Allowed.

Appeals: Allowed by either party within 10 days. Heard in district court as a new trial; jury trial allowed if request within ten days of appeal notice.

Evictions: Yes.

Jury Trials: Not allowed before magistrate. If case is not assigned to a magistrate, plaintiff may request jury trial within 5 days of receiving notice of nonassignment, and defendant may make request either before or at the same time as filing answer.

Notes: (1) Rules of evidence apply.

(2) Counterclaims over $4,000 not allowed.

NORTH DAKOTA

Court: Small Claims Court (district court).

Statutes: N. D. Cent. Code §§ 27-08.1-01 to 27-08.1-08.

Court Information: *www.courts.state.nd.us/court/forms/small/forms.htm*
Dollar Limit: $5,000.
Where to Sue: County where the defendant resides. For bad checks or less than $1,000 owed on credit: county where defendant resides, has a place of business, or where act or transaction occurred. If defendant is a corporation, LLC, or partnership, where it has a place of business or where the subject of the claim arose.
Service of Process: Disinterested adult or certified mail.
Defendant's Response: Defendant must return form requesting hearing within 20 days of service. Defendant must file and serve counterclaim at least 48 hours before hearing.
Transfer: Defendant may transfer case to regular civil court procedure if request made within 20 days of service.
Attorneys: Allowed.
Appeals: Not allowed.
Evictions: No.
Jury Trials: Not allowed.
Notes: Plaintiff may not discontinue once small claims process is begun; if plaintiff seeks to discontinue, claim will be dismissed with prejudice (plaintiff cannot refile claim).

OHIO

Court: Small Claims Division (municipal and county courts).
Statutes: Ohio Rev. Code Ann. §§ 1925.01 to 1925.18.
Court Rules: Ohio Rules of Appellate Procedure, Rule 4.
Court Information: *www.clevelandheightscourt.com/main.html* [Cleveland Heights] *www.courtclerk.org/small_claims_guide.htm* [Hamilton County, Cincinnati]
Dollar Limit: $3,000.
Where to Sue: County in which the defendant resides or has place of business, or obligation arose. Actions involving notes can be brought only where obligation was incurred.
Service of Process: Sheriff, certified mail by clerk, return receipt.
Defendant's Response: No written answer required. Must file and serve counterclaim at least 7 days before trial date.
Transfer: To regular civil court procedure upon defendant's counterclaim over $3,000 or motion of the court. Either party may request transfer, but must file an affidavit stating grounds of defense.
Attorneys: Allowed.
Appeals: Must be filed within 30 days. Heard in court of appeals.
Evictions: No.
Jury Trials: Not allowed except in county court.
Notes: Claims limited to recovery of money; some consumer complaints also allowed.

OKLAHOMA

Court: Court: Small Claims Procedure (district court).
Statutes: Okla. Stat. Ann. tit. 12, §§ 1751 to 1773.
Court Information: *www.okbar.org/publicinfo/brochures/sccbroc.htm*
Dollar Limit: $4,500.
Where to Sue: County in which the defendant resides, or contract or debt was entered into. In automobile or boat accident cases, where one or more of the parties resides or where the accident occurred. A corporation may be sued in a county in which it has an office or where the act or omission occurred.
Service of Process: Certified mail by clerk, return receipt. Plaintiff may request personal service by sheriff or other disinterested adult.

Defendant's Response: No formal written answer required. Defendant must file counterclaim at least 72 hours before appearance date.

Transfer: Allowed to regular district court on a defendant's request or counterclaim over $4,500, unless both parties agree in writing to stay in small claims court. Defendant must make a transfer request at least 48 hours prior to the time ordered for her appearance and answer.

Attorneys: Allowed, but can't charge more than 10% of judgment in uncontested cases.

Appeals: Allowed by either party within 30 days. Heard by Oklahoma Supreme Court on law only, not facts.

Evictions: No.

Jury Trials: Not allowed unless claim or counterclaim is more than $1,500. Then either party may demand a jury trial at least 2 working days before time set for defendant's appearance.

Notes: Suits to recover personal property (*replevin*) are allowed.

OREGON

Court: Small Claims Department (circuit or justice court).

Statutes: Or. Rev. Stat. §§ 46.405 to 46.425; 46.441 to 46.488; 46.560 to 46.570; 55.011 to 55.140.

Court Information: *www.osbar.org/public/legalinfo/1061.htm*
www.ojd.state.or.us/uni/home.nsf/small_claims.htm

Dollar Limit: $5,000.

Where to Sue: County where defendant resides or can be found, where injury or damage occurred, or where contract or obligation was to be performed.

Service of Process: Plaintiff may choose certified mail or personal service by sheriff or court-approved adult. (In justice court, if claim is over $50, must use personal service.)

Defendant's Response: Defendant must answer within 14 days of service to avoid default. If counterclaim is over $5,000, must file motion to transfer to regular circuit court or counterclaim will be ignored.

Transfer: To regular docket or other appropriate court if counterclaim is more than $5,000 and defendant requests transfer; or, in circuit court, if defendant demands jury trial.

Attorneys: Not allowed without judge's consent.

Appeals: From circuit court, no appeal. From justice court, allowed by defendant (or plaintiff, on counterclaim) within 10 days. Heard in circuit court as a new trial.

Evictions: No.

Jury Trials: If claim is over $750, defendant may request jury trial. Request must be made at same time as answer, within 14 days of service.

Notes: Plaintiff must reply to defendant's counterclaim within 20 days of service.

PENNSYLVANIA

Court: District Justice Court; Philadelphia Municipal Court.

Statutes: 42 Pa. Cons. Stat. Ann. §§ 1123(4); 1515; 1516.

Court Rules: Pennsylvania Rules of Civil Procedure for District Justices, Rule 201 to 324, 1002; Philadelphia Municipal Court Rules of Civil Practice, Rule 101 to 144.

Court Information: *http://courts.phila.gov/pdf/brochures/small-claims-court.pdf* [Philadelphia]
www.co.delaware.pa.us/consumeraffairs/howtosue.pdf

Dollar Limit: $8,000. $10,000 in Philadelphia Municipal Court.

Where to Sue: Individual: wherever defendant can be served or where act or transaction occurred. Corporation or partnership: where it regularly conducts business or has a principal place of business or where act or transaction occurred.

Service of Process: Writ server, sheriff, or constable; registered, certified, or first-class mail. If registered mail is refused, first-class mail is valid service.

Defendant's Response: Defendant must file counterclaim at least 5 days before hearing date (district justice court); at least 10 days before trial date (Philadelphia Municipal Court).

Transfer: If defendant's counterclaim is over $10,000, may bring suit in court of common pleas within 30 days (Philadelphia Municipal Court). There is no provision for transfer from district justice court.

Attorneys: Allowed. Corporations must be represented by an attorney if claim is more than $2,500 (Philadelphia Municipal Court).

Appeals: Allowed by either party within 30 days. Heard in court of common pleas as a new trial.

Evictions: Allowed.

Jury Trials: Either party can request a jury trial and case will be transferred (district justice court). Not allowed except on appeal (Philadelphia Municipal Court).

Notes: (1) Rules of evidence apply except for ordinary business receipts, bills, statements, or estimates (district justice court).
(2) If claiming more than $2,000 personal injury or property damage, must submit a verified (signed under oath) statement of claim (Philadelphia Municipal Court).

RHODE ISLAND

Court: Small Claims Court (district court).

Statutes: R.I. Gen. Laws §§ 10-16-1 to 10-16-16; 9-12-10 (appeals).

Court Rules: District Court Rules of Small Claims Procedure, Rule 1.00 to 7.01.

Court Information: *www.courts.state.ri.us/district/smallclaims.htm*

Dollar Limit: $1,500.

Where to Sue: District where either party resides; if plaintiff is corporation, where defendant resides.

Service of Process: Certified or registered mail; if mail is undelivered, then by process server. Certified or registered mail that is refused is still valid service.

Defendant's Response: Defendant must file written counterclaim either before or on the date set for answering.

Transfer: Allowed to regular district court procedure on defendant's counterclaim over $1,500, if judge decides that the counterclaim has merit.

Attorneys: Allowed; required for public corporations and private corporations with assets of $1 million or more.

Appeals: Only defendant has right to appeal. Must file within 2 days. Heard in superior court as a new trial. Exception: In a consumer plaintiff claim, if manufacturer or seller defendant loses by default, no appeal allowed.

Evictions: No.

Jury Trials: No provision.

Notes: Consumers may bring claims for contracts and for damages connected with retail products or with services.

SOUTH CAROLINA

Court: Magistrates Court; Charleston County, Small Claims Court.

Statutes: S.C. Code Ann. §§ 22-3-10 to 22-3-320; 15-7-30; 18-7-10 to 18-7-30.

Court Rules: South Carolina Administrative and Procedural Rules for Magistrates Court, Rule 1 to 19.

Court Information: *www.scbar.org/pdf/public/magbook.pdf*
www3.charlestoncounty.org/docs/magistrates/summfaq.htm

Dollar Limit: $7,500.

Where to Sue: County where defendant resides at the time claim filed. Corporation or insurance company: county where it has an office for conducting business.

Service of Process: Sheriff or disinterested adult; certified or registered mail.

Defendant's Response: May answer in writing or orally any time within 30 days after service (5 days for claims of $25 or less). Must file counterclaim within 30 days (5 days for claim of $25 or less).

Transfer: Counterclaims over $7,500 will be transferred to court of common pleas.

Attorneys: Allowed.

Appeals: Must be filed within 30 days. Heard in county or circuit court on law, not facts.

Evictions: Yes.

Jury Trials: Either party may request jury trial in writing at least 5 days before trial date.

SOUTH DAKOTA

Court: Small Claims Procedure (Circuit or Magistrates Court).

Statutes: S.D. Codified Laws Ann. §§ 15-39-45 to 15-39-78, 16-12B-6, 16-12B-12 to 16-12B-16, 16-12C-8, 16-12C-13 to 16-12C-15.

Court Information:
www.sdjudicial.comindex.asp?title=smallclaimsprocedures&category=procedures&nav=94
www.ag.state.nd.us/brochure/smallclaim.pdf

Dollar Limit: $8,000.

Where to Sue: County in which any defendant resides, or injury or property damage occurred. Corporation, partnership, or LLC, at its principal place of business.

Service of Process: Certified or registered mail first, return receipt (service is binding on defendant who refuses to accept and sign for the letter). If undeliverable, then service must be made by sheriff or disinterested adult who is a county resident.

Defendant's Response: No formal written answer required.

Transfer: Allowed at judge's discretion on defendant's petition for regular civil or jury trial. (Plaintiff may request transfer in response to counterclaim.) Must make petition at least 5 days prior to appearance date and provide affidavit giving reasons that justify transfer. Appeals are allowed by both plaintiff and defendant if case transferred.

Attorneys: Allowed.

Appeals: Not allowed.

Evictions: No.

Jury Trials: Not allowed. Must apply for transfer.

Notes: Uncontested claims may be heard before a clerk magistrate instead of a judge.

TENNESSEE

Court: Court of General Sessions.

Statutes: Tenn. Code Ann. §§ 16-15-501 to 16-15-505; 16-15-710 to 16-15-735; 16-15-901 to 16-15-905.

Court Rules: Tennessee Rules of Civil Procedure, Rule 38.03.

Court Information: *www.co.shelby.tn.us/county_gov/court_clerks/gen_sessions_court/civil/civfaq.htm*
www.knoxcountyorg/gsjudges/jurisdiction.htm

Dollar Limit: $15,000; $25,000 in Shelby and Anderson Counties. No limit in eviction suits or suits to recover personal property.

Where to Sue: District nearest to defendant's residence. For collecting debt from out-of-state defendant, suit can be brought where plaintiff resides. Eviction suits brought where property is located.

Service of Process: Disinterested adult, plaintiff's attorney, or certified mail.

Defendant's Response: No formal written answer required.

Transfer: Defendant may request transfer to circuit court at least 3 days before hearing (must provide affidavit that defense is either substantial, complex, or expensive enough to require transfer).

Attorneys: Allowed.

Appeals: Allowed by either party. Heard in circuit court as a new trial. May demand jury trial within 10 days after appeal filed.

Evictions: Yes.

Jury Trials: Not allowed except on appeal or transfer.

Notes: Tennessee has no actual small claims system, but trials in general sessions court are normally conducted with informal rules.

TEXAS

Court: Small Claims Court (justice court).

Statutes: Tex. Gov't. Code Ann. §§ 28.001 to 28.055.

Court Rules: Texas Rules of Civil Procedure Rule 523 to 544, 556 to 574b.

Court Information: *www.dallascounty.org/html/departments/jp_courts/index.html*
http://dentoncounty.com/dept/main.asp?Dept=41&Link=167
www.williamson-county.org/JP/index.html#SmallClaimsProcedures

Dollar Limit: $5,000.

Where to Sue: Precinct in which defendant resides or county where obligation was to be performed. Corporations and associations may be sued where they have representatives.

Service of Process: Sheriff, constable, process server, or (with court approval) disinterested adult. Certified mail by clerk of the court.

Defendant's Response: Defendant must file a written answer on or before 10:00 a.m. on the next Monday after 10 days from service of process.

Transfer: Transfer allowed to another precinct in same county upon written motion of defendant, or defendant's affidavit supported by 2 county residents or by consent of both parties.

Attorneys: Allowed.

Appeals: Allowed by either party within 10 days. Heard in county court as a new trial.

Evictions: No.

Jury Trials: Either party may demand a jury trial by filing request at least one day before hearing date.

Notes: (1) No lenders of money at interest may sue in small claims court.
(2) If a default judgment is entered against defendant or plaintiff for failure to appear, either party has 10 days to file a written motion to show good cause for setting aside default.

UTAH

Court: Small Claims Department (justice or district court).

Statutes: Utah Code Ann. §§ 78-6-1 to 78-6-15.

Court Rules: Utah Rules of Small Claims Procedure, Rule 1 to 12, A to K.

Court Information: *www.utcourts.gov/howto/smclaims*

Dollar Limit: $7,500.

Where to Sue: County in which the defendant resides or debt was incurred. Corporation can be sued where it has resident agent or office or place of business.

Service of Process: Sheriff, constable, or certified mail or courier service, return receipt requested.

Defendant's Response: No answer required. Must file counterclaim at least 15 days before trial.

Transfer: To district court upon defendant's counterclaim over $7,500.

Attorneys: Allowed. Businesses and individuals may also be represented by attorneys.

Appeals: Either party may appeal within 30 business days of receiving notice of entry of judgment. Heard in district court as a new trial.

Evictions: No.

Jury Trials: Either party may demand a jury trial.

Notes: Either party may file a request to set aside a default judgment within 30 days.

VERMONT

Court: Small Claims Procedure (superior court).
Statutes: Vt. Stat. Ann. tit. 12, §§ 5531 to 5541.
Court Rules: Vermont Rules of Small Claims Procedure, Rule 1 to 14.
Court Information: *www.vermontjudiciary.org/courts/superior/smclaims.htm*
Dollar Limit: $3,500.
Where to Sue: County in which either party resides, or act or omission occurred.
Service of Process: Sheriff, constable, disinterested adult (with court's permission), or certified mail, return receipt.
Defendant's Response: Defendant must give written or oral answer within 20 days of service to avoid default.
Transfer: Not allowed.
Attorneys: Allowed.
Appeals: Allowed by either party within 30 days. Heard in superior court on law, not facts.
Evictions: No.
Jury Trials: Defendant may request jury trial at least one day prior to appearance.
Notes: Counterclaims over $3,500 allowed, but recovery is limited to $3,500.

VIRGINIA

Court: Small Claims Division (district court)
Statutes: Va. Code Ann. §§ 16.1-77 to 16.1-80, 16.1-92 to 16.1-113, 16.1-122.1 to 16.1-122.7.
Court Information: *www.courts.state.va.us/pamphlets/small_claims.html*
www.courts.state.va.us./gdc/gdc.htm
Dollar Limit: $2,000, small claims division; $4,500 to $15,000, general district court (no limit in evictions or rent owed).
Where to Sue: District in which defendant resides, is employed, or regularly conducts business; where act or omission occurred; or where property is located.
Service of Process: Sheriff or adult approved by court.
Defendant's Response: No formal written answer required. May file counterclaim any time before trial.
Transfer: Any time before return date on service of process or up to 10 days before trial, defendant may request transfer to circuit court upon filing an affidavit stating substantial grounds for defense. Must pay court costs up front.
Attorneys: Not allowed in small claims division; allowed in general district court.
Appeals: Allowed by either party within 10 days (on cases over $50). Heard in circuit court as a new trial; on appeal either party may request jury trial.
Evictions: Yes.
Jury Trials: Not allowed (except in appeals).
Notes: Friend or relative who is not an attorney may represent any party incapable of understanding or participating on their own.

WASHINGTON

Court: Small Claims Department (district court).
Statutes: Wash. Rev. Code Ann. §§ 12.36.010 to 12.40.120; 3.66.040.
Court Rules: Washington Civil Rules for Courts of Limited Jurisdiction, Rule 1 to 86.
Court Information: *www.courts.wa.gov/newsinfo/resources/?fa=newsinfo_jury.scc&altmenu=smal*
www.metrokc.gov/kcdc/smclhome.htm [King County]

Dollar Limit: $4,000.

Where to Sue: County where any defendant resides. Corporation, where it transacts business or has an office.

Service of Process: Sheriff or deputy, constable, disinterested adult, or certified or registered mail return receipt requested.

Defendant's Response: No formal written answer required.

Transfer: Allowed only upon judge's decision, following a hearing.

Attorneys: Not allowed without judge's consent, unless case transferred from regular civil court. (Applies also to paralegals.)

Appeals: Within 30 days. The party who files a claim or counterclaim cannot appeal unless the amount claimed exceeds $1,000, and no party can appeal unless the amount claimed is $250 or more. Heard in superior court as a new trial.

Evictions: No.

Jury Trials: Small claims court is generally informal, but either party has the right to demand a jury trial. Must be made in writing, filed with the court, and served upon the other party.

Notes: (1) May sue to recover money only.

(2) Defendant with counterclaim over $4,000 may file separate suit in superior court at the same time as filing a small claims action.

WEST VIRGINIA

Court: Magistrate Court.

Statutes: W. Va. Code §§ 50-2-1 to 50-6-3; 56-1-1.

Court Rules: Rules of Civil Procedure for Magistrate Courts, Rule 1 to 21.

Court Information: *www.state.wv.us/wvsca/prose/faq.htm*
www.state.wv.us/wvsca/prose/guide.pdf

Dollar Limit: $5,000.

Where to Sue: County in which any defendant resides or can be served, or where act or omission occurred. West Virginia corporations, where principal office located; other corporations, where they do business. For eviction suits, county where property is located.

Service of Process: Sheriff or disinterested adult.

Defendant's Response: Defendant must appear or file written answer within 20 days of service to avoid default (30 days if service is made on defendant's attorney or agent).

Transfer: Allowed if all parties agree to remove to circuit court, or by any party for claims over $300. Also allowed at magistrate's discretion if defendant requests transfer in her answer or within a reasonable time.

Attorneys: Allowed.

Appeals: Allowed by either party within 20 days. Heard in circuit court. If original trial was by jury, appeal is on law only, not facts; if original trial was without a jury, appeal is a new trial (also without a jury).

Evictions: Yes.

Jury Trials: Either party may demand a jury trial if claim is over $20 or involves possession of real estate. Must be made in writing within 20 days of service of defendant's answer.

WISCONSIN

Court: Small Claims Action (circuit court).

Statutes: Wis. Stat. Ann. §§ 799.01 to 799.45; 421.401; 808.04.

Court Information: *www.courts.state.wi.us/circuit/pdf/small_claims.pdf*

Dollar Limit: $5,000. No limit in eviction suits.

Where to Sue: County in which any defendant resides or does substantial business. County where contract claim arose or, if claim arose from consumer transaction, county where contract was signed or where purchase or loan took place. For landlord-tenant claims, county where property is located.

Service of Process: Certified mail by court clerk, return receipt requested; sheriff, process server, or disinterested adult.

Defendant's Response: No formal written answer required.

Transfer: Upon defendant's counterclaim over $5,000, case will be tried according to regular circuit court civil procedure.

Attorneys: Allowed.

Appeals: Allowed by either party within 45 days. Heard in court of appeals on law, not facts. No appeal from default judgment. A motion for a new trial must be made within 20 days of judgment.

Evictions: Yes.

Jury Trials: Either party may request a jury trial.

Notes: Either party may request that a different judge be assigned the case; must be filed in writing on the day the summons is returned or within 10 days after the case is scheduled for trial.

WYOMING

Court: Small Claims Case (circuit court).

Statutes: Wyo. Stat. §§ 1-21-201 to 1-21-205, 5-9-128, 5-9-135 to 5-9-143.

Court Rules: Rules and Forms Governing Small Claims Cases, Rule 1 to 7, Form 1 and 2.

Court Information: *www.courts.state.wy.us/wyoming_court_rules.htm*
www.courts.state.wy.us/overview.htm#_iii_other_state

Dollar Limit: $3,000 (small claims case); $7,000 (regular circuit court).

Where to Sue: County in which defendant resides or can be served. For Wyoming corporations, county where corporation has principal office of place of business; for out-of-state corporation, where cause of action arose or plaintiff resides.

Service of Process: Sheriff or deputy, disinterested adult. Certified mail, return receipt (by court clerk if defendant lives in the same county as court).

Defendant's Response: No formal written answer required.

Transfer: No provision.

Attorneys: Allowed. If one party appears with an attorney, the other party is entitled to a continuance to obtain one.

Appeals: Allowed by either party within 10 days. Heard in district court on law only, not facts.

Evictions: Yes.

Jury Trials: Either party may demand jury trial. ■

INDEX

CATALOG

...more from nolo

	PRICE	CODE
BUSINESS		
Buy-Sell Agreement Handbook:		
Plan Ahead for Changes in the Ownership of Your Business (Book w/CD-ROM)	$49.99	BSAG
The CA Nonprofit Corporation Kit (Binder w/CD-ROM)	$59.95	CNP
Consultant & Independent Contractor Agreements (Book w/CD-ROM)	$29.99	CICA
The Corporate Minutes Book (Book w/CD-ROM)	$69.99	CORMI
Create Your Own Employee Handbook	$49.99	EMHA
Dealing With Problem Employees	$44.99	PROBM
Drive a Modest Car & 16 Other Keys to Small Business Success	$24.99	DRIV
The Employer's Legal Handbook	$39.99	EMPL
Everyday Employment Law	$29.99	ELBA
Federal Employment Laws	$49.99	FELW
Drive a Modest Car & 16 Other Keys to Small Business Success	$24.99	DRIV
Form Your Own Limited Liability Company (Book w/CD-ROM)	$44.99	LIAB
Hiring Independent Contractors: The Employer's Legal Guide (Book w/CD-ROM)	$34.99	HICI
How to Create a Noncompete Agreement	$44.95	NOCMP
How to Form a California Professional Corporation (Book w/CD-ROM)	$59.95	PROF
How to Form a Nonprofit Corporation (Book w/CD-ROM)—National Edition	$44.99	NNP
How to Form a Nonprofit Corporation in California (Book w/CD-ROM)	$44.99	NON
How to Form Your Own California Corporation (Binder w/CD-ROM)	$59.99	CACI
How to Form Your Own California Corporation (Book w/CD-ROM)	$34.99	CCOR
How to Get Your Business on the Web	$29.99	WEBS
How to Write a Business Plan	$34.99	SBS
Incorporate Your Business	$49.95	NIBS
The Independent Paralegal's Handbook	$29.95	PARA
Leasing Space for Your Small Business	$34.95	LESP
Legal Guide for Starting & Running a Small Business	$34.99	RUNS
Legal Forms for Starting & Running a Small Business (Book w/CD-ROM)	$29.99	RUNS2
Marketing Without Advertising	$24.00	MWAD
Music Law (Book w/CD-ROM)	$34.99	ML
Nolo's California Quick Corp	$19.95	QINC
Nolo's Guide to Social Security Disability	$29.99	QSS
Nolo's Quick LLC	$24.95	LLCQ
Nondisclosure Agreements	$39.95	NAG
The Small Business Start-up Kit (Book w/CD-ROM)	$29.99	SMBU
The Small Business Start-up Kit for California (Book w/CD-ROM)	$34.99	OPEN
The Partnership Book: How to Write a Partnership Agreement (Book w/CD-ROM)	$39.99	PART
Sexual Harassment on the Job	$24.95	HARS
Starting & Running a Successful Newsletter or Magazine	$29.99	MAG
Take Charge of Your Workers' Compensation Claim	$34.99	WORK
Tax Savvy for Small Business	$36.99	SAVVY
Working for Yourself: Law & Taxes for the Self-Employed	$39.99	WAGE
Your Limited Liability Company: An Operating Manual (Book w/CD-ROM)	$49.99	LOP
Your Rights in the Workplace	$29.99	YRW
Your Crafts Business: A Legal Guide	$26.99	VART
CONSUMER		
How to Win Your Personal Injury Claim	$29.99	PICL
Nolo's Encyclopedia of Everyday Law	$29.99	EVL
Nolo's Guide to California Law	$24.95	CLAW
Trouble-Free Travel...And What to Do When Things Go Wrong	$14.95	TRAV

Prices subject to change.

ORDER 24 HOURS A DAY @ www.nolo.com
Call 800-728-3555 • Mail or fax the order form in this book

ESTATE PLANNING & PROBATE

	PRICE	CODE
8 Ways to Avoid Probate	$19.99	PRO8
9 Ways to Avoid Estate Taxes	$29.95	ESTX
Estate Planning Basics	$21.99	ESPN
How to Probate an Estate in California	$49.99	PAE
Make Your Own Living Trust (Book w/CD-ROM)	$39.99	LITR
Nolo's Simple Will Book (Book w/CD-ROM)	$36.99	SWIL
Plan Your Estate	$44.99	NEST
Quick & Legal Will Book	$16.99	QUIC

FAMILY MATTERS

	PRICE	CODE
Child Custody: Building Parenting Agreements That Work	$29.99	CUST
The Complete IEP Guide	$24.99	IEP
Divorce & Money: How to Make the Best Financial Decisions During Divorce	$34.99	DIMO
Do Your Own California Adoption: Nolo's Guide for Stepparents and Domestic Partners (Book w/CD-ROM)	$34.99	ADOP
Get a Life: You Don't Need a Million to Retire Well	$24.99	LIFE
The Guardianship Book for California	$39.99	GB
A Legal Guide for Lesbian and Gay Couples	$29.99	LG
Living Together: A Legal Guide (Book w/CD-ROM)	$34.99	LTK
Medical Directives and Powers of Attorney in California	$19.99	CPOA
Using Divorce Mediation: Save Your Money & Your Sanity	$29.95	UDMD

GOING TO COURT

	PRICE	CODE
Beat Your Ticket: Go To Court and Win! (National Edition)	$19.99	BEYT
The Criminal Law Handbook: Know Your Rights, Survive the System	$34.99	KYR
Everybody's Guide to Small Claims Court (National Edition)	$26.99	NSCC
Everybody's Guide to Small Claims Court in California	$26.99	CSCC
Fight Your Ticket ... and Win! (California Edition)	$29.99	FYT
How to Change Your Name in California	$34.95	NAME
How to Collect When You Win a Lawsuit (California Edition)	$29.99	JUDG
How to Seal Your Juvenile & Criminal Records (California Edition)	$34.95	CRIM
The Lawsuit Survival Guide	$29.99	UNCL
Nolo's Deposition Handbook	$29.99	DEP
Represent Yourself in Court: How to Prepare & Try a Winning Case	$34.99	RYC
Sue in California Without a Lawyer	$34.99	SLWY

HOMEOWNERS, LANDLORDS & TENANTS

	PRICE	CODE
California Tenants' Rights	$27.99	CTEN
Deeds for California Real Estate	$24.99	DEED
Dog Law	$21.95	DOG
Every Landlord's Legal Guide (National Edition, Book w/CD-ROM)	$44.99	ELLI
Every Tenant's Legal Guide	$29.99	EVTEN
For Sale by Owner in California	$29.99	FSBO
How to Buy a House in California	$34.99	BHCA
The California Landlord's Law Book: Rights & Responsibilities (Book w/CD-ROM)	$44.99	LBRT
The California Landlord's Law Book: Evictions (Book w/CD-ROM)	$44.99	LBEV
Leases & Rental Agreements	$29.99	LEAR
Neighbor Law: Fences, Trees, Boundaries & Noise	$26.99	NEI
The New York Landlord's Law Book (Book w/CD-ROM)	$39.99	NYLL
New York Tenants' Rights	$29.99	YRW
Renters' Rights (National Edition)	$27.99	NYTEN
Stop Foreclosure Now in California	$29.95	CLOS

IMMIGRATION

	PRICE	CODE
Becoming a U.S. Citizen: A Guide to the Law, Exam and Interview	$24.99	USCIT
Fiancé & Marriage Visas	$44.95	IMAR
How to Get a Green Card	$29.99	GRN

ORDER 24 HOURS A DAY @ www.nolo.com
Call 800-728-3555 • Mail or fax the order form in this book

	PRICE	CODE
Student & Tourist Visas	$29.99	ISTU
U.S. Immigration Made Easy	$44.99	IMEZ

MONEY MATTERS

101 Law Forms for Personal Use (Book w/CD-ROM)	$29.99	SPOT
Bankruptcy: Is It the Right Solution to Your Debt Problems?	$19.99	BRS
Chapter 13 Bankruptcy: Repay Your Debts	$34.99	CH13
Creating Your Own Retirement Plan	$29.99	YROP
Credit Repair (Book w/CD-ROM)	$24.99	CREP
Getting Paid: How to Collect from Bankrupt Debtors	$24.99	CRBNK
How to File for Chapter 7 Bankruptcy	$34.99	HFB
IRAs, 401(k)s & Other Retirement Plans: Taking Your Money Out	$34.99	RET
Money Troubles: Legal Strategies to Cope With Your Debts	$29.99	MT
Stand Up to the IRS	$24.99	SIRS
Surviving an IRS Tax Audit	$24.95	SAUD
Take Control of Your Student Loan Debt	$26.95	SLOAN

PATENTS AND COPYRIGHTS

The Copyright Handbook: How to Protect and Use Written Works (Book w/CD-ROM)	$39.99	COHA
Copyright Your Software	$34.95	CYS
Domain Names	$26.95	DOM
Getting Permission: How to License and Clear Copyrighted Materials Online and Off (Book w/CD-ROM)	$34.99	RIPER
How to Make Patent Drawings Yourself	$29.99	DRAW
Inventor's Guide to Law, Business and Taxes	$34.99	ILAX
The Inventor's Notebook	$24.99	INOT
Nolo's Patents for Beginners	$29.99	QPAT
License Your Invention (Book w/CD-ROM)	$39.99	LICE
Patent, Copyright & Trademark	$39.99	PCTM
Patent It Yourself	$49.99	PAT
Patent Pending in 24 Hours	$29.99	PEND
Patent Searching Made Easy	$29.95	PATSE
The Public Domain	$34.95	PUBL
Trademark: Legal Care for Your Business and Product Name	$39.99	TRD
Web and Software Development: A Legal Guide (Book w/ CD-ROM)	$44.95	SFT

RESEARCH & REFERENCE

Legal Research: How to Find & Understand the Law	$39.99	LRES

SENIORS

Choose the right long-Term Care: Home Care, Assisted Living & Nursing Homes	$21.99	ELD
The Conservatorship Book for California	$44.99	CNSV
Social Security, Medicare & Goverment Pensions	$29.99	SOA

SOFTWARE

Call or check our website at www.nolo.com for special discounts on Software!

LeaseWriter CD—Windows	$129.95	LWD1
LLC Maker—Windows	$89.95	LLP1
PatentPro Plus—Windows	$399.99	PAPL
Personal RecordKeeper 5.0 CD—Windows	$59.95	RKD5
Quicken Legal Business Pro 2004—Windows	$79.95	SBQB4
Quicken WillMaker Plus 2004—Windows	$79.95	WQP4

SPECIAL UPGRADE OFFER—Get 35% off the latest edition of your Nolo book

It's important to have the most current legal information. Because laws and legal procedures change often, we update our books regularly. To help keep you up-to-date we are extending this special upgrade offer. Cut out and mail the title portion of the cover of your old Nolo book and we'll give you 35% off the retail price of the NEW EDITION of that book when you purchase directly from us. For more information call us at 1-800-728-3555. This offer is to individuals only.

Order Form

Name

Address

City

State, Zip

Daytime Phone

E-mail

Item Code	Quantity	Item	Unit Price	Total Price

Method of payment

☐ Check   ☐ VISA   ☐ MasterCard
☐ Discover Card   ☐ American Express

Subtotal	
Add your local sales tax (California only)	
Shipping: RUSH $9, Basic $5 (See below)	
"I bought 3, ship it to me FREE!" (Ground shipping only)	
TOTAL	

Account Number

Expiration Date

Signature

Shipping and Handling

Rush Delivery—Only $9

We'll ship any order to any street address in the U.S. by UPS 2nd Day Air* for only $9!

* Order by noon Pacific Time and get your order in 2 business days. Orders placed after noon Pacific Time will arrive in 3 business days. P.O. boxes and S.F. Bay Area use basic shipping. Alaska and Hawaii use 2nd Day Air or Priority Mail.

Basic Shipping—$5

Use for P.O. Boxes, Northern California and Ground Service.

Allow 1-2 weeks for delivery. U.S. addresses only.

For faster service, use your credit card and our toll-free numbers

Call our customer service group
Monday thru Friday 7am to 7pm PST

Phone	1-800-728-3555
Fax	1-800-645-0895
Mail	Nolo 950 Parker St. Berkeley, CA 94710

Order 24 hours a day @
www.nolo.com

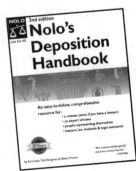

Remember:

Little publishers have big ears.
We really listen to you.

Take 2 Minutes & Give Us Your 2 cents

Your comments make a big difference in the development and revision of Nolo books and software. Please take a few minutes and register your Nolo product—and your comments—with us. Not only will your input make a difference, you'll receive special offers available only to registered owners of Nolo products on our newest books and software. Register now by:

PHONE
1-800-728-3555

FAX
1-800-645-0895

EMAIL
cs@nolo.com

or **MAIL** us
this registration card

------------------------------- fold here -------------------------------

NOLO Registration Card

NAME	DATE

ADDRESS

CITY	STATE	ZIP

PHONE	EMAIL

WHERE DID YOU HEAR ABOUT THIS PRODUCT?

WHERE DID YOU PURCHASE THIS PRODUCT?

DID YOU CONSULT A LAWYER? (PLEASE CIRCLE ONE)   YES   NO   NOT APPLICABLE

DID YOU FIND THIS BOOK HELPFUL?   (VERY)   5   4   3   2   1   (NOT AT ALL)

COMMENTS

WAS IT EASY TO USE?   (VERY EASY)   5   4   3   2   1   (VERY DIFFICULT)

We occasionally make our mailing list available to carefully selected companies whose products may be of interest to you.
❏ If you do not wish to receive mailings from these companies, please check this box.
❏ You can quote me in future Nolo promotional materials.
    Daytime phone number _____.

NSCC 10.0

Nolo
in the
NEWS

"Nolo helps lay people perform legal tasks without the aid—or fees—of lawyers."
—USA TODAY

Nolo books are ..."written in plain language, free of legal mumbo jumbo, and spiced with witty personal observations."
—ASSOCIATED PRESS

"...Nolo publications...guide people simply through the how, when, where and why of law."
—WASHINGTON POST

"Increasingly, people who are not lawyers are performing tasks usually regarded as legal work... And consumers, using books like Nolo's, do routine legal work themselves."
—NEW YORK TIMES

"...All of [Nolo's] books are easy-to-understand, are updated regularly, provide pull-out forms...and are often quite moving in their sense of compassion for the struggles of the lay reader."
—SAN FRANCISCO CHRONICLE

fold here

- -

Nolo
950 Parker Street
Berkeley, CA 94710-9867

Attn: **NSCC 10.0**